Softly, *with Feeling*

EDWARD BERGER

Softly, *with Feeling*

JOE WILDER *and*
the BREAKING *of* BARRIERS
in AMERICAN MUSIC

Foreword by WYNTON MARSALIS

TEMPLE UNIVERSITY PRESS PHILADELPHIA

TEMPLE UNIVERSITY PRESS
Philadelphia, Pennsylvania 19122
www.temple.edu/tempress

Copyright © 2014 by Temple University
All rights reserved
Published 2014

Text design by Kate Nichols

Library of Congress Cataloging-in-Publication Data

Berger, Edward, author.
    Softly, with feeling : Joe Wilder and the breaking of barriers in American music / Edward Berger ;
foreword by Wynton Marsalis.
        pages cm
    Includes bibliographical references, discography, and index.
    ISBN 978-1-4399-1127-3 (cloth : alk. paper) — ISBN 978-1-4399-1129-7 (e-book)   1. Wilder, Joe.
2. Jazz musicians—United States—Biography.   3. Trumpet players—United States—Biography.
I. Title.
    ML419.W522B57 2014
    788.9'2165092—dc23
    [B]

                                                                                                    2013043283

♾ The paper used in this publication meets the requirements of the American National Standard for
Information Sciences—Permanence of Paper for Printed Library Materials, ANSI Z39.48-1992

Printed in the United States of America

2 4 6 8 9 7 5 3 1

*In both classical music and jazz music, sometimes you can play
something and it just touches your heart. You have no idea when
this is going to happen. The music is so beautiful that it seems to
come from just someplace unknown to you, but at the moment it
happens, you just feel so happy about it.*

—JOE WILDER

Contents

Photograph gallery follows page 99

Wynton Marsalis and Wilder, Jazz at Lincoln Center, January 2011.
(Photo by Ed Berger.)

Foreword
Wynton Marsalis

I didn't know about Joe when I was coming up. Even though my father is a musician, I was like all the other kids in my neighborhood—we didn't know much about the history of the music. I wasn't aware of it at the time, but Joe Wilder set the table. His struggles made it easier for me and many others. When I got to New York in the early 1980s, I found out about Joe. Everywhere I went people would talk about him. I was like a grandson to a lot of the older guys, and they were always letting me know about the history. They treated me as a family member, not like they were preaching to an outsider. They told me, "You need to know about Joe Wilder, who he is, and what he did." Milt Hinton may have been the first to tell me about Joe, about his classical playing and how he made it possible for me and others. You don't always see the battles—you don't always know the struggles—and that's why this book is so important.

Touring with Joe in 1992 with the Lincoln Center Jazz Orchestra was a great education for me. I sat next to him every night and listened very intently. He was playing third, and I was playing fourth. Every night after the gig, I would sit on the stage with Joe, and he would teach me various techniques. I would ask him about playing with the plunger mute, playing with the hat, his way of playing vibrato and attacking notes, the different ways of throwing the note out and catching it. I mean every night—we'd be the last ones there! We would sit down together for twenty-five or thirty minutes and talk about the music. But beyond that, just being around Joe, I learned a lot by observing him and in general conversation: the way he would play his parts, the feeling and dignity he had. Everybody in the band loved him, and cats would be smiling whenever he played a solo because he has that characteristic sound and feeling. There is also the integrity with which Joe played the parts. You would start to notice the whole note, the half note, the unglamorous attention to detail, and the professionalism and seriousness of playing under all conditions. The collegial way he functions in the context of a group was instructional for me.

His style is classic. He pays great attention to thematic development, which is the mark of a supremely intelligent musician. He plays in the center of the time—he'll play behind it or on top of it. He has a variety of approaches and techniques. He can play quarter notes and longer notes; he can play shorter notes and faster runs. He plays great in all the registers and has mastered all technical aspects of the trumpet—questions of attack, endurance, flexibility. He has a sound and vibrato that is his alone and can't be described. When you hear it, you know it's him. The same type of dignity and personal grandeur that he has as a man is in his sound. The truth of his playing is what it's all about. When he joined the Juilliard faculty in 2002, of course I was in favor of it, but they didn't need me to convince them. Victor Goines and everybody else knew who he was and what he would mean to the program. They knew how giving he is in terms of his knowledge and how he wants the legacy of the music to continue.

Beyond the excellence of his playing, as a man he has such dignity and feeling and is so engaged and intelligent. He brings a warmth to every situation. He loved my kids, who were very young at the time, and was constantly looking out for them. He would tell me, "You've got to be attentive to your kids." He's always talking about family and the importance of savoring moments together.

Everything that Joe went through isn't readily apparent because he's always so dignified and positive. But I know that his struggles made it a lot easier for the rest of us, and I love him. Joe is soulful. You're always happy when you see Joe Wilder.

Preface

One of the pitfalls of writing about someone I have grown very close to is a presumed loss of objectivity. My only defense is that I got to know Joe Wilder precisely because of my admiration for his music and not the other way around. Hearing him first on record and then at various events in and around New York, it began to dawn on me that here was a musician with a completely original sound and a style that utterly defied the arbitrary categorizations in which jazz fans and critics like to indulge. Like so many who have heard him, I was captivated by his ability to enhance and embellish a melody while remaining true to its essence. Time and again, I witnessed Joe Wilder somewhat diffidently approaching the microphone—seemingly embarrassed at being the center of attention. Within a few bars, he would win over an audience, not by bombast or pyrotechnics, but through the sheer beauty of his sound, the clarity of his thoughts, and the ability to "tell a story" on his instrument with both wit and feeling. And at the conclusion of yet another succinct yet perfect musical statement, Joe would shyly acknowledge the applause with a fleeting smile, and quickly turn away, clearly anxious to escape the limelight.

Joe represents a unique confluence of experiences and qualities that make him an exemplary person as well as an extraordinary musician. Growing up in Philadelphia during the Depression, he was nurtured by loving and concerned parents and an extended family that lived nearby. Like most Americans, white and black, the Wilder family struggled financially, but his parents valued education and saw to it that Joe and his brothers had every opportunity to succeed in school. His father, Curtis, then a part-time musician who delivered coal, among other jobs, to make a living, was a major influence, overseeing Joe's early musical development and instilling in him the strict standards of deportment for which he later became known and which enabled him to avoid the pitfalls that consumed so many musical colleagues of his generation. Caring teachers, such as cornet virtuoso Frederick D. Griffin and Alberta Lewis, orchestra director at what was then called the William T. Tilden Junior High School, in Philadelphia, had a profound effect on the youngster, as did the many renowned musicians Joe encountered while playing on the *Parisian Tailor's Colored Kiddies' Radio Hour.* On that program, Joe and his fellow young performers had the extraordinary experience of being backed by musicians from many of the leading black bands of the 1930s. The encouragement he received from these mentors, Louis Armstrong among them, would manifest itself many decades later in Joe's own work with students at all levels.

The fact that Joe grew up in a diverse working-class neighborhood in Philadelphia certainly helped him acquire the ability to get along with people of all backgrounds. As an African American musician coming of age in 1930s America, Joe was subjected to indignities on almost a daily basis and, on occasion, to far more serious dangers. But he emerged from these experiences without bitterness, with his dignity, humor, and most important, his humanity intact.

Just as race did not define Joe Wilder's life, I did not intend it to be the focal point of this book. But in relating his story, it became clear that race affected his career at almost every turn. From his travels with both black and white bands on the road in the 1940s, his experiences as one of the first African American marines during World War II, his pioneering role in integrating the Broadway and network orchestras in the 1950s, and his penetration of the insular world of classical music, race was a constant thread, and so it inevitably plays a major role in this narrative. But just as music remained paramount in Joe's life, I hope his experiences and achievements as a musician emerge as the central theme.

In telling the Wilder story, I wanted to place his life and work within a broader historical and musical context, which led to many digressions, including sometimes lengthy excursuses on the history of integration in the military, Broadway, the network studios, and the symphony, as well as asides on such topics as society orchestras, the jazz repertory movement, and the jazz party phenomenon. I hope readers will find this background information interesting in and of itself and useful in understanding Joe's contributions.

Joe was not an activist, in the sense that he did not seek out battles. But when confronted with injustice at all stages of his career, he refused to back down, whether the perpetrator was black or white, a powerful bandleader, club owner, contractor, or music industry executive. In addition, none of his achievements came at the expense of someone else. As in most fields, self-promotion and internal politics play a role in the music business, especially in the highly competitive world of the studios. But such behavior is anathema to Joe, who, as far as I can determine, never lobbied for any job. His place in the leading big bands and his breakthroughs on Broadway, in the studios, and in the classical world all came as a result of his musical abilities, not his connections.

It can be dangerous to equate a musician's character with his or her style of playing. But as I came to know Joe Wilder, I soon found out that the warmth, sophistication, humor, and compassion that characterize his music are simply a reflection of the man himself. Joe's sterling personal qualities are legend. He, along with such friends and colleagues as Milt Hinton, Benny Carter, Hank Jones, and George Duvivier, spent much of his career defying commonly held stereotypes of both African American musicians and jazz players. In talking with Joe's musical peers, friends, employers, and students, I can honestly say that the most critical remark I could elicit was Dick Hyman's comment, "He always dressed a bit more formally than he needed to."

Although Joe Wilder's contributions to this work were enormous and his reminiscences constitute perhaps its most valuable component, it is not an autobiography. I, therefore, am responsible for all interpretations of events, as well as any errors.

Acknowledgments

My first debt is to Joe Wilder, who patiently shared the details of his remarkable life story. Joe answered all of my questions during countless hours of discussion in person and over the phone. As always, his motivation was not to call attention to himself but to give credit to those who helped him along the way and to remember the many musical friends and colleagues who inspired him and are no longer able to tell their own stories. My relationship with him is something I will always cherish. The entire Wilder family has been very encouraging. Joe and his wife, Solveig, have always treated me as family during my many visits to their home, as have their daughters, Elin, Solveig, and Inga.

My colleagues at the Institute of Jazz Studies (IJS) and the Dana Library at Rutgers–Newark provided a great deal of support and assistance. Since retiring in 2011 from IJS—largely to work on this book—for the first time, I was able to use the institute as an outside researcher, affording me a new perspective on the depth of its resources and the unfailing helpfulness of its staff. Vincent Pelote, Tad Hershorn, the late Annie Kuebler, Bob Nahory, Elsa Alves, Joe Peterson, April Grier, Christian McFarland, and Dan Faulk all responded to my frequent requests. Similarly, my colleagues at the reference desk of the Dana Library have always been extremely accommodating. Natalie Borisovets, Ka-Neng Au, Roberta Tipton, and Ann Watkins provided many leads and tracked down a number of obscure sources. Dana Library's technology gurus Mark Papianni and Chris Singh were always willing to solve my many computer issues, as were my brothers, Ken and Larry, and my friend Doug

Blair. Dan Morgenstern, my longtime friend and colleague, offered many valuable suggestions and sage advice.

I am indebted to librarians, archivists, and staff members at several other institutions: Larry Appelbaum (Library of Congress), Margaret Crull (New York City Commission on Human Rights), John Gardner (Manhattan School of Music), Wolfram Knauer (Jazzinstitut Darmstadt, Darmstadt, Germany), Alfred Lemmon (Williams Research Center, Historic New Orleans Collection), David M. Ment (Municipal Archives, City of New York), Gabryel Smith (New York Philharmonic Archive), the Microforms Service of the Princeton University Library, and the Indiana University William and Gayle Cook Music Library.

I am especially grateful to Barbara Steinberg, who gave me access to the papers of her father, conductor Benjamin Steinberg, which were invaluable in telling the story of the Symphony of the New World. Barbara opened her Laredo, Texas, home to me. I am happy to report that this valuable collection has now become part of the New York Public Library's Schomburg Center for Research in Black Culture. The following individuals all also contributed much to this work: George Avakian, David G. Berger, Bill Kirchner, Jeff McMillan, Lynne Mueller, Randy Sandke, Phil Schaap, A. P. Tureaud, and Kenny Washington.

I thank the following friends and colleagues of Joe Wilder who graciously shared their memories and insights: Van Alexander, Max Bennett, Eddie Bert, Alfred Brown, Leon Cohen, Ray Crisara, Bill Crow, Jim Czak, Buddy DeFranco, Mat Domber, Peter Duchin, Dominick Farinacci, Victor Goines, Jimmy Heath, Dick Hyman, Harold Jones, Rebecca Kilgore, Ken Kimery, Brandon Lee, Mundell Lowe, Nancy Marano, Kermit Moore, Rigmor Newman, Henry Nowak, Glenn Osser, Jimmy Owens, Monk Rowe, Loren Schoenberg, Berisford "Shep" Shepherd, Andy Stein, Warren Vaché, Michael Weiss, Frank Wess, and Harriet Wingreen. Their contributions greatly enriched the narrative. Wilmer Wise, in addition to supplying much new information and many leads, was a source of encouragement throughout the project. I am forever indebted to Earl Madison for sharing, for the first time, his perspective on the historic 1969 lawsuit against the New York Philharmonic that so deeply affected his life and career.

I thank Loren Schoenberg for his careful reading of the manuscript, which resulted in many improvements both in style and content (and saved me from several gaffes). Micah Kleit, executive editor at Temple University Press, expertly guided this work through the publication process, and Sara Cohen, rights and contracts manager, provided much support along the way. Rebecca Logan of Newgen supervised the book's production with care and understanding, and I cannot imagine a more skillful and conscientious copy editor than Merrill Gillaspy. Finally, I am deeply grateful to Wynton Marsalis for his warm and insightful foreword.

The Making of a Musician

Philadelphia (1922–1938)

oe Wilder was born on February 22, 1922, in Colwyn, Pennsylvania, a small township between Philadelphia and Darby. He was delivered—most likely in the family home on Front Street—by Dr. Edward Pratt Woolard, a white obstetrician, whom the family respected (Joe's youngest brother, Edward, was named for him). Joe's father, Curtis—his real name was Carpenter Curtis Wilder, but preferring "Curtis," he dropped "Carpenter"—was born November 23, 1900. In 1910, he had been sent by his family from their home in Winfall, North Carolina, to live with relatives in Philadelphia. "They didn't want him growing up and sharecropping like the rest of them were doing," Joe recalled.[1] Eventually, Curtis's parents, James (born c. 1878) and Tarnetta (born c. 1884), joined their son in Philadelphia. Joe was named for his great uncle Josephus, James's older brother.

Wilder (*second from left*) with fellow students of Frederick D. Griffin, Philadelphia, 1934. *(Wilder Family Collection.)*

Joe's mother, Augustine, was born on May 10, 1903, in Philadelphia. Her father, Lewis Mosley, was born in Pennsylvania in 1874, and her mother, Frances, was born in South Carolina in 1882. The 1920 U.S. Census lists Lewis's occupation as a laborer in an ice plant. Augustine, sixteen at the time of the 1920 census, was listed as a "machine hand" in a candy factory.

Both the Wilders and the Mosleys settled in Colwyn, renting row houses at 210 and 214 Front Street, next to the tracks of the Baltimore and Ohio Railroad. It was here that Joe's parents, Curtis and Augustine, known to all as Gussie, met and eventually married. Curtis's father moved his own family to nearby Saybrook Avenue, and apparently Curtis and Gussie took over the house at 210 Front Street, where Joe and his three brothers were born. The other three or four adjoining row houses were occupied by black families as well.

Joe's paternal grandfather, James Wilder, worked for the Fels Naptha soap factory, located on Island Road, which separated Philadelphia from Colwyn. Raw materials for soap production were delivered via the nearby railroad, and James was in charge of the workers who hoisted barrels of resin, the smell of which permeated the nearby community. "Even though he didn't make much," Joe said, "he saved enough money to eventually buy the building he lived in and two others on Saybrook Avenue."

Gussie would become a mainstay of the community—active in her church and women's social organizations. "She was a very gregarious and friendly person," Joe recalled. "She was very compassionate—if someone in the neighborhood was sick, she would always cook for them and have us bring the food over." She took courses in nursing and became a midwife and eventually became licensed as a beautician as well.

Curtis was undoubtedly Joe's greatest influence. Presaging Joe's own military service, during World War I, Curtis lied about his age and joined the Navy. From May until the war's end in November 1918, he served as a mess attendant—one of the only assignments available to black sailors at the time—aboard a troop ship, the U.S.S. *Orizaba*. Curtis was on board when the ship brought back celebrated bandleader James Reese Europe and his band from France in 1919. During his sixteen round-trips to Europe from the ship's home port of Hoboken, New Jersey, Curtis was also called upon to fulfill other duties: "If there was any shooting out at sea, my station was down in the bottom of the ship—not to have pleasure—but to send bags of gun powder up to the gunners. At seventeen, I did not realize the monumental danger we were in deep below the water line of the ship."[2]

Curtis reenlisted and served again during World War II, this time as a musician. Nearly forty-two years of age, in October 1942, Curtis enlisted by traveling to New York from Philadelphia, where he had been working on the Navy base. After taking a test on tuba, he was designated musician second class, and after basic training, he was assigned to the Pasco Naval Air Station Band, a twenty-three-piece all-black group in Pasco, Washington. In addition to a busy musical schedule, the unit had other duties. "If the wheat fields would catch on fire, the members would have to go and help to put it out and save the raw food on many occasions," he recalled.[3] Curtis was discharged in January 1945. "Any member who was 45 years of age and came from a defense job could get out and go back," he recalled. "I was glad to get in and was glad to get out."[4]

Growing up, Joe recalled his father doing various jobs—mostly as a truck driver. "When I was little more than a toddler, my father was driving a stucco truck for a company in Colwyn," he explained. "They would deliver the stuff to the builders. If we behaved, he let me and my brothers sound the truck's air horn." But more significantly, Curtis Wilder was also a musician and saw to it that his sons had every opportunity to develop their own musical talents.

Curtis began on cornet but switched to sousaphone, probably in the mid-1920s. "I never remembered him playing the cornet, but that was his first instrument," Joe recalled. "He played it well enough to perform in the church—things like the 'Inflammatus' and a lot of the established cornet solos." Curtis's teacher was a noted Philadelphia African American cornet soloist named Frederick D. Griffin, who would later teach Joe as well. After trying a sousaphone, Curtis fell in love with it and gave up the cornet. He continued to receive instruction from Griffin on the new instrument. He later explained to Joe that the sousaphone was coming into vogue over the tuba because audiences liked the novelty of having the bell pointed at them rather than upward. As was the case with many sousaphone and tuba players in the 1920s, Curtis began to double on string bass. "He studied bass violin at the Philadelphia Settlement School with a fellow from the Philadelphia Orchestra and learned to play quite well," Joe remembered. "It was kind of unusual because those guys usually didn't have black students. He was an Italian, and my father loved him. He also loved my father because he was so studious."[5]

Curtis remembered that his first professional engagement came in 1928, with an orchestra led by Raymond Smith, a celebrated violinist and bandleader: "I was selected to play bass for Raymond Smith's dance band on a steady job, which was my first one. It was my first professional one. It was at Brewer's Café in Camden, New Jersey. I was very proud as though I was with the Philadelphia Orchestra."[6]

Drummer and arranger Berisford "Shep" Shepherd, who went on to a distinguished career with Benny Carter, Artie Shaw, and Earl Bostic, among others, grew up in Philadelphia. Five years Joe Wilder's senior, he recalled playing a couple of engagements with Joe's father, who impressed him with his musicality and technique: "He was the very first string bass player I worked with who was not slapping the strings. And he had a great sense of being part of a rhythm section."[7] Although he played regularly as a sideman in a variety of local musical groups, music was not Curtis Wilder's main source of income. He continued to drive the stucco truck as well as make deliveries for local coal companies. He would not become a bandleader himself until after World War II.

In addition to his musical abilities, Joe Wilder inherited his devotion to learning from his father. He remembered Curtis, who died at the age of one hundred on September 19, 2001, as "having studied his whole life. He took correspondence courses in sociology and mathematics from the University of Chicago and the University of Pennsylvania. My stepmother used to get annoyed with him and say, 'You're eighty years old! Why are you studying all that stuff?' He'd answer, 'Because yesterday I didn't know something, and today I know it.'" Curtis constantly stressed the need for education to his sons. "If we had a question about something we were studying in school, he wouldn't just give us the answer," Joe recalled. "He'd tell us to look it up, so we would retain it better than if someone just gave us the answer."

Other than the Wilders and their immediate neighbors on Front Street, the population of Colwyn was almost entirely white. The U.S. Censuses of 1920 and 1930 show only two other African American families residing in the Borough of Colwyn. In 1915, the Borough Council of Colwyn adopted an ordinance prohibiting "colored people from residing in those sections of the borough now exclusively occupied by white families," even though Colwyn was "known as one of the progressive boroughs in Delaware County."[8] The *Philadelphia Tribune*'s front-page coverage noted that members of the council felt the ordinance to be constitutional because it also prohibited white families from settling in black sections of the borough. The *Tribune* surmised that the reason "such an iniquitous measure should even be considered in Pennsylvania" could be attributed to the fact that "this little town is made up of some poor white people, some foreigners, some southerners." It noted that "it is difficult to find any appreciative number of native born white Pennsylvanians afflicted with such mean sentiment," adding that "they as a rule are pleased when colored people show a tendency to save money, buy property and evidence a desire for better home environments." The unsigned article concluded that "the great State of Pennsylvania . . . is more humiliated by the passage of such laws than are the people of color. Because such steps are steps backward."[9]

It is unclear whether this ordinance was ever enforced or was even still in effect by the time the Wilders arrived in Colwyn, probably in 1918 or 1919.[10] Several white families lived near the Wilders' Front Street home, and the white and black children used to play freely together, as indicated by some surviving Wilder family photos. "We were all little kids—we didn't know black and white," Joe said. "We weren't going into restaurants and being told we wouldn't be served."

Joe's best friend was a young white girl named Helen Gibbons, who was the daughter of a friend of his mother. Joe and Helen walked over the railroad bridge together every day to the Colwyn Public School, where he and his brothers were among the only black students: "We were treated like all the other kids, until one day when I was coming out of school and one of the kids saw me and said something like, 'Look at the nigger.' Helen heard what the kid said and went over and said something to him. He got smart with her, and she slapped him. He said he was going home to get his family and threatened to jump her." When Helen's mother found out what had happened, she told Joe, "If anybody ever calls you that again, you jump on him and try to beat the living daylights out of him!"

In 1929, when Joe was seven, disaster struck the family: "Helen and I were coming back from school, and we heard the siren calling the volunteer firemen. We could see billowing smoke, so we started to follow it. When we crossed over the footbridge, we saw that it was my own house that was burning! My mother was outside hanging clothes on the clothesline and managed to get back into the house and save my brothers' lives." It turned out that Joe's younger brother, Edward, had inadvertently caused the blaze while playing with a kerosene lamp. Fortunately, no one was hurt, but the entire row of houses was destroyed. In the aftermath, Joe remembered seeing the firemen removing the remains of the family piano and his father's melted sousaphone.

The Wilders moved in temporarily with Joe's paternal grandfather, James, and his family, who had by then settled nearby on Saybrook Avenue in Philadelphia. The move was devastating to Joe: "I thought my life was over, and I would never see Helen and my other friends again." Shortly afterward, Curtis, Gussie, and their four sons moved again—to a rented house nearby at 2018 South Seventieth Street, an integrated working-class neighborhood in Paschall, in Southeast Philadelphia. Despite his fears, Joe did maintain a lasting friendship with the Gibbons family, although he and his brothers were forced to endure the taunts of intoxicated patrons in an Irish bar they had to pass on their way to the old neighborhood in Colwyn.

After the fire, Joe and his brothers attended the Harriet Beecher Stowe School. The elementary school, which had expanded from a one-room schoolhouse, was integrated and, according to Joe, there were approximately fifty black students. Joe's maternal grandfather, Lewis Mosley, had been a student there, and Joe even was taught by one of his teachers, a Miss Hess. "She was the oldest teacher in the school system—she was ninety when she taught us," Joe remembered. "When she found out who my grandfather was, she treated me like I was somebody special."

For the most part, Joe enjoyed the new school and was a good student. But as a young African American, he could not hide his disgust at certain traditions that he found offensive:

> In the assembly, they used to make us sing all these old-fashioned Stephen Foster songs with "nigger" in them. For example, when we sang "Old Black Joe," all the kids would turn and point to me, and I would get furious. One teacher saw that I couldn't conceal my anger, and she asked me, "Why are you sitting there looking like a black cloud?" That really got to me, and I said something, so she sent me to the principal's office. The principal, Mrs. Dever, sent me home and said, "Don't come back without your mother." When I told my mother what had happened, she was livid. She said, "We're going back to the school *now*!" When we got to her office, the principal said, "Your son caused a disturbance at the assembly." And my mother answered, "I understand that the teacher said he looked like a black cloud. I don't appreciate that, and I don't want people referring to him like that." So they got together with the teacher, and while she didn't apologize, she agreed not to say it again.

Gussie had to make another visit to the school when Joe questioned a teacher's remark that the blacks in America were not as black as those in Africa. After eluding the teacher, who was chasing him with a yardstick, Joe was sent home by the principal and told once again not to return without his mother. And again, Gussie stood up for her son. "She didn't encourage us to challenge the teachers, but she would support us," Joe said. "She would reason with them, and that's how she was able to resolve any problem." Principal Dever told Gussie that her son "seems to be a very nice young man," adding, "but you know, he's very sensitive." Principal Dever decided that added responsibility might be helpful to the youngster, so she appointed him to the school's Safety Patrol, a coveted position. When she was replaced as principal by Mr. Kelly, an Army veteran, he taught the patrol members how to march and made Joe the patrol lieutenant: "I got a badge, and I was out there every morning at seven thirty, even in the snow, seeing that the kids crossed the street safely. I was like a big hero! The cop who was supposed to be on duty knew I'd be there, so he wouldn't even bother to show up. He told me, 'You've been helping me, and I'm gonna take care of you!'"

As a youngster, Joe inherited his love of cooking from watching his mother and his grandmothers in the kitchen:

> [One day] I thought I'd surprise my mother and make a cake for her. I put in all the ingredients and put the cake in the oven. It smelled just tremendous, but when I took it out of the oven, it was the same size as it was when I put it in. I hadn't put in any baking powder! You could have dropped it on the floor, and it would've bounced this high and wouldn't break. My mother thought it was so funny, and my brothers rode me to death![11]

He eventually mastered the art of baking and became famous for his fabled cheesecakes, often bringing samples to recording sessions to share with his fellow musicians.

Joe's legendary sense of decorum and propriety were certainly a product of his upbringing. While his parents were not "that strict," they set definite rules for Joe and his brothers: "First you had to do your homework; then you could go out and play." And transgressors were swiftly punished with a leather strap. Joe vividly recalled an incident involving a "skatemobile," a homemade but more elaborate predecessor of the skateboard:

> We used to skate down the middle of our street, which was quite busy. A couple of kids got killed when someone came around the curve and didn't see them. My father was really hard on us about that. We had two cops in the neighborhood, one black and one white. The black cop was called "Swifty" because you would see him here, and then you'd go to the other part of the neighborhood, and he'd be there when you arrived! The white cop was called "Sneaky" because all of a sudden he'd be on top of you, and you wouldn't know where he came from. So Sneaky came up and saw me on the street with my skatemobile. He grabbed me and took me to my house and rang the bell. My father came to the door, and he said, "The kid is out there in the middle of the street, and you know how dangerous that is." My father thanked him and said, "I'll take care of it." He got the leather strap, and I got a few welts on the fanny, and that was it.

Although the Wilder boys were generally well behaved and well liked in the neighborhood, they would occasionally get into some mischief, including attempting to drive their father's car: "He used to park it on the lot next to our house. My brothers and I would take the brake off and push it a couple of feet and then push it back so when he came home, it was where he had left it. We'd pretend we were driving."

Gussie Wilder was a religious woman and saw to it that Joe and his brothers attended services and Sunday school at the Phillips Brooks Episcopal Church on Lombard Street in downtown Philadelphia. "She was sincere about her religion, but she never beat people over the head with it," Joe recalled. Their minister, the Reverend Young, made an impression on Joe, who briefly entertained the notion of becoming a clergyman. "But at one time, I wanted to be a policeman," he said, "and that didn't work out either!" Drummer Shep Shepherd, who attended Sunday school with Joe, already saw in him the sense of decorum for which he would become famous: "He developed rapidly because he was a smart young man and didn't waste time with foolishness. Even as a kid, he took care of business."[12]

Joe's father's family were devout Baptists: "My paternal grandmother was a member of what we used to call the 'Holy Roller' church," Joe said. "They would get a storefront, put a cross in the window, and call it a church. We used to laugh at them, but their faith got them through the Depression and the period leading up to it." The youngster was impressed with the music he heard there, however: "They would swing! The tambourines would be wailing, and they'd be singing loud and making up hymns as they went along." Joe's uncle, Norton B. Wilder, his father's younger brother, was a bishop, and served as pastor of the Prayer of Faith Temple in Lynchburg, Virginia, for almost fifty years, until his death in 2000. His son, Joe's cousin Norton J. Wilder Sr. (1940–2012), was a Baptist minister who had a distinguished career in law enforcement. He served as Philadelphia's deputy mayor and "drug czar," as well as in various posts with the Drug Enforcement Administration in Washington.

As was the case in Colwyn, Joe remembered having both white and black friends in Philadelphia. His immediate neighbors on South Seventieth Street included families of various ethnic groups that got along well for the most part:

> There was a Polish family across the street and the Kocherspergers, who were German-Irish next door, and we were all very close. My mother and those ladies were always talking together in the backyard. Of course, there were always some idiots, but we just ignored them. My brothers went to mostly white schools, and they had white friends who would come over to our house for lunch. One day, my younger

brother Calvin went with one of his friends to his house, and when his mother came in and saw him, she said, "Don't you ever bring one of those people in here again!" My brother couldn't understand why somebody would say something like that.

According to the 1930 U.S. Census, the heads of households on South Seventieth Street worked in a variety of professions, and included janitors, railroad and factory workers, house painters, postal workers, and a minister. Saxophonist Jimmy Heath, who was four years younger than Joe and also grew up in Philadelphia, noted, "Philadelphia was not completely segregated. We had other ethnic groups on our block. I remember an Italian family on the corner and a Jewish family nearby."[13] Clarinetist Buddy DeFranco, Joe's contemporary and high school classmate, who grew up in South Philadelphia, also valued the area's diversity: "There were Jewish neighborhoods next to Italian neighborhoods next to black neighborhoods. That was a good quality about the music in that area because black, white, people of different ethnic groups played together. We'd rehearse in each other's homes. There was a common feeling among all of us as musicians."[14] And trumpeter Wilmer Wise, one generation removed from Joe, recalled, "I didn't really have any racial problems as a kid. I have a kindergarten picture of my class in 1941 or 1942, and it was totally integrated. My elementary school class and junior high school were totally integrated. We lived in row houses in South Philly, and on one side we had an Italian family and on the other a Jewish family. As a kid, I spent more time in those houses eating three or four dinners every night. I had a wonderful experience as a kid in Philadelphia."[15]

Drummer Shep Shepherd had a similar multicultural experience. He grew up in a predominantly Jewish neighborhood in Northwest Philadelphia:

There was one street behind Diamond running parallel known as Edgely, with brick row houses. That one block from Twenty-Ninth to Thirtieth was primarily black, and most of those people went out into the rest of the neighborhood to do what they used to call "day's work"—domestic work. They were very nice houses—tiny but nice. I went to Blaine School in the same neighborhood with the rest of the kids. I didn't understand very well then why my friends Abie and Hymie couldn't come out and play with me on Saturdays.[16]

The crushing economic effects of the Depression, however, made life difficult for both white and black families. Jimmy Heath remembered his family being on welfare at one point and going to pick up food at a distribution center near the Wilder home.[17] And Joe remembered the breadlines in his neighborhood, and how before school, he would accompany his father to Yeadon, an affluent Philadelphia suburb, to "go through the trash cans looking for stuff we could sell at the junkyard—old lamps, newspapers." Joe also recalled how his next-door neighbor, Sam Kochersperger, who was an engineer for the Baltimore and Ohio Railroad, helped provide the Wilders with free coal: "He would tell us what day and time he would be coming by on his train, and we would walk on the side of the tracks south toward Darby. There was a steep incline, and the train would slow down, and Mr. Kochersperger would drop some coal onto the track. He would signal with the horn to let us know it was okay, and we'd start collecting the coal in bags we brought with us."

Although the Wilders and other African Americans clearly lived harmoniously with whites in many areas of Philadelphia, conflict certainly existed, and violence was not unknown by any means. Joe remembered that both of his grandfathers used to travel to South Philadelphia in search of work during the Depression. "They had to go by trolley along Gray's Ferry Avenue past the naval hospital," he recalled. "A lot of Irish and Poles and Italians lived in that area, and when they saw these black guys on the trolley car, they would start throwing rocks. So my grandfathers and some of their friends brought their own rocks and got off the trolley and started retaliating when they were attacked. After that, they left them alone." Joe and his brothers also had their share of altercations with both white and black kids in the neighborhood or at school. Joe often found himself on the losing end, until his Uncle Norton taught him how to box. Using his newly acquired skill, he was able to get the best of an Italian classmate who had referred to Joe Louis as "that nigger" after the boxer had defeated Primo Carnera in June 1935. Joe Louis was a hero in the black community, and his honor had to be defended at any cost.

Musical Beginnings

As a musician himself, Curtis Wilder naturally tried to instill his love of music in his four sons. Curtis taught the eldest boy, Curtis Jr., to play bass, and he became a professional musician, performing and recording with many jazz, pop, and rhythm-and-blues groups throughout the 1940s, 1950s, and 1960s, including the popular Do Ray Me Trio, the Counts and Countess (with pianist Alma Smith), and the Evans-Faire Trio. Curtis Jr. was also a fine vocalist and used to perform duets with singer Damita Jo (DeBlanc) (for whom Janet "Damita Jo" Jackson was named). Curtis Jr. was a member of Damita Jo's group when he died of cancer in 1963. Joe regretted not having had the chance to play with his brother, but both were on the road, and their musical paths rarely crossed, with one notable exception: "Once when we were both in Los Angeles—I think I was with Jimmie Lunceford—we were staying at the same hotel, and we jammed with a guitar player and recorded a couple of things in the room. We had a good time. I don't know what ever became of the recordings."

Joe's two younger brothers had talent but were not as serious as Curtis Jr. and Joe. "Calvin [1923–2007], who was next to me in age, could sit down at the piano and play just by ear," Joe said. "My youngest brother, Edward, was doing pretty well on drums without reading any music. My father was always trying to teach them to read, and they'd make fun of him, and he'd get hacked." In addition to encouraging his sons' musical development, Curtis Sr. also imparted lessons about deportment and promptness that were to remain with Joe for life: "He would tell my brothers and me, 'Just because you're a Negro, doesn't mean you have to be late. It's better to show up an hour early than one minute late.'" When someone would praise Curtis Sr.'s musical abilities, he would say, "I knew other bass players who played just as well; the difference is that I would show up on time!"

The bands with which Joe's father played used to rehearse at the Wilder home. "The other kids used to come and sit on our porch and listen to some good music for free," Joe recalled. "I heard the horns playing and must have shown some reaction." One day his father came home with a case and handed Joe, who was seven or eight at the time, an old but serviceable Holton cornet, which he had bought in a pawn shop. Joe was initially disappointed because he had harbored a secret admiration for the trombone: "My paternal grandparents lived directly across from the Saint Clements Catholic School, and they had a marching band. I used to watch these guys out front with the trombone slides going in and out, and I thought that was the greatest thing I'd ever seen!"

Curtis had a wide range of musical tastes and exposed his sons to all kinds of music: "We used to listen to the radio, and we'd hear Baja bands from Mexico, and I can remember my father saying, 'My goodness, listen to those rascals double- and triple-tonguing!' As we'd listen, my father would always call our attention to things. Duke Ellington was one of his favorites, but he also liked Guy Lombardo. The other musicians would laugh at him and say, 'How can you like a band like that?' He thought they were great because they played so well together and everyone had the same vibrato."

Curtis arranged for one of his fellow band members, Henry Lowe, to give Joe his first lessons. "He was a good trumpet player but not an exceptional one," Joe observed. Disappointed with his son's slow progress, Curtis sent Joe to Frederick D. Griffin, who had been his own cornet and sousaphone teacher. The dignified Griffin was a local legend who had been a cornet soloist in the Ninth and Tenth Cavalry bands during World War I. He was heard regularly on Philadelphia radio stations playing concert cornet pieces with pianist W. Franklin Hoxter, another noted African American Philadelphia musician. The Philadelphia Rapid Transit Company sponsored both a white and a black band, and Griffin was conductor of the latter, which was also heard regularly on WCAU radio in Philadelphia.[18]

Griffin was in demand as both a leader and featured soloist with the many local African American musical groups in Philadelphia in the 1920s and 1930s. For example, in March 1930, he directed the debut performance of the Symphony Orchestra Club at the Elks auditorium. Curtis Wilder was a member of the orchestra, and the *Philadelphia Tribune* singled him out for his "solo of bygone days 'Asleep in the Deep' rendered on double B flat bass horn."[19] "Fred Griffin was very fond of my family," Joe remembered, and Griffin respected Joe's father for his devotion to music. The previous November, Griffin played cornet solos at the wedding of Joe's Aunt Myrtle, his mother's sister.[20] A review of a 1931 performance by Griffin at the Shiloh Baptist Church called him "Philadelphia's best known concert cornetist and trumpeter," and noted that his performance of Herbert Clarke's "Bride of the Waves" was "a clever demonstration of what can be done with a trumpet when in the hands of a clever player" and was "greeted with much applause."[21] "Mr. Griffin could play all those things from the Arban trumpet exercise book[22] and all the Herbert Clarke cornet solos absolutely perfectly," said Joe.

Griffin played bravura solo cornet pieces with roots in classical music and in the popular marching bands of the era, especially that of John Philip Sousa. The repertoire developed by such cornetist-composers as Herbert L. Clarke (1867–1945) comprised technically challenging set pieces, often played with piano accompaniment. Many of these works were adaptations of folk tunes or popular songs of the day and became immensely popular in the late nineteenth and early twentieth centuries. With the advent of radio, by the mid-1920s, cornet soloists, such as Del Staigers (1899–1950), who played first chair with Nat Shilkret's Victor Salon Orchestra from 1926 to 1942, were featured prominently on broadcasts. Joe Wilder, who was just beginning his own musical studies, heard these programs, and the virtuoso approach of Staigers and the other featured cornetists was to have a profound and lasting effect on his own stylistic development. Their technique not only influenced him as a trumpet player but would later contribute to his unique jazz improvisational approach.

Each week, Joe would make the trip downtown to Griffin's studio at the Elks Club. "My father was paying Mr. Griffin 50 cents a lesson," Joe recalled. "This was pre-Depression, and it was a chore to get the money together. Mr. Griffin was a wonderful teacher, very strict but compassionate, and he had tremendous ears. He could hear a bad note five blocks away! If he was sitting next to you and you made a mistake, you'd get a fist on your leg: 'Don't you know that's a D-flat, not a C?' But he was a very affectionate man . . . and he helped me a great deal."[23] At that early stage, the youngster was simply interested in playing the trumpet and drew no stylistic distinctions: "I had no concept of what was jazz and what was classical. I was just trying to learn to play the notes."

While continuing his study with Frederick D. Griffin, Joe also took some lessons from trumpeter Cliff Haughton, whose brother, Chauncey, was a well-known saxophonist with Cab Calloway, Chick Webb, and other leading orchestras. "He played lead and could improvise some," Joe noted. "He was an exceptionally fine player and helped me a great deal." Haughton provided Joe's first formal training in jazz—not so much in improvisation but in phrasing within jazz arrangements, a skill that would soon serve him well and one that Fred Griffin, even though he was a gifted teacher, was unable to impart. "Mr. Griffin was strictly classical," Joe said, "so that most of the students he taught who played jazz used the same stiff classical approach for everything."

Under Griffin's strict tutelage, the youngster began to progress rapidly. "I thought it was great that you could see these notes and play them," he said. "And when I'd hear them, I'd think of what Mr. Griffin had played, and I felt like I was getting somewhere." Joe also became an inveterate practicer, a habit he continued into his nineties. "I practiced all the time," he said. "There were two white families that lived down the block from us. The Andersons were Swedish and were older and quite wealthy because they had a Rolls-Royce. The other family was the Elliots, who were very nice people. I would practice up in the bathroom, which had a window that opened toward the lot between our house and the Elliots', and Mrs. Elliot would always say, 'Joseph, will you stop playing that so-and-so cornet!' One time I swore at her, and she told my mother, and after she got done with me, I never did that again!"

Apparently, the trumpet was not the only instrument Joe practiced. The youngster would sneak up to the bedroom and play his father's sousaphone after he went off to work: "The mouthpiece is quite large, and the more I played, the more my embouchure would puff up. When my father came home from work, he would ask me to play some of the trumpet exercises I was learning, and I couldn't get a note out of the trumpet mouthpiece! He couldn't understand what was going on until one day he came home early and caught me fooling around on the sousaphone. He just laughed and said, 'Now I know what the problem is!'"

It was not long before Joe played in public for the first time. His nemesis, Principal Dever, decided that he should play taps at the school's Armistice Day celebration: "There was such a reaction to my playing that I thought, 'Gee, this is not a bad thing to do.' It might have been at that point that I decided I might like to be a professional musician." He would soon be heard by much larger audiences and backed by some of the leading orchestras of the day.

Colored Kiddies of the Air: "Little Louis" Meets Pops

Philadelphia was home to the Parisian Tailoring Company, which in the early 1930s made uniforms for many of the leading black orchestras. "These weren't military-type uniforms," Joe recalled, "but sports jackets and slacks. And when these guys traveled, people would see what they had on and would say, 'Where did you get that from?'" With business booming, as a way of paying back the community, Eddie Lieberman, the company's chief cutter and a manager of musical acts on the side, devised a plan for a black children's radio show to compete with the predominantly white *Horn and Hardart Children's Hour*, sponsored by the well-known restaurant chain. Sam and Harry Kessler, who owned the tailoring company, agreed to sponsor the new program, and the *Parisian Tailor's Colored Kiddies' Radio Hour* debuted on Sunday, March 27, 1932, on Philadelphia's station WPEN.[24]

Joe, who had just turned ten, auditioned for the program and became a regular. His close childhood friend, Percy Heath Jr., who would later become the outstanding bassist with the Modern Jazz Quartet, also appeared on the program. Although he played violin as a child, Heath switched to bass because as Joe remembered, "He lived in a kind of rough area, and he said every time he was on his way to school, these black kids would see him and say, 'Look at the sissy with the violin,' and they would challenge him and make fun of him. Being named Percy didn't help either!'" On the radio show, however, Percy played neither violin nor bass but appeared as a singer. Percy once described his vocal style as "singing sepia Eddie Cantor," and remembered Joe "playing his trumpet with the plunger then, *at 13 years old, man!*"[25] Younger brother Jimmy Heath remembered Percy scat singing on the program: "Percy always had a gift of gab, and he would do things in the street—people would call it rap now."[26] Jimmy was only five when the program debuted but remembered hearing his brother and Joe Wilder: "Joe was outstanding on trumpet, and Percy was just cuttin' the fool!"[27] Joe was a frequent visitor at the Heath home and developed a crush on Percy's older sister Elizabeth. "I was around twelve years old and announced that I was going to marry her, which is what I knew people did when they liked someone," Joe said. "Jimmy still kids me about that today!"

The *Colored Kiddies* radio show emanated from the stage of the Lincoln Theatre, on Broad and Lombard Streets, Philadelphia's main venue for leading black performers. Duke Ellington, Jimmie Lunceford, Louis Armstrong, Fletcher Henderson, and Fats Waller were just some of regular headliners at the Lincoln in the mid-1930s. What was most extraordinary about the radio show is that the children were backed by members of these legendary orchestras. Because of Pennsylvania's blue laws, there could be no regular performances in clubs or theaters on Sunday. As Joe put it, "We could go out and shoot each other on Sunday, but we weren't allowed to play jazz!" So as part of their contracts with the theater, the visiting bands were obligated to play behind the youngsters during the one-hour broadcasts on Sunday mornings. "We had the joy of having every name band—Duke Ellington, Cab Calloway, Fletcher Henderson, Earl Hines, Count Basie, the Mills Blue Rhythm Band— play for us on their day off," Joe said. "They would improvise backgrounds for whatever we played, and they encouraged us. It was unbelievable!" Although the bandleaders themselves didn't usually play, they did come to the rehearsals to make sure that their musicians fulfilled the terms of their contracts. "They were all very nice to me," Joe said. "Because I was one of the only kids who was playing an instrument, they would always talk to me—especially the trumpet players." For example, Ed Lewis, a mainstay of Count Basie's trumpet section, told him, "Kid, you're going to be all right!" He also remembered that when Crawford Wethington, a saxophonist with the Mills Blue Rhythm Band, saw his cornet, he told him, "Kid, you don't want to go out there with your instrument all tarnished!" Joe recalled, "He took the cornet, cleaned it up, polished it, and gave it back to me before the program started. It looked brand new, and for a week, I was afraid to touch it!" In typical fashion, three decades later, Joe sought out the saxophonist, who by then had left music and was working for the Transit Authority in New York, to thank him.

The *Colored Kiddies* show was an immediate hit. The African American press gave it extensive coverage. In its review of the April 10, 1932, performance, which drew a live audience of more than two thousand, the Baltimore *Afro-American* reported:

> The audience was made up of both white and colored, with the former showing a most courteous interest in the proceedings. To hear these kiddies on the air affords one a splendid hour of entertainment, but to see them before the mike, some not half as tall as the instrument, and facing a crowd of over 2,000 people, gives one a thrill and makes you feel proud of them.[28]

The reviews included Joe Wilder's first press notice: "A Louis Armstrong in the making was uncovered, in the person of Joseph Wilder, ten-year-old trumpet player."[29] Joe and the other "kiddie" performers showed tremendous poise appearing for the first time before such a large audience, although he admitted, "I didn't know there were that many people out there. I was standing back stage, and they just said, 'It's time to go on,' so out I went!" He also credited Ruth Mosely, the pianist who accompanied him and the other musical acts, with helping them through the ordeal: "She was a tremendous person and was like a mother to us."

By the April 24, 1932, show, the *Philadelphia Tribune* reported overflow crowds at the Lincoln Theatre, "causing many thousands to be turned away" and prompting WPEN officials to try to secure the larger Convention Hall for future performances. The paper again named Joe Wilder as one of "those whose creditable performance added considerable versatility to an interesting and most pleasing broadcast."[30] Joe continued to be praised in the *Tribune* for his performances, and the April 28, 1932, issue contained a short feature on him with a photo of a cherubic, round-faced ten-year-old Joe holding his trumpet. The article noted that the young musician also sold the *Tribune*, stating, "Joseph, the very energetic young son of Mr. and Mrs. Curtis Wilder, pays for his music lessons from his profits. If you have attended or tune in on the children's hour at the Lincoln Theatre on Sunday mornings you have heard Joseph play his cornet." Prophetically, the article concluded, "The TRIBUNE predicts a great musical career for Joseph."[31] Apparently, Joe's budding celebrity adversely affected the young man's usual modest demeanor, for he recalled that his father felt compelled to take him aside and say, "Joseph, for a ten-year-old cornet player, you play very well. But there are a lot of other ten-year-olds who play very well, too." He left it at that, "Joe recalled, "but I got the message!"

The talented youngsters included singers, dancers, and even comedians, some of them as young as two years old. Some of the "kiddies" went on to professional careers, including singer Ida James, who later worked with Erskine Hawkins; Mary Louise Jones, who sang with Cab Calloway; Leon James, who joined Whitey's Lindy Hoppers in the 1930s and toured with the Ink Spots in the 1940s as "Poke" of the Moke and Poke dance team; and James Cross and Eddie Hauptman, who formed the comedy duo of Stump and Stumpy (Hauptman was later replaced by Harold Cromer). Some of the youngsters began making appearances outside of the radio program. Joe recalled that Eddie Lieberman took him and several other "colored kiddies" to perform at a synagogue on Broad Street in Philadelphia: "He had taught Ida James how to sing 'Eli, Eli,' and she did it so beautifully that the whole congregation was crying." Joe also played a cornet solo at the Union Tabernacle Church on a program sponsored by the Paschall Social Club in December 1934.[32]

Joe explained that he was not improvising at all on these programs: "I would be playing the first trumpet part to some popular stock arrangement, like 'The Waltz You Saved for Me'—just reading the melody note for note. And the people thought that this was great! They called me 'Little Louis,' not because I played anything like Louis Armstrong but just because I played the trumpet." Armstrong, himself, was one of the visiting stars who appeared regularly at the Lincoln Theater, and Joe got a chance to meet him.

Louis Armstrong first appeared at the Lincoln Theatre in December 1932 and made several other visits in 1933 and 1936.[33] Joe's encounter with Armstrong most likely took place in February 1936. On Friday, February 21, Armstrong opened a week at the theater with Luis Russell's band, which also backed the *Colored Kiddies* for its weekly broadcast. The *Philadelphia Tribune* noted that Armstrong and his troupe "comes to Philadelphia direct from Connie's Inn on Broadway . . . and promises ninety minutes of the hottest and most spectacular entertainment ever presented on any stage."[34] The article also underscored the rigors endured by performers of that era, noting that Armstrong would be presenting five shows daily, the first beginning at twelve thirty in the afternoon. Louis, himself, did not play for the *Kiddies* broadcast but, according to Joe, was present for the Saturday rehearsal at which he heard the youngster play. "He was very nice to me that day," Joe recalled. "He gave me a pass to the theater and told me, 'Young man, you want to hear Pops play, you come every day.'"

Joe certainly knew who Armstrong was but did not fully appreciate the significance of this encounter until much later: "I knew he was a great personality, but I didn't realize how great his stature was as a musician." The youngster went to hear Armstrong's show the day of the rehearsal and once more during the week. "I was impressed, but I didn't understand that what he was doing was as great as it was because I was still trying to play like Del Staigers," Joe said. "I do remember being impressed with his version of 'Tiger Rag,' where he played one hundred high C's in a row. It was just great!"

Even as early as the mid-1930s, some members of the black community were disturbed by Armstrong's stage persona. "My father and many other black musicians in Philadelphia thought he was an Uncle Tom because he was always smiling and showing his teeth," Joe remembered. "Hearing them talk, I felt that way, too, for a time. I just didn't know any better." In time, however, his admiration for Armstrong grew, and he came to understand what obstacles the trumpeter had overcome. He learned to place Armstrong's onstage demeanor in context. Many years later, Joe was in the orchestra for the NBC *Kraft Music Hall* television show when Armstrong appeared as a guest in September 1967. During an interview segment, Joe recalled that Armstrong became very serious and said, "Everyone thinks that Pops is a 'Tom,' but in those days you could be lynched if you didn't play the game—you didn't know if you would live or die." Joe noted, "He looked so sad that I had tears in my eyes hearing him tell about it."

Looking back, Joe realized that Armstrong had made a greater impression on him than he thought at the time: "I guess he influenced me obliquely, because his cadenzas and things like certainly made an impression. Even today, when I'm improvising and I want to embellish something, I think in terms of what Louis Armstrong did." Joe never forgot Armstrong's kindness during that first meeting and kept the pass the trumpeter had given him. Over the years, Joe and Armstrong would meet periodically. "I think he took pride in the fact that I had made it in the studios," Joe said, "and he always remembered me as the kid trumpeter in Philadelphia. He would tell me, 'I always knew you were going to make it!'"

At the time of his meeting with Armstrong, Joe was about to turn fourteen and was gaining some celebrity thanks to his radio appearances. In announcing the *Colored Kiddies* show for August 16, 1936, the *Philadelphia Tribune* included Wilder—still known as "Joseph"—in a short list of "well known kiddie stars" to be featured with "a supporting cast of over one hundred and fifty children" in a revue called "Dixie in Harlem."[35] Unfortunately, Joe could not escape the kind of offensive material he had objected to a few years earlier in elementary school. One of the numbers in the show was "That's Why Darkies Were Born." Although the song had been recorded by Paul Robeson and the lyrics have a certain sarcastic connotation, the "sensitive" fourteen-year-old no doubt found it distasteful.

Joe and a hundred other young performers traveled to Atlantic City in early September 1936 for an outing sponsored by the Parisian Tailor's Sam Kessler. The *Philadelphia Tribune* singled out Joe's performance in a swing trio, consisting of his friends Eddie Lambert on guitar and John Cook on washboard: "When they started to swing 'Robins and Roses,' even Old Neptune rose from the bottom of the sea and started to truck."[36] The *Kiddies' Hour* concept was becoming so popular that a rival show began broadcasting from the stage of the new uptown Nixon Grand Theater in August 1936.[37] Although some of the child performers seemed to appear on both programs, Joe did not recall ever playing on the Nixon Grand show, which was produced by Harry Slatko, who had managed the Lincoln Theatre until March 1936, when he came under attack for mistreating the employees.[38] The Lincoln show began to refer to its troupe as the "Original Parisian Tailor's Colored Kiddies."[39] Joe continued to appear on the program at least until his first year of high school. He is listed in a display ad for a *"Parisian Tailor's Kiddie Hour"* broadcast on October 23, 1938, from the "WPEN Ballroom,"[40] and was mentioned (as "Joe," not "Joseph") in a list of "stars" from the same show after it aired.[41]

William T. Tilden Junior High School

In 1935, after graduating from Harriet Beecher Stowe Elementary School, Joe entered the William T. Tilden Junior High School. Named for the father of the Philadelphia-born tennis star of the 1920s and 1930s, the school (now Tilden Middle School) is still located on Elmwood Avenue, not far from the Wilder home on Seventieth Street. The neighborhood and the school were integrated, and once again, Joe had both white and black friends. The school also had a dedicated music teacher, Alberta Lewis (born "Schenbecker"), who directed the orchestra and had a profound effect on Joe's musical development. "It was with Mrs. Lewis that I started to make progress playing orchestrally," Joe said. "She's the one who introduced us to classical music. We would play excerpts from the *Pirates of Penzance* and other things that were pretty advanced for kids our age." The orchestra gained a reputation and soon began to receive invitations to play at other schools, some of which were segregated. Joe recalled traveling with the group to a nearby school, only to be confronted by one of the teachers, who asked, "Why would you bring a nigger into our school?" Lewis responded by threatening to take the orchestra and leave, and the performance continued. "I had many experiences like that as a kid," Joe said, "but there were always people like Mrs. Lewis who were trying to eliminate those situations."

Alberta Lewis believed in social justice and tried to confront segregation whenever she could. During the summer, she taught music at Girard College in Philadelphia. The school, which provided free tuition for students in grades one through twelve, was founded in 1833 through provisions in the will of Philadelphia shipping magnate Stephen Girard, who restricted enrollment to "poor, white, male orphans." It remained segregated until 1968.[42] In the summer of 1938, shortly before Wilder entered the Mastbaum School, Lewis decided to bring Joe and another of her African American students, pianist William Hamilton, to perform at Girard. Joe understood the significance of this act because he remembered that his father, who used to deliver coal to the college, was not allowed on the grounds even for that purpose: "They dug a big hole on the sidewalk outside the school so they could deliver the coal through a chute without coming on the campus." Undoubtedly,. Lewis felt by having two talented black students perform, she could combat some of the stereotypes and prejudices of her all-white Girard students. Following the performance, Joe remembered receiving a letter from each of the students thanking him for playing for them. Joe subsequently returned for another performance. His appearance was significant enough to merit mention in the *Philadelphia Tribune*.[43] While the segregated nature of the college was not mentioned, the significance of the visit by the sixteen-year-old Joe was certainly not lost on the paper's African American readership. Stephen Girard would probably not be pleased to know that his school's current enrollment is around 80 percent African American.

In the Tilden school orchestra, the other trumpet player was Rosario Pino, who became Joe's closest friend. The Pinos lived on the other end of Seventieth Street, and the two boys would walk to and from school together. Although for the most part the white and black students at Tilden got along, there were unpleasant incidents. On one occasion, Joe remembered that some-one or something incited a near-riot, which escalated until white and black students were fighting one another in the street in front of the school. As Joe and Rosario approached the mob, they turned to each other and said, "What are we going to do now?" But as they drew nearer, the crowd parted to let them through. "They knew we were friends and, for some reason, just let us pass," Joe said.

Joe played first and Rosario second cornet in the school orchestra. "He had a brand-new Blessing cornet, and I had a used Holton, which was okay but wasn't as good as the Blessing," Joe said. "One day Rosario came in and said, 'I was talking to my dad, and we decided that since you're playing first trumpet, I ought to let you play the Blessing, and I can play the second parts on your horn.' It was such a heartrending thing, and I never forgot it." Rosario and Joe remained lifelong friends until Rosario's death in 2004.

While playing in the Tilden school orchestra, Joe was attracted to the sounds of other instruments and tried to duplicate them on the trumpet: "I would hear a clarinet solo or a violin solo, and after the rehearsal, I'd be off in the corner playing what the clarinetist or string player had played." Sometimes the youngster would overdo it, and Lewis would interrupt and say, "Joseph, stop playing, or you'll be too worn out to do the concert tonight!" Joe began a lifelong regimen of practicing pieces written for other instruments. This method helped him gain flexibility on the trumpet, which paid off when he began working in the studios:

Once I was subbing at CBS, and we were doing something with an opera singer. The music had a French horn part, but we had no French horn player in the staff orchestra. They gave it to the trombone players, but they didn't know how to transpose it, so I told Lou Shoobe, the contractor, that I could play it on my flügelhorn, if they really needed it. So I played it, and he couldn't get over it. Then he gave the trombone players a hard time about it, so they wanted to kill me!

Joe's ability to play things that he heard was aided by the fact that he had perfect pitch, which he discovered around the age of twelve:

I was sitting around one day listening to a jazz program on the radio with my father, and he said, "Joseph, what key do you think they're in?" I could hear the chords in my ear, and I said, "I think it's B flat." I was right, and then he started playing other things for me, and that's how we found out I had absolute pitch, as it was called. It didn't mean much to me at the time, but a few years later, I understood what it meant. Even today, I'll start humming something I heard, and it'll turn out to be in the key in which I heard it initially. It can be advantageous, but other times it can work to your detriment. You can get so dependent on it that you think whatever it is, you can hear it, but there are some intervals that are so far apart that you can get all fouled up.

By the time he turned thirteen or fourteen, Joe began to accompany his father on some of Curtis's musical jobs, even sitting in on occasion. "He would tell me, 'We have three trumpet parts, but we only hired two trumpets, so you sit there next to Mr. Beckett [lead trumpeter Leroy Beckett], and if you think you can read the notes, then you try to play, but don't play anything that you can't read because I don't want Mr. Beckett to get angry.'" Joe recalled that Beckett was not too thrilled with this arrangement: "About the fourth time he took me with him, Mr. Beckett was standing with one of the other musicians, and when he saw me, he said louder than he realized, 'Oh, my God! Here comes Wilder with that damn kid again!'"

Another adult who began to take the youngster with him on gigs was Percy Heath Sr., father of Joe's friends Percy Jr. and Jimmy. "My father was an auto mechanic and would play clarinet on weekends when he'd get it out of the pawn shop," Jimmy said. "He used to play in the Woodsmen's marching band and would take Joe with him."[44] Joe was already a good reader and recalled that the senior Heath liked to tease his fellow band members by saying, "Look, this little kid can out-read all of you!" Joe noted, "They hated my guts and hated him even more for bringing me!"

While in junior high, Joe also recalled being taken by the older brother of a friend to play in a black nightclub called Hawley's in Darby. "Blind Jimmy played the piano there," Joe said. "He was a very fine musician and would be playing different pop tunes of the day, and I'd play the melody with him. I looked older than I was, so nobody questioned it."

By junior high school, Joe Wilder had already accumulated a wealth of musical experiences. In addition to receiving a solid musical grounding from teachers like Frederick Griffin and Alberta Lewis, the youngster had performed in public before large audiences and had met and been encouraged by some of the leading jazz figures of the day. Over the next two years, he would further hone his skills and complete the transition from student to full-time working musician.

From Student to Pro (1938–1943)

Mastbaum

As he was about to graduate from Tilden Junior High School in 1938, Joe Wilder remembered that the guidance counselor tried to steer him into an industrial course in high school but that his music teacher, Alberta Lewis, intervened and convinced him to take an academic path. Meanwhile, she arranged for him to audition for the Mastbaum Vocational and Technical School in Germantown, which was renowned for its music program. The audition took place at the University of Pennsylvania, and Wilder chose to play a well-known 1908 cornet solo piece, "I Am Waiting for You Darling at the Old Red Mill," composed by Ernest S. Williams. (Wilder would use the same piece for his audition in 1950 at the Manhattan School of Music.)

Wilder passed the audition and in the fall of 1938 enrolled at Mastbaum, where he was one of only a handful of African American students; another was pianist Sam Cosby, the uncle of Bill Cosby. The curriculum at Mastbaum at that time was entirely classical, despite the fact that among Wilder's classmates

---

Wilder as a member of Lonnie Slappey's Orchestra, Pennsauken, NJ, November 1940. *(Wilder Family Collection.)*

were future jazz stars trumpeter Red Rodney and clarinetist Buddy DeFranco. "Buddy and Red were always experimenting with jazz," Wilder recalled. Rodney, in particular, liked to push the envelope with the staid Mastbaum faculty. "He was like a rebel, and he'd play jazz just to annoy the teachers," Wilder said. "He was a nice kid, but wild!" DeFranco agreed, "Red was wild by our standards. Joe and I were more conventional and sedate. Red was a little edgy. He made a little noise, but he never got in real trouble."[1]

"A lot of the Mastbaum students entered the Curtis Institute when they graduated, and some went on to the Philadelphia Orchestra or the Baltimore Symphony," Wilder said. Jazz was not only excluded from the curriculum, it was not tolerated on the premises. "If they caught you playing jazz, you were in real trouble," Wilder said. "Some guys would be playing a symphony and add a seventh to the last chord and the conductor would get furious! He'd start an investigation to find who did it. He knew that only the jazz guys would do something like that." Once again, Rodney was the instigator, according to DeFranco: "He'd throw in some jazz once in a while and [conductor and school director] Maier Levin's baton would go flying in his direction!"[2]

DeFranco and some of the other jazz-minded students formed a swing band, which at first had to rehearse outside the school grounds. Eventually, however, attitudes changed. "The conductors got to the point that they acknowledged the swing band and supported it," DeFranco recalled. "It had to change because of the quality of the band and the popularity of swing."[3]

Although he played in the student-formed swing group, Wilder was not given to jazz experiments and was certainly not inclined to challenge the rules at Mastbaum. For one thing, he was still primarily interested in a career as a classical musician. "I was more into the Arban book," Wilder said. "The thought that I couldn't play with a symphony because of segregation didn't occur to me, although I must have known about it." Moreover, as one of the few black music students in the school, he felt the pressure to be on his best behavior. Saxophonist Leon Cohen, who attended Mastbaum with Wilder and later worked with him on staff at ABC, recalled that even then Wilder displayed his legendary sense of propriety: "He never cursed and always came to school in a suit and tie, even on the hottest summer day."[4] And DeFranco said, "As a person, Joe never seemed to change—he was always very dapper, well dressed, well spoken, even in high school—and he always had a good sense of humor."[5]

Wilder described his playing in the symphonic band at Mastbaum: "They had a symphony orchestra, but there were so many trumpet players and wind players that they had no way to use us all, so they made us the symphonic band, under the direction of Ross Wyre. We played violin music—symphonic concert music that had been transcribed for wind instruments. It was a beautiful band." The trumpet section consisted of three solo cornets and three each in the first, second, third, and fourth chairs. Although he was named to one of the three solo cornet chairs, Wilder felt he was not yet in the same league as his two colleagues. "The other two guys could double- and triple-tongue," Wilder said. "I could 'stumble-tongue,' but by listening to them, I learned."

Wilder constantly sought to improve his skills while he was a student, just as he did throughout his career. During the nearly two-hour daily commute by trolley and then subway from his home in Philadelphia to Germantown, he would study the music: "I'd look at it, and in my ears I could hear what the symphonic band was playing, and I would relate what I heard to what I saw on the paper. I got to the point where I could sight read almost as well as anybody in the band." DeFranco commented, "One thing that really impressed me was his dedication. He practiced all the time."[6]

DeFranco noted that Wilder was also making progress as a jazz player: "Once in a while I did jazz gigs with him outside of school. He was not improvising a lot in the beginning—he would just play the orchestration. But as time went on, he began to delve into improvising more and more. And he always had good ears, so he picked it up quickly."[7] At that early stage—indeed throughout his career—Wilder's classical training was a primary influence on his improvisational style. "His demeanor, his attitude, and his approach to playing jazz were all very much aligned with his 'legitimate' playing," De-Franco said.[8]

The teenager made a quantum leap in both his ability as an instrumentalist and in his overall knowledge of music theory at Mastbaum. Although he was not playing jazz—at least not in school—Wilder was introduced to the theory of "tonal magnetism," which was in vogue at the time: "It helped explain why you would be drawn to a certain harmonic closure to a phrase," and the theory would prove useful in his later career as an improviser. Wilder also began to make the transition from cornet to trumpet. "I had to get used to playing trumpet after I'd played cornet for so long," he said. "With the cornet, the bell is only a few inches from your face. The trumpet was strange to my ears because of the longer distance."

Despite playing by the rules and going out of his way not to make waves, Wilder's stay at Mastbaum was not without incident. The York Band Instrument Company, which supplied the instruments at Mastbaum, sent a representative to photograph the school orchestras for their catalog. Wilder took his customary seat on the stage with the other two solo cornetists in the symphonic band. When school director Maier Levine came in and saw him, Wilder recalled him yelling, "Hey, Wilder! What are you doing up there? Get down there where you belong!" Wilder tried to explain, to no avail, that he had been playing in the solo section all semester. "He just wouldn't let up," Wilder said. "Finally, the guys in the orchestra—Buddy DeFranco, Leon Cohen, Robert Little, and the others—started screaming at him [Levine], 'He's been here all along!' He said, 'Oh, really? Let me hear you play the C-sharp scale—two octaves! Now play a melodic minor.'" After Wilder successfully passed this impromptu test, Levine relented and let him stay. "It was really dumb because that's what they were teaching us!" Wilder noted.

Saxophonist-composer John LaPorta, who was a senior when Wilder entered Mastbaum, recounts this incident in his autobiography, but it differs in the details and, perhaps in deference to the memory of Levine, downplays any racial overtones:

> Maier Levine, although normally a pleasant man, was out of sorts on this particular day. Nothing the orchestra did pleased him. About half way through the rehearsal, he stopped the orchestra and pointed his baton at the young Afro-American playing third trumpet. "I'll bet you don't even know your major scales," he said sarcastically. "Play an A flat major scale for me." Joe Wilder sat up straight, took a deep breath and played a perfect two octave A flat major scale in rapid sixteenth notes. Then, politely, he asked Maier, "Would you like any other?" Without another word, our amazed conductor turned to the rest of us and continued with the rehearsal.[9]

Although devastated by the incident, which would eventually contribute to his decision to leave the school, Wilder was encouraged by the strong verbal support he had received from his fellow students. "You don't forget that," he said. "People like that have enabled me to overcome a lot of the problems I faced. No matter how angry I might get, you can't make generalizations and apply them to everybody."

DeFranco recalled this incident and a few similar ones involving Wilder: "Once in a while there was some friction, some funny attitudes, but over time, the fact that we were all playing the same music brought us together." He added, "Of course we all stood up for Joe because we admired him so much—his performance, his approach and his demeanor. Everybody liked him."[10] DeFranco noted, "Joe taught me the meaning of tolerance and acceptance."[11]

Percussionist-arranger Shep Shepherd also attended Mastbaum. Five years Wilder's senior, he graduated in 1937, a year before the trumpeter entered the school. One of only a handful of African American students, Shepherd also recalled the school's rigid anti-jazz policy maintained by its director: "To Maier Levine, anything that was not classical or symphonic wasn't worth anything and was taboo. He didn't even want anyone to blow a saxophone in his orchestra. Ross Wyre was more flexible because he had played some jazz in his day."[12] Although he stopped short of accusing Levine of racist tendencies, he acknowledged that the incident between Maier Levine and Wilder did not surprise him.

At Mastbaum, students were required to learn a second instrument, and following in the steps of his father, Wilder chose the bass. He studied with an outside teacher who taught at the Philadelphia Settlement School. "He didn't like me to begin with," Wilder said. "There are certain ways to hold your arm and fingers, and I was so short that I couldn't get my elbow up as high as he wanted it, so he came over and smacked my elbow up. I told him if he did that again, I'd knock his head off, and that was the end of the bass lessons!"

Despite his continued commitment to classical music, at some point during his tenure at Mastbaum, Wilder's goals began to shift slightly, as it began to dawn on him that a career with a major symphony orchestra was not realistic for an African American musician coming of age in the late 1930s and early 1940s. "I still hoped to join a symphony orchestra but perhaps on a lower level," he said. In addition, a family crisis made it imperative that he begin to earn more money. So while continuing his classical studies at Mastbaum, the trumpeter began to work in some of the many local Philadelphia jazz groups.

While Joe was at Mastbaum, his parents divorced. His father had had an affair with a singer, whom he later married. It was completely out of character for Curtis Sr., whose behavior until then had been beyond reproach and from whom Joe had acquired his own high moral values. But that one transgression was enough. Gussie never forgave him, and the marriage was over. With his characteristic sense of responsibility, Joe, who was only fifteen or sixteen at the time, regretted that he was unable to save the marriage. "If I had been older, I would have tried to reason with them and settle it," he said. "But my mother had told all her friends, and these so-called friends would never let her forget it." Joe and his brothers were devastated. His older brother, Curtis Jr., never forgave his father and refused to have anything further to do with him. Joe tried to maintain some contact, but his father's absence was a major void. "I felt so sorry for him because he was basically a good-hearted person who had made one mistake," he said. Wilder also noted that even after the divorce, his parents were still "fond enough of each other so that when my father got sick and had to have an operation, my mother went to the hospital to see him. And when my mother was sick, he went to the hospital several times to see her." And eventually, Joe and his father became close once again and would remain so until Curtis's death.

The divorce put an additional financial strain on the family, and Joe began to take whatever musical jobs he could find to supplement the family's income while continuing his studies at Mastbaum. Fortunately, there was plenty of work. The black population of Philadelphia had almost doubled between 1920 and 1930, creating a great demand for entertainment and spawning the vibrant music scene to which Joe Wilder was exposed in the 1930s.[13] As early as 1932, the *Philadelphia Tribune* called the city "the new Mecca for the theatrical world," citing an "evacuation" of black performers from Harlem because of the Depression: "With the Lincoln, Pearl, Standard, Forrest, Mastbaum, and the Nixon Grand all featuring colored bands and performers quite considerable relief is offered, and how they are pouring into the Quaker City is nobody's business."[14] The author of the *Tribune* article listed more than a hundred performers he claimed to have encountered during the prior seven days alone, "while passing to and fro on the theatre streets of Philadelphia, on our visits to the various dance halls and cabaret restaurants." Among those listed were Louis Armstrong, McKinney's Cotton Pickers, Duke Ellington, Bubber Miley, Benny Moten, Clara Smith, the Mills Brothers, Eubie Blake, Alberta Hunter, and Benny Carter.[15]

In addition to the larger theaters, which presented the nationally known swing bands and stage shows, dozens of fraternal organizations, lodges, social clubs, and dance halls turned to the abundant supply of local talent for entertainment. "The black community was trying to build itself up, and these events were an important part of the peoples' lives," Wilder said. Thanks to his already impressive musicianship and reading ability, the teenaged Wilder found himself in great demand. At first he was paid two dollars for a dance that might last all night, but as he gained experience, his fee was raised to three dollars. Unable to improvise at first, playing with these local groups—especially the smaller ensembles that did not have written arrangements—proved invaluable in helping him develop his jazz skills. "I didn't even know that I was playing jazz!" he said.

One of the popular groups with whom Wilder worked was a big band led by Jimmy Gorham. Wilder had been playing with a society orchestra led by the distinguished African American concert violinist Josh Saddler, but was drawn to the exciting swing of Gorham's band. "The guys in that band had tremendous ears, absolute pitch," Wilder said. "Shep Shepherd would copy an Ellington or Basie or Lunceford record note for note, and every instrument would be correct." According to Shepherd, his transcriptions may have been a little too accurate for the leader: "Gorham once said to me, 'Don't bring any more of those records in here—you've got the band sounding just like Jimmie Lunceford!' He was after something else, so I give him credit."[16]

Whereas playing with Gorham was far more thrilling for the young trumpeter than playing with the more staid orchestra led by Saddler, the paychecks were less frequent. "Some nights we wouldn't get anything, and Jimmy would tell us he'd make it up the next night," Wilder said. "My father asked if I was sure I'd made the right decision."

Gorham's band played an engagement at the all-white Warwick Hotel in Philadelphia for a lady who was throwing a party. "This was only the second time that a black band played in the hotel—my father happened to be in the band that first played there years earlier," Wilder said. "And after that engagement, the white union local told the hotel that if they hired any more black bands, they would bar any white bands from playing in there." But the hostess specifically requested Gorham's band, which was a big hit with her guests. "During the intermission," Wilder recalled, "she came over to compliment Jimmy and said with a deep Southern accent, 'Mr. Gorham, I just want to tell you that my guests all enjoyed y'all's music. Most of them have never heard a hot nigger band before!' There was a silence in that band room, and then the guys started asking each other, 'Did she say what I think I just heard?' They lit into that woman to the point that some of us actually felt sorry for her because she really didn't mean to offend us."

Gorham gave occasional solo opportunities to the young trumpeter, who at the time was infatuated with the plunger style of Ellington trumpet star Cootie Williams. "One of the first times I got to solo was on the melody of 'The Waltz You Saved for Me,' the Wayne King thing, at a society dance," Wilder said. "So I played it with the plunger, and the guys in the band were breaking up. One of the trumpet players took me off to the side when we got through and said, 'Joe, you don't have to play everything with the toilet plunger!'"

Nevertheless, the seventeen-year-old trumpeter was developing an approach of his own—one that set him apart from the average big-band trumpeter of the day. Shep Shepherd, who in addition to his arranging, played drums in the Gorham orchestra, already saw some of the characteristics that would mark Wilder's later distinctive style, notably his incorporation of classical technique and motifs: "At that early stage, he was very influenced by his teachers, who in turn had been influenced by the symphony orchestra, so he had an 'up' on many other trumpet players. He could combine his classical knowledge in a jazz solo in interesting ways. That made him stand apart from all the guys who were just trying to sound like Louis Armstrong."[17] Shepherd also noted the contributions Wilder made to the section and the ensemble as a whole: "He could play a first part on sight and he played in tune. To play jazz with that kind of intonation set you apart in those days. Most of the guys had taught themselves, and playing in tune didn't make any difference to them."[18]

Now that he was regularly employed as a working musician, Joe Wilder joined Musicians Union Local 274, the black Philadelphia local, which had been established in 1935 (Curtis Wilder was a founding member). At age sixteen, he passed the musical entry test with ease; the fact that he was a student of Fred Griffin, who was well known and respected, did not hurt. As in most major cities (New York being an exception), Philadelphia had separate white and black musicians unions. Local 77, Philadelphia's white union, controlled employment in the larger white hotels and the Philadelphia Orchestra, while the black Local 274, handled the predominantly black theaters and smaller neighborhood clubs. In her thorough study of Local 274, Diane Delores Turner noted the importance of the black locals in the cultural life of the community, "With the establishment of colored locals, Black musicians were able to perpetuate their cultural identity and articulate a Black perspective through their music. Black locals also reinforced the cohesiveness that African-American musicians developed through their music. Colored musicians' unions functioned as unions but also as cultural and fraternal institutions."[19] For this reason, after passage of the Civil Rights Act of 1964, when the American Federation of Musicians launched efforts to merge the nation's separate musicians unions, many black members opposed these mergers. Apart from losing an important cultural and social institution, they felt that amalgamation would also hurt black musicians economically. They would lose control over the jobs they had, while still being excluded from the traditionally white venues. As Shep Shepherd put it, "With all the politicking going on, the jobs were still segregated."[20] Consequently, Philadelphia's Local 274 became the last black local to hold out; its refusal to merge resulted in its expulsion from the American Federation of Musicians in 1971.[21]

The Harlem Dictators

Working until all hours of the night and then having to make the long commute to Germantown in time for early classes at Mastbaum began to take a toll on the teenage Wilder. "I'd be half asleep in a history class, and the teacher would ask me who was president when some event took place," Wilder said. "One of the other students would wake me up and whisper, 'Louis Armstrong,' or something like that, so that's what I answered, and everyone would laugh!" By the spring of 1939, it was clear that he could no longer maintain this grueling schedule, and Wilder left Mastbaum after only one year to became a full-time working musician. Apart from the need to help support his family, Wilder's decision to leave school was hastened by the unpleasant incident with Maier Levine and the Mastbaum orchestra photo.

The 1940 U.S. Census (recorded on April 16 of that year) lists the eighteen-year-old Joseph's occupation as "musician" and confirms the fact that he was no longer in school. With Curtis Sr. no longer residing in the family home at 2018 Seventy-First Street, Gussie (Augustine) is named as head of household. Her occupation is listed as "seamstress" for the WPA, one of several jobs she pursued to make ends meet.

During the summer of 1940, Wilder began playing with another local band, the Harlem Dictators, which was modeled after the popular John Kirby Sextet. The band had two trumpeters, and even though the other trumpeter, Billy Jones, was also the group's leader, Wilder found himself playing all the intricate lead parts as well as the improvised solos. "Billy Jones would just sit there," Wilder said. "He didn't want to exert himself as long as I didn't know any better! At one point, I'd played so much that my embouchure went dead. For almost a month, I could barely play a note." Charlie Shavers, the virtuoso trumpeter and arranger with Kirby's group, learned about the Harlem Dictators and even came by to hear them during an engagement in Baltimore. "He was very encouraging to me," Wilder remembered.

The Harlem Dictators frequently played in Annapolis, Maryland, whose Fourth Ward was home to a vibrant African American community. From the 1920s through the 1940s, its nightspots attracted "local and national talent that most other blues and jazz lovers traveled to Washington, Philadelphia, or New York to hear."[22] It was during an Annapolis engagement with the Harlem Dictators at Eudie Legum's Washington Hotel that Wilder met Charlie Parker for the first time. Parker was part of the band in a troupe led by Banjo Burney, which was playing in a different venue, most likely the Wright Hotel. "Banjo Burney was a slick operator," Wilder said. "He would put a whole package together to play in a nightclub—he had the band, the singers, the dancers, the comedians. The club or hotel owner would just pay Banjo Burney, and he would deliver a whole show." During the day, Parker would sit in the window of his hotel room practicing incessantly. "He'd play all these popular tunes in every key," Wilder said. "Then he'd play them fast and slow, and everybody said, 'This guy is crazy!' But that's how he developed what we came to know as bebop. He was very friendly to me, although we didn't speak too much then."

While playing with the Dictators, Wilder met Lillian Wykoff, a young lady from Annapolis who came to hear the band at the Washington Hotel. They began dating and eventually married in 1943.

Another of the local bands with whom he worked regularly was a small group led by pianist Lonnie Slappey. With Slappey, Wilder's improvisational skills improved, as he was called on to solo more extensively than he had with Jimmy Gorham's orchestra. Moreover, he was replacing Frank Galbreath, an experienced soloist with whom he would later work in Lucky Millinder's band. "Frank was so creative and had a style all his own," Wilder said. The band's book featured the trumpet extensively. "I had to learn how to improvise because Frank was a genius at that stuff. He loved Louis Armstrong, and he even talked like Louis," Wilder added. "He could come up with some of the most interesting improvisations, and I tried to do some of the things he did. It was a great opportunity for me."

The drummer with the Slappey band was Rudy Traylor, who went on to a distinguished career with Earl Hines and Jimmie Lunceford and later as a studio musician and producer. Much to the amusement of his fellow musicians, Wilder would vocally replicate Traylor's intricate drum licks: "I sounded like a whole drum set, and Rudy would say, 'You're stealing my stuff!'"

In Slappey's band Wilder began to acquire a reputation as a prankster, mastering the art of the "hotfoot." "I learned it from the guys in the band," he recalled. "We'd go into a restaurant, and I'd get down on my knees on the floor, light a wooden match, and slip it under the foot of the person in the next booth, and all of a sudden they'd start screaming. We used to pull this in a restaurant on Broad and South Street, where some of the worst thugs in Philadelphia hung out. If they had found out it was us, we would never have gotten out of there alive!" Eventually, Wilder's conscience—and sense of self-preservation—prevailed, and he abandoned the hotfoot for less risky practical jokes.

Around this time Wilder had the chance to play with another of his idols, Roy Eldridge, who was appearing at the Downbeat in Philadelphia. "He had heard me play somewhere and invited me to come by and sit in," Wilder said. "So I went down, and he said we would play 'After You've Gone,' which was a big hit for him at the time. I said, 'I can't play at that tempo,' and he said, 'Well, I'll play one, and then you play one,' so I played along with him and got through it. Although he was very competitive, he was very kind to me by not making me play three or four choruses in a row. He could play ten choruses, and all of them would be different!"[23]

Leaving Home: Les Hite

In 1941, Wilder accepted an offer to join a nationally known touring band: Les Hite's orchestra. Hite's organization had been based in Los Angeles, where it built a solid reputation during a nearly decade-long residency in the 1930s at Sebastian's Cotton Club. Lionel Hampton was one of the band's notable sidemen, and Louis Armstrong fronted the group for several landmark recordings in 1930. By 1941, Hite was seeking a wider audience by touring the Midwest and Northeast. Wilder was recommended to Hite by the arranger Walter "Gil" Fuller, who was writing for the orchestra and had heard the trumpeter while he was with Jimmy Gorham's band in Philadelphia. Almost simultaneously, Wilder received an offer from another top bandleader, Earl Hines, who was looking for a replacement for trumpeter Benny Harris. Harris had become unreliable because of a spiraling drug problem, and Wilder was suggested by band members Budd Johnson, Pee Wee Jackson, and Billy Eckstine, who had also heard Wilder in Philadelphia. Wilder greatly admired the Hines orchestra, which he had seen several times at the Lincoln Theatre, but by the time he received Hines's telegram, he had already accepted Les Hite's offer. In addition, he felt uncomfortable replacing Benny Harris, whom he had gotten to know and considered a friend.

In November 1941, the nineteen-year-old Wilder boarded a bus in Philadelphia for East Lansing, Michigan, to join Les Hite's orchestra. This was Joe's first time away from home—other than a brief trip to Virginia with the Harlem Dictators—and Gussie was at the bus station to see him off: "My mother was standing there at the side of the bus, which was loaded with strangers, lecturing me through the window. 'Now you behave yourself, and whatever you do, don't do anything to embarrass our family!' I'm sinking down in my seat hoping nobody would see me!"

After meeting up with the band in East Lansing, Wilder spent the first week learning the new music. Once again, his sight-reading skills, honed at Mastbaum, served him well. "The guys in the band thought I was a genius because I could come in and read the music right away," he said. "I wasn't even thinking about it because that's what I'd been doing and had studied in school." His skills were not always appreciated by some of the older musicians who may have felt threatened by the precocious youngster. "There were some guys in the band that were really mean," Wilder recalled. "During intermission, we would leave our horns on our seats on the bandstand. At one show, when I came back and picked up the horn and tried to play, I almost popped my eardrums. They had turned the valves around so no air was going through. And these guys were all laughing."

While the band could swing, by the time Wilder joined the orchestra, Hite was cultivating a more sedate and sweeter approach. "It was a good band, but it was more like a commercial orchestra because we were basically playing white dances." Wilder said. "It was very seldom that we'd play for a black dance." In a feature on Hite in the Baltimore *Afro-American* in January 1942, the leader referred to his band's style as "mood" music, and the writer added, "He plays what the dancers want—when they want it: sweet ballads, novelties, rhumbas, tangos, and congos [*sic*]."[24]

Wilder was playing lead trumpet exclusively, but he did get some solo opportunities on ballads. Hite had commissioned arranger Van Alexander, who went on to become a noted composer in Hollywood, to provide some of the ballad charts. "In those days, the first trumpet player would play an eight- or sixteen-bar solo leading into the ensemble," Wilder said. "He'd write these beautiful, flourishing trumpet lead-ins. I got a tremendous amount of experience by playing first trumpet on his arrangements." Alexander's work for Chick Webb, including Ella Fitzgerald's 1938 hit "A-Tisket, A-Tasket," raised the profile of the young arranger. "Through that I gained a little momentum in my fledgling career," Alexander recalled. "I was asked to write arrangements for different bands at the Savoy, like Teddy Hill and Don Redman."[25] Les Hite was one of the black bandleaders who sought him out. Alexander arranged about a dozen pieces for Hite and remembered rehearsing the band on his charts in a New Jersey club—probably the Chatterbox. "He had a wonderful band, with musicians like Joe Wilder and Marshal Royal,"[26] Alexander said. "I didn't pick out the tunes to arrange. Les would give me a list of tunes because I wouldn't be presumptuous enough to just arrange anything I wanted to. The tunes he gave me lent themselves to the lush kind of arrangement that I produced for them."[27] It was on one of those "lush" pieces that Wilder played his first recorded solo—a full-toned, eight-bar melody statement on "I Remember You," made for the Hit label in April 1942. The flip side, "Jersey Bounce," was far more celebrated because it contains one of the essential early Dizzy Gillespie solos and, consequently, has been reissued many times on LP and CD. As of 2013, however, "I Remember You" remains a rarity, with the original 78 its only issue.

Gil Fuller, who had recommended Wilder to Les Hite, was also writing for the band. Fuller was a versatile arranger, who became associated primarily with bebop through his later work for Dizzy Gillespie. But at that early stage, he was deeply influenced by Sy Oliver's writing for the Jimmie Lunceford band. "He would write arrangements that were almost note for note stolen from a Jimmie Lunceford thing he'd copy and give to Les [Hite]," Wilder said. "A couple of times I said innocently, 'You know this sounds just like so-and-so,' and Gil would come over and nudge me and say, 'Keep quiet, fool! Les doesn't know any better—leave it alone!'"[28]

Although Wilder missed his family, he enjoyed traveling. "I was fascinated by the geography of the different states we passed through," he said. "We traveled mostly by bus—a Western Flyer, which was a small, fast, and very maneuverable vehicle. We traveled in pretty good style, staying in some nice hotels or in private homes." One of the places where Wilder stayed during the band's Northeastern swing in early 1942 was the Newark home of Dorothy Foster, whose daughter, Gail, remembered Joe's good manners and his appreciation of her grandmother's cooking, especially her cornbread.[29]

In January 1942, Hite's orchestra became the first black band to play at the Chatterbox in Mountainside, New Jersey. Helped by regular broadcasts over the Mutual network, the band was held over an extra four weeks and received much press coverage, especially for a piece called "Blackout," which "created as much pandemonium . . . as the famous panic caused by Orson Welles's dramatization of an invasion by the Martians. Some of the realistic air raid effects, especially the zooming of bombers by the trombones, caused residents in nearby houses to black their windows hurriedly."[30]

The band had some excellent players, including Britt Woodman on trombone, with whom Wilder enjoyed a lifelong friendship; his brother, Coney, on piano; and high-note trumpet specialist Walter Williams. Wilder also got along well with the leader: "Les Hite was a nice man—a very low-key kind of a guy. He was a saxophone player himself, and he rehearsed the band and played a ballad on occasion. He treated me very nicely, or should I say put up with me." Wilder was referring to his penchant for practical jokes, which sometimes rankled the older members of the orchestra. The leader's patience was tested even more after a brilliant new trumpeter, John Birks "Dizzy" Gillespie, whose nickname was well earned, joined the orchestra in March 1942.

Wilder had first met Gillespie several years earlier, when the trumpeter had played with Joe's father in a Philadelphia band led by Frankie Fairfax. "Everyone in the Fairfax band was in my father's age group, so they had never seen anyone with a sense of humor like Dizzy's," Wilder said. Gillespie, who was still a teenager but five years older than Joe, befriended the youngster. "He used to kid me because I was a little kid and always had a bowtie. But he was always very nice to me." Even at that early stage, Wilder could detect something new and different in Gillespie's style. "I remember hearing him say to some other musicians in Philadelphia, 'I can't play the high things like Roy Eldridge, but I'm going to play as articulately as I can,'" Wilder said.

By the time he joined Les Hite, Gillespie was gaining fame for his advanced trumpet style as well as for his zany humor, which had a deleterious effect on his young section mate, Joe Wilder. "He was always saying things to crack me up," Wilder said. "When you're nineteen, everything is funnier than it should be, and just when Les Hite gave the down beat, Dizzy would give the punch line. I'd be laughing so hard I couldn't play a note!" With his lead trumpet player incapacitated, Les Hite was understandably perturbed: "He'd be yelling at me, 'Junior! Play! I'm gonna fire you if you don't play!' And as he's screaming, I see Dizzy sitting there like he had a halo over his head—playing as if nothing had happened."

Humor aside, Wilder found playing with Gillespie a highly stimulating musical experience. "He was one of the most wonderful section mates you could have," Wilder said. "He could read like mad, and whatever phrasing you wanted to use, he would follow. Or he would suggest that we play a figure a certain way, and it would always be an improvement over the way it was written."

Gillespie's antics eventually led to his being fired by Hite and to Wilder's own departure from the band shortly thereafter. Gillespie crossed the line during an engagement at the Howard Theatre in Washington, DC, in May 1942. Hite was standing up front and doing a little dance with his back to the band. Gillespie, from his perch in the trumpet section, began imitating each of the leader's moves. "The audience was cracking up," Wilder recalled. "Les had this big smile on his face, thinking, 'I'm really killing these people!'" Whenever the leader turned around to direct the band, Gillespie would quickly sit down with his customary angelic expression on his face. At one point during the second day of the engagement, however, Hite turned more quickly and caught Gillespie imitating him. "Les was a very nice man but very sensitive," Wilder said. "He was so angry he just seemed to swell up to double his size. He shook his head and gritted his teeth. And when we came off the bandstand, he said, 'That's it! Everybody's fired! You've got your two weeks' notice!'"

Hite actually wanted to get rid of Gillespie and not the entire band. But Hite was wary of firing him because of the famous incident in which Gillespie had pulled a knife on Cab Calloway when the bandleader unfairly accused the trumpeter of throwing a spitball at him. "So when we went in to get paid at the end of the week," Wilder recalled, "he told each of us individually, 'That notice doesn't apply to you. I'm just trying to get rid of Dizzy. You know, he cut Cab, and I don't want to take any chances.'" But between the time Hite had fired the band and the time he revoked the notice only a couple of days later, Wilder had already received a call from Lionel Hampton inviting him to join his orchestra, and he accepted.

Lionel Hampton

Wilder was originally brought in to the Hampton band in May 1942 as a temporary replacement for first trumpeter Karl George, who had to leave for a few weeks on personal business.[31] Thanks to his work with Les Hite, Wilder was becoming known for his abilities as a lead player, and several members of Hampton's band recommended him to the leader as someone who could step in and sight-read the first trumpet parts. Wilder had a clear understanding of his role and enjoyed the responsibility that went with the lead chair:

The first trumpet player is supposed to look at the music and decide how he wants to play it. The other members of the trumpet section and the rest of the orchestra in general follow what he does. Of course, the first alto player decides certain things for the reed section, and the rhythm section likewise. But the key to most of it is the first trumpet player. He decides how to phrase things. He doesn't necessarily say anything to the other players; he just does it, and the other guys listen to him and try to emulate what he's doing. The first trumpet player, for the most part, sets the style.

When Karl George returned, Hampton decided to keep Wilder and expand the trumpets from three to four. So Wilder became a permanent member of a formidable section that included George, Ernie Royal, and Joe Newman. Packed with young up-and-coming stars, such as tenor saxophonists Illinois Jacquet and Dexter Gordon, Wilder found Hampton's band to be a far more swinging unit than Hite's:

Although Les Hite's band, musically, was a very fine orchestra, it was more or less commercial. When I went with Lionel Hampton's band, I couldn't believe the things they were playing! I was very happy because this had to be the best band and the youngest band on the scene, and they were playing music that was so different—it wasn't bebop yet, but it was so much more modern and swinging than what I was accustomed to. When they got ready to play "Flying Home," you had to be there to see what it did to the audience. Vernon Alley was a thundering bass player from the days when the guys were proud of their calluses. He would play a figure leading in, and by the time we came in, the people were screaming. I felt it just couldn't get any better.

Karl George had reclaimed his position as lead trumpeter, but during a rehearsal, after he had trouble with a new piece, Wilder was reassigned the role. "Fred Norman came in with an arrangement on 'I Left My Heart at the Stage Door Canteen,'" Wilder recalled. "He had written it in concert E, which put the trumpets in F sharp. Because it was written in that key, it was kind of awkward to play, and Karl George was fighting his way through it. Finally, Karl said, 'I don't want to play this thing,' so Hamp told him to give it to me. So I played it, and Hamp said, 'Well, look here, Gates. You're going to be my first trumpet player.'" Although he was the section lead, Wilder was not a high-note specialist, so those parts were assigned to Ernie Royal.

It took some time for Wilder to adapt to the difference in phrasing from the Les Hite style to the more forceful and dynamic approach of the Hampton orchestra. "[Lead trombonist] Fred Beckett was on my case because I was playing the notes but in the style of Les Hite," Wilder said. "But after three or four weeks, I caught on as to how they phrased things. Les's was more a ballad band, while Hampton was all about swinging!"

Although Wilder would not record commercially with Hampton until his return to the band in 1946, following his military service, he is present on an Armed Forces Radio Service transcription made in Hollywood in October 1942. Wilder takes two full choruses on "The Great Lie," an Andy Gibson–Cab Calloway swing opus, loosely based on "Fine and Dandy," that found its way into the books of several leading bands in the 1940s, including those of Charlie Barnet and Jimmy Dorsey. This relatively extended solo is a fascinating missing link in the study of the evolution of Wilder's solo style. It is his first recorded improvised solo; his eight bars on Les Hite's "I Remember You," recorded some six months earlier, is strictly a melody statement. Wilder's playing on the Hampton transcription confirms the observations of fellow musicians Shep Shepard and Buddy DeFranco—and the trumpeter's own recollections—that his early jazz improvisations were largely based on classical techniques and motifs. His "Great Lie" solo is an impressive technical display of rapid-fire patterns, skillfully executed over the chord changes, but only hinting at the beginnings of the more spontaneous "jazz" approach to come.

The impact of the Hampton band of 1942 is conveyed by a review of a typical performance on October 26 at Natatorium Park in Spokane, Washington:

> Early arrivals were treated to one of the hottest impromptu jam sessions ever held in the Pacific Northwest. Each member of the band "took a ride" in this session, improvising and displaying technique seldom heard in these parts. When the solos were completed the whole ensemble fell in with the brass "hitting" in a solid groove, the reeds weaving a mellow pattern, and the rhythm section slightly on the heavy side. Following this the sextet played a number which exasperated the jazz fans leaving them limp.[32]

Although Wilder played first trumpet, he also had opportunities to solo and is singled out in the review along with saxophonists Arnett Cobb and Jack McVea, violinist Ray Perry, pianist Milt Buckner, and trombonist Fred Beckett. Naturally, Hampton was the main focus, "stealing the show time and again with his instrumentations" on vibraphone, piano, and drums.[33] Six weeks earlier, in a review of the band's appearance at the Casa Mañana in Culver City,

California, *Billboard*'s Sam Abbott describes the opener, "Bugle Call Rag," as an "all-outer," during which "Joe Wilder turns in some top trumpeting," and notes a featured spot on "Mushmouth."[34] A few days later, the same writer describes Wilder's "hot trumpet" on "Hour of Parting" at a September 23 performance at the Orpheum Theatre in Los Angeles.[35] And few months later, in a general paean to Hampton, Leonard Feather cites the band's "great trumpet quartet—Joe Newman, Joe Wilder, Joe Morris and Lamar Wright, Jr."[36]

While at the Casa Mañana, Wilder approached Hampton about a raise. At the time, he was earning eleven dollars a night, while everyone else in the band was paid at least fifteen and some considerably more. Hampton told him to see his wife, Gladys, who held the purse strings. Gladys told him to see the notorious Joe Glaser, who was booking the band. Wilder made an appointment to see Glaser in his Los Angeles office, and when he introduced himself and told Glaser the reason for his visit, Glaser replied, "Who the hell do you think you are?" Wilder returned to Hampton and announced that if his salary demand was not met, he would be returning to Philadelphia the next day. Gladys authorized the raise.

While Wilder admired Hampton's consummate musicianship and indefatigable spirit, the trumpeter's exhilaration at being at the center of this musical powerhouse was quickly dampened when he observed how the bandleader and his wife condescended to and outright bullied the musicians. "They were just ignorant people," Wilder said, "and they liked to pit one musician against another. We'd be on the bus, and Lionel would be sitting in the front reading his Bible, and two guys would start a verbal altercation in the back. Lionel would say, 'Hey, Gates! Why don't y'all get out of the bus and fight?' Here he's reading the Bible and encouraging two guys to fight each other for no reason! It was entertainment for him."

Through the years, many musicians were especially critical of Gladys. "She was always telling us that she was 5 percent Indian—one of those African Americans who are always trying to find something that separates them from the rest of us," Wilder said. He recalled an incident when Gladys withheld a telegram informing trombonist Al Hayes of the death of his uncle so that he wouldn't leave the band to attend the funeral. To some extent, Wilder's role as lead trumpet made him less expendable and shielded him from some of the abuse. "They kind of lightened up on me," he said, "but I despised them for what I saw them doing to other people, especially to those they felt weren't too important to the band."

The Hamptons' legendary parsimony when it came to musicians' pay and the couple's lack of concern for their employees' working conditions was a constant source of irritation. In December 1940, two years before Wilder joined the band, Dexter Gordon described a "mutiny" because Gladys was "economizing" and had forced the band to tour in a small, unheated bus.[37] And in 1988, some five decades after Wilder had left the band, a similar uprising occurred when a new generation of Hampton musicians refused to board a plane for a Japanese tour until they received the pay and benefits stipulated by the Musicians Union. In a statement eerily reminiscent of the attitude Wilder perceived in the 1940s, Hampton's manager, Bill Titone, who had taken over after Gladys's death in 1971, justified this treatment by saying, "He [Hampton] is not just a leader who waves a baton, he is a star. . . . They are getting to play with a living legend."[38]

Wilder's strict morals and clean lifestyle were at odds with the self-destructive habits he encountered in many of his fellow band members—habits that would claim far too many of his friends over the years. "When I got into Lionel Hampton's band, these guys were doing everything!" he said. "Every place you went, someone was smoking pot or sticking a needle into his arm." Wilder became something of a crusader in trying to convince his friends to curb their excesses. "Dexter Gordon and Lamar Wright Jr. were my buddies because we were all in the same age group," he said. "They nicknamed me 'Reverend' because I was always telling them that they'd get tired of pot and would go on to something stronger. They'd come to my room in the hotel and say, 'Hey, Rev! Come down and preach to us!' and Dexter would blow marijuana smoke at me and crack up! They were really good guys, but once they got hooked, that was it. They went from pot to cocaine, and I saw what it did to them."

It was during his tenure with Hampton that Wilder also earned his reputation for never swearing, a source of wonder—and amusement—for his fellow musicians, who would offer him ten dollars if he would just utter a single four-letter word. He never collected.

Although Wilder had certainly faced discrimination in his travels with Les Hite, the Hite orchestra had toured primarily in the Northeast and the Midwest. With Hampton, he faced even greater indignities during the band's forays into the Deep South:

> We traveled mostly by bus but sometimes by train. During the war, there were travel restrictions, but you could get transportation if you promised to do a free performance at a military base if there was one nearby. We did a lot of those. Once, we were down in Valdosta, Georgia, at a base, and we met a lot of mostly white soldiers who were from the North. They gave us a big greeting, and we're all hugging each other when the military police came up and drew a line on the ground and said, "All the whites on this side, all the Negroes on the other side, and anybody that crosses that line is going to jail!"

One of the most serious incidents involved Illinois Jacquet:

> We were in Alabama, and Illinois was late getting to the station, and the train was getting ready to pull out. Illinois didn't have time to run down and get his luggage and stuff into the black coach. So he just got on the first step that was open. He started walking through the white cars, and this conductor, who looked like the Kentucky colonel, hit him and said, "Boy, what do you think you're doing back here?" Illinois said to him, "Who you calling 'boy'?" and kept walking. The guy pulled out a pistol and followed him into the black coach. Illinois was talking back to him, and several of our guys who carried pistols stood up. Our road manager, who was a very nice red-haired Texan named Mack O'Connell, came into the coach just as this guy was threatening to blow Illinois's head off. Mack shouted, "What's going on here?" The conductor said, "Cap'n, is them your niggers?" And Mack said, "Yeah, why?" "Well, you better teach 'em how to behave down here!" the conductor replied. Meanwhile, Red Farrington, the band boy, was standing right behind the conductor with a switchblade. Mack O'Connell quieted the whole thing down. He was a nice guy. A lot of guys didn't like him because he had a southern drawl. A lot of us were turned off by the accents, but some of these guys were the nicest people you could run into.

On another occasion, the band played a dance at Alabama State University in Montgomery, a black school. When it was over, the young people milled around talking with the musicians. "The sheriff arrived with his men and told everyone to leave," Wilder said. "They started shooting their pistols in the air, yelling like you would herd cattle."

Accommodations were always problematic, especially in the South. In the larger cities, the band was able to stay in black hotels, but elsewhere the musicians were housed in private homes. "There was a network that had been set up through the bands who had played previously," Wilder recalled.[39] Their hosts were not always as hospitable as the Foster family in Newark had been. "Sometimes we'd be staying in places that were filthy, and we couldn't do anything about it," Wilder said. "Some of the blacks [in the South] were almost as bad as some of the rural whites and had the attitude: 'You come down here with your smart northern ideas, and we gonna have to tell the Ku Klux Klan!'"[40]

Wilder had mixed feelings about his time with Hampton. Surrounded by some of the most gifted young musicians of the day, he found the music to be both challenging and stimulating. Even though he was leading the section, he had ample solo opportunities and, by all accounts, was rapidly developing a style of his own. On the other hand, he found the treatment of the musicians by Lionel and Gladys demeaning and the travel, particularly in the South, infuriating. Before he could even consider making a career change, however, the draft intervened, and Wilder's life was about to enter a new and even more challenging phase.

Integration of the Armed Forces

The Montford Point Marines
(1943–1946)

J oe Wilder's tenure in the Hampton orchestra was interrupted for a period of three years, during which he was part of the first group of African Americans in the U.S. Marine Corps. Before President Harry S. Truman desegregated the U.S. Armed Forces by executive order in 1948, African Americans had served in predominantly segregated military units in all wars dating back to the Revolution. Despite frequent attempts to relegate them to menial, noncombat activities, many black soldiers served with great distinction and valor, including such celebrated units as the 369th Infantry Regiment (known as the Harlem Hellfighters) in World War I and the Tuskegee Airmen in World War II. Before World War II, the Marine Corps was the least progressive of the military branches in its policies toward African Americans. Indeed, with the exception of a handful of black soldiers who fought with the Continental Marines during the Revolutionary War, there were no black Marines

---

Wilder at Montford Point, Camp Lejeune, NC, 1945. *(Wilder Family Collection.)*

until 1942, even though the Corps was under the aegis of the Secretary of the Navy, a branch that had long admitted blacks. In June 1941, when President Franklin Roosevelt signed Executive Order 8802, which banned "discrimination in the employment of workers in defense industries or government because of race, creed, color, or national origin" and established a Committee on Fair Employment Practice, the first step toward acceptance of African Americans into the Marines had been taken. The edict was met with resistance from Marine Corps Commandant Major General Thomas Holcomb, who stated, "If it were a question of having a Marine Corps of 5,000 whites or 250,000 Negroes, I would rather have the whites."[1] Nevertheless, "under pressure to make some move, General Holcomb proposed the enlistment of 1,000 Negroes in the volunteer Marine Corps Reserve for duty in the general service in a segregated composite defense battalion. The battalion would consist primarily of seacoast and antiaircraft artillery, a rifle company with a light tank platoon, and other weapons units and components necessary to make it a self-sustaining unit."[2]

Opening the Marine Corps to African Americans was by no means the same as integrating it. To receive the first black recruits in August 1942, separate facilities were hastily constructed at Montford Point, a remote area in the far western sector of the vast Marine complex near Jacksonville, North Carolina, that would soon be known as Camp Lejeune. In the words of military historian Bernard C. Nalty, "To ensure segregation, General Holcomb proposed to funnel all blacks through a single training facility, with their unit gradually taking form as the men completed the courses of instruction. . . . Insofar as possible, black Marines would train and serve in isolation."[3] Some 20,000 black Marines passed through Montford Point between 1942 and 1949, when the Corps was finally fully integrated.[4]

Musicians, like all Americans, found their lives disrupted by the draft. Wilder had been classified 1-A for quite some time before setting out for California with the Hampton orchestra late in 1942. To delay his induction, he had transferred his Selective Service registration to California, but by the time the Los Angeles draft board attempted to contact him, the band had already left for the East Coast. Two days after he arrived back in Philadelphia, the local board notified him to report. "They had assumed, and rightly, that I was doing this to avoid going in, so they had been tracking my movements," Wilder said. When he reported, the sergeant asked him what he did for a living. "When I told him I was a musician, he said, 'That won't do you any good because they're not accepting any more noncombatants, so you can go into the Navy, the Army, or the Coast Guard.' But then he said, 'Wait a minute. They've just started taking Negroes into the Marine Corps. Would you be interested?' So

I said, 'Well, since they're not taking any more musicians, yeah, why not?' I figured if I had to learn to fight, the Marines might not be a bad idea. I wasn't thinking in terms of being one of the first African American Marines or anything."

There was one other African American candidate for the Marines at the recruiting office, and the sergeant took the man and Wilder aside and warned them about some of the obstacles they would face. Wilder recalled him telling them, "I want you all to know, you're going down South. There's going to be some rough conditions down there." To Wilder he added, "You've been playing with a band—you know what it's like!"

The Selective Service officers screened potential candidates, and those chosen for the newly formed African American Marine unit were generally better educated and more motivated than the average war-time draftee. In her survey of blacks in the military, *American Patriots*, Gail Buckley notes, "The black recruits, 75 percent of whom had some college education, included specialized technicians, teachers, ROTC grads, and even Army professionals who had relinquished commissions for the Corps."[5]

Wilder left the Hampton band in Baltimore in April 1943, an event noteworthy enough to garner a brief mention in the *Pittsburgh Courier*.[6] Although he had grown increasingly disgusted with treatment of the musicians by the Hampton organization, he had built close friendships with many of his bandmates and was sad to leave them. He had also formed a close bond with the band's singer, Dinah Washington, whom he greatly respected as an artist and a person. One indication of the singer's honesty involved "Record Ban Blues," a song that Wilder had a hand in creating during his tenure with Hampton. "I would often contribute some figures or backgrounds for the bands I was with, but never got any credit when they were recorded," Wilder noted. "Record Ban Blues" was not recorded until 1947, when Washington sang it backed by Cootie Williams's band. When the music was copyrighted, Wilder and fellow Hampton trumpeter Joe Newman, were both listed as composers along with the singer.

Lionel Hampton himself was more concerned by the inconvenience of having to replace his lead trumpet player. Wilder explained, "Lionel was mad at me because his personal doctor, Arthur Logan, had told me to take a whole fistful of aspirin tablets the night before I reported, so that when I got there, my heart would be racing. A lot of guys did that, but I didn't want to."

A few days later, Wilder found himself aboard a train headed south to begin his Marine training at Camp Lejeune. Wilder and the one other black Marine recruit were sitting with all the white recruits as the train left Philadelphia. "We're having a good time because we were all from Philadelphia," he said, "but when we got to Washington, the MPs came in and marched me and the other black guy to the front of the train behind the coal car. That was disturbing even to the white recruits, who couldn't understand why we couldn't sit with them anymore. We could hardly breathe with all the soot and everything, and we rode like that all the way to North Carolina."

Although the morale was high among the black recruits, the conditions and treatment they encountered at Montford Point tested them severely. The hastily assembled living quarters were primitive even by military standards, with the recruits living in tents until barracks were eventually erected. It was not only uncomfortable but dangerous. "This was in rural North Carolina, and there were rattlesnakes and copperheads," Wilder recalled. "They sent out units to clear out as much as they could, and they would spread gasoline to kill off the snakes. It was a long time before it was cleaned up." Wilder's first and only "kill" involved a snake outside the USO in Jacksonville. "We were out on the street just wasting time, and here comes a water moccasin. I beat it with a stick and killed it right there on the road!"

In its coverage of the arrival of the first black Marine recruits the year before, the Baltimore *Afro-American* presented a rather rosy picture of the conditions at Montford Point, referring to its "scenic" location and listing such facilities as a "huge recreation building," which apparently had yet to be built.[7]

Many of the new black recruits were not only encountering the virulent racism of the South for the first time but faced the opposition of some officers who considered their very presence an assault on the sacred traditions of the Marine Corps. At Montford Point, the African American recruits were almost completely isolated from the white Marines, many of whom routinely referred to the black base as "Monkey Point." "There was no interaction with the white Marines," Wilder said. "For instance, when they had a movie, they would reserve three rows in the back for the blacks, and this was for a base that was entirely black except for the officers!"

Black Marines were frequently harassed by both military and local police while traveling to and from the base. Wilder recalled an incident involving two of his fellow Montford Pointers who were detained while on leave after completing boot camp:

> They get to the bus station in Jacksonville, and the Army or Navy patrol sees them and asks, "What are you doing in Marine uniforms?" They ended up having some altercation, and they put them in jail and kept them there for almost the entire period of their leave. When they were finally released and returned to the base, they were admonished for making a scene!

Wilder remembered an incident he himself was involved in upon returning to Montford Point after being on leave. He and some fellow African American Marines were first in line to board the bus from Jacksonville, but white passengers were allowed ahead of them, and there was no more room. After spending the night in the city jail, the black Marines arrived back at the base two hours late and were punished by being confined to the camp for two weeks. Frustrated by the ongoing transportation problems, some of the Montford Point Marines eventually took matters into their own hands: "Angry black Marines, at the risk of violence from the local police, might commandeer a bus, remove the driver, and take it to the gate nearest Jacksonville, where the transit company could retrieve it on the next morning."[8]

Wilder recalled that when the Fifty-First Battalion of African American Marines was traveling to the West Coast to join the war effort in the Pacific, they were denied entrance to a restaurant in the Atlanta train station. "Colonel Stevens, who was in charge of the battalion, told his men to 'lock and load!'" Wilder said. "He was so mad he told them to go in and wreck the place, which they did. By the time they got to California, the word had already reached the command post about what they had done, and they stripped the colonel of his command."

At first, there were no ranking African American Marines, so the training was carried out entirely by white drill instructors. Although, as Gail Buckley points out, the white instructors "were chosen from the least openly racist . . . the traditional welcome to Marine recruits—'I'm going to make you wish you had never joined this damn Marine Corps'—was given new significance for Montford Pointers."[9] General Holcomb, in an uncharacteristic display of sensitivity, "was aware of the adverse effect of white noncommissioned officers on black morale, and he wanted them removed from black units as soon as possible."[10] However, he told his commanders, "It is essential . . . that in no case shall there be colored noncommissioned officers senior to white men in the same unit, and desirable that few, if any be of the same rank."[11]

As blacks began to move up in the ranks at Montford Point, many of them replaced whites in positions of authority, but this did not necessarily mean better treatment. "Some of them were even harder on the recruits because they wanted to show the whites how mean they could be," Wilder said. And he recalled how this harsh approach resulted in the deaths of a couple of the black Marines:

> Five or six of them would take you out in the woods and beat you half
> to death if you questioned them. One guy lined up the whole platoon

and asked, "How many of you can swim?" They told those that could to fall in. Then they told the rest of us to forward march toward the river with our rifles held over our heads. They marched us down the bank and into the water. As the water got close to our necks, they started cracking up. When it got to our chins, they finally said, "Platoon, halt!" Once they pulled this stunt, and a couple of the guys went under and drowned. There was a big investigation, and they called the drill instructors on the carpet and chewed them out. But they kept on doing it.

Not all of the white officers were against the integration efforts, and several actively worked to improve conditions for the black recruits. "Many of them were exceptionally nice and did what they could to make conditions better," Wilder said. "They took some awful lumps for it." Even some of the Southern officers were supportive, and Wilder learned a lesson that would be repeated at several junctures in his career—that a Southern accent did not necessarily equate with racism. "Our commanding officer, Colonel [Samuel A.] Woods, was tall and very dignified, with white hair. He was from the Deep South and was a very fine man," Wilder noted. From the beginning, Woods showed respect for the black Marines, and soon after the arrival of the first recruits in August 1942, he predicted they would "make excellent Marines worthy of following in the footstep of their illustrious predecessors."[12] Not long after Wilder arrived, he witnessed Colonel Woods's efforts to improve the treatment of the Montford Point Marines:

> The "N" word was being thrown at us all the time, and Colonel Woods had had it up to here. He called a sit-down on the drill field to address all the troops, white and black, and [pointing at the black troops] said, "I want everybody to know, these are *my* Marines. They're Marines like any other Marines on this United States Marines base, and you had better show some respect!" As of that moment, some of the problems stopped. He was always trying to boost the morale.

The situation regressed when Major General Henry L. Larsen assumed command of Camp Lejeune in June 1943, upon his return from the Pacific. Wilder recounted an incident that infuriated the entire contingent of black Marines:

> We were all required to sit on the drill field so Larsen could address us. He said, "When I came back here and saw women Marines, war

dogs, and *you* people wearing *our* globe and anchor, I knew there's a war going on!" Everyone started booing and walking away, but they couldn't do anything to us because how could you put a whole battalion of people in jail? There wasn't a guy on the base who couldn't quote his whole speech verbatim!

Another spontaneous demonstration by the black Marines occurred when longtime Secretary of War Henry L. Stimson, who had strongly resisted integration, resigned in 1945 because of poor health. "We all celebrated," Wilder recalled. "It was like the atmosphere in the black community after a Joe Louis victory. They wanted to court-martial everyone, but there were too many of us."

In addition to Colonel Woods, another supportive white officer whom Wilder encountered was Bobby Troup, the celebrated songwriter-pianist. Lieutenant (later, Captain) Troup, who had already had hit songs recorded in the early 1940s by Glenn Miller and Tommy Dorsey and would later write the famous "Route 66," was the entertainment and morale officer at Montford Point, and he had earned the respect of the black Marines for his tireless efforts to improve conditions. Troup was responsible for Wilder's transfer to the band, which ultimately led to his spending his entire three-year military stint at Camp Lejeune. "At the end of boot camp, you spent a week on the rifle range, Wilder said. "I made sharpshooter, so they put me in Special Weapons." Although they only met at Montford Point, Wilder and Troup had known of each other's musical accomplishments. "He told the commanding officer that, as a professional musician, I would be much more useful as a member of the Marine band," Wilder said. "So the general had me transferred. If I'd stayed in Special Weapons, they would have shipped me out in a hurry!"

Wilder played in the headquarters (marching) band and the dance band, both composed entirely of African Americans. The white bandmaster, Paul B. Jackson, and his assistant, Staff Sergeant George Dowdy, were also sympathetic to the black Marines. "They knew what we were going through and did as much as they could to make things more pleasant for us," Wilder said. Unfortunately, Jackson was an alcoholic and was frequently not up to leading the band, so he would put Dowdy in charge. With Dowdy's departure to a battalion overseas, Wilder would take charge of the band whenever Jackson was indisposed. After marching the band to headquarters, Wilder would report to the appropriate general following strict protocol: "I'd say, 'Sir! Sergeant Wilder reporting with the Montford Point Marine Band as instructed!' I'd do everything by the book, and as I turned around and did a snappy about-face, I heard the general say to one of his assistants, 'Now that's my kind of Marine!'"

While Wilder led the band, bandmaster Jackson would stand to the side where he could not be seen. "He would make sure we were playing the right number of flourishes, depending upon how many stars the general had," Wilder said. The black marching band was much in demand for the many formal events and ceremonies throughout Camp Lejeune, and Wilder recalled that when Marine legend Lieutenant General Lewis Burwell "Chesty" Puller was to be honored in a ceremony, he specifically asked that the Montford Point band play for him. The Baltimore *Afro-American* reported, "For sweet or swing, fans of the fifteen-piece Montford Point Camp dance band . . . swear there is none smoother in these parts."[13]

With Dowdy's departure, Troup officially appointed Wilder assistant bandmaster, and he was promoted to staff sergeant. In addition to playing, Wilder rehearsed the band and selected much of the music. One of his duties was to march the band to the flagpole every morning for the playing of the national anthem and back again in the evening. During one of these marches, Wilder encountered some white Marines and overheard one of them say, "Look at that nigger over there! He's got three stripes, and I've been in the Marine Corps seven years, and I'm a PFC!" Wilder was so infuriated that he was driven to violate his own policy of never swearing. Much to the amusement of his band members, he retorted, "You dumb son of a bitch! You're white! You could be president of the United States if you weren't so goddamn ignorant!"

The degree of separation between the white and black Marines was illustrated by an incident Wilder experienced involving his friend drummer Stanley Kaye, who was also stationed at Camp Lejeune. Kaye and Wilder had gotten to know each other while Wilder was touring with Les Hite and Lionel Hampton. When they learned that they were on the same base, they attempted to meet for dinner. "They wouldn't let us eat together on the base," Wilder said. "We saw each other a couple of times, and Stanley said, 'Can you imagine? We're down here being trained to kill for our country, and we can't even eat together! What are we fighting for?'"

One group of whites with whom the blacks were allowed to mingle was a contingent of Dutch Marines, who had already seen combat and had been sent to Camp Lejeune for further training. "The white Marines would make fun of them, so they sent them over to us since they couldn't get along with the other whites," Wilder said. "They loved the black Marines and even stayed on the base during their leaves because they wanted to be buddies with us. That really made the Southerners mad!"

A musical highlight of Wilder's Marine Corps service was the chance to play with Louis Armstrong, who brought his orchestra to entertain the troops at Montford Point. One of Armstrong's regular trumpeters was taken ill, so Wilder joined the section for the entire show, sight-reading the parts. Armstrong remembered him from the *Colored Kiddies'* radio show in Philadelphia, as well as from subsequent meetings while Wilder was touring with Les Hite and Lionel Hampton. "Louis treated me like I was family, which surprised the guys on the base," Wilder said. "I enjoyed every minute of it!"

Wilder began to move up the ranks fairly rapidly. "I was a private for quite a while," he said. "But every few months you would get an evaluation, and mine were always very high, so I kept getting promoted. I ended up a tech sergeant with five stripes."

The morale of the black Marines was bolstered by the success of their sports teams in base competitions, the results of which were regularly reported in the African American press. "The black Marines were winning all the boxing matches, and the football and basketball teams were beating all the other teams," Wilder said. "Our football team had Claude 'Buddy' Young, who later played for the Baltimore Colts, and Dan Bankhead [who later became the first African American to pitch in the major leagues] was on the baseball team. Even though the white teams also had some major league players, the Montford Point teams kept beating them." The black teams were not allowed to compete in the Marine Corps athletic league, so contests with the whites were called "exhibitions." Nevertheless, some base authorities found the domination by the black athletes unacceptable and devised a scheme to end it. "They started putting the best black athletes in 'depot companies' and sending them to protect military installations in Alabama, Georgia, and California," Wilder said. "When Bobby Troup and several other white officers protested, they were told by the general, 'I suppose y'all want to keep your boys with you. Well, I can't keep your boys with you, but I can keep you with your boys,' and they shipped them all off to combat duty in the Pacific." Troup was deployed even though his wife was about to give birth to twins—usually cause for a postponement. Wilder learned of this because he had gotten to know some of the other officers, who were musicians, like Troup. "They would let me come play with them—we used to do some John Kirby arrangements," he said. "It made me always remember that I knew white people who were fighting as hard as we were to eliminate all of this, much to their own detriment."

Before deploying to the Pacific, Troup, who by then had been promoted to captain, asked Wilder if he would be interested in becoming his field sergeant major. Wilder told him, "Captain Troup, anything you want me to, I'll do my best, but if you're asking me if I really want to go, I'll be honest and tell you that the only place I want to go is home." Troup replied, "You're the only guy I've spoken to who's been forthcoming enough to say exactly what he feels," and he removed Wilder's name from the list of candidates. "That's probably why I'm here today!" Wilder observed.

Before being shipped out, Troup used his songwriting talents to express the sentiments of many of the Marines—both white and black—about the town of Jacksonville, North Carolina:

> *Take me away from Jacksonville,*
> *'Cause I've had my fill and that's no lie.*
> *Take me away from Jacksonville,*
> *Keep me away from Jacksonville until I die.*
> *Jacksonville stood still,*
> *While the rest of the world passed by.*

"He would sing it on the base, and all the guys would break up because neither the white nor the black Marines liked North Carolina," Wilder said. "Once we were playing with the black band at the USO, and the mayor of Jacksonville was there as a guest. When Bobby Troup came in with some of his fellow officers, the mayor said, 'Captain Troup, I wonder if you'd honor us by singing that song you wrote about Jacksonville.' Bobby said, 'Sir, I don't think you really want to hear that.' They insisted, and now all the rednecks are applauding, so Bobby went to the piano and did it. I thought they were going to get a rope and hang him!" Troup's impact was such that at his memorial service in Encino, California, in 1999, representatives of the Montford Point Marines came to pay their respects:

The most impactive speeches were given by the Montford Point Marine representatives who came to honor Bobby's service in the Marines. It seems that Captain Troup was the first white officer to be given command of an all black unit in Jackson, North Carolina. When Bobby came in, the men were living in tents, with filthy latrine conditions, and nothing anywhere to relieve the stress of their condition. (This was in the days where a black in Jackson had to cross the street or literally stand in the gutter while a white walked by.) Captain Troup took a "haul ass" attitude, and with the help of the men, created Quonset huts, new latrines, a nightclub, a basketball court and team, a boxing ring, a jazz band, an orchestra, and get this . . . he somehow maneuvered a friend to come and install a miniature golf course. Soon, the other (white) units (who had given an intolerable time to the unit before Bobby's arrival) suddenly wanted to come and hang out in their area. Those who spoke said that Bobby didn't recognize color . . . only soul.[14]

Despite heroic efforts by sympathetic white officers like Bobby Troup, morale was not aided by frequent reports of German prisoners of war receiving better treatment in the South than black servicemen. Wilder recalled one incident in particular that offended him and his fellow African American Marines: "Some of the German POWs were held in the brig on our base, and black Marine MPs were assigned to escort them to Fort Benning, Georgia, by train. The German prisoners would be allowed to eat in the dining car, while the black Marines couldn't. And the Germans are laughing at them, saying, 'Ach, sie schwarze, sie können nicht mit uns essen!' [Oh, you blacks, you cannot eat with us!] It was infuriating!"

During his stint in the Marine Corps, Wilder was able to renew his passion for photography. As a youngster, he first became fascinated by the photographic process when his older brother, who was in high school, brought home some photographic plates he developed. Wilder signed up for an extracurricular course in junior high school but was not allowed to take the class:

> The teacher was not very friendly. She asked me what I was doing there, and when I told her I wanted to learn photography, she asked me if I had a camera. When I said I didn't, she asked, "Will you be able to buy one?" This was during the Depression, and I was lucky to have a piece of bread to eat on my way to school in the morning, so I told her, "Well, I don't think so," and she said, "Then there's no sense in wasting your time or mine now, is there?" And that was that.

Wilder later found out that they had cameras available to lend to students, but he was never offered one. Nevertheless, he never lost his interest and at Montford Point he met a fellow Marine who was a portrait photographer from Philadelphia. "He was a tremendous photographer, who used to do portraits of all the well-known black artists," Wilder said. Wilder asked him to be on the lookout for a camera he might be able to use. "Sure enough, he returned from a leave with an old Rolleiflex that he had found in a pawn shop," Wilder said. "It used 127 film and had an f/7.7 fixed-focus lens. Everything was sharp on this thing from, like, two and a half feet to infinity." Thus began a lifelong hobby. "After I came out of the service, I bought a Kodak reflex, and after that my brother gave me a Leica, which I traded in for a Hasselblad many years later." Wider voraciously devoured books on photography and eventually set up a darkroom in his apartment. He was rarely spotted without his camera at recording sessions, concerts, and other events. Although his photos have appeared in magazines, newspapers, and album covers, the most frequent beneficiaries of his skill are his friends and colleagues with whom he has generously shared thousands of prints through the years. In 2010, Wilder successfully made the transition to digital photography, when he purchased a Nikon D7000.

Wilder was discharged from the Marines in April 1946, almost three years to the day after he had entered. During the discharge process, the captain tried to convince him to reenlist. "They said they would make me a master sergeant if I stayed in for another three years," Wilder said. "I must have said something the captain found offensive because he said, 'Hold it, sergeant! Don't get too smart here—you're not discharged yet!' I didn't make anymore wisecracks."

4

Big Band Odyssey (1946–1950)

Hampton Redux

The Serviceman's Readjustment Act of 1944, better known as the GI Bill (of Rights), guaranteed veterans the right to return to their previous jobs after military service, and a month after his discharge in April 1946, Joe Wilder rejoined Lionel Hampton. Unfortunately, he found the conditions in the band had not changed much since his departure for the Marine Corps in 1943. Three years older and having attained a position of some authority in the military, Wilder himself had changed, however, and was even less inclined to accept what he viewed as exploitation during his second stint with the orchestra:

> When I rejoined the band, all the things that I disliked from before came to the surface. I was not a favorite of Hampton's because I would

Wilder solos while Lionel Hampton watches, 1943.
(Wilder Family Collection.)

speak out about certain things, and they resented that. We'd play a dance after driving two or three hundred miles to get there, and instead of letting us go to the hotel and check in, Lionel would have us go to the hall for a rehearsal. Then we'd play for four hours, and we'd be ready to pack up, and he'd say, "Hold it, Gates. They want us to play another hour." By that time, I had some knowledge of the union rules, and I'd ask, "Lionel, do we get paid for the extra time?" After that, my name was mud, but they needed me; otherwise I would have been fired.

Perhaps a bit intimidated by his new assertiveness, Lionel and Gladys Hampton avoided direct confrontation with Wilder. "In fairness, they seldom did anything to me personally," he said. "And musically, Hampton did some wonderful things, but it was just the way they treated the guys in the band that got to me."

Onstage, some of the extramusical antics in which the band was expected to participate now seemed silly to him. "We always had to be doing something, like throwing the horns into the air," Wilder said. "I did it halfheartedly, and Hamp would say, 'What's the matter, Gates?' One time I threw mine up, and I looked directly into the spotlight, and the horn landed on the floor right on the bell. The thing was crushed! Lionel thought it was funny and said, 'Keep that in!'"

Wilder was dismayed to find the situation for black musicians on the road had not improved much either. He recalled an incident in Des Moines, Iowa, when he and fellow Hampton trumpeter Duke Garrette were refused service in a Chinese restaurant and staged their own sit-in some fourteen years before the famous Greensboro, North Carolina, lunch counter incident that helped launch the civil rights movement: "We were sitting at a window table, and the Chinese manager told us, 'If I serve you, the white people won't come in here.' I told him, 'You mean to say, I just came out of the Marine Corps, and you're telling me you can't serve us?' So we just sat there until it was time to go back and play the show. And after each show that day and the next, we went back and sat there. They still wouldn't serve us. We weren't part of any movement or anything—we were just really hacked!"

Although, as in Des Moines, Wilder often confronted racism and took a stand as an individual, he never participated in any marches or other formal actions for fear that he would lose his temper. "If I saw a cop beating up on somebody or turning a hose on them, I would have found some way to get even, and I would be dead," he said. "Having been born in Pennsylvania, I'd been subjected to prejudice but not the kind of things that happened in the South."

Within a few months of his return to the Hampton band, Wilder's dissatisfaction had grown to the point that he decided to leave: "Having been in the Marine Corps and having learned to assert myself, I could see all the things I had despised about being in Hampton's band, and I realized, 'I can't stay here.'" Wilder felt that, eventually, he might get into a confrontation with Lionel and Gladys that might damage his reputation, so during an engagement in Newark, New Jersey, he gave his two weeks' notice. This probably occurred at the end of October, when the band was appearing at Newark's Adams Theater.[1] Wilder was so anxious to free himself of the Hampton yoke that he resigned with no other job awaiting him.

In September 1946, about a month before leaving Hampton, Wilder made his only commercial recordings with the band, during three sessions, for Decca, in Los Angeles—his first since making his recording debut with Les Hite some four years earlier. His longest solo, a full chorus on "Double Talk," with an octet from the Hampton band, was not released until decades later, on LP.[2] An entirely improvised performance based on "I Know That You Know," it opens with a muted solo by Wilder that shows tremendous dexterity at a rapid tempo. It has a distinctly boppish feel, as noted by Gunther Schuller, who felt that "on 'Double Talk,' Hampton broke through into the bop ranks." Schuller also cites Wilder's "new modern-oriented solo work."[3]

Jimmie Lunceford

After giving his notice to Lionel Hampton, Wilder did not have to wait long for an offer to materialize. Jimmie Lunceford, who had been one of Wilder's early idols, contacted him, and by the end of November 1946, Wilder joined the orchestra.[4] "I think Jimmie was looking for someone to play lead," Wilder said. "[Trumpeter] Reunald Jones Sr. was in the band. He and I were pretty good friends, and I think he recommended me." Wilder joined the band at the Strand Theater in Philadelphia. "Jimmie had known my dad because they were both Masons, and I remember him telling my father, 'I'll take good care of your son,'" Wilder said.

By the mid-1940s, the Lunceford band was no longer the iconic swing powerhouse it had been during the previous decade. Lunceford was not the only bandleader trying to weather shifts in popular taste and economic changes that affected the entertainment industry in the postwar era. In 1946, the year Wilder joined Lunceford, no less than Woody Herman, Benny Goodman, Tommy Dorsey, Benny Carter, Harry James, and Les Brown all gave up their big bands.[5] Lunceford struggled to keep the orchestra going. As Lunceford biographer Eddie Determeyer notes, "For a while the Jimmie Lunceford band functioned as a telephone orchestra, which meant that whenever a gig turned up, the agency started calling the musicians. Gradually more substitutes, not familiar with the book, began to move in. This resulted in rather uninspired performances and recordings during 1946 and into 1947."[6] But by the time Wilder joined, the orchestra was on the upswing, a fact not usually acknowledged by the jazz histories but hinted at by its last, albeit it relatively few, recordings. "Jimmie wanted the band to sound the way it had originally sounded, with the same kind of phrasing," Wilder said. In an attempt to recapture his orchestra's former glory, the leader made several significant personnel changes, which raised the orchestra's musical level. Wilder replaced William "Chiefy" Scott[7] and took the lead chair, with high-note specialist Paul Webster, Reunald Jones, Bob Mitchell, and Russell Green completing the trumpet section. Al Grey, a young and dynamic talent, was added to the trombone section. Russell Green felt this brass section was Lunceford's finest,[8] and Wilder agreed. As Determeyer points out, "It was, no doubt, one of the few trumpet sections in the business whose members were all good soloists and good lead men."[9]

The newcomers joined such Lunceford stalwarts as saxophonists Joe Thomas and Earl Carruthers and pianist Eddie Wilcox to form a much improved orchestra. "It wasn't up to the level of the original band yet," Wilder noted. "We were different people, different personalities, but it had just begun to come together and knit very closely. The guys knew each other, and they began to play together extremely well. Jimmie was very happy with the band at that point. It was on its way up. And had he lived, it would have gone completely back to its original level." And bassist George Duvivier, one of the band's chief arrangers in its last incarnation, said, "Unfortunately, that particular band never got the chance to record, so people always talk about the Lunceford orchestra declining. But by 1947, things were on the upswing, and that band was absolutely roaring!"[10]

Lunceford was a taskmaster and rehearsed the band intensively to acclimate the new members. Wilder found the transition relatively easy, however, since he had long admired the Lunceford orchestra and was familiar with its music. In fact, once the bandleader learned that Wilder had served as assistant bandmaster in the Marines, Lunceford occasionally asked him to lead the rehearsals. Wilder was also flattered when the leader gave him a transcription of Freddie Webster's solo on "Street of Dreams," which the legendary trumpeter used to play during his tenure with the band a few years earlier. "Jimmie wanted me to play it, but we never got around to doing it because we were mostly playing dances," Wilder said. "Freddie and I were very friendly, and I loved to hear him play. He was a nice guy and very serious about playing the trumpet."

In sharp contrast with his time in Lionel Hampton's band, Wilder was now working for a man he deeply respected, both as a bandleader and a person. "I was very impressed with Jimmie," he said. "He was a straightforward guy, a real stickler for making time and deportment." Wilder welcomed the discipline for which Lunceford was well known. "I appreciated it because he was very aware of the problems of the black community and particularly black performers, and he insisted that the guys deport themselves in a certain way," he explained. "It was such a highly regarded orchestra, and wherever we went, we were treated with great respect because of the tone that he set." Wilder also noted a similarity in conducting style between Lunceford and Paul Whiteman, whose father, Wilberforce, perhaps not coincidentally, had been Lunceford's music teacher in high school in Denver: "I think that he sort of tried in some ways to emulate Paul Whiteman. I think that's one of the reasons he used the big, long baton."[11]

The band members shared the leader's concern with projecting a dignified image and were quick to challenge old stereotypes, whether the source was white or black. Wilder recalled an incident during which the band was accompanying the legendary dancer and entertainer Bill "Bojangles" Robinson, who was beloved by white audiences but was considered a bully and something of an Uncle Tom by many blacks, especially the younger generation:

We were in a big theater in Boston. The audience was all white except for some black school kids, who were in the highest part of the balcony. Bojangles was telling all these stories involving "darkies," and the kids started booing. So he stopped everything and said, "The way you're behaving is why they don't want Negroes in the theaters." Those of us in the trumpet section just couldn't believe what he was saying, but the rest of the audience enjoyed it because it was so derogatory. When he started all this race business to ingratiate himself with the audience, we brought out our mutes and started making noise so you could hardly hear what he was saying. He was so mad that he threatened to shoot us, but we kept on doing it! There was a blues singer on the bill, and when she started singing about eating corn bread and biscuits with the butter just "oooozing out," we did the same thing to her!

Lunceford's dignified appearance and stately manner commanded respect, and he knew how to deal with the problems that black musicians habitually faced on the road. Wilder recalled an incident that took place in an Indianapolis hotel:

We were trying to check into a hotel, and they looked at us and said, "Not here! No more black bands in this hotel because these people don't know how to act." Eddie Vinson's band had just stayed there, and apparently, guys had gone to the local five-and-ten and shoplifted, and some of them had left the hotel in the middle of the night to keep from paying. So Jimmie told them, "This is not just any Negro band. This is the Jimmie Lunceford Orchestra, and we don't have people like that." The clerk was embarrassed and said, "Okay, Mr. Lunceford," and that was it!

Because of his commanding presence, Lunceford was even able to persuade segregated restaurants to serve his band on the road. "When we were touring down South, Jimmie would tell us to wait outside the restaurant while he went in first," Wilder said. "He would introduce himself and ask if they would serve us. Because of his dignified manner and the respect he commanded, they would usually agree."

Lunceford's deep concern about the image of blacks in general and musicians in particular led to his emphasis on punctuality. "He insisted that wherever we went, we should set an example," Wilder said. "He would tell us, 'If the bus leaves at 8:00 A.M., don't come at 8:15 or 8:30 because if we're rolling down the street, and you're back there yelling, we're not going to stop. You get to the job in whatever fashion you can get there, and if you don't make it, you're fired.'" But because he was fair and his rules were not capricious or arbitrary, even the transgressors did not take it personally. "It was amazing to think that when the bus was supposed to leave at two o'clock, it left at two o'clock! And everyone was on it!" George Duvivier recalled. "Rehearsals were always on time. If any sort of discipline had to be meted out, it was always done with good humor."[12]

Wilder recalled Lunceford's unique method of dealing with a band member who might over-imbibe on occasion and start to doze on the bandstand:

Jimmie would come up to him with his baton under his arm and say, "This one's on you." A couple of months later, we'd finish a job, and Jimmie would tell us, "Guys, don't go back to the hotel. We're all going to go to a restaurant and have a little party." He'd tell us to order whatever we wanted, and when we finished, we're all telling him, "Thanks, Jimmie, that was really nice of you." And Jimmie would say, "Don't thank me. So-and-so was drunk on such-and-such date, so he didn't get paid, and that's the money that's paying for the party!"

Lunceford was a trained pilot, as was pianist Eddie Wilcox, and the two used to fly to gigs in Lunceford's two-engine Cessna. Wilder recalled flying with them from New York to Boston and back. "I was the only passenger," he said. "The rest of the guys were afraid to fly. When we took off from Westchester Airport, the sky was filled with clouds, and you couldn't see anything. All of a sudden, we got up above the clouds, and it was so clear I couldn't believe it. I thought to myself, 'This is as close as I've ever been to God.' When we were returning to Westchester Airport, as we were descending, all of a sudden, Eddie Wilcox sees these trees and yells, 'Pull up, pull up!' Jimmie got us back up in a hurry!" Wilder's recollection of his bandmates' reluctance to fly with their leader is at odds with a report in the *Philadelphia Tribune* that said Lunceford was planning to give flying lessons to his musicians during their two-week stint at the Coronet Club in Philadelphia. "Members of the Lunceford band . . . all share the enthusiasm of their boss for flying," the article blithely reported, concluding, "It may not be too long before the entire Lunceford entourage will be zooming through the skies in echelon."[13]

The revival of the Lunceford orchestra, to which Joe Wilder contributed, came to a halt on July 12, 1947, with the leader's sudden death in Seaside, Oregon.[14] The band had played the night before at McElroy's Spanish Ballroom in Portland.[15] During intermission, the musicians had encountered a problem getting served at a restaurant across the street, a disturbing experience the band members had not anticipated in Oregon.[16] Wilder remembered the incident:

We had about forty minutes' break, and after we sat there [in the restaurant] for about twenty minutes, we noticed that nobody was paying any attention to us. Finally, somebody said, "Can we get some service?" and the owner told us, "We don't serve you people in here." We started arguing and said, "This is Oregon—not the South." She made a phone call, and the next thing we know, four cops descended on the restaurant. They came in with their hands on their pistols and asked what was going on. They were so harsh that some of the other patrons in the restaurant told them, "Those fellows haven't done a thing! All they did was asked to be served!" So the cops backed off a little. We said to the sergeant in charge, "This is the state of Oregon. Aren't they supposed to serve us?" He said, "Yeah, they are," and turned to the owner and told her, "If you're not going to serve them, you have to be closed." So she walked over to the door and pulled the curtain down with the sign that said "closed." And that was it. We didn't eat and just went back and played.

The next day, things only got worse. The band traveled by bus to Seaside, about eighty miles northwest of Portland, to play a dance at the Bungalow, a skating rink, which was transformed into a ballroom on weekends and where many leading bands—both white and black—had played over the years.[17] Lunceford had agreed to sign autographs at a local record store before the show. He was accompanied by Wilder and trombonist Al Cobbs. "He had signed a couple, and all of a sudden, he spun around and just fell, like he had a dizzy spell or something," Wilder said. Eddie Rosenberg, the band's road manager arrived, and they rushed Lunceford to Seaside Hospital.

Knowing nothing yet about the fate of their leader, the band members were in for a shock when they learned that the management of the Bungalow was attempting to dissuade black patrons from attending the evening's festivities. "They had offered our valet fifty dollars if he would stand out in front of the ballroom and discourage the black couples from buying tickets," Wilder said. "Of course, he refused to do it, and he told us about it." Wilder along with fellow trumpeter Reunald Jones Sr., angry about the attempt at barring blacks from the dance and concerned about the condition of their absent leader, convinced their fellow musicians not to play. Finally, the management relented and agreed to allow black patrons into the venue, and the band played for the time remaining until intermission. Meanwhile, Rosenberg had returned but did not disclose that Lunceford had died, which the band only learned when saxophonist Kirt Bradford called the hospital. Overcome by grief and furious at Rosenberg, the band somehow finished the Seaside engagement. "We were in a state of shock," Wilder recalled. "Jimmie had just had a physical to renew his pilot's license, and he had passed it with flying colors."

Although the cause of death was deemed a heart attack by the coroner, rumors began to fly. Some band members contended that, apart from the incident the day before in Portland, Lunceford and some of his musicians had also been refused service at a Seaside restaurant before the leader went to sign autographs at the record store. After a verbal altercation with Lunceford himself, the management relented and agreed to serve the musicians beef sandwiches, which were somehow tainted and resulted in several members of the band, including the leader, falling ill, leading biographer Determeyer to surmise, "It is not too far-fetched to maintain that Jimmie Lunceford was poisoned for being the proud black man that he was."[18]

The band was booked for twelve more one-nighters before returning to New York. Determeyer recounts, "To add injustice to incredibility, July 12 happened to be payday. Lunceford had carried the payroll in his pocket, and owed his management a certain amount of money. But, mysteriously, the money had vanished. . . . Depressingly, the band had to play an extra seven performances before it had covered the debt plus the fare back to New York."[19]

"We didn't want to continue the tour and wanted to go right back to New York to be there for Jimmie's funeral," Wilder said. "But Eddie Rosenberg convinced us to finish the tour." This was a decision Wilder still regrets: "It was kind of cruel, actually. And in fact it was almost an affront to Jimmie's stature for us to do it. There were a lot of ill feelings about that."[20]

They band eventually completed the tour, returning to New York after Lunceford's funeral. Ed Wilcox and Joe Thomas tried to keep the orchestra together, serving as coleaders of what must have been one of the first "ghost bands." Wilder remained with group for a short period, which included a stint at the Savoy Ballroom.

Dizzy Gillespie

After leaving the Lunceford organization in late 1947, Wilder was reunited with his good friend Dizzy Gillespie, whom he had known growing up in Philadelphia and with whom he had played in Les Hite's orchestra. In 1946, Gillespie had formed a pioneering big band devoted to the modern sounds he helped create with Charlie Parker. In addition to translating bebop into the big band vocabulary, Gillespie was fascinated with the Afro-Cuban sounds, which the legendary percussionist Chano Pozo brought to the orchestra. Even though Wilder was of the same generation as the young beboppers, the music he had been playing with Hampton and especially Lunceford was vastly different from that which he now encountered with Gillespie: "It was a real challenge. It was pretty much all bebop. Even when we did a standard, Dizzy or someone else would arrange it in the bebop style, but it was always done very well. It was a hard book to play, but once you learned the phrasing, it was a lot of fun." While the style may have been a radical change, Wilder's technical abilities, honed by his classical training, eased the transition to the rapid tempos and intricate lines Gillespie's charts demanded. Wilder found some of his section mates "ghosting" the notes—not articulating them precisely: "When I came in, I started playing these things as they were written, and the other guys would ask me how I did it, so I told them, 'Play it slower until you get it, and then go a little faster.'"

Although Wilder quickly adapted to the section work, he was less satisfied with his initial attempts at improvising within the bebop context. "Because of my classical training, I could play fast," he said, "so if I ran out of ideas, I could get 'technical' and start double- and triple- tonguing and try to make it as 'jazzy' as I could, even if it didn't exactly relate to the tune we were playing.

But the classical element remained, and it sounded somewhat corny. But after a while, I got away from that." With Gillespie, Wilder was able to demonstrate his skill with mutes, especially his creativity with the plunger: "Guys would use the plunger, but it was always 'doo-wah, doo-wah, doo-wah,'" Wilder recalled. "I would try to come up with different figures—some simple, some complicated—that related to the song harmonically and rhythmically. And sometimes I'd infuse some excerpt from a classical piece that fit. Dizzy always appreciated that."

In addition to his brilliance as a trumpet player and his advanced musical conception, Gillespie was also a great entertainer, and his singing, dancing, and comedy added greatly to the popularity of his orchestra and probably helped make the band's progressive charts more palatable to the general public. Wilder, of course, was familiar with Gillespie's sense of humor from their time together in Les Hite's band; it was Dizzy's clowning that ultimately, if inadvertently, led to Wilder's departure. Now, as the leader himself, Gillespie was in a different role and was forced to exert some discipline, but this by no means altered his basic personality. "It was a joy playing in Dizzy's band," Wilder said. "He might have been the leader, but he was always one of the guys in the band. He was very tolerant, but he wanted the music played right. He knew what he wanted, and he'd rehearse until it was that way."

Gillespie's discipline did not always extend to his own promptness, however. "As far as being on time, he was the worst in the band!" Wilder recalled. "When we were at the Apollo, Dizzy invariably would show up late for the first show." On those occasions, he would designate Wilder to take the trumpet solos in his absence. "I didn't try to play what he played, but I got the chance to get out there and play something of my own. He was very nice to me." Wilder even contributed the piece "Ool-ya-koo" to the band's repertoire, albeit without credit. He explained, "In the trumpet section, we used to play different backgrounds for something that Dizzy or someone else was playing." Wilder added, "I used to play [hums 'Ool-ya-koo']." The idea came from the Baptist church, when the minister would start preaching and the members would respond. So Dizzy used it and called it "Ool-ya-koo." Apparently, this uncredited appropriation of his riff rankled Wilder. Two years later, soon after he joined Herbie Fields's band, he mentioned it to *Down Beat* Chicago correspondent Pat Harris, who reported, "A little miffed at first, [the] incident now has taken its place in his store of anecdotes about the music biz—a collection to which many other musicians could add similar experiences."[21]

At the Apollo, Wilder remembered the leader complaining that his band members were not sufficiently engaged in the entertainment aspects of the show: "Dizzy called a meeting and told us, 'I'm out there dancing and doing all these different things, and you guys are sitting back there like a bunch of choir boys! Do something! Put some life in the band!'" Wilder took it on himself to work up some routines with his section mates, trumpeters Lammar and Elmon Wright and Dave Burns. "Backstage they had some props, like a hand truck and a policeman's uniform with the billy club and the cap," Wilder said. "So I'd put on the uniform and wheel Elmon out on the hand truck, like he's my prisoner, while Dizzy's out there dancing. When we got to the other side, I'd give Elmon the uniform and the hat and club, and I'd get on the truck, and Elmon would hold me by the neck. And the people would start screaming!" Among other pranks, Wilder and his cohorts raised the seats of the trombone players so that they could not sit down. He also supplied his bandmates with "all-day sucker" lollipops, which they had in their mouths when introduced by the leader. "Finally, after a couple of shows," Wilder said, "Dizzy called another meeting and told us, 'It's okay, guys, just go back to what you were doing before.'"

While a hit with audiences, Gillespie's antics upset some critics in much the same way as did the stage persona of another great trumpeter-entertainer, Louis Armstrong. *Down Beat*'s Michael Levin, in his report on Gillespie's September 29, 1947, Carnegie Hall concert, with Charlie Parker and Ella Fitzgerald, found the band "a unit which plays with profound conviction and enthusiasm." But Levin said of Gillespie, "No one, not even in Carnegie Hall, would want him to work without the showmanship so necessary to appeal to large crowds. But this doesn't mean that he has the license to stand on a platform doing bumps, grinds and in general often acting like a darn fool."[22]

Unfortunately, Wilder never recorded with Gillespie's band, joining sometime after the RCA Victor date of August 22, 1947, and leaving before the next Victor session on December 22. "The band wasn't working that much, and although they wanted me to go to Europe with them, I'd had a better offer from Lucky Millinder," Wilder said. Wilder was also disgusted by a comment made by the son of Moe Gale, who was booking the European tour. When Wilder told him that the pay was below what he could accept, Gale replied, "But you can have all the white girls you want over there."

Upon his departure, Wilder remembered that he and Gillespie had a slight misunderstanding about his uniform: "When I told him I would return it, he said, 'No, you can keep the uniform, but you have to pay for it.' I reminded him that when I was a kid in Philadelphia, he used to give me advice about the music business. And one of the things he told me specifically was that when you join a band, you tell them up front that you do not buy the uniform. You wear it while you're working, and you give it back when you leave." Dizzy's wife, Lorraine, took Wilder's side, telling her husband, "You've got the brains of a gnat's behind!" That ended the discussion.

Lucky Millinder

After leaving Gillespie, Wilder joined Lucky Millinder's band in late 1947 or early 1948.[23] Wilder had been recommended by his friends and former band-mates Frank Galbreath and Reunald Jones Sr., both members of Millinder's trumpet section at the time. Millinder, who first came to prominence with the Mills Blue Rhythm Band, was not a musician but was respected for his ability to assemble and lead top-notch ensembles. By the late 1940s, he was moving in the direction of rhythm and blues, but his orchestra retained a jazz sensibility, and he sought out interesting arrangements for the band. "Lucky had a great and a very unusual book," Wilder recalled. "He would go out and get arrangers who wrote in completely different styles. He would get them to write a lot of daring things because he had guys in the band who could play that stuff. It was one of the most interesting big band books to play, yet little is known about it because we didn't do many recordings." In a piece preview-ing the band's upcoming appearance at the Apollo (March 26–April 1, 1948), *Down Beat* correspondent Pat Harris described what the audience could look forward to based on the band's recent engagement at the Regal Theater in Chi-cago: "They will hear Blue Skies, on which a melodic trumpet solo [possibly Wilder] immediately precedes a growl chorus, a version of Rachmaninoff's Second Piano Concerto which includes everything, even boogie, and vo-cals ranging from the tenor trills of former Wings Over Jordan singer Paul Breckenridge to the much more earthy work of saxist-singer Bull Moose Jack-son and Annisteen Allen."[24] Although Millinder could not read music, he had good musical instincts and keen ears. "He had been a dancer in Chicago, and he knew what moves to make, and he was very adept at setting a certain tempo," Wilder said. The ability to choose the perfect tempo served Millinder well when the band played the Savoy Ballroom opposite the formidable Savoy Sultans, a small group known for getting patrons out of their seats and onto the dance floor.

At his first rehearsal with the band, Wilder, who was playing lead and sight-reading the charts, inadvertently embarrassed his fellow section mates:

> Lucky stopped me and said, "Hey, Fess"—he called everyone "Fess."
> "That's not what we play here!" I said, "Well, Lucky, I'm playing what I see written." So he had me play it again, and then he looked at Frank Galbreath and the other guys and asked, "What have you guys been playing? Is that what's there?" Apparently, whatever they didn't want to read or didn't like, they would just make up something! Lucky didn't know the difference. After that, Lucky thought I was a genius

and made me the straw boss, and I rehearsed the band. It's a wonder the other guys didn't kill me!

Millinder's orchestra was unusual in that as many as seven of his musicians—nearly half the orchestra—were white. Even more remarkable was the fact that Millinder regularly toured the South with this integrated group. As he told *Down Beat*, "I like the south. . . . We go through West Virginia, North and South Carolina, all through there. Those people don't see bands as often as people up north do. They'll pay two, two-fifty to hear a band because they can only do it every month or two. They're wonderful to us, treat us better because we're strangers, you know."[25] Despite his cordial receptions in the past, Millinder was apprehensive about his upcoming Southern swing, scheduled for June 1948: "Tour before the last we had seven white boys in the band and no trouble anywhere, but recently there's been talk of trouble and turmoil and the Klan marching again, so I don't have a mixed band now."[26]

Apparently, Millinder decided to ignore these warnings because Wilder recalled making that Southern tour with as many as five white members in the band. To forestall any problems in accommodations, both the black and white musicians stayed in private homes. Despite the real dangers posed by touring with a mixed band, the contradictions of segregation produced occasional humorous moments. Wilder recalled one such incident:

We were in Charleston and were waiting for the ballroom to open. Up comes the sheriff's car, and the sheriff gets out and asks, "Who's in charge here?" Lucky says, "I am." "Well, I'm tellin' you, boy, there ain't gonna be no mixed bands down here in Charleston, South Carolina!" And Lucky says, "Well this isn't a mixed band." The sheriff looks around and says, "You mean to tell me those aren't white musicians over there?" "No," says Lucky. So now the sheriff walks up to each white musician and asks, "You colored?" And each guy said yes. He looked at the deputy in disbelief. He gets to Porky [Solomon] Cohen, our first trombone player, and says, "Now, you gonna tell me that you're colored, too?" And Porky, who had a pronounced lisp, answers emphatically, "Why, thertainly!" We were almost doubled over laughing. Finally, he turned to the deputy and said, "Well, if they all say they colored, ain't nothin' we can do about it," and they got in the car and drove off! Many years later, whenever I'd run into Porky in New York in the middle of the theater district, I'd ask him, "Are you . . . ?" And he'd say, "Why thertainly!"

While with Millinder, Wilder suddenly found himself in the unlikely role of leader of a Latin "band within a band" at the 845 Club in the Bronx. "Lucky was a shrewd operator and persuaded the owners that he could bring in two bands, and it would only cost them a little more than they were paying for one," Wilder said. "One would be a Latin band because of all the Hispanic people living in that neighborhood." Millinder made Wilder the leader of the small group, billing him as José Wildez and His Afro-Cuban Orchestra. Wilder recalled, "We wore ruffled shirts with big bowties and played all this authentic Latin music. The band was quite a hit until people started coming up to the bandstand and talking to me in Spanish, which I couldn't understand. Someone yelled out, 'Man, he ain't Spanish!' and everyone started to get upset. The hoods that were running the place felt that they'd been had!"

Although Wilder made no studio recordings while a member of Millinder's orchestra, an extraordinary unissued air check of the band, with Wilder backing Billie Holiday, survives. The program was part of an NBC series, *Swingtime at the Savoy*, that debuted on July 28, 1948, with Ella Fitzgerald as special guest.[27] That show includes a bombastic rendition of Aram Khachaturian's *Sabre Dance*, arranged by Henry Glover, with Wilder playing the opening and closing melody. Hosted by Millinder and Noble Sissle (with no less than Langston Hughes as a script writer), the fast-paced half-hour variety show was designed to showcase top black artists in live broadcasts, re-creating a typical evening at the legendary Savoy Ballroom (the show actually emanated from the NBC studios). Wilder remembered it as an "experiment," and *Billboard* noted that the show was replacing *National Minstrels*, a "Mr. Bones" type of show that had been originally scheduled as an outlet for Negro talent. The reviewer, Sam Chase, offers a cautionary note: "The webs [networks] themselves may have no color line, but they and sponsors and agencies long have worried about the reaction to such a show in the corn pone belt."[28] *Swingtime at the Savoy* was a "sustaining" program, meaning it had no commercial sponsorship. The NAACP endorsed the new program, as the originally scheduled *National Minstrels* had elicited complaints from community groups, a number of which felt that "the minstrel characterization was not the best possible choice."[29]

Billie Holiday was the special guest on the broadcast that aired August 18, 1948. She sang her famous "Billie's Blues" with Wilder's plunger-muted obbligatos prominent behind her throughout. Wilder recalled how he came to play with her: "She wanted a trumpet to play behind her, and when she saw me, she said to Lucky, 'I want that short little cornet player over there.' And Lucky said, 'Well, he's my first trumpet player; Frank Galbreath is my hot man. He'll play behind you.' And she repeated, 'No, Lucky, I want that little short cornet player to play behind me!'" Millinder finally relented, and Wilder may be heard in what amounts to an extended duet with the singer, as he fashions a string of imaginative blues accompaniments. Upon hearing the recording decades later, Wilder noted that his boldly aggressive fills ran completely counter to his philosophy of tasteful, unobtrusive accompaniment for singers: "I just got carried away!" Wilder had played a similar role behind Holiday the year before, while he was with Jimmie Lunceford: "We were in Philadelphia, and she was a guest. She sang 'God Bless the Child,' and I played the fills behind her—that's how she knew me. She was always awfully nice to me."

Wilder participated in a couple of Millinder studio sessions in 1949 and 1950, after he had left the band. Guitarist Mundell Lowe recalled his first meeting with Wilder at a Millinder session for Victor on January 3, 1949: "When I first got to New York, through John Hammond, I was thrown in with a lot of black players, including Lucky Millinder. We seemed to get along okay, so that became my main thrust in jazz for a long time. I remember being taken with Joe because of his very melodic style. I thought to myself, 'I didn't know trumpet players could do that sort of thing!' Later, he reminded me a lot of Brownie [Clifford Brown]."[30]

While a member of Millinder's orchestra, Wilder received a very tempting offer. "The phone rang at three on a Sunday morning. It was Duke Ellington!" Before Ellington could go any further, Wilder blurted out, "My father was one of your greatest fans. I've been listening to you since I was a little kid!" Ellington said, "I'm trying to get someone to come into the band, and the guys told me you can play with the plunger. Would you be interested?" Wilder replied, "Would I be interested? You can't believe how flattered I am. This is just unbelievable!" Wilder recalled that Johnny Hodges and Harry Carney had heard him with Les Hite's band and, apparently, had recommended him to Duke. After talking for a while, Wilder finally got around to asking Ellington about the salary. "Well, you know, Joe baby, there ain't a lot of money around these days," the Maestro answered cryptically. "He never mentioned a figure," Wilder recalled, so he told him, "I'm playing first trumpet with Lucky, and he pays me a little extra for that and for rehearsing the band, so I'll come for exactly the same amount." When Wilder named the figure, Ellington said he was sorry, but he could not match it. "I would have loved to play with him," Wilder said, "but I had a family to support, and it didn't make much sense for me to come for less than I was making."

Sam Donahue

After leaving Lucky Millinder in the fall of 1948, Wilder joined bandleader Sam Donahue's orchestra, replacing Doc Severinsen. Wilder met up with the all-white band in Washington, DC, at the Club Kavakos on Eighth and H Streets in northeast Washington. The club (which advertised itself as "the home of the world's largest glass of beer") was segregated, even though it would be the site of Charlie Parker's legendary recorded appearance with "The Orchestra" in 1953 and had hosted many other leading black jazz artists.[31] As was his custom, Wilder arrived at least an hour early and was the first musician to enter the club. "When I walked in, there were people sitting at the bar, and all the heads turned around as if to say, 'Who in the world is this?'" Wilder recalled. "The bartender asked me if I was lost, and they sent me to wait in the band room. I'm sure they were relieved when the rest of the guys arrived, and they were all white."

Despite this inauspicious beginning, Wilder's acceptance by the musicians and the leader could not have been warmer. Born in 1918, Donahue was a talented saxophonist (and trumpeter), who had played with Gene Krupa from 1938 to 1940. In 1942, he took over leadership of Artie Shaw's Navy band, which he honed into a highly respected unit. After the war, Donahue formed his own civilian band, which he continued to lead into the early 1950s. When Wilder joined the group, he found it profoundly influenced by the music of Jimmie Lunceford, so the transition was easy for him. "Sam was a Lunceford fanatic," Wilder said. "It was like I never left Jimmie!" Wilder greatly respected Donahue, both musically and personally. "Next to Jimmie Lunceford, I guess he's the band leader I liked most. He was just wonderful," Wilder said. "At no point do I ever remember feeling there was something odd about me being in the band. And Sam set the tone."

Although Wilder was particularly close to his fellow members of the trumpet section—Fern Caron, who played lead, and the Faffley brothers, Bill and Don—he got along well with everyone in the band. More important, from the leader on down, his fellow musicians were unswerving in their support when faced with the problems of an integrated band on the road in the late 1940s. "We were in Harrisburg, Pennsylvania, and we arrived early, so we went to a pool hall to kill time," Wilder explained. "All of a sudden, this black guy who was sweeping the floor sidles over to me and says, 'The boss doesn't want you to shoot pool in here.' I told him to tell the boss to get lost. Then the boss himself came over and told me to leave. The guys in the band all left with me. These guys had never been confronted with segregation until I joined the band, but they didn't hesitate." The same scenario played out in restaurants that refused to serve Wilder: "Sam Donahue would say, 'Okay, guys. That's it. Let's go.' And we'd get back on the bus and go someplace else. The guys in the band would actually apologize to me! I felt sorry for *them*. It gave me the chance to see how other people were affected by what I was being subjected to. I had a tremendous bond with those guys."

Herbie Fields

After leaving Sam Donahue's orchestra in early 1949, Wilder played briefly with a group led by drummer Cozy Cole. Billed as "Cozy Cole's Cu-Boppers," the band, which included Cozy's brother, June, on piano, clarinetist Tony Aquaviva, and tenor saxophonist George "Big Nick" Nicholas, recorded for the obscure Candy label in February 1949, as well as four sides for Decca, with vocalist Bob Marshall.[32] Reflecting the prevailing Afro-Cuban influence popularized by Chano Pozo and Dizzy Gillespie, the group included two veterans of Dizzy's 1947 orchestra, Bill Alvares on bongos and Diego Iborra on congas. As Cozy Cole recalled, "[The band] wasn't too popular, because we were far out. We were playing some really modern stuff. . . . [I]t was a nice sounding band, I thought. I don't imagine the public did."[33] Wilder traveled with the group to play in Chicago at the Music Bowl. As Cole noted, the public failed to respond, and the second week of the two-week engagement was canceled. The club shut down, and the musicians filed a claim with the local American Federation of Musicians.[34] The band was scheduled to appear at the Howard Theatre in Washington, DC, after leaving Chicago. Despite the problems in Chicago, *Down Beat* predicted a bright future for Cole's combo: "A bop trumpeter [Wilder], a bongo player . . . that's the thing, man."[35] The two issued Candy sides, "La Danse" and "Stardust," give a good indication of the Afro-Cuban bebop-inflected music played by the group. On "La Danse," Wilder takes a wild up-tempo chorus full of the double- and triple-tonguing he remembered using on similar pieces with Gillespie.

In July 1949, Wilder received a call from saxophonist-bandleader Herbie Fields, inviting him to join his septet. When Wilder joined, the band included Bobby Burgess on trombone (later replaced by Frank Rosolino), Joe Gatto on piano, Rudy Cafaro on guitar, drummer Gene Thaler, and bassist Dante Martucci, who became Wilder's roommate on the road. Red Kelley soon replaced Martucci, with Max Bennett eventually filling the bass chair. Bennett, who joined Fields at the age of twenty and went on to a career as one of the most sought-after studio players on the West Coast, recalled the circumstances of Wilder's arrival: "Joe replaced Doug Mettome,[36] a wonderful trumpet player, but he had a drug problem. He couldn't go on the road because he couldn't find a connection, so that's when Joe joined the band. Joe fit in really well. He had a really warm, fat tone and a lot of facility—I enjoyed his playing very much. And he was so easy to get along with."[37]

Down Beat correspondent Pat Harris noted Wilder's arrival in the band in his Chicago Band Briefs column: "He has a smooth, limpid tone not too common among bop trumpeters, and a nice drive." Harris called the band "solidly good, without a weak spot. It jumps. The guys like to work together, they like to play, and they're not above showing it on the stand."[38]

As in Sam Donahue's band, Wilder was once again the only African American in the Fields group (drummer Fred Radcliffe, who was black, had played with Fields but left the band before Wilder joined). Although he had no problems with his bandmates, who were supportive, there were the inevitable incidents while on the road. "Of course, it was still in the 1940s, and prejudice was rampant," Max Bennett remembered. "Naturally, we hated it. We all tried to protect each other, but there were probably a lot of things that happened to Joe that he would never mention to us because he didn't want to burden us with them."[39] Although Wilder appreciated the support and friendship of his fellow musicians, he was disappointed with the leader's failure to stand up for him when confronted with discriminatory treatment in service or accommodations. "Once we were in [New] Philadelphia, Ohio, and we pulled up to a restaurant," Wilder said. "When they gave us the routine about not serving 'those people,' Herbie turned to me and said, 'Okay, Joe. Stay in the car—we'll bring you something.'" This was in sharp contrast to the way Sam Donahue, Wilder's former bandleader, had handled similar situations.

Fields, a rising star who had recently left Lionel Hampton's orchestra, was, to say the least, an extroverted soloist. "Fields' problem is restraint; he'll start out fine in a Chu Berry-Herschel Evans mold, then get carried away," Dan Morgenstern writes in describing the saxophonist's work on the famous 1940 to 1941 jam session recordings made by Jerry Newman. "And that's the way things remained with him—when he was featured with Lionel Hampton a few years later, restraint was hardly the reason why Hamp showcased him."[40] Personally, he was a flamboyant character, whom Wilder found hard to take. "I wasn't that fond of Herbie—he was a little strange," Wilder said. "He was a prima donna, and as the leader, he didn't want to be on the stand when we started. So we'd be out there playing whatever we couldn't play while he was there and were a big hit with the early arrivers." Although there are no recordings of the group with Wilder, a live release from the Flame Club in Saint Paul, after trumpeter Doug Mettome had returned to the band, bears out Wilder's recollection. Fields does not play on the opening three numbers of the set.[41]

Fields stressed showmanship, a holdover from his tenure with Hampton, and expected his musicians to contribute to the entertainment portion of the show. "He liked to work you to death," said Max Bennett.[42] The extramusical show business demands were one reason Wilder left Hampton, so he was less than enthusiastic about this aspect of the group's performances. Apparently, other band members shared his reluctance. In his *Billboard* review of the band's performance in Chicago in August 1948, Johnny Soppel noted, "While jazz blowing is good, it's [Fields's] terrific showmanship that brings down the house. While his sidemen are improved showmen, they could still give the energetic Fields more of a hand if they'd synchronize their action with what the Victor artist is doing."[43] Fields played all the reed instruments, including the unwieldy bass saxophone on occasion. "Because he wasn't really a great accomplished jazz musician, his style was sort of a mishmash," Bennett recalled. "At least half or even 75 percent of what he did was for show. I always felt that he had the potential to be a better musician than he was. He let showbiz get in the way."[44] Wilder and Bennett used to commiserate and coined the phrase "to the delight of the audience and the embarrassment of the band" in reference to Fields's onstage behavior. The leader responded to the frequent criticism by telling *Down Beat*, "My jumping around on the stand isn't merely commercial. I do it to give the guys the beat, and the audience, too—and it's working."[45]

By the time Wilder joined the band, Fields was apparently making an effort to curb some of his excesses, prompting a reviewer to observe, "Herbie has toned down the honks and squeals that went with his antics for so long. He's still not the greatest saxist in captivity, but he's leagues closer than before."[46] The band drew good crowds wherever they played, except when they were booked in a black section of Los Angeles. "Nobody showed up," Max Bennett said. "We were pretty much a white band, not what you'd call today a funk band."[47]

Musically, the band's repertoire included "Dardanella," a recent hit record for Fields on Victor, as well as some rhythm-and-blues pieces, a direction Fields would take increasingly in later years. "We were also playing some of the more accessible bebop things but not the really involved ones," Wilder said. "I felt pretty comfortable with them, although they were challenging." In his review of the band's appearance at the Blue Note in Chicago in August 1949, *Down Beat*'s Pat Harris noted, "Herbie's is the band that ought to have the Bop for the People tag," the name used by Charlie Ventura's small group, which attempted to bring the new music to a wider audience.[48] "With Herbie, there were arrangements, but they were loose," Max Bennett said. "As I recall, we didn't have any music when I joined. In a situation like that, you start doing your own arranging, and it just kind of gels."[49] The Flame Club live recording displays many of these effective "head" arrangements, as well as the leader's frenetic solo style.

Fields fancied himself a lady's man and liked to boast to his musicians that he could get any woman he wanted, including the band members' wives. "My first wife and my son were in Milwaukee with me, and a couple of the other musicians and their wives were there," Wilder said. "Herbie made a remark to the effect that he could 'make it' with any one of them. [Guitarist] Rudy

Cafaro, who had been a boxer, said, 'If you ever make a move on my wife, I'll knock your head off!'" And the great female jazz singer Chris Connor, who sang with the Fields group, would often seek Wilder's and Cafaro's assistance in warding off the leader's advances.

The band toured the Midwest extensively, playing clubs like the Flame in Saint Paul, Minnesota, and similar places in Detroit and Milwaukee, some with alleged mob ties. Fields had a big following in Chicago, and the band fulfilled regular residencies at the Silhouette Club (nicknamed the "Stiletto" by the musicians) and the Blue Note.

The band was back in Chicago at the Silhouette in early November 1949 playing opposite Charlie Ventura's unit. "Billed as a battle of the bands, the opening night came to a decision after the second set," wrote Pat Harris. "And it wasn't in favor of little Herbie. Other than a Joe Wilder trumpet solo on *Tenderly*, it was a throwback to a Fields we haven't, fortunately, heard much of recently."[50] At the Silhouette, Wilder had to deal with some hecklers in the rather unruly crowd:

> Some of the local college kids would come in there, and whenever I would take a solo, they would just keep repeating "nigger." This happened a few times, and finally, I walked over to them and said, "I know you probably don't understand just how offensive this is. At some point, you're going to say something like that in the wrong place, and you'll end up getting yourselves hurt." The next time they came in, they didn't say anything, and the time after that, they actually were friendly to me.

As the group consisted of only seven pieces, much of the travel was by private cars, driven by the band members, which could sometimes be perilous. "I used to ride in Herbie's car with him and his girlfriend," Wilder said. "I'm sitting in the back, and he'd be going ninety miles an hour after he'd been drinking. All of a sudden, I'd wake up and see that we're on the wrong side of the divider line. And I'd yell, 'Herbie!' We're lucky we didn't have a head-on collision."

Disaster finally struck when the band left Chicago after the Silhouette engagement to return to New York. Wilder, trombonist Frank Rosolino, and Max Bennett were traveling in Bennett's new Chevy convertible. They were somewhere in Ohio, with Wilder dozing in the backseat next to Bennett's bass, when Rosolino, who was driving, fell asleep. The car left the road, landed in a field, and flipped over, crushing the roof before righting itself again. "Frank Rosolino was unconscious," Wilder recalled. "The windshield had broken, and pieces of the glass were pressing on his head. Max and I managed to get him out. When a state trooper came, he couldn't believe we had been in that car. We had chips of glass in our heads but were okay." They had to leave the car in Ohio and eventually made their way to New York by bus. After appearing with Fields at Bop City on Broadway for a couple of weeks, in November of 1949, Wilder left the band. The accident, and other near misses over the years, prompted Wilder to begin to seriously consider other musical outlets that would enable him to get off the road. Herbie Fields himself would not live another decade; he committed suicide in 1958, at the age of thirty-nine.

5

New York (1950–1953)

Noble Sissle and the Diamond Horseshoe

The immediate means by which Wilder was able to leave the trials of life on the road was an extended engagement with veteran composer-bandleader Noble Sissle at Billy Rose's Diamond Horseshoe in New York. An alumnus of James Reese Europe's 369th Regimental Band, Sissle (1989–1975) was best known for his collaborations with Eubie Blake on such groundbreaking black Broadway shows as *Shuffle Along* (1921), which produced the hit song "I'm Just Wild about Harry." In 1938, impresario Billy Rose opened a new nightclub in the lower level of the Paramount Hotel on Forty-Sixth Street and Broadway, and he immediately booked Sissle to lead the orchestra.[1] "It quickly became noted for his [Rose's] then unique formula of cheap food and drinks and scantily clad chorus girls, maintaining its popularity for decades."[2] Sissle was a regular at the club through the 1940s and had become an institution by the time Wilder joined his show at the end of 1949.

Original cast recording of *Guys and Dolls*, December 3, 1950; Wilder and trombonist Benny Morton are the two African American orchestra members.
(Wilder Family Collection.)

Artistically, Wilder paid a steep price to for his decision to leave the road. The Diamond Horseshoe represented a radical change from the progressive music Wilder had recently played with Gillespie, the bop-inflected style of Herbie Fields, or even the more traditional swing of Jimmie Lunceford and Sam Donahue. The club's entertainment was a throwback to the earlier vaudeville and even minstrel era, an anachronism by 1950. When Wilder joined Sissle, the show at the time was called *Banjo on My Knee*. A review in the *Toledo Blade* paints a depressing picture of what Wilder encountered each night:

> For this memory minstrel show, Rose has recruited many veterans of the minstrel days and for his interlocutor he has chosen spry 72-year-old Frank Evans, who was once a minstrel fledgling with Thatcher, Primrose and West in 1887. He not only sings and cracks jokes as the interlocutor, but also does a tap dance on roller skates. . . . This "looking back" revue of minstrel days revives many of the old vaudeville numbers which were specialties between acts of the colorful burnt cork revues at such old time theaters as Koster and Bials, Niblo's Gardens and the Palace. . . . Other than [Frank] Evans and [Harry] Armstrong, the show offers such minstrel veterans as blind W.C. Handy playing his immortal "The St. Louis Blues," Noble Sissle singing his own song, "I'm Just Wild About Harry," and several old time dancers tripping highly through such minstrel steps as soft shoe, sand dance, 1875 time step and the corkscrew.[3]

In an extended four-part article in *Collier's Weekly*, Maurice Zolotow describes the Diamond Horseshoe as "the first port of call in New York for the peasant thirsting for big-city excitement . . . right up there alongside the Metropolitan Museum of Art, Grant's Tomb and the Empire State Building." He also unveils a not very flattering portrait of Rose and his taste in entertainment:

> Rose's métier is the spectacular, the flashy, the ponderous, the garish. Being a little man, who stands five feet three inches in his elevator shoes and refuses to be measured in his stocking feet, Rose suffers from the disease of giantism. He is not happy unless his shows are running riot with huge casts, with hordes of lush show girls, with lots of clanging symphony, with novelty act following upon novelty act.[4]

Not only was the music archaic, but the treatment of musicians at the Diamond Horseshoe also harkened back to an earlier era. "The band had to wear circus costumes, and we had to march from the bandstand to the end of the club and then back onto the bandstand," Wilder said. At twenty-eight, the trumpeter was the youngest member of an orchestra in which most of the members were his father's age or older and were less inclined to stand up for their rights. Wilder, particularly after his Marine Corps service, had become more outspoken when he felt he or his fellow musicians were being mistreated, as evidenced by his dealings with Lionel and Gladys Hampton. "The guys in Noble Sissle's band were easily intimidated," he recalled. "We'd be in there rehearsing things over and over until somebody in the band would say to Noble, 'I think the guys need a break.' 'No!' Billy Rose would say. 'I'm paying them—play it over!' You dared not talk above a whisper. You had to behave in a certain manner; otherwise it might jeopardize Noble's position as the bandleader. It was brutal."

Wilder was also dismayed at the treatment of the "Long Stem Roses," the show's chorus girls, all of whom were more than six feet tall. "They were seminude, and they could appear legally in front of an audience as long as they didn't move around," he said. "They might turn in a certain position and stay there for two choruses; then they could move in another direction, and as long as there was no continual motion, they were within the laws of decency." Apparently, Rose made some further demands: "One night we came off for intermission, and one of the girls in the cast was standing there crying. [Fellow trumpeter] Wendell Culley asked her what was wrong, and she said, 'Mr. Rose told me it's my turn in the bed tonight.' And if they didn't acquiesce, they'd get fired."

Not only was the audience all white, but it catered to a large Southern contingent. Wilder recalled one evening when Dr. Ralph Bunche, the noted African American scholar-diplomat and winner of the 1950 Nobel Peace Prize, entered the Diamond Horseshoe. "They seated him behind a pillar," he said. After it was pointed out to management that Bunche was "no ordinary Negro," they attempted to move him to a better seat. "You put me here—I'll stay here," Bunche replied.

Another visitor was Alabama Governor Jim Folsom, who came in and asked, "Where's that blind boy who plays the cornet?" "He was talking about W. C. Handy!" Wilder said. The dignified Handy, known as "the father of the blues," had been a regular at the Diamond Horseshoe since the early 1940s. In a 1943 piece in *Negro Digest*, Langston Hughes describes the then sixty-nine-year-old icon's nightly trip to the club after a full day of work at his publishing company: "At midnight, he speeds down Riverside Drive toward the Diamond Horseshoe for the last show. When the lights come up for the finale, the incredibly sweet notes of the 'St. Louis Blues' flow from that golden trumpet. . . . A mighty lot of energy, race pride, will-to-create, love of music and all people—went into the making of the 'St. Louis Blues.' It is a great song and he is a great man."[5]

Handy was still playing the "St. Louis Blues" some seven years later when Wilder encountered him at the Diamond Horseshoe:

> We'd listen to Mr. Handy every night, and I could hear that he was struggling. It sounded like he was blowing his brains out, but the sound was so thin. I thought his horn might have needed to be cleaned, so when he finished that set, I said, "Mr. Handy, has anyone cleaned your trumpet for you?" He said, "No, not in many years." So I asked him if he would like me to do it, and he said, "Would you do that for me, young man?" I said I'd be proud to, so I took it between shows and put it in the sink. There was like a tube of saliva collected inside. When I put the brush through there, it came out like an inner tube! The valves were green. I don't know how he even got a sound out of it. So I cleaned it out and put oil in the valves and gave it back to him. He didn't play a note until the next show. Well, the difference was unbelievable. The guys in the band looked up and wondered what had happened to him! His neck wasn't puffed out, and you could really hear him. He never forgot that. Every night he would ask, "Where's that nice young man who cleaned my trumpet for me?"

Wilder's sense of humor helped him deal with some of the indignities of life in the Diamond Horseshoe. As was evident during his time with Dizzy Gillespie, Wilder was becoming something of a prankster, a quality not always appreciated by his older, staid band mates. For example, every night, before the musicians would begin marching through the club, Wilder would surreptitiously drop some towels into the bell of the tuba player's horn. "The people in the back were complaining that they couldn't hear the tuba," Wilder said. "I did this to him about eight nights in a row, until I dropped in a towel that was all wet, and he felt it hit the bell and realized it was me all along! He was such a nice guy he just broke up laughing." But his jokes were not always appreciated by the older musicians:

> They thought I was a nut because I saw humor in things they couldn't deal with. We had a big Southern clientele, and having this black orchestra there, they would come up to us and say, "Hey, boy, can you play 'Ol' Man River' or 'Old Black Joe'?" and all these minstrel songs with "nigger" in them. So I made up a pricelist of requests: "Ol' Man River"—$50 without the verse; with the verse, which had "Niggers all

work on the Mississippi"—$150. I made up copies and gave them to everyone in the band. I'd be cracking up, but Noble and the rest of the guys couldn't understand that kind of humor.

While the conditions at the Diamond Horseshoe were in many ways demeaning and the music moribund, the engagement, which probably lasted into the spring of 1951, allowed Wilder to remain in New York. It turned out to be a pivotal point in his career because it enabled him to both work in Broadway orchestras and to further his formal education.

Breaking Barriers on Broadway

African Americans have had a long history on Broadway, going back to the turn of the century with such pioneering productions as Bob Cole's *A Trip to Coontown* (1898) and Will Marion Cook's *Clorindy, or The Origin of the Cakewalk* (1898) and *In Dahomey* (1903). After a hiatus, the 1920s brought a new wave in black musicals, including *Shuffle Along* (1921) and *The Chocolate Dandies* (1924), the landmark collaborations by Noble Sissle and Eubie Blake, as well as productions by such black composers as James P. Johnson (*Runnin' Wild*, 1924), Fats Waller (*Keep Shuffling*, 1928, and *Hot Chocolates*, 1929), and many others. Most if not all these shows involved black musicians, sometimes appearing onstage. But it would be another two decades before a black musician played in the orchestra of a nonblack production. That distinction would seem to belong to the bassist Al Hall. Hall (1915–1988), who began as a violinist and preceded Wilder at the Mastbaum School in Philadelphia, originally aspired to a career in classical music but, as was the case with many black musicians of his era, soon became discouraged by the lack of opportunities. He went on to a distinguished career with many leading jazz groups, including Teddy Wilson, Mary Lou Williams, and Erroll Garner, and later with Alberta Hunter and Doc Cheatham. In 1947, he made history by playing in the orchestra of the George Abbott production of *Barefoot Boy with Cheek*, which opened in April and ran for some three months at the Martin Beck Theater. Coincidentally, Hall, as Wilder some five years later, was working at the Diamond Horseshoe (in *Venus on the Half Shell*, a typical Billy Rose revue, featuring a seven-foot blonde named Siri) when he got the offer. Pianist Herman Chittison recommended Hall to Milton Rosenstock, the show's musical director. Rosenstock had been the musical director for Irving Berlin's *This Is the Army*, a 1942 musical that featured some black entertainers and, consequently, "got a flair for what the black performer had to offer," as Hall himself put it, adding, "So when he got this show [*Barefoot Boy with Cheek*], he wanted a half and half orchestra, half white and half black, and he posted a sign at the Union and they made him take it down."[6]

Several of the black musicians recommended to Rosenstock, including saxophonist Eddie Barefield, trombonist Benny Morton, and drummer Jimmy Crawford, were touring with bands and were unavailable, so Hall became the only African American in the orchestra. This significant breakthrough seems to have gone unnoticed in the press at the time, although *Down Beat* alluded to it by publishing a photo, by noted jazz photographer William Gottlieb, of Hall with Rosenstock and four white members of the show's orchestra playing cards in the dressing room. The caption states, "It's been a long time coming; but the pit bands of Broadway musical shows are finally getting hip. One of the pioneers is *Barefoot Boy With Cheek*."[7] The caption goes on to name the musicians, Hall included, and cites their past big band affiliations. It is unclear whether the magazine considered the show a "pioneer" because it included jazz players in the pit or because one of them was black. Shortly after *Barefoot Boy* closed, Hall played in the orchestra of another George Abbott Broadway production, *High Button Shoes* (October 1947–July 1949), for which Rosenstock also served as musical director.

At the time of Hall's breakthrough, the cultural division of the National Negro Congress held a conference on equal rights for African Americans in the entertainment industry.[8] The African American opera singer Kenneth Lee Spencer, who chaired the theater committee, cited a report compiled by unnamed researchers commenting on the dearth of black musicians in Broadway orchestras, noting, "Of eight musical shows on Broadway, only one has Negro musicians in the pit."[9] That one was presumably *Barefoot Boy*, with Al Hall.

A few months later, in November 1947, Leonard Bernstein wrote a piece in the *New York Times* titled "The Negro in Music: Problems He Has to Face in Getting a Start." Although primarily concerned with the absence of black musicians in symphony orchestras (we examine his remarks on that subject later on), Bernstein noted, "There are no Negroes playing in any of the pit orchestras of the Broadway musicals. Exception: last season 'Beggar's Holiday' (because Duke Ellington wrote the score) used five Negroes in the orchestra."[10] This drew a correction from Peggy Phillips, a press agent and representative at the time of the Theatre Guild, who noted that the Rodgers and Hammerstein musical *Allegro*, then at the Majestic Theatre, had two black musicians in the pit orchestra: Winston Collymore (violin) and William Taylor (string bass).[11] Collymore (1903–2002) studied at Juilliard and had a long career on Broadway and in the recording studios, including eleven years as a member of the Radio City Music Hall orchestra.[12] Bassist William Taylor was the noted jazz bassist Billy Taylor, who played with Duke Ellington from 1935 to 1940.

In her letter, Phillips also noted, "To my knowledge, 'Allegro' is the only musical current on Broadway which employs Negro musicians in the pit."[13]

Wilder on Broadway

Shortly after joining Noble Sissle's band at the Diamond Horseshoe, Wilder received an offer to do his first Broadway show, *Alive and Kicking*, which opened at the Winter Garden Theatre on January 17, 1950. Wilder is not sure who recommended him for the orchestra. Since rehearsals were to begin immediately, he needed Noble Sissle's permission to leave the Diamond Horseshoe without giving the customary two weeks' notice. Sissle, of course, had been a key figure in the "Black Broadway" efflorescence some three decades earlier, and he recognized the significance of this opportunity. "He was very nice about it and was very proud that I was asked to do it," Wilder said. "He told me, 'I'll let you go, young man, but if you're away for more than five weeks, I'll have to get a permanent replacement.'" Even though the show lasted six weeks, closing on February 25, Sissle allowed Wilder to return to the Diamond Horseshoe. "I have to give Noble Sissle credit. I wouldn't have gotten into the theaters at all were it not for him," Wilder said.

Overall, Wilder's initial reception on Broadway was positive, although he did encounter some hostility at the first rehearsal. "Oddly enough, some of it was from the violin players, who had no reason to object, since they were on the other side of the orchestra," he said. The musical director of *Alive and Kicking* was Lehman Engel, and he was supportive. "He was from Mississippi and had a great sense of humor," Wilder recalled. "He was a very nice man and a talented conductor, and it was good for me that I started out with somebody like him." The wind players on the whole were receptive. "Once they determined that you were able to do what was required, any problems began to diminish," Wilder said. Wilder was playing third trumpet, with Jimmy Blake on second trumpet and Hy Small on lead. Small, who had been a student of Harry Glantz's, principal trumpet with the NBC Symphony under Arturo Toscanini, went out of his way to make Wilder feel comfortable. Wilder occasionally got to play an improvised solo, filling in for his colleague Jimmy Blake:

He [Blake] and Lehman used to imbibe a little bit. They would fill Coca-Cola bottles with gin, and as the show would be going on, they'd be sipping. Jimmy had an improvised solo to play, and maybe four or five bars before it, he'd turn to me and say, "You want to play the solo?" So I'd jump in and play it. That was understood between him, me, and the conductor.

Wilder's main problems came from the stagehands. "They were like an arm of the Ku Klux Klan, and tried to make it uncomfortable," Wilder said. "But there were so many other people who were just as nice as they were nasty, so that got me through a lot of it. And after a while, everybody just worked together, and it was okay."

Playing in the orchestra for a Broadway show was markedly different from Wilder's work in jazz bands, although, once again, he was able to draw on his classical training and experience. "It was a different kind of music, and it required a different kind of discipline," he said. "When you were playing in a dance orchestra, you had an opportunity to improvise, so you had a freedom of expression that you didn't have in a musical. In a musical, you had someone directing almost every note you played, and you had to conform to the wishes of the conductor. Of course, you're still playing the same notes, so it's not that big a difference." He also noted that *Alive and Kicking* differed from the typical Broadway show in that it was a "revue," meaning it didn't have a set musical book: "They would try something new every day, and if it worked, they would keep it as part of the show."

Wilder also had to learn the idiosyncrasies of each show's conductor: "You had to know if a certain conductor's upbeat is going to be indicative precisely of the tempo because you couldn't always be sure that what he did was what he meant." One might think that playing the same music night after night without the respite of improvisation might soon become tedious, but as would later be the case in his work as a studio musician, Wilder found new ways to challenge himself in the Broadway pits: "You would try to play it as well today as you did yesterday." He recalled the words of Anton Coppola, his conductor in the show *Silk Stockings*: "Let's do an opening-night performance tonight!" Wilder tried to oblige every night. And he learned another essential lesson: not to watch the stage from the orchestra: "A lot of times the girls would be wearing flimsy costumes, and you might miss a cue!"

Alive and Kicking closed on February 25, 1950, and Wilder returned to the grind of the Diamond Horseshoe. In November, he received a call to do another Broadway show, and once again, he approached Noble Sissle about taking time off. Anxious to see African American musicians succeed, Sissle continued to be accommodating, allowing his first trumpet player to leave while again cautioning him that if the show lasted more than four weeks, he would have to find a permanent replacement. The show turned out to be the original *Guys and Dolls*, which ran for more than three years. Needless to say, Wilder never returned to the Diamond Horseshoe.

Guys and Dolls was the first hit produced by the team of Cy Feuer and Ernest Martin, who would go on to create such Broadway successes as *Silk*

Stockings and *How to Succeed in Business without Really Trying.* Feuer's son, Jed, recalled that his father, who began his career as a trumpet player, had recently heard Wilder, possibly at the Diamond Horseshoe: "It was 1950, and he had heard a sensational trumpet player with whom he was very impressed. The trumpet player happened to be African-American, and Cy hired him to be one of the four trumpets in *Guys and Dolls.* This was not easy, and it did not go over well at all, but that was the way it was going to be because Cy saw it that way."[14] This time Wilder, who played second trumpet, was not the only black musician in the orchestra; Benny Morton, a veteran of the Fletcher Henderson, Chick Webb, Don Redman, and Count Basie bands, was on trombone, and Billy Kyle, whom Wilder had known growing up in Philadelphia and had been a mainstay of the John Kirby Sextet, was the pianist. As was the case when Al Hall broke the Broadway color barrier three years earlier, *Down Beat* noted the presence of Wilder, Morton, and Kyle in the *Guys and Dolls* pit but not the fact that that they were African Americans. It cited them along with several white musicians as jazzmen who were members of the orchestra.[15] On December 3, 1950, less than two weeks after *Guys and Dolls* opened, Wilder played on the original cast recording for Decca. He can be heard playing a delicate four-bar muted solo passage on "My Time of Day," sung by Robert Alda.[16]

Although Wilder's tenure in the comparatively short-lived *Alive and Kicking* had been relatively smooth, he found the cast and the production team of *Guys and Dolls* even more supportive. From composer Frank Loesser, producers Cy Feuer and Ernie Martin, to the musical director Irving Actman and the contractor Henry Topper, Wilder and his fellow black musicians were accepted and made to feel at home. Unfortunately, the problems with the stagehands persisted. "'Nigger' was the order of the day with them, and they shunned anybody who tried to be friendly toward you," Wilder said. During these incidents, Wilder was heartened by the intervention of some of his fellow band members, especially trumpeter Johnny Granada. "If someone used the 'N' word, Johnny would be all over him," Wilder recalled.

Despite the overall predominantly positive attitude the African American musicians encountered in New York, they could not escape the realities of prejudice elsewhere. Toward the end of its run, *Guys and Dolls* was scheduled to go on the road for a six-week summer stint in Washington, DC, at the National Theatre, opening on June 29, 1953.[17] The orchestra was to be made up of some of the New York musicians, with added players from Washington. Some of the local musicians refused to sit next to African Americans in the pit. Apparently, the producers decided to make pianist Billy Kyle assistant conductor, so that he would be allowed to play. "They finally accepted him because he wouldn't be sitting in the section next to them," Wilder said. But

Wilder and trombonist Benny Morton were left behind, which begs the question, why didn't the show's management cancel the engagement?

After a brief hiatus while he toured with Count Basie, Wilder would return to Broadway in 1955 with *Silk Stockings*. A much longer hiatus took place while he was on staff at ABC, before he resumed working on Broadway in the early 1970s (these shows are discussed in later chapters). The table on the following page summarizes Wilder's Broadway show engagements.

Manhattan School of Music

One advantage of working steadily in New York was that Wilder was able to go back to school. He greatly valued education and always regretted his premature departure from Mastbaum, even though it had been necessary to help support his family. Like his father, Wilder was always studying on his own, whether it was languages, music, photography, or other subjects. While playing with Noble Sissle at the Diamond Horseshoe in 1951, he applied to the Manhattan School of Music and was admitted. "They didn't care if I had a high school diploma, and the GI Bill paid for it," he recalled. Wilder attended classes full time during the day, and he worked at the Diamond Horseshoe and later in the Broadway orchestras at night.

Apart from simply wanting to prove he could earn a college degree, Wilder felt he had unfinished business. His early aspirations as a classical musician had been cut short by the lack of opportunities for African Americans and the need to help his family financially. He also wanted to better himself as a well-rounded musician:

> I felt I didn't have enough depth, musically. I also wanted to shore up
> my ability to do classical playing, particularly in the areas of transposition and orchestral repertoire. I was fortunate to be assigned to Joseph Alessi Sr., the grandfather of Joe Alessi, who's the first trombone
> player with the [New York] Philharmonic. I studied orchestral repertoire with William Vacchiano, who was the first trumpet player with
> the Philharmonic at that time. These were two wonderful men who
> had no prejudices. If they took you on as a student, they stuck with you
> until you gained something from it. They were very fatherly toward
> you, as helpful as they could be.

Wilder especially remembered playing duets from the Pietsch book of operatic excerpts with Vacchiano: "He would have me play the first part, and he would play the second part. You can imagine how encouraging that was." Wilder

JOE WILDER'S PARTICIPATION IN BROADWAY SHOWS

Name	Preview Date	Opening Date	Closing Date	Theater	Role
Alive and Kicking		Jan. 17, 1950	Feb. 25, 1950	Winter Garden	3rd trumpet
Guys and Dolls		Nov. 24, 1950	Nov. 28, 1952	46th Street	2nd trumpet
Can-Can		May 7, 1953	June 25, 1955	Shubert	sub
Silk Stockings		Feb. 24, 1955	Apr. 14, 1956	Imperial	1st trumpet
Most Happy Fella		May 3, 1956	Dec. 14, 1957	Imperial, Broadway	1st trumpet
Man of La Mancha		June 22, 1972	Oct. 21, 1972	Vivian Beaumont	1st trumpet
Lorelei	Jan. 17, 1974	Jan. 27, 1974	Nov. 3, 1974	Palace	sub
Shenandoah	Dec. 23, 1974	Jan. 7, 1975	Aug. 7, 1977	Alvin, Mark Hellinger	1st trumpet
Timbuktu	Feb. 9, 1978	Mar. 1, 1978	Sept. 10, 1978	Mark Hellinger	1st trumpet
Angel	May 4, 1978	May 10, 1978	May 13, 1978	Minskoff	1st trumpet/ contractor
Annie Get Your Gun		Summer 1978	Summer 1978	Jones Beach	2nd trumpet
Ballroom	Dec. 1, 1978	Dec. 14, 1978	Mar. 24, 1979	Majestic	1st trumpet
I Remember Mama		May 31, 1979	Sept. 2, 1979	Majestic	2nd trumpet
Peter Pan	Aug. 10, 1979	Sept. 6, 1979	Jan. 4, 1981*	Lunt-Fontanne	2nd trumpet
Reggae	Mar. 11, 1980	Mar. 27, 1980	Apr. 13, 1980	Biltmore	1st trumpet/ contractor
Camelot	June 30, 1980	July 8, 1980	Aug. 23, 1980	New York State, Lincoln Center	1st trumpet†
42nd Street	Aug. 18, 1980	Aug. 25, 1980	Jan. 8, 1989	Winter Garden, Majestic, St. James	2nd trumpet

Source for dates and theaters: Internet Broadway Database (http://www.ibdb.com).

* Wilder left before the show closed.

† Wilder was hired as 1st trumpet but left before the show opened.

became a favorite of Vacchiano's, and when his teacher heard of openings in symphonies, he would bring them to Wilder's attention and suggest that he audition. "He would mention places like the Dallas or San Antonio Symphonies, and when I would tell him they would never hire me, he just couldn't understand it."

Not everyone at the Manhattan School was as sympathetic. When Wilder auditioned for the school's symphony orchestra, he encountered an obstacle in the person of Harris Danziger, the conductor. "I don't think it had so much to do with race as it did the kind of music you were coming from," Wilder said. "If he knew you played jazz or commercial music, he just had no use for you, and he didn't hesitate to let you know it. He was just convinced that nobody who had been playing in a dance band could play classical music." Wilder auditioned several times and was told, "Well, you know, Mr. Wilder, you played it very well, but we don't use that concept in the symphony orchestra." Finally, at a rehearsal during which Wilder filled in for the absent principal trumpet, the conductor kept criticizing his phrasing until Wilder could stand it no more: "I told him, 'Wait a minute! Each time I come to play you tell me that I'm not using the right concept. Just tell me the way you want it phrased, and then if I don't do it, you're certainly justified in saying that I don't belong here.' He slammed the baton and yelled, 'Get him out of here!' Then he went to the dean and told him he didn't want me in the orchestra. So that was it. I was out."

Although there were no other African Americans in the orchestra at the time, he emphasized that white musicians coming from a jazz or commercial music background received the same treatment from Danziger, although no one had challenged him openly as Wilder had. "He was a nice enough man, and I later studied conducting with him," Wilder said. "But he just had this thing about dance music." To their credit, the school administrators realized they had a problem and diplomatically removed Danziger as conductor, replacing him in 1952 with Jonel Perlea, who had conducted at La Scala and the Metropolitan Opera. Also, the school instituted blind auditions for the symphony orchestra, with all candidates playing the same repertoire behind a screen to hide their identities. Wilder again tried out, playing for three judges: Simeon Bellison, clarinetist with the New York Philharmonic; John Clark, bass trombonist with the NBC Symphony; and Perlea. "To my surprise, they gave me the principal chair," Wilder said, adding with customary modesty, "There were a couple of guys who probably could have done a better job than I did, but they were so nervous about it." Although the school was integrated, Wilder may have been the first African American to hold a principal chair in the orchestra.

Wilder was anxious to make a good impression on Perlea, but at one rehearsal things went terribly wrong:

> We were doing the *Leonore* overture, and there's a trumpet solo in the middle of it. So Mr. Perlea gives the cue, and I play the first trumpet part. I think I'm playing it pretty well, but he's standing up there shaking his head and says, "This is not correct. Can we please do this again?" So we do it again, and I say to myself, "Maybe I didn't play it loud enough." So I play it louder, and again, he says, "This is not correct!" So he starts to walk through the orchestra, and the second trumpet player nudges me and says, "Joe, it's trumpet in D!" I didn't see the transposition and was playing it in the wrong key! When the conductor had gotten almost to me I said, "Maestro, can we please do it just once more?" So I played it again, and this time he gets a big smile on his face and says, "This is correct." He was always very nice to me and made a joke about it afterward.

Unlike many conservatories and universities of that era, the Manhattan School of Music was not outwardly hostile to jazz and jazz musicians. Wilder's fellow students included pianist John Lewis, drummer Max Roach, and trumpeter Donald Byrd. As was the case with Wilder, they came to improve their overall musicianship, not their jazz playing. As classical trumpeter Henry Nowak, Wilder's friend and fellow student at the Manhattan School, noted, "That was an age when there was a big gulf between the two kinds of musicians: 'legitimate,' as they called them, and jazz."[18]

In addition to music courses, at the Manhattan School Wilder studied other subjects, including European history and German, at which he excelled. He also studied Italian for a semester, fulfilling another dream deferred. Because of his deep friendship with Rosario Pino, his fellow trumpet player in the Tilden Junior High orchestra in Philadelphia, he had attempted to sign up for an extracurricular Italian class at the school. "Rosario used to invite me to his house, and his grandmother, who was Sicilian, didn't speak any English," Wilder said. "I thought if I studied Italian, I'd be able to talk to her." When he tried to enroll, the teacher asked him whether he was planning to go to college: "I said I didn't know. I didn't see how I could, as we were fighting through the Depression, and we barely had food to eat. So she told me, 'In that case, there's no sense in your wasting your time or mine,' and that was it. I always felt bad about that because I thought that, by learning Italian, I could show the Rosario family how fond I was of them." Wilder, who ultimately became fluent in Swedish, saw a connection between his facility for languages and the fact that he is a musician: "As a musician, you hear things and retain them because you've been trained to listen to different types of music. It gives you a definite advantage."

After graduating from the Manhattan School of Music in May 1953 with a Bachelor of Arts in Music (Trumpet), Wilder planned to pursue a master's degree, but once again, economic necessity intervened. By this time, Joe and his wife, Lillian, had a son, Joseph Jr., and Wilder could not spare the time and expense of pursuing a graduate degree. In addition, the marriage was in trouble, and his situation at home with Lillian was becoming unbearable. So at the end of 1953, Wilder broke his vow never to travel again and accepted an offer to join Count Basie's band—"going back on the road for a little respite," as he put it.

On the Road Again

Count Basie (1953–1954)

By the end of 1953, when Wilder joined the Basie orchestra, it had made the transition from the "Old Testament" band of the 1930s and 1940s—a freewheeling unit sparked by the improvisational genius of such singular soloists as saxophonists Lester Young and Herschel Evans and trumpeters Buck Clayton and Harry Edison—to the "New Testament" band, a well-oiled swing machine shaped by such gifted arrangers as Neal Hefti, Ernie Wilkins, Frank Foster, and Frank Wess. "The arrangers had a lot to do with the success of the band," Wilder said. "Frank Foster, Frank Wess, and the others knew the Basie style, and they would write arrangements that contributed to that style." Neal Hefti, who perhaps was most responsible for the "New Testament" Basie sound, was a particular favorite of Wilder's: "When we used to get calls to do jingles or a record date, and they said it was for Neal Hefti, I'd say, 'I'll be there!' You knew it was going to be a lot of fun musically."

Joe and Solveig, Conference of the International Association for Jazz Education, Toronto, January 2008. *(Photo by Ed Berger.)*

Wilder was brought in to the Basie orchestra both to play parts and to share the trumpet solo work with Joe Newman, his friend and section mate from the Lionel Hampton band of a decade earlier. At his first rehearsal at New York's Birdland, Wilder recalled how Newman, normally very protective of his solo space, generously divided up the band's charts with the newcomer:

> Joe was handing me one thing after the other, and they all had trumpet solos on them. After rehearsal, I was talking to Marshal Royal, and I said, "It's so nice of Joe to give me all these things with trumpet solos." And Marshal said, "Well, let me see some of the tunes." When I showed him the stack, he said, "Joe, we haven't played those things in five years!"

After a few weeks of playing with the Basie orchestra with no solo opportunities, during a performance, Wilder finally took action:

> I got a piece of paper, and I wrote a note: "Dear Count, could I play sixteen bars of anything?" And I signed it, "The Trumpet Player Second from the Drums." I folded it up and handed it to Marshal Royal, and he passed it to Count. Count stopped playing, looked at the note, and then looked up at me and said, "You want to play? Play!" And he let me play a couple of choruses of whatever we were playing. From that point on, he always gave me some solos to play.

At his first record session with Basie, on December 12, 1953, Newman played all the trumpet solos, with the exception of Wilder's short statement on the bridge of the lovely and aptly titled Neal Hefti piece "Softly, with Feeling," seemingly tailor-made for Wilder's lyrical style. Wilder made the most of his opportunity; it is hard to imagine anyone investing more beauty and feeling in eight bars of music.

His return to the road with Basie was an improvement over Wilder's extended big band odyssey of the previous decade. In addition to better travel conditions and accommodations, Wilder found the even-tempered leader very easy to work for: "I loved Count. You had to like him. It was such a pleasant atmosphere. He wanted guys to be on time and to do what they were supposed to do on the job, but I never saw him go off on anybody. He was just an easygoing person. That's why the band played so well and had that real free feeling."

Frank Wess recalled one incident in which Basie expressed mild disapproval. As did many of the big bands, the Basie orchestra had its own softball team, and Wilder was one of the stars. Although they usually played other bands or the waiters from Birdland in Central Park, Wess recalled a tour in Virginia: "Basie had just gotten us some new [band] uniforms, and while we were sitting in the bus before the gig, members of the team went outside to practice. Basie looked out the window and said, 'Look at them out there playin' ball in my new uniforms!'"[1]

Although Marshal Royal was the straw boss and led most of the rehearsals, there was no doubt as to who was in charge of the band. Despite his minimalist conducting style, Basie was able to exert complete control over his orchestra from the piano bench with subtle signals and gestures that often went unnoticed by the audience. "Count would play an introduction, and we knew exactly at what point to come in," Wilder said. "And while he was playing piano, he would point to the band to accent certain things that we were doing. It was very simple, and most people didn't even realize that he was really giving cues to the band." Basie was also a master at setting tempos. "He had tremendous musical sense," Wilder said. "Like Lucky Millinder, he knew tempos like you wouldn't believe."

In March 1954, about four months after Wilder had joined, the Basie orchestra embarked on a monthlong tour of Europe, Wilder's first trip abroad. Wilder almost did not make the trip. "I told Basie I couldn't go for the money he was offering," Wilder said. "After he called several times, I told him, 'If you pay the taxes and the union dues, I'll take what you're offering me.' He said, 'You got a deal.' After we were in Europe for a while, Count came to me and said, 'You made a good move there. I wish I'd made one like it!'"

The itinerary included much of Scandinavia, West Germany, Holland, Belgium, France, and Switzerland.[2] One significant difference between the Basie tour and most of Wilder's previous big band experiences was that the Basie orchestra was performing in a concert setting, not for dances. While Joe Newman was still taking the bulk of the solos, Wilder was also featured. Reviewing one of the band's concerts in Sweden, Carl-Erik Lindgren described him as "a distinctive and personal soloist with a mellow, round tone and bold intervals in his originally constructed phrasing. He didn't seem as involved rhythmically, employing an almost dreamy phrasing—an odd mixture of the underrated Joe Thomas, Bunny Berigan and Clifford Brown."[3]

By that time, Wilder had become a serious photographer, and the European tour provided him with new opportunities and subjects. As Frank Wess recalled, "I had a little Minox at the time, but Joe Wilder had all kinds of cameras. He had a big press camera, so I asked him to take some pictures for me, and he gave me a whole lot of pictures of the Eiffel Tower and all the points of interest."[4]

For Wilder, the most significant moment of the European tour occurred in mid-March in Gothenburg, Sweden:

We had played a concert in the opera house and were signing autographs when I happened to look over and saw this very pretty girl. She had on a leopard tam and a coat to match. I said, "Gee, that girl is cute." There was a guy there who saw me looking over, and he said, "Would you like to meet her?" I said, "Yeah, I would!" So she came over and asked me for an autograph. She spoke very little English, but we stood there and talked, with the Swedish fellow translating. When we were getting ready to leave, I asked if I could get her address. I remember walking her to the train to say good-bye.

Thus began a remarkable love story and a long-distance courtship of three years. The young lady was Solveig Andersson, a twenty-one-year-old who had traveled by train with a friend from her small town of Säffle, in the Värmland province of Sweden, to attend the concert. "I was not a big jazz fan, but my best friend was," Solveig said. "They had just started a little jazz society in my hometown, and she was a member. She had heard of Count Basie coming for a concert and was very excited and asked me to come along. In the beginning, I wasn't that keen on going—the tickets were very expensive, and it was quite a distance from my hometown. But she talked me into it."[5]

At the concert, Solveig was not too impressed with the soloists until one of the trumpeters stepped forward: "He played a ballad, and I really enjoyed it! My girlfriend told me his name was Joe Wilder." Her recollection of their meeting afterward at the train station was somewhat more dramatic than Wilder's account:

As we were waiting in the station around two in the morning, the musicians came in with all these girls—now they're called groupies—all around them. A sailor came and sat down next to me on the bench. He was drunk and started swearing and carrying on about the musicians and calling them the "N" word. I yelled at him, "You have some nerve! Here you are sitting here drunk and dirty, and you have the nerve to talk about them like that!" He yelled, "You damn whore!" and grabbed me so that all the buttons of my coat came off. Joe saw this, and he came over and asked, "Are you okay? Can I help you?"

Their brief conversation, through a translator, was cut short when Count Basie came running and announced that the train was leaving for Oslo, the band's next stop. Solveig hurriedly scribbled her address, and then she and her friend stood and waved as Wilder and the Basie entourage pulled out of the station. "I never thought anything more would happen," Solveig said. "We took our train and got home about eight o'clock in the morning on a Sunday. I lived with my parents, and I went to my room and went to sleep. After about an hour, my mother woke me up and told me I had a telegram. This was 1954 in my hometown in Sweden. We had never seen a telegram before! My mother asked, 'What have you done?' I told her, 'You know me; I never do anything!'"

The telegram was from Wilder inviting Solveig to come to Copenhagen for a concert. "There was no way we could make it," she recalled. "I figured since I hadn't answered his telegram or come to the concert, I wouldn't hear from him anymore, but a month later he sent me a postcard from New York. Then he sent me a long letter, and where I worked there was one person who spoke English, and she translated that letter."

This was the start of a three-year correspondence, problematic at the beginning because of the language barrier, which Wilder was determined to overcome: "I had a friend who knew the librarian at the Swedish consulate, Gudren Ebenfelt. She gave me weekly lessons at the library and told me what books to get. She happened to be from the same section of Sweden [Värmland] as Solveig, so they spoke the same dialect."

Although she had grown up in a small town in a relatively isolated area, thanks to her parents, Solveig early on had developed a social conscience and was determined to broaden her horizons:

> I had grown up not knowing anything about racism. My father had shown us pictures of black people because we had never seen a black person in person. I grew up during the war, and my father used to talk about how wrong what was happening to the Jews was. Then when I was sixteen, I started doing fund-raising with the United Nations, traveling with UNESCO. I finally got to see what this other world was like, and I was fascinated. The first place was Paris, and I saw black people for the first time. So I wasn't thinking in colors, and it didn't matter to me what color a person was. That's how I was raised by my parents. Then I traveled a lot—to Spain, to Morocco—and learned more and more about other people and about racism, and I spoke about it at home.

Over the following three years, the correspondence between Joe and Solveig intensified. "During the last year, we wrote each other almost every day," Solveig said. "And through the letters, we got to know each other very well." When she realized how serious her son was about the relationship, Wilder's mother, Gussie, also began corresponding with Solveig. Finally, in the spring of 1956, Wilder proposed and sent an engagement ring in the mail. Solveig accepted and made plans to travel to New York to marry a man with whom she had spent no more than a few minutes in a train station some three years earlier. Wilder had laid the groundwork by writing regularly to Solveig's parents. "He kept sending my parents cards, so they got an idea about what a wonderful man he was, and they trusted my opinion," she said. "He even wrote to my father and asked for my hand." But other members of the family were incredulous: "My uncles had a family meeting before I left, and some of them said, 'This is crazy! The girl has gone insane! She doesn't know anybody, her English is limited, and to go to a complete strange man, who was married before and has a son—the whole thing is insane!'" But Solveig's parents had faith in their daughter's judgment and ended the discussion by saying, "It's up to her."

Solveig's cousin and best friend, Ingrid Swedberg, who was fluent in English, insisted on accompanying her to America. So on January 4, 1957, the two young ladies traveled to Gothenberg, spending the night in a Salvation Army hotel before setting sail for New York early the next morning on the M.S. *Kungsholm*. "The day we left was a very sad day," Solveig remembered. "When I said good-bye to my family, I didn't know if I would ever see them again."

The situation was not made any easier when, on the morning of their departure, Solveig discovered that her impending marriage had become a news story. "I'm not paranoid, but when we went to breakfast the next morning, people were looking at us in a strange way," she said. "Then we saw a newspaper, and there was a picture of me on the first page with the caption, 'Marries Negro.'" When they finally boarded the ship, they found two journalists sitting on the bed in their cabin, cameras in hand. Even Solveig's parents were besieged by the press. Although much of the attention was simply motivated by curiosity, some of the articles were negative and even racist, and Solveig received occasional hate mail. Such lack of tolerance is surprising because Sweden later became known as something of a haven for expatriate American black jazz artists looking to escape the discrimination they faced at home. But as Solveig noted, in the 1950s, Sweden was a far more ethnocentric place, and intolerance, even outright racism, was not unknown, especially in the more rural areas.

When Solveig arrived in New York on January 14, 1957, hope chest in hand, she could not immediately spot Wilder. But Ingrid suddenly called out, "There is Joe!" Solveig explained, "And she had never met him!" Before they could get married, Wilder had to address the problem of his marriage to Lillian, from whom he had been estranged for several years, so he traveled to Mexico and obtained a divorce.

Solveig, who immediately fell in love with New York City, stayed in a hotel until they married on June 9, 1957, her twenty-fifth birthday. Wilder, who had been raised an Episcopalian, had hoped to have the ceremony at the Church of the Transfiguration, better known as the "Little Church around the Corner" on East Twenty-Ninth Street, between Madison and Fifth Avenues. But when he went to see the rector, he discovered that the church would not accommodate an interracial marriage, so the ceremony took place at the Mount Olivet Baptist Church on 120th Street and Lenox Avenue in Harlem. The Reverend Adam Clayton Powell Jr., whom Wilder had met at various events, had been scheduled to officiate but had suffered a heart attack while preaching a few days earlier. Instead, they were married by Clay Maxwell Sr., the church's longtime pastor, who the year before had arranged a visit there by the Reverend Martin Luther King.

The Scandinavian press was still fascinated by the marriage and sent a photographer to the church. "Our picture was on the cover of *SE*, the biggest magazine in Sweden, and in the *Göteborgs-Posten*," Solveig said. "I was very unhappy because many of the things they wrote weren't so nice." Joe added, "It wasn't necessarily negative, but they sensationalized it." Overall, the *SE* cover story was upbeat and positive in tone, although the intimate cover image of Solveig and Joe kissing was certainly provocative for the times. The photo spread inside showed the couple at the marriage ceremony, flanked by Solveig's cousin Ingrid and Wilder's best man, the noted classical trombonist and educator John Swallow. There were also attractive images of the couple in Central Park and in the spacious new apartment on Riverside Drive and 141st Street, where the couple moved the day of the wedding. The Wilders still live there some fifty-six years later. Of course, the interracial marriage was the entire raison d'être for the piece. One headline proclaimed, "'He alone taught me to be happy,' says the girl from Säffle about her bridegroom, the black trumpeter." There were also sympathetic quotes from Solveig's parents. Her father, Oskar, said, "One is white, the other black. The important thing is that they're happy." To Joe, he added humorously, "Don't be sorry that you're dark-skinned. People sit in the sun and bake themselves to be the same color as you." Joe's new mother-in-law, Eli, simply said, "There could be no kinder son-in-law than Joe."[6]

In August, the couple traveled to Sweden for a honeymoon and so that Joe could meet Solveig's family for the first time. Again, he had prepared in advance to facilitate his acceptance. "Solveig had sent me pictures of almost everybody in the family, and I was determined that I would know who everybody was when I got there," Wilder said. Of course, his study of Swedish was a huge factor in easing his transition into the family. Solveig's family was amazed not only that Wilder was fluent in the language but also that he spoke their own dialect, thanks to his teacher's Värmland roots. "One of our most famous poets, Gustav Fröding, was from Värmland," Solveig said. "Joe had learned his poems and would recite them to me in our own dialect. I thought it was so charming!"

Wilder's introduction to the family was a complete success. "They all loved him," Solveig said. "My father got a bicycle for him, since we all rode bicycles in Sweden, and he painted it red, white, and blue! And they put a big American flag in the room where we stayed." Wilder enjoyed a special bond with his father-in-law. "We were very close," he said. "He wrote beautiful poetry. He was a master gardener. And he loved our kids. Just a great person."

Overall, Wilder did not experience any problems with the general public, other than the genuine surprise and curiosity with which he was met. He recalled walking through Säffle one day, when he passed a group of teenagers who yelled out in Swedish, "Hey! Look at the Negro!" Wilder turned around and beckoned them to him and said (in Swedish, of course), "I'm a guest in your town, and it's not very courteous to greet a guest like that. I'm not angry with you, but would your parents approve of what you just did?" The next day, Wilder passed the same group, and this time they politely greeted him with the respectful "farbror" (uncle).

The only downside of the visit was the continued obsession of the press with the interracial marriage. "My in-laws didn't know how to deal with it and were intimidated by the reporters, so they did what they asked," Wilder recalled. Even after they returned to New York, the harassment continued. "There was a guy from Denmark who came and interviewed us in one of the big hotels on Park Avenue," Wilder said. "He wrote that we lived in the worst ghetto he had ever seen, even though at the time we moved into our apartment, I was the only visible African American!" Even after decades of marriage, Solveig was approached during a visit by a Swedish reporter looking for a follow-up: "He said, 'The people are curious about how it went for you.' We'd been married fifty-three years, and they still wanted to write about it from that point of view. I said I didn't give interviews anymore."

Remarkably, the Wilders' romance was not the only one born on that March day in 1954 in Gothenburg. Joe Newman, Wilder's friend and bandmate in the Basie trumpet section, met his future wife, Rigmor, at the same concert. Rigmor, a Gothenburg native, and Joe Newman corresponded even longer than Joe Wilder and Solveig had before Rigmor came to the United States in 1960, although her future husband did make a couple of trips to Sweden during the intervening years. They were married in 1961, and in 1965, the Newmans cofounded Jazz Interactions, a nonprofit jazz advocacy organization that did much to promote jazz education over the following two decades. Rigmor recalled that her marriage to an African American did attract some attention in her native country but not the prurient interest that Solveig encountered, probably because she lived in Gothenburg, a major city. "We had more problems in the States," Rigmor recalled. "The first year I was here, I traveled with the [Basie] band, and there were some places I couldn't go."[7] Rigmor also recalled an incident involving an album Newman had recorded in Gothenburg in October 1958 with several of his fellow Basieites. *Counting Five in Sweden* was originally issued on the Swedish Metronome label. The album cover consisted of a lovely color photo of Rigmor and Joe together in Gothenburg. "The idea was that Joe was counting my fingers because he had a quintet," Rigmor said. Shortly after the album was reissued in the United States on World Pacific, *Jet* reported, "Dealers and distributors in all parts of the country have refused to display and promote the album because it showed a Negro man with a white girl."[8] The cover was withdrawn and replaced by one with a picture of Newman alone.

Wilder remained with Basie for about a month after returning from Europe, leaving the band after the end of its Birdland engagement on May 12, 1954. "I left reluctantly because Basie and all the other guys were very nice to me," Wilder said. "But it occurred to me that I wasn't making enough money to do some of the things I wanted to do." And of course, despite improved travel conditions, Wilder was again growing weary of life on the road. Although he remained very fond of Basie, Wilder was disturbed by the bandleader's response, even though it was probably meant as a joke: "When I gave him my notice at Birdland, he said, 'I knew you wouldn't stay too long because you can go out and play with them white folks!'"

Wilder certainly did not leave a large recorded legacy as a soloist with the Basie orchestra. Including his classic eight bars on "Softly, with Feeling" from the studio recording of December 12, 1953, his total solo output on issued Basie recordings and air checks up until his final appearance with the band at Birdland amounted to thirty-two bars of music. But on the Birdland broadcast of April 29, 1954, Wilder's swan song with Basie, he was the featured trumpet soloist; one wonders whether Joe Newman, who normally would have played in most of these spots, was absent, or perhaps the leader was giving Wilder some time in the spotlight before his imminent departure.

Photo Album

Curtis Wilder, U.S. Navy, World War I. *(Wilder Family Collection.)*

FACING PAGE, BOTTOM: Wilder *(left)* with brother and neighborhood friends, Colwyn, PA, ca. 1929. *(Wilder Family Collection.)*

Joe (*center*) with older brother, Curtis Jr., and neighborhood friends, Colwyn, PA, ca. 1927. *(Wilder Family Collection.)*

Lionel Hampton's band: Teddy McRae, Dinah Washington, and Wilder;
Tick Tock Club, Boston, 1943. *(Wilder Family Collection.)*

———

Wilder and Louis Armstrong, Camp Lejeune, ca. 1944.
(Wilder Family Collection.)

Joe (*left*) with brothers Edward and Calvin; mother, Gussie; and son Joey,
Philadelphia, ca. 1945. *(Wilder Family Collection.)*

Wilder (*top row, left*) with Dizzy Gillespie's orchestra, Detroit, 1947;
Chano Pozo is on conga. *(Wilder Family Collection.)*

———————

Wilder as "José Wildez," leader of Latin band within Lucky Millinder Orchestra,
Club 85, Bronx, New York, 1948. *From left to right:* Reunald Jones Sr., Wilder,
Russell Jacquet and friend. *(Wilder Family Collection.)*

From left to right: Wilder, Frank Rosolino, Herbie Fields, and a policeman jokingly warning against disturbing the peace with bebop, Silhouette Club, Chicago, 1949. *(Rutgers Institute of Jazz Studies collection, Rutgers–Newark, NJ.)*

———

Cozy Cole's Cu-Boppers: June Cole [?] (pianist, pictured with bongos, *back row*), Wilder, Billy Taylor Sr. (bass), Tony Aquaviva (clarinet), Big Nick Nicholas (tenor sax), Cozy Cole (drums), Bill Alvarez (percussion, *far left*), and Diego Iborra (percussion, *far right*); Chicago, 1949. *(Wilder Family Collection.)*

Earle Warren, Freddie Green (*seated*), and Lester Young; "The Sound of Jazz," 1957. *(Photo by Joe Wilder.)*

Coleman Hawkins, Pee Wee Russell, Henry "Red" Allen, Vic Dickenson, and producer Robert Herridge (*far left*); "The Sound of Jazz," 1957. *(Photo by Joe Wilder.)*

Curtis Wilder with granddaughters Elin (*left*), Solveig (*right*), and Inga (*seated*), ca. 1970. *(Photo by Joe Wilder.)*

Solveig, late 1960s. *(Photo by Joe Wilder.)*

Alec Wilder, early 1960s.
(Photo by Joe Wilder.)

Louis Armstrong, NBC *Kraft Music Hall*, New York, 1967.
(Photo by Joe Wilder.)

Hank Jones and Wilder, Birdland, New York, 2009. *(Photo by Ed Berger.)*

––––––––

Wilder with Jimmy Heath, rehearsal, JVC Festival, Kaye Playhouse, Hunter College, New York, 2003. *(Photo by Ed Berger.)*

Wilder with Frank Wess, Birdland, New York, 2001. *(Photo by Ed Berger.)*

LEFT: Buddy DeFranco and Wilder, Statesmen of Jazz recording session, Nola Studios, New York, December 2003. *(Photo by Ed Berger.)*

RIGHT: Wilder with Warren Vaché, Nola Studios, New York, 2002. *(Photo by Ed Berger.)*

Wilder performing at the Village Vanguard, New York, February 2006. *(Photo by Ed Berger.)*

Wilder and Satchmo cutout during a visit to the Louis Armstrong House Museum, Corona, Queens, New York, March 2013. *(Photo by Ed Berger.)*

7

Back on Broadway and into the Studios (1954–1957)

Silk Stockings **and** *Most Happy Fella*

After leaving Basie, Wilder returned to freelancing in New York. In addition to working in Broadway show orchestras, he was exceptionally busy in the recording studios. Between 1954 and 1956 alone, he took part in more than forty sessions ranging from jazz and vocal dates and experiments in the nascent "Third Stream" movement to Broadway musical soundtracks, as well as, in January 1956, his own first album as a leader.

Wilder achieved a new milestone when in February 1955, he became the first African American to play first chair for a Broadway show—Cole Porter's *Silk Stockings*. Like *Guys and Dolls*, *Silk Stockings* was a Feuer and Martin production. Cy Feuer, who early in his career had supported himself as a trumpet player, was well aware of Wilder's musical abilities, as well as his sterling personal qualities. He also had learned that, on occasion, Wilder and lead trumpeter Stan Fishelson had switched parts in *Guys and Dolls*, Feuer and Martin's

---

Wilder plays a solo backed by Count Basie Orchestra, ABC-TV telethon, ca. 1958.
From left to right: Joe, Al "Jazzbo" Collins (emcee), Count Basie, Frank Wess, Eddie Jones, Ernie Wilkins. *(Wilder Family Collection.)*

earlier show. "Stan was a good, strong player, but he didn't like to play in some of the hard keys," Wilder said. "Robert Alda was singing some things like 'My Time of Day' in E concert, so Stan would pass the lead trumpet part over to me. That's how I ended up playing the solo on the recording. The conductor found out one night and said to Stan, 'We're paying you extra for lead trumpet. What other parts is he playing lead on?' It turned out I was playing lead on about six other pieces." So when it came time to pick the orchestra for *Silk Stockings*, Feuer thought of Wilder for the first trumpet chair.

Feuer and Wilder had become friends, and because of the great success of *Guys and Dolls*, when putting together his new production, Feuer was able to operate with little interference from the show's financial backers:

> After *Guys and Dolls*, we just called up on the phone and they sent in their money. And we never let anybody invest too large because we didn't want to have any discussion. And we were very arrogant, we wouldn't let anybody read anything or hear anything either, because I don't want some pants manufacturer telling me what he thinks of the score.[1]

But one person Feuer felt he had to consult before assigning Wilder to the first chair was the show's composer, Cole Porter. The producer later told Wilder that when asked if he would have any objection to a black musician playing first trumpet in his show, Porter responded, "Can the man play my music?" When told that he could, the composer simply said, "That's all that matters." Wilder was overwhelmed, and although he did meet Porter at rehearsal, he was unable to fully express his gratitude: "I did tell him I was very flattered at being hired, but I was too shy to go up to him and tell him just how much I appreciated what he'd done."[2]

Wilder was one of three African American musicians in *Guys and Dolls*, but he was the only black member of the orchestra in *Silk Stockings*. Wilder got on well with his fellow musicians and enjoyed the full support of the show's production team. He even starred on the *Silk Stockings* softball team, which won the first Broadway Show League championship in 1955. But once again, there were problems with the stage crews and theater personnel, especially when the show went out of town. For example, before opening in New York, *Silk Stockings* previewed in Philadelphia, with rehearsals scheduled in the venerable Lulu Temple on Broad Street. To show its appreciation, the theater's management invited the cast to an opening-night party, but the invitation stated, "No Negroes or Japanese," a crude attempt to exclude Wilder, a black couple that worked in the wardrobe department, and the show's head electrician, who was Japanese. "When Cy Feuer saw it, he said, 'Anybody who goes to that party can consider themselves fired!'" Wilder recalled. "And nobody went. The stars, Don Ameche, Hildegard Knef,[3] and none of the other principals of the show went."

Wilder also encountered hostility from the local contractor: "He saw me and asked the road contractor for Feuer and Martin who I was. When he told him I was their first trumpet player, the guy said, 'Of all the trumpet players in the world, why would you bring a nigger here?' And this was in my dear old hometown of Philadelphia!" Wilder faced similar reactions from local crew members during the show's runs in Boston and Detroit, where he was confronted by a house detective after escorting Hildegard Knef back to the hotel following a performance.

In her autobiography, Knef reports on an incident that occurred at a celebration of the one-year anniversary of the opening of *Silk Stockings*:

We had decided to have the *Silk Stockings* [one-year] birthday party yesterday, Saturday the 25th [of February 1956]. [Don] Ameche and I rented a restaurant and invited everyone connected with the show from the cashiers to the stagehands. Only Lela [the costume person] and a Negro who plays second [*sic*] trumpet excused themselves with weak arguments that all ended with, "You'll see, it's better we don't . . ." Finally I persuaded them. The restaurant had a doorman. "Niggers ain't allowed in," he barked. "We've rented the restaurant," I said, louder than necessary. "I'll call the newspapers, coming from a German it'll make a nice scandal." After making a phone call he opened the door and hissed, "The boss says we make an exception just for today," then let go of the knob, slamming the door into the trumpeter's back.[4]

Wilder's recollection of this event differs in detail but not in substance from Knef's account. He remembered entering the restaurant with fifteen cast members, with the maître d' ignoring Wilder as the man undercounted how many guests were to be seated. After correcting him several times, Don Ameche said, "I think I know what's going on here," and he and Knef decided to take the party elsewhere.

Silk Stockings closed on April 14, 1956, after a run of more than a year at the Imperial Theatre. Less than three weeks later, Wilder was back at the Imperial as first trumpeter for a new show, Frank Loesser's *Most Happy Fella*. He faced an almost identical situation at the show's opening-night party, when he was told to use the kitchen entrance of New York's famous 21 Club. As with *Silk Stockings* in Philadelphia, the show's management backed Wilder to the hilt: "When I called Frank Loesser's office and told them what had happened, Mr. Loesser called the club and told them, 'Mr. Wilder, the fellow who was just there, is not only a guest; he's our first trumpet player, and he's in charge of the musicians who are going to play tonight. If you don't want him there, we're going to cancel the whole thing.'"

Wilder emphasized that, as unpleasant as these incidents were, the support of the cast and his fellow musicians helped him to persevere and to emerge without bitterness:

> I would be lying if I said I didn't resent the attitude towards me or towards other black musicians. I had to grit my teeth and say, "If I hit this guy, I'm gonna louse it up for anybody else who happens to be a black musician." You finally realize that it's them, not me. I mean, it's their problem, not mine. The people I was working with took the curse off of any of the things that happened. I knew I was sitting next to people who didn't condone that sort of thing, so I kept reminding myself that everyone isn't alike. And I ended up with a lot of friends from those times. I would think of all the people I grew up with who weren't like that. We're all going to encounter bigotry and racism in some form or other because that seems to be the norm, no matter where you go. But you can't let yourself get mired down in it. And you can't hold it against everybody who happens to be of the same ethnic background. I also found that the more you have contact with people, even those that resent you, the more you find that there's something redeemable in everybody if you give yourself a chance to get to know them.

Wilder remained grateful to producers Feuer and Martin, who had hired him for both *Guys and Dolls* and *Silk Stockings*. He enjoyed a long friendship with Cy Feuer and even gave trumpet lessons to his son, Jed, a musician and composer. When Feuer died in 2006, the *New York Times* obituary cited his role in integrating Broadway by his hiring of Wilder.[5] A few months later, Wilder spoke at a memorial for Feuer at the Lunt-Fontanne Theatre on Broadway, relating the story of the party in Philadelphia, at which Feuer forbade the cast from attending because of the discriminatory note on the invitations. Among many others paying tribute were Neil Simon, Jimmy Breslin, and Joel Grey.[6]

While working in Broadway orchestras in the mid-1950s, Wilder still hoped to eventually return to classical playing. He was able keep his hand in it thanks to a rehearsal orchestra assembled by cellist-conductor Jascha

Fishberg. "He would get some of the fellows in the theater orchestras to come early on Wednesdays, when we had matinees, and he'd pass out some of the symphonic arrangements," Wilder recalled. Eventually, Wilder was assigned the first trumpet chair in that rehearsal orchestra.

The Urban League: Integrating the Music Industry

In the fall of 1956, at the same time that Wilder was playing first trumpet in the orchestra for *Most Happy Fella*, a committee of African American musicians approached the Urban League of Greater New York to expand opportunities for minority musicians in all areas of the music industry. The League's Industrial Relations Department undertook a study to determine the "qualifications, experience and availability of the Negro professional musician." In May 1958, the Urban League issued a brief but telling report titled *Job Status of the Negro Professional Musician in the New York Metropolitan Area*. It was prepared by G. Douglas Pugh, the League's industrial relations secretary. Pugh (1923–2010), who began his career as a civil rights worker, majored in music at Columbia, where he also earned an M.B.A. He went on to hold a number of high positions in New York State labor organizations.[7] For the report, information from black musicians was gathered via questionnaires and follow-up interviews. In addition, white musicians, conductors, and union officials were interviewed. The report does not specify how many members of either group were surveyed.

Pugh's report examined the employment situation in seven musical areas: (1) symphony orchestras; (2) pit orchestras (Broadway musicals); (3) radio-television staff musicians; (4) presentation house pit orchestras; (5) club, hotel, and society dates; (6) recording companies; and (7) advertising agencies.

Regarding the situation in the Broadway pit orchestras, the report indicated, "Negro musicians are usually employed when the musical has a Negro theme or the star of the production is a Negro. Employment for the Negro musician is most often secured at the insistence of the Negro headliner, a liberal producer, theatre owner, or pressures exerted by the Negro musician."[8] As previously noted, the "liberal producer" scenario certainly contributed to bassist Al Hall's 1947 breakthrough in *Barefoot Boy with Cheek* and Wilder's getting hired for *Guys and Dolls* and *Silk Stockings*.

Responding to the paranoia engendered by McCarthyism, the Urban League report said that "red baiting or using the communist smear technique is one of the most onerous means used against liberal white conductors who are willing to employ qualified Negro musicians in pit orchestras of Broadway musicals."[9]

The report's section on Broadway musicals concludes by stating that from 1956 to 1958, there were twenty-six shows on Broadway, employing approximately 650 musicians, of which 14 were African American. Seven of the black musicians were in the shows *Mr. Wonderful* and *Jamaica*, both of which "featured a Negro headliner."[10] The issue of discrimination against women was not raised in the report.

After deciding to come off the road, with the exception of his few months with Count Basie in 1953 and 1954, many of Wilder's professional musical pursuits—from his studies at the Manhattan School of Music to his work in Broadway orchestras—were leading him away from jazz. Although he felt uncomfortable in the competitive jam session environment, he still wanted to keep up his jazz skills and began to frequent some of the famous after-hours musician hangouts, Minton's Playhouse in particular:

> My first wife and I were having problems, so rather than go home and argue, I'd go by Minton's on my way from the theater and sit in. Carmen McRae was the house piano player, and all these top-notch guys would come by. Occasionally, Sarah Vaughan would show up. I was never one who could play fifteen choruses. Besides, I wasn't improvising all that much—I was sitting in a pit reading notes. So I was easily intimidated. Fats Navarro would come up there, and it was like a guillotine cutting your head off! Everything they played would be so creative. Every once in a while I'd get up the nerve to go up and play.

There are many stories about how musicians at jam sessions would handle would-be sitters-in whose nerve exceeded their talent, and Wilder remembered one such Minton's legend:

> There was a saxophone player who they nicknamed the "Demon." He was one of the worst saxophone players ever, but he'd stand in front of the bandstand with his tenor, and finally someone would say, "Okay, Demon. You want to play?" Once he got up there, he'd stay there forever. So [Eddie] Lockjaw Davis, who was assigned to keep things orderly, would say, "Come on, Demon. You gotta let the other guys play!" Demon would just ignore him and go right on playing. So he'd go and get Teddy Hill, who was the manager, and he'd come up and stand in front and say, "Demon, get off my bandstand!" and Demon

would go off and sulk. They went through this same routine every time he got up there.

Wilder also remembered frequenting the Flame, an after-hours joint on Eighth Avenue and 110th Street. "We used to call it the Bucket of Blood, because somebody was always getting into a fight outside," he said. "Big Nick Nicholas was in charge, and Hot Lips Page would come in there often. Now how are you going to stand up and play next to someone like that?" Wilder recalled that there were so many pianists, bassists, and drummers lining up to play for free that the owner eventually fired the rhythm section.

Although Wilder modestly dismissed his own abilities as a "jammer," an effusive account by Woody McBride, columnist for the *Philadelphia Tribune*, of his impromptu appearance with trombonist Bennie Green at the Show Boat one night in 1954 indicates that he could more than hold his own in such situations:

Joe was asked to ascend the stage for a little jam session. Nonchalantly he doffed his coat and hat, revealing a stunning tuxedo with full regalia, shuffled to the stand and—whammo—blew them off the stage. This mad hatter's got the mind of Dizzy Gillespie, the tonation of Clifford Brown, the versatility of Charlie Shavers, and the poise and showmanship of Louis Armstrong. Oh, what a man! A Philadelphia boy, too.[11]

Developing a Style: Recordings in the 1950s

Settling in New York and working on Broadway and, later, in the network studios enabled Wilder to take part in a wide variety of recording sessions in the mid- to late 1950s. By the close of 1955, Wilder had been featured—often extensively—on jazz dates under leaders Frank Wess, Pete Brown, Oscar Pettiford, Urbie Green, Al Cohn, Ernie Wilkins, Hank Jones, and Johnny Richards. In contrast, his entire pre-Basie (1942–1953) recorded oeuvre consists of nine solos, only two of which exceed twelve bars in length.

The paucity of recorded solos makes it difficult to assess exactly what Wilder sounded like as a jazz player early in his career; although, as may be inferred from descriptions of others as well as the extant recordings, he always had a beautifully full sound. His very early up-tempo solos—namely, "The Great Lie" (1942) and "Double Talk" (1946), with Lionel Hampton, and "La Danse" (1949), with Cozy Cole—are highly technical and show great dexterity but are ultimately formulaic, a characteristic Wilder himself acknowledged. Always realistic and often far too modest about his own abilities, Wilder downplayed his jazz improvisatory skills, acknowledging that much of his solo work early in his career derived from patterns and techniques he had mastered through his classical training. His description of what he felt were his short-comings during his tenure with Dizzy Gillespie in 1947 bears repeating here:

> Because of my classical training, I could play fast, so if I ran out of ideas, I could get "technical" and start double- and triple-tonguing and try to make it as "jazzy" as I could, even if it didn't exactly relate to the tune we were playing. But the classical element remained, and it sounded somewhat corny. But after a while, I got away from that.

By the mid-1950s, Wilder had definitely gotten away from that, as evidenced by the spate of solos he recorded in a relatively short period. It was becoming clear that, as technically impressive as his up-tempo solos could be, Wilder's musical essence found its truest expression at slower tempos, particularly in ballads, where his lyricism and gift of embellishment—not to mention his ravishing sound—were fully revealed. Wilder's guiding principle in improvisation was always to tell a story:

> Growing up in Philadelphia, that's what the guys on the bandstand would say. Then in music schools, I learned, if the melody is simple, you can dress it up on top. If it's busy on the bottom, then you play something simple on top. This was a kind of a rule of thumb that we used. . . . And I always listen. When I hear a melody that I like, I'll think, "I wonder what I could do to enhance that a little bit differently but still keep the character of it." I try to play something that enhances the basic idea of the piece. It's almost as if you're a continuation of what the composer had in mind.

Wilder also gave a lot of thought to how he might fashion a solo on a particular piece: "When I go to bed, I may stay awake for two hours thinking about some tune that I don't know too well. I start humming it in my head and figuring out things to do harmonically and lyrically, so the next time I play it, I'll have an idea of what I might want to do."

Wilder's solos of the period also display his penchant for musical quotation, a practice he continued to employ throughout his career. These fleeting interpolations, while often drawn from the classical repertoire, could come from anywhere: other jazz pieces, popular songs, and even folk or country music. In the wrong hands, this practice can become a crowd-pleasing indulgence, but Wilder's quotes are usually subtle, in good taste, and more important, make sense musically. "I try to do it where it really harmonically relates—superimposing it, not imposing it," he said.[12]

Although Wilder knew his own strengths lay in melodically based improvisation, he could appreciate more adventurous styles that departed from the conventional harmonic and rhythmic contours of a piece. "Guys like Fats Navarro and Dizzy Gillespie had the kind of minds that enabled them to come up with things that were as interesting as the tune itself," he said. "Dizzy's musical thoughts were so well organized that you enjoyed what he played no matter how daring." Musically, Wilder felt a strong affinity with another rising star, trumpeter Clifford Brown:

> He had everything that you would expect or want to have as a trumpet player. He had the sound, he had the harmonic knowledge, he had the technique, and he had the range—just unbelievable! I mean, you listen to the things that he did today, and you say, "How could he have even thought of these things?" And he showed you didn't have to stick a needle in your arm to be a genius.

It was on ballads that Wilder could fully realize his storytelling abilities, eschewing the formulaic patterns that he recognized as a weakness in his improvisational approach early in his career. At times, Wilder's sound takes on a certain fragility, which imbues his playing with deep emotion and even a sense of vulnerability. This may seem something of an anomaly for a musician who spent much of his early career as a lead trumpeter, but Wilder did not fit the mold of the classic powerhouse big band first trumpet, either physically or temperamentally. First, he was never a high-note specialist, preferring the horn's middle and lower ranges, where he could cultivate his distinctively rounded and full sound. "I usually played lead," he said, "but if there was something that was high and beyond what I did, they would give that part to the guy whose specialty that was, like Ernie Royal [with Hampton] or Reunald Jones [with Lunceford]."

The most significant of Wilder's flurry of recordings in the mid-1950s was his first album as leader, *Wilder 'n' Wilder* for Savoy, recorded in January 1956. One would think that this might have been a fairly momentous occasion in the life of a musician, especially one who, despite his achievements and growing celebrity, at age thirty-four had yet to lead a date. But as was customary with the budget-conscious Savoy and its notorious owner, Herman Lubinsky, the album was made in one three-hour session without rehearsal or any advance preparation. "You'd just get a call to come out to the studio," Wilder said. "You didn't know with whom you'd be playing. You didn't know what you would be playing. We'd get there, and they'd say, 'You guys just improvise something.' So we'd sit there, and we'd improvise and talk about how we would play some riff or something on it."

This low-budget, impromptu method of making a jazz album was by no means unique to Savoy, and musicians of the caliber of Wilder, Hank Jones, Wendell Marshall, and Kenny Clarke, Wilder's collaborators on *Wilder 'n' Wilder*, were certainly capable of coming up with something worthwhile on the spur of the moment. What may have been unique, however, was the fact that Wilder was not informed that he was to be the leader until *after* the session was over and producer Ozzie Cadena approached him with a contract. "As leader, they would pay you double—maybe two hundred dollars instead of one hundred dollars," Wilder said. "And you never got a royalty. I don't think I knew anybody who got a royalty from Savoy during that time. You were lucky if you got a couple of extra records! We used to laugh about it after it was all over. On the other hand, it gave a lot of us the opportunity to play things that we felt we'd do pretty well on."

Although Savoy could not resist the pun and called the album *Wilder 'n' Wilder*, the title chosen decades later for the reissue CD, *Softly with Feeling*, was far more descriptive of the music, which featured three ballads ("Prelude to a Kiss," "Mad about the Boy," and "Darn That Dream"), two medium-tempo pieces ("My Heart Stood Still" and "Cherokee"), and an improvised blues in waltz time ("Six Bit Blues"). Despite the impromptu nature of the date (or possibly because of it), it is the most extensive showcase to date for Wilder's abilities as an improviser. Although the ballads may be most revealing of Wilder's own sensibilities, the stunning version of "Cherokee" shows just how far he had evolved as a pure jazz player. Since the 1940s, "Cherokee" has been played at breathtakingly fast tempos—a test piece for jazz players at cutting contests. It was also the basis, of course, for one of Charlie Parker's most celebrated recordings, "Ko-Ko," also made for Savoy in 1945, eleven years before Wilder's version.

Wilder approached "Cherokee" in a very different manner, playing it at a medium tempo (180 bpm), even slower than composer Ray Noble's original 1938 recording for Brunswick. This tempo enables Wilder to fully incorporate the melodic embellishments, witty asides and interpolations, and the thematic development that are the hallmarks of his style, while carefully adhering to the song's harmonic structure.

Wilder first got the idea of playing "Cherokee" at the slower tempo after hearing a broadcast by Fred Waring and his Pennsylvanians: "He had a wonderful choral group with Bobby Hackett playing cornet and guitar, and they did it as a ballad. It was so beautiful. So when someone suggested Cherokee at the date, I thought of that tempo."

Wilder was fortunate in having the ideal rhythm section for the *Wilder 'n' Wilder* session. Wilder has always been extremely sensitive to his accompaniment, and Hank Jones, Wendell Marshall, and Kenny Clarke provided the kind of responsive and creative support that enabled him to move in any direction, knowing that they would follow. Two months earlier, on November 8, 1955, Wilder had recorded with the same trio on another Savoy session, under the leadership of Ernie Wilkins. That album, *Top Brass*, featured five trumpeters: Ernie Royal, Idrees Sulieman, Ray Copeland, Donald Byrd, and Wilder. *Down Beat*'s review called Wilder's ballad feature, "Willow, Weep for Me," "one of the most movingly lyrical solos ever recorded."[13] And three weeks later, on November 29, 1955, Wilder and Jones recorded another favorite of the bop era in a version that foreshadowed their treatment of "Cherokee." Their ballad version of "How High the Moon" completely transformed another traditionally up-tempo jam-session vehicle, with Wilder's solo a quintessential example of his melodic inventiveness.[14]

Down Beat was equally enthusiastic about Wilder's own debut as a leader. In his four-and-a-half-star review of *Wilder 'n' Wilder*, Nat Hentoff wrote, "Joe has a beautiful, proud-to-be-brass tone; conception that is fresh and always building; and above all, that flowing singing lyricism with drive and swinging strength. . . . In an era when many styles blur into each other, Wilder is maturely his own man."[15] *Billboard*'s review stated that "trumpeter Wilder, on the basis of this program, should become a much bigger jazz name," adding, "He gets a gorgeous, full tone and plays like a warmer, tastier edition of Charlie Shavers. His is a singing, emotional style especially suited to ballads."[16]

Wilder credits pianist Hank Jones for much of the success of *Wilder 'n' Wilder*: "Hank is one of these guys whose sense of music and harmonic structure pulls you in directions you wouldn't ordinarily go. That's one of the reasons it came off as well as it did." Jones remained perhaps Wilder's favorite pianist; the two often worked together, right up until the pianist's death in 2010.

Like Parker on "Ko-Ko," Wilder does not play the melody of "Cherokee"; nor does he devise an alternative contrafact, a new melody based on the song's chord changes. Rather, the performance begins with two improvised choruses by Wilder, followed by two at the hands of pianist Hank Jones, a chorus of four-bar trumpet trades with drummer Kenny Clarke, a chorus of trades between Jones and bassist Wendell Marshall, and a final improvised chorus by Wilder.

Oddly enough, although the melody is never stated, the tune is still called "Cherokee," contrary to Savoy's usual practice. In his relentless efforts to avoid paying royalties, Herman Lubinsky preferred to have his artists record originals, which he would publish and for which he would pay royalties at a lower rate or not at all, as Wilder noted. This practice was clearly illustrated by the well-known aborted take of Parker's "Ko-Ko," which is cut short by Savoy producer Teddy Reig after the group launches into the "Cherokee" head. It is also interesting to note that "Six Bit Blues," seemingly completely improvised blues in waltz time, is credited to Ozzie Cadena, who produced the Wilder session.

"Cherokee" shows that by 1956 Wilder had essentially already arrived at the individual and immediately identifiable solo style that would characterize his playing for the next five decades. The trumpeter combines elements of his classical technique, including octave leaps, double- and triple- tonguing, and a pure tone and precise articulation (not to mention frequent direct quotes from the classical repertoire) with such jazz devices as half-valve effects, smears, growls, and blue notes. Wilder's solos, above all, tell a story, achieving the narrative quality he had sought since his early days in Philadelphia. Even as he creates such a commanding and imaginative improvisational tour de force as "Cherokee," the fragile aspect of Wilder's sound is also evident, including some occasional faltering moments in the upper register, which give his playing an even more affecting quality. These fleeting technical lapses may simply have been fatigue, especially in "Cherokee," which because of its extended sixty-four-measure structure, may represent Wilder's longest sustained solo playing on record. Moreover, as was the custom, the album was made in one three-hour session, and it is unlikely that Wilder took time off from *Silk Stockings* to ensure his embouchure was well rested for the Savoy date.

Wilder's singular 1956 version of "Cherokee" continued to influence trumpet players of later generations. Jimmy Owens (born in 1943), who came to prominence in the 1960s, adapted Wilder's solo for his trumpet ensemble. "I was hip to Joe Wilder because I had his record of 'Cherokee,'" Owens said. "Unlike Clifford Brown, where the tempo was [*demonstrates rapid tempo by tapping his hand on his thigh*], Joe played it at a medium tempo and expressed his ideas in such a way that I fell in love with it."[17]

Wilder's friend, cornet star Warren Vaché (born in 1951), remembered his first hearing of *Wilder 'n' Wilder*:

A friend of mine had that wonderful album, and he loaned it to me so I could tape it. I was just knocked out. That was the sort of trumpet playing I had always wanted to do. "Cherokee" was exceedingly memorable. It's so intelligent, so well executed; there's such a sense of humor about it. It's got everything I could conceive of putting in a solo. Joe's sound is just the way he his—it's honest, it's heartrending. It's the man speaking his voice through the trumpet.[18]

Writer Will Friedwald, in a 2007 appreciation of Wilder appropriately titled "The Greatest Trumpeter You've Never Heard," reported that Jon Faddis (born in 1953), who started out as Dizzy Gillespie's protégé, "acknowledged that [Wilder's] 'Cherokee'. . . was a solo that he played over and over as a young trumpet student."[19] Faddis added, "His playing is extremely logical; his solos are like compositions unto themselves."[20] Friedwald also noted, "I've heard Wynton Marsalis play Mr. Wilder's arrangement of 'Cherokee' many times, and even though it's not much of an 'arrangement' per se, it's clear that Mr. Marsalis is using Mr. Wilder's performance as a starting point."[21] Trumpeter Nicholas Payton, who came to prominence in the 1990s, after listening to "Cherokee," commented, "When I first heard this, I didn't really know much about Joe Wilder. . . . This is an example of some of the great musicians who have been in our music but have never really gotten the opportunity to get their due. He was a great player, and I think he deserves to be listened to."[22] Finally, Jeremy Pelt, one of the leading trumpeters of the current generation, said, "The most famous version of 'Cherokee' is Clifford Brown's but I also like Joe Wilder's version . . . because his ideas are so melodic and fresh, the way he approaches every chord. [*Sings part of Wilder's solo.*] And he does some trumpet stuff that will grab the ear of any discerning trumpet technophile. I transcribed his 'Cherokee' solo. That always got to me."[23]

Wilder was also attracting admirers from other musical spheres. Rolling Stones drummer and sometime jazz performer Charlie Watts, while discussing his love for jazz, said, "I was 14 when I bought my first Charlie Parker record. In those days it was a big deal to know who was on a record. If somebody couldn't recognize that it was, say, Joe Wilder playing trumpet without seeing the label, they'd had it. You didn't talk to the bloke."[24]

Wilder 'n' Wilder was recorded by Rudy Van Gelder, the legendary engineer, in his original studio in his parents' home in Hackensack, New Jersey, before he moved to a new facility in Englewood Cliffs in 1959.[25] Wilder recorded frequently in both locations and got to know Van Gelder fairly well. Wilder appreciated the fine sound Van Gelder achieved but found the engineer's rigidity off-putting at times:

I always like to get to a date early so that when we start, I'm warmed up and ready to go. I drove out to Rudy's one very cold night and got there sooner than I expected to. The date was supposed to start at eight o'clock, and I got there at about seven fifteen. I rang Rudy's bell, and he comes to the window and says, "Who is it?" I said, "It's Joe Wilder, Rudy. I'm doing the date tonight." He said, "Well, the date starts at eight, Joe," and he shut the window and left me standing out there freezing! Fortunately, my car had a heater! Once you got in, it was pretty comfortable. It was very relaxed until he would say, "Don't put your hands on my microphone!" But the results sounded pretty good. He was good at capturing what we were doing.

In addition to his own first album as leader, between 1955 and 1958, Wilder also played on Savoy sessions led by Ernie Wilkins, Hank Jones, Marlene Ver-Planck, A. K. Salim, Mort Herbert, and Billy VerPlanck.

Recordings like *Wilder 'n' Wilder* make it abundantly clear that by the mid-1950s Wilder had perfected a truly personal approach to jazz improvisation, drawing on his classical training and his by-then extensive experience touring with a wide variety of jazz orchestras. Unlike his early efforts as a jazz improviser, Wilder no longer used his classical technique as a crutch to get him through a solo; rather, he incorporated it as a natural component of a wholly original concept and sound. Warren Vaché noted:

> Classical training allows you more freedom and flexibility, more accuracy, and more strength. That's what comes through in Joe's playing. He knows the literature of the trumpet and the physicality of playing the trumpet. He's mastered both of them, so anything he plays is informed by that mastery. The classical approach has also given him a somewhat more sophisticated way of thinking about harmony and melody. While his approach to the trumpet may be classical in conception, he's a jazz musician, and what you're hearing when Joe Wilder plays a solo is the essence of the man. He's taken all of that nonsense you have to study for a hundred and fifty years and sings through that instrument with his own unique voice.[26]

From Mainstream to Third Stream

In the mid-1950s, Wilder took part in a number of challenging recording sessions loosely categorized as "Third Stream," a somewhat nebulous term denoting attempts at combining elements of jazz and classical music. Gunther Schuller, who coined the phrase in 1957 and was a leading exponent of the genre, described it as "a concept of composing, improvising, and performing which seeks to fuse, creatively, jazz (and other vernacular musics) with contemporary classical concepts and techniques."[27] Schuller's definition is necessarily broad, as Third Stream efforts vary widely in the degree to which they incorporate these elements, especially improvisation. Moreover, some Third Stream passages that sound improvised or random may actually be written. As bassist George Duvivier, who played on Schuller's celebrated *Jazz Abstractions* album in 1960 (with Eric Dolphy and Ornette Coleman), noted, "When you listen to the overall work, it may sound as if everyone came in whenever they felt like it. But everything was meticulously written out—every entrance. It was extremely demanding to read. You couldn't lose your place and hope to pick it up from the melody."[28]

These experiments were a departure from the often superficial early "symphonic jazz" efforts of the 1920s, many of which exhibited the trappings of jazz and "serious" music without penetrating the core of either. The 1930s saw groups like the John Kirby Sextet and soloists like Art Tatum adapting classical pieces for performance. Of such attempts, critic Terry Teachout wrote, "Some of these arrangements were banal, others ingenious, but nearly all trivialized the original material on which they were based."[29] As Schuller himself wrote, "The lifting of external elements from one area into the other is happily a matter of the past. At its best Third Stream can be an extremely subtle music, defying the kind of easy categorization most people seem to need before they can make up their minds whether they should like something or not."[30] Schuller also observed that the Third Stream movement's true ancestry may lie in the prescient 1941 compositions of Paul Jordan for Artie Shaw: "Evensong" and "Suite No. 8."[31]

Wilder enjoyed the challenge of the Third Stream experiments, although he found some of the efforts to be pretentious and contrived. Wilder's combination of classical technique, sight-reading ability, and improvisational skills suited him well to the genre. Between 1955 and 1960, he played on several albums containing works by Schuller, John Lewis, Johnny Richards, Tom Talbert, and others with Third Stream ties. The best known of these is probably the landmark 1956 Columbia release *Music for Brass*, performed by the Brass Ensemble of the Jazz and Classical Music Society, with Miles Davis, J. J. Johnson, and Wilder billed as soloists. The Society was founded by Schuller and Lewis to "bring together musicians in both the 'classical' and jazz fields."[32] The album predated Schuller's use of the term "Third Stream," and in his annotation, he makes no attempt to characterize his work or those of the other composers as a synthesis of the two musics; in fact, he refers to the pieces by J. J. Johnson, John Lewis, and Jimmy Giuffre as "jazz scores." Of his own *Symphony for Brass and Percussion*, years later Schuller noted, "There isn't one jazz thing in that whole piece, not even one jazz rhythm, and it's atonal, completely, almost 12-tone." And of Wilder's participation, he said, "He was a completely classically trained musician. He could play anything. That's why he is on the recording [*Symphony for Brass and Percussion*]."[33]

Unless the discographies are mistaken, however, Wilder does not play on the Schuller piece, only on the works by J. J. Johnson and John Lewis. On Johnson's *Poem for Brass*, Wilder solos after Miles Davis (flügelhorn) and the composer (trombone) in a lyrical ballad section in the second movement. (Forty years later, Johnson reprised this melody as "Ballad for Joe" on his *The Brass Orchestra* [Verve 314-537-321, CD], with Wilder again stating the theme.) Wilder also plays in the ensemble on John Lewis's *Three Little Feelings* but does not solo.

A year earlier, Wilder had been far more prominently featured on an equally challenging but lesser known early Third Stream recording by composer-arranger Johnny Richards. *Annotations of the Muses*, an extraordinary three-part suite for a nine-piece ensemble, was seemingly tailor-made for the eloquent and lucid improvisations of Wilder and guitarist Johnny Smith. Released as a ten-inch LP on the obscure Legende label (a subsidiary of Roost), the recording was not reissued until 2006, and it never received the attention it merited as one of the most successful attempts at melding elements of jazz and classical, retaining the salient qualities of both with none of the synthetic gravitas sometimes associated with the genre. In his rave review of *Annotations of the Muses* in the *Washington Post and Times-Herald*, Paul Sampson wrote, "The only thing pretentious about the work is its title."[34]

Wilder recalled the rehearsal process for the *Annotations* project: "We would rehearse in sections—the brass, the rhythm, etcetera. And you're listening and wondering, 'What's going to happen? Can he put this together?' And when we finally heard the whole thing, you sat there with your mouth open! How could anybody think that way? It was tremendous! Johnny Richards was a genius!" He also described his own approach to the improvised solos in the piece: "You had to try to play something that remains in the idiom of the piece itself. You try to think in terms of the body of the piece and to play something that feels it's a part of it."

Wilder was also heavily featured on *Bix, Duke, Fats*, composer Tom Talbert's 1956 album for Atlantic (1250, LP). Talbert, a highly talented and original composer-arranger, put his own stamp on pieces by Bix Beiderbecke, Duke Ellington, and Fats Waller. The three Beiderbecke pieces, "Candlelights," "In a Mist," and "In the Dark," owe as much to Debussy as they do to anything in the jazz tradition and were, in a sense, precursors of the Third Stream. Talbert's imaginative reworkings were a perfect showcase for Wilder and underscored some similarities between Beiderbecke's and Wilder's styles—notably a lyrical, understated approach—that had not gone unnoticed through the years. Remarkably, this connection was first pointed out to Wilder as early as 1942, by no less a qualified observer than the wife of saxophonist Frankie Trumbauer, perhaps Beiderbecke's closest musical associate. Wilder recalled meeting her:

> I was playing a dance with Les Hite's band in Topeka, Kansas. One of the patrons came up afterward and said to me, "You know, you sound a lot like Bix Beiderbecke." I had certainly heard him on record but didn't know it was him. She said, "If you have time before you leave, come by my house—I've got a lot of records by Paul Whiteman, and Bix Beiderbecke is on some of them." She turned out to be Frankie Trumbauer's wife. She also told me she had a son [Bill] a couple of years younger than me who would like to meet me. So I went to visit, and among the things she played for me was "In a Mist," so it was a real thrill for me to play that with Tom Talbert.

Wilder had recently played on an album Talbert had arranged for singer Patty McGovern,[35] and he was Talbert's first choice for *Bix, Duke, Fats*. As Talbert wrote of Wilder in the liner notes, "With his highly developed harmonic sense and a taste which, like good manners, eludes you until you realize everything has been done just right, he creates a mood we all too seldom hear." Years later, he added, "Joe Wilder did an absolutely terrific job on the Beiderbecke pieces. . . . They were originally piano solos so the intervals are not typical jazz intervals and, as I said, so exposed with these lean backgrounds. And he played it just beautifully."[36] And in his discussion of *Bix, Duke, Fats*, Talbert's biographer, Bruce Talbot, notes, "To complete the spell, he [Talbert] had the benefit, once again, of one of the most original, sublimely inventive, and consistently underrated trumpeters of the post-World War II era."[37]

Contemporaneous reviews were equally laudatory. *Down Beat*'s Dom Cerulli awarded *Bix, Duke, Fats* a maximum five stars and noted, "Wilder emerges as a trumpet man of stature and delicacy. His taste and flexibility are particularly evident on the Beiderbecke pieces."[38] Some fifty years later, Wilder was featured on Talbert's final two recordings: *This Is Living* (1997, Chartmaker PDP14480) and *To a Lady* (1999, Essential Music Group 1000).

As was the case with his "Cherokee" solo, Wilder's striking contributions to the Talbert recording were not lost on players of a younger generation. In another *Jazz Times* "Before and After" blindfold test, "In a Mist" was played for trumpeter Terence Blanchard, one of the leading musicians to emerge in the 1980s. When told the soloist was Wilder, he said:

You listen to him or someone like Henry "Red" Allen, they had sounds. And that's not an easy melody to play on the trumpet. Not easy at all. The difficulty is not in the fingering; it's in the embouchure, because you have to make these wide leaps. It's about your flexibility. . . . It's being able to play those wide intervals and hit the center of the note. I mean, you listen to him play and you go, wow, if it were only that easy. . . . Joe Wilder, isn't that something?[39]

In 1958, Wilder took part in another historic recording project, *Legrand Jazz* (Columbia CL1250, LP), featuring the writing of the talented French pianist and composer Michel Legrand, who was just coming into prominence as a film scorer. Similar in concept to Talbert's *Bix, Duke, Fats*, Legrand's album assembled three all-star groups to interpret his singular and challenging orchestrations of famous jazz compositions across several eras. Like Talbert's recording, Legrand's album included works by Waller, Ellington, and Beiderbecke (both contained "In a Mist"), albeit with very different instrumentations and approaches. Legrand managed to enlist Miles Davis, John Coltrane, Bill Evans, Ben Webster, and many other luminaries for his project. Wilder was part of a group that included fellow trumpeters Ernie Royal, Art Farmer, and Donald Byrd. Wilder is the first trumpet soloist on Dizzy Gillespie's "Night in Tunisia," which also features a series of exciting four- and then two-bar trades among the trumpeters. In his annotation to the 1986 CD reissue, British critic Max Harrison found Wilder's contribution "especially shining."[40] Harrison also noted that "one is sadly reminded of how reputations rise and fall. Thus Joe Wilder, who played so beautifully on the third session, is now largely forgotten, while Bill Evans and John Coltrane, long since recognized as crucial influences on jazz, were not mentioned on the front of the sleeve of the original issue."[41] While Harrison is correct with regard to the subsequent ascendancy of Evans and Coltrane, he may be overstating both Wilder's celebrity in 1958 and his obscurity in 1986.

Wilder summed up his feelings about the Third Stream and related musical experiments in which he took part during this period, saying:

I found it to be a challenge, and I enjoyed it because there was something different about it. Composers, people like Johnny Richards, J. J. Johnson, and Gunther Schuller, were writing things that expressed their feelings and reflected what they would have played if they had been doing the actual playing. It gave them the opportunity to say, "This is the way I think," rather than simply having someone like me improvise around the harmonic structure.

In addition to his participation in these challenging Third Stream projects, during the mid-1950s, Wilder was in great demand by vocalists. In 1955 and 1956, he was featured on recording dates with Lena Horne, Marlene VerPlanck, Carmen McRae, Mary Ann McCall, and Chris Connor, among others. Also, in 1956, he was reunited in the studio with Dinah Washington, his old friend from the Lionel Hampton band. Wilder recalled that when the singer entered Capitol studios and saw only a few black faces in the orchestra, she threatened to call off the date unless more black musicians were included.

As a result of this flurry of recording activity in the mid-1950s, Wilder's name began to surface in the *Down Beat* critics' polls. In 1956, he was tied with Thad Jones for seventh place in the trumpet category, and in 1957, he tied for sixth (with Chet Baker, Kenny Dorham, and Doc Evans)—behind Dizzy Gillespie, Miles Davis, Louis Armstrong, Ruby Braff, and Roy Eldridge.

8

On Staff

African American Musicians
and the Network Orchestras
(1957–1964)

B y 1957, Wilder's multifaceted career was flourishing. Happily married and about to start a family, he had left the road and forged a successful career in New York, where he was playing lead trumpet in *The Most Happy Fella* on Broadway and in constant demand for both pop and jazz record dates. But there were still new musical worlds to conquer, one of which was the rarefied realm of the network staff orchestras.

From the 1930s until the early 1970s, network radio (and later television) staff orchestras represented a lucrative and steady source of employment for many New York musicians. In 1958, each of the three major networks, CBS, NBC, and ABC, maintained full-time staff orchestras of approximately sixty-five musicians.[1] Staff musicians were paid a regular salary, for which they remained "on call" for whatever musical needs might arise. These involved

---

Wilder at a record date, Nola Studios, New York, 2002. *(Photo by Ed Berger.)*

regular daily or weekly assignments on ongoing radio or television programs, as well as specials. Studio work required a high degree of musicianship: the ability to sight-read and to double (especially for reed players). It also called for considerable stamina and versatility. The last quality was essential, as musicians were required to play all types of music, often within the same program. Staff work demanded certain personal qualities as well. Dependability was first and foremost; showing up late was not an option and would quickly lead to dismissal. Deportment was also stressed; musicians arriving in less than optimal playing condition would not last long. Finally, musicians had to be willing to forgo personal glory and attention. Although studio musicians were sometimes featured, most of their work was anonymous and uncredited, recognized only by their peers.

Although African American musicians had been featured stars on radio going back to the 1920s, and occasionally, black stars like Louis Armstrong and Fats Waller had even hosted their own programs, it was not until the 1940s that they were able make inroads into the regular network staff orchestras. In 1942, John Hammond, producer, talent scout, and champion of civil rights, launched a quest to obtain network staff positions for several prominent black artists. As often was the case, Hammond's patrician lineage gave him the entrée needed to effect change. Hammond contacted Larry Lowman, a vice president of CBS and a jazz fan, who was married to his cousin Kathleen Vanderbilt Cushing: "I told Larry that there was not one Negro musician on the staff of any radio station in the city, or, I believed, in the entire country."[2] Hammond was regularly editorializing about the issue in *Music and Rhythm*, which he coedited. As early as December 1941, the magazine had called attention to the fact that, although Local 802 was integrated, the union had done nothing to secure studio work for black musicians in New York, even though it "has contracts guaranteeing radio and pit band employment. . . . It seems odd that with so many outstanding Negro sidemen not one of them can land a job in radio."[3] The unsigned article, undoubtedly by Hammond, also noted that network studio orchestra musicians earned from $200 to $400 a week. And in May 1942, Hammond railed, "The bars against Negroes are nothing less than appalling. . . . Not a single Negro is employed in a radio staff orchestra, major symphony group, legitimate theatre pit, or with one exception, a leading hotel. Hitler himself could do no better if he were supervising employment."[4] A month later, Hammond secured a meeting with David Sarnoff, head of NBC, to plead his case. He pointed out that Sarnoff had "just been appointed to the President's Fair Employment Practices Committee . . . which was established to end the very sort of discrimination practiced at NBC."[5] With his customary zeal, Hammond proclaimed, "Putting an end to discrimination in the music industry will act as an incentive to those people all over the world who are now engaged in a war against Fascism."[6]

After the meeting with Sarnoff and the representatives of NBC's two networks, the Red and the Blue, Hammond reported, "They hemmed and hawed, and finally agreed to employ [trumpeter] Bill Dillard, [bassist] John Simmons, and one other Negro on a trial basis. They were used sparingly during the summer of 1942, and the week after I went into the Army all were promptly fired."[7]

Hammond had greater success at CBS. In July 1942, a banner headline in *Music and Rhythm* announced the end of discrimination in the network radio studios.[8] The unsigned article, again probably by Hammond, goes on to say that Network officials had "long been troubled by the fact that no Negro musician has ever been employed on a steady basis by their network, and they have gone to work to form a mixed dance band to be regularly featured on all popular CBS programs."[9] The article made it clear that no white musicians would lose their jobs as a result of this effort; the black musicians were being added to the staff.

By late July, these initiatives spearheaded by Hammond led to the employment of six African Americans in a studio band led by Raymond Scott, music director at CBS. They included Cozy Cole (drums), Emmett Berry (trumpet), Benny Morton (trombone), and Israel Crosby (bass).[10] Cozy Cole also cites bassist Billy Taylor and saxophonist George Johnson as being part of this original contingent of black musicians at the network.[11]

Raymond Scott might, at first, seem an odd choice for this pioneering role. A talented arranger and composer, Scott's "Quintette" came to prominence in the late 1930s, featuring clever, highly stylized, and oddly titled arrangements that downplayed improvisation. But by all testimony, he proved adept at leading the new integrated CBS band, which featured some of the most powerful swing players of the era. Scott named Duke Ellington as his primary inspiration, and he looked upon his collaboration at CBS with the black players as "a great opportunity to pay him back."[12]

Cozy Cole described his tenure at CBS: "You gained an awful lot of experience there with Raymond [Scott]. . . . You used to free lance up there with different conductors. Play all different styles of music."[13] Along with Hammond, Cole credited CBS contractor Lou Shoobe with making the breakthrough in the studios possible. He also was very positive about the reception accorded him and his fellow African American musicians: "[There] wasn't any sort of prejudice or anything else evident up there when you were playing, because they all treated you beautiful. . . . Raymond and all the guys in the band, you know, just everybody up there just treated you wonderful, so you didn't feel that pressure at all."[14] Cootie Williams was one of those originally recruited by Scott for CBS, but the trumpet star ultimately decided that he could make more money leading his own band, and Emmett Berry was hired instead.[15]

The African American press devoted extensive coverage to the CBS breakthrough. In a piece carried by the *New Journal and Guide* and the *Chicago Defender*, Harold Jovien reported on the first broadcast by the mixed band on a show titled *Jump Time—Raymond Scott's Orchestra*, which aired on August 18, 1942: "The closed door prohibiting colored musicians from playing in radio studios bands has suddenly been flung open."[16] Hammond, himself, in a *New York Times* piece, wrote:

> Tucked away amid soap operas some rather startling music comes out of the Columbia Broadcasting System at odd times in the morning and afternoon. It is the new music of Raymond Scott, a band composed of top-flight instrumentalists, preponderantly Negro. Because housewives' tastes lean mostly to the hillbilly and sentimental forms of music the exuberance of the Scott band has been something of a problem for many of the stations affiliated with CBS, but somehow the network has had enough courage to keep the band and to feature it in spots assuring it of a more general audience.[17]

One of the black musicians who reportedly turned down an offer to join CBS was multi-instrumentalist-arranger-composer Benny Carter.[18] But earlier in 1942, Carter had been hired by conductor Mark Warnow to arrange for the immensely popular CBS program *Your Hit Parade*. (Coincidentally, Warnow was the older brother of Raymond Scott, who had changed his name from Harry Warnow.) During an association that lasted several months, Carter prepared four arrangements a week for *Your Hit Parade*. The caption under a photo of Carter and Warnow in *Down Beat* proclaimed that Carter's hiring marked "an end to racial discrimination in the network studios, for before Mark [Warnow] took on the great colored ace Negroes were not allowed in the studios."[19] The *Pittsburgh Courier*, the African American weekly, described this breakthrough as "perhaps one of the most important events in the progress of Negro music."[20] Carter did not play in the studio orchestra for the show, although he did record as a featured soloist with Warnow's orchestra for Victor in February 1942.

It is unclear just how long Scott's integrated band endured at CBS. The group was certainly still on the air in May 1943, when it teamed up with Frank Sinatra for a broadcast.[21] The band also appeared outside the studio when it fulfilled a two-week engagement at the Roxy Theatre in November 1942. The group included Emmett Berry, George Johnson, Billy Taylor, and Cozy Cole, along with white pianist Mel Powell. The *Atlanta Daily World*, another African American paper, declared, "It not only showed real democracy but it proved to be one of the finest small bands yet," adding, "the boys get along well with each other."[22]

Unfortunately, as Hammond himself noted, his success at integrating the network orchestras was short lived. As with similar attempts over the years to end segregation in Broadway orchestras and in the classical world, pressure by individuals like Hammond, organizations such as the Human Rights Commission, and later on, campaigns by the musicians themselves brought attention to the issue and succeeded in achieving some progress. But as soon as the pressure waned, most of the gains proved temporary, and the situation tended to revert to its previous status. Thus, by 1947, the National Negro Congress noted that "only one Negro musician, [drummer] Specs Powell, makes a living with network house bands."[23] Powell had been hired by Raymond Scott in 1943 to replace Cozy Cole at CBS. As Cole reported, "When I left, I took Specs Powell up there because Raymond wanted another colored drummer."[24] The case might be made that Gordon "Specs" Powell, who remained with CBS until 1972, was, in fact, the first African American to be hired as a regular member of a network orchestra, as it is unclear just how fully the black musicians hired the year before at John Hammond's behest were integrated into the overall musical activities of the network. Powell, on the other hand, worked at CBS for decades on a variety of programs, including the *Ed Sullivan Show*, *Jackie Gleason Show*, and *Candid Camera*.[25] Powell also played on Arthur Godfrey's *Talent Scouts* program. (Godfrey even interrupted his Christmas show in 1952 to salute Powell while the drummer was recuperating from eye surgery.)[26]

Unlike Cozy Cole, who glowingly reported on his full acceptance at the network, Powell met with some resistance, especially early on. Dan Del Fiorentino interviewed the drummer for the National Association of Music Merchants (NAMM) oral history project. Del Fiorentino recounted the interview:

> He often found himself alone even in the large 30-piece orchestra. After a break one evening, Specs returned to his drum set to find a noose on it. During my interview with Specs, I asked him what he did and he recalled, "I looked around the room at the faces of anger and realized no one person put it there—they all did. Then I picked up my sticks and did my job."[27]

By 1954, a decade later, the situation had not improved. In a wide-ranging series of five articles, *New York Amsterdam News* theater editor Alvin "Chick"

Webb surveyed the plight of African Americans in the entertainment industry. In his opening salvo, Webb asserted that "discrimination against Negroes is still rampant in the TV and radio industries." He accused NBC and CBS of "paying homage to the Southern viewer and ignoring the potential 15-billion dollar Negro market."[28] In his November 13, 1954 column, Webb reported on the results of a questionnaire on the employment of African Americans he had sent to twenty-one radio and seven television stations in the New York area. He found CBS to have the most African Americans, noting that out of a total of approximately three thousand employees, about three hundred were black—and only seven of those were musicians.[29] In the next installment, Webb names the seven: pianist Teddy Wilson, bassist Milt Hinton, drummer Specs Powell, trombonist Tyree Glenn, trumpeter Jimmy Nottingham, "Averill Snow" (probably a misprint for bassist Arvell Shaw), and drummer Joe Marshall. Robert E. Kalaidjian, director of personnel relations, described their status as "employed on a regular daily or weekly contractual basis," which suggests that they were not salaried staff orchestra members.[30] This was corroborated by Milt Hinton, who noted that when he left Louis Armstrong's All Stars in 1954 to join CBS, "[Lou] Shoobe hired me as a freelance musician. I wasn't on staff, which meant I got paid by the show and didn't have any other commitments to the network."[31]

In his final installment, Webb reported that, together, New York's twenty-three radio and television stations, including networks and local outlets, employed a total of forty African Americans as "regular performing personnel."[32] Although not defined, one would assume this category would include on-air personnel, such as emcees, announcers, reporters, and musicians. In the wake of Joseph McCarthy's anti-Communist witch hunts, the Coordinating Council for Negro Performers, founded by a group of black actors in 1952 to improve the number and image of African Americans on television, noted in its report:

> When Negroes are omitted from the American scene [radio and television], the impression is given that Negroes have no place in American life. By the same token, if he is pictured exclusively as a clown, a buffoon, a stereotype, we are saying in effect that he is restricted to this position in our American society and this is not good propaganda for a nation on whose shoulders the leadership of a floundering world has been thrust. Communists and exponents of other ideologies will certainly make the most of it.[33]

Bassist Milt Hinton pointed out another reason why, in the 1950s, black musicians sought entry into the studios: "Integration of the studios became even more important with the breakup of the big bands because a lot of the work switched to the studios."[34]

Wilder Joins ABC

Joe Wilder's entrée into the network studios came about in much the same manner as his breakthroughs on Broadway and later in the classical world. Someone heard him, recognized his talent, and decided that he would be an asset. Throughout his career, Wilder's self-effacing nature and aversion to self-promotion prevented him from engaging in the not uncommon practice of lobbying for a gig or a position. In this case, the person responsible for Wilder's eventual hiring at ABC was the well-known trumpeter Billy Butterfield. Butterfield (1917–1988), a veteran of the Bob Crosby, Artie Shaw, and Benny Goodman orchestras, had a beautiful tone and a lyrical approach to ballad playing not unlike Wilder's. From the early 1940s, he worked as a staff musician at both ABC and NBC, an association that continued into the 1950s. In 1955, he and Wilder happened to be together on a record date for a singer. "As usually happened on those dates, each of the trumpet players would play some of the lead parts," Wilder said. "When we finished, Billy said, 'You know, the way you play, you ought to be getting a lot of work here in town. If I ever get a chance to throw something your way, I'm going to do it.'"

About six weeks later, Butterfield called Wilder to say that he needed to take off from a show at ABC for a special engagement and that he had spoken to Frank Vagnoni, the network's contractor, who agreed to excuse him as long as he could get someone to "cover the chair." Butterfield suggested Wilder. "I didn't have to audition," Wilder recalled. "I just came in and played backgrounds for a mystery drama, *The Whistler*, that they were recording live."

When he arrived at the studio, Wilder was met by a very dignified gentleman who told him to stop by his office when he was through with the show. "I had no idea who he was; I thought he was one of the guys in the crew putting me on," Wilder said. "We read through the music once and then did it on the air. The show went okay, and when I got through, I packed up and went home." A few days later, Wilder received a call from Vagnoni's secretary asking about his availability for half a dozen additional dates. She also told him that the contractor had expected him to come by his office on the previous date and that Wilder should go straight there when he arrived for the next session. Wilder recalled, "When I got there, Mr. Vagnoni looked at me and said, 'Mr. Wilder, how do you expect to succeed in the music business if you don't know a contractor when you see one?' He never let me forget it!" Vagnoni must have found it unusual—and perhaps refreshing—that, in a business in which people were always scheming to gain access to him to solicit work, Wilder had failed to respond to a direct invitation—especially when the contractor had intended to ask the trumpeter whether he would be interested in a regular staff orchestra position at ABC, should an opening occur. Over the following two years, Wilder was called to sub from time to time at the network. Finally, in 1957, while he was playing in the orchestra for the Broadway show *The Most Happy Fella*, Vagnoni, true to his word, offered him a regular staff position, which he accepted.

When Wilder joined the network, he was the only African American in the orchestra, although he would soon be joined by Ernie Royal, his friend and former trumpet colleague from Lionel Hampton's band, and by violist Al Brown, with whom Wilder would later work in the Symphony of the New World. Vagnoni was the ideal contractor to help ease Wilder's entry into the studios. "There were some members of the orchestra that resented the fact that they hired me," Wilder said, "but over a period of time, I'd look up, and one by one these people would be gone. Mr. Vagnoni systematically got rid of all the guys that might have caused a problem!" Wilder emphasized that most of the musicians were receptive, especially his fellow brass players: "We all wanted to do the best job we could, and if you could contribute to it, you were welcome. But I was aware that, as a black musician, I had to be on top of things."

The contactor wielded tremendous power at a network. He not only hired the musicians and assigned them to the various programs but was usually present to supervise the sessions, working closely with the orchestra conductors and arrangers. The only exceptions were "commercial" or "outside" shows in which "an Arthur Godfrey, Patti Page, etc., can usually demand what musicians they will include in their package."[35] As conductor Glenn Osser, with whom Wilder worked for many years at ABC, noted, "The contractor was the head guy, not the bandleader. The musicians got [paid] a certain amount, and the leader got one and a half. The contractor got double."[36] So having Frank Vagnoni on his side was a tremendous help in Wilder's transition to the network staff orchestra. "Mr. Vagnoni was one of the most wonderful employers you could ever have had," Wilder said. "The management respected the musicians, we respected them, and it was because Frank was in the driver's seat." Wilder also appreciated the fact that the contractor stood up for his musicians. "When we did *Music for a Summer Night*, we had this one conductor who was always browbeating the orchestra," he recalled. "Nobody could do anything right, and these were some of the top classical players in the country. Mr. Vagnoni was at one of the rehearsals, and when we finished, the conductor said, 'Okay, I'll see you tomorrow.' And Frank went up to him and took the baton and said, 'No you won't!' He told him, 'You don't mistreat the musicians, not at this studio!'"

Wilder's talents and musical skills were a perfect match for the demands of a network staff orchestra, as they had been for the Broadway pit bands. His reading ability and instrumental technique, of course, were the most important assets. But unlike in the Broadway orchestras, his ability to improvise and transpose and his flexibility to adapt to any musical situation gave him an advantage over the studio players who came from strictly classical backgrounds. Although most of the work at the studios involved playing written music, there was a frequent need for improvised solos. In addition, some situations required some spur-of-the-moment musical legerdemain. Pianist Hank Jones played on countless studio dates of all types. He noted, "We used to arrive at a session to accompany a vocalist and find there were no parts—just one copy of some sheet music! So we'd find a key, make up an introduction, figure out some kind of a chord progression, and then you'd go."[37]

Not all veterans of the big bands were qualified—either musically or temperamentally—for studio work. As bassist Milt Hinton, another studio stalwart, said, "There was a big difference between playing in the bands and in the studios, and a lot of the guys couldn't handle the transition. . . . In Cab's [Calloway's] band you'd have one guy who only could play second trumpet. He might never have to get above A. The band was famous, so he was famous and made a good living. They would stay at one level and thought it would go on forever. After ten or fifteen years, when the band broke up, they were lost."[38] Jazz players like Wilder and Hinton, who chose to enter the studios, were often criticized by their fellow musicians for "selling out." Trumpeter Ray Crisara, Wilder's friend and colleague at ABC, said, "They were jealous because they weren't strong enough players to do what Joe was able to do."[39]

At the network, Wilder worked closely with staff arrangers and conductors, including Buddy Weed, Ralph Herman, and Glenn Osser. Wilder became a favorite of Osser's, who joined ABC as a staff conductor in 1947 and remained with the network for nearly three decades. Osser used Wilder whenever possible for a variety of work both within and outside of ABC. "When I first heard him play, I said, 'This guy is something!'" Osser recalled. "No matter what came up, there wasn't anything that I wouldn't give Joe to play. I liked his tone; I liked his improvising. Sometimes I would write things out, and he would play them exactly the way I would have if I were a player myself. He was one of the favorites amongst the guys. Everybody loved Joe."[40]

The Studio Life

The 1950s and 1960s represented a peak for studio musicians. In New York, a pool of roughly two hundred players were responsible for a significant portion of the music heard on television and radio, commercial jingles, and a wide range of pop recordings of all types. These accomplished musicians labored anonymously for the most part, developing their own community, culture, and support system. Most of these players probably did not originally envision studio work as their ultimate goal in music. Those with a classical background may have seen themselves on the concert stage, performing with a major symphony orchestra. Those coming out of the jazz and big band world may have aspired to lead their own groups, making their marks as creative improvisers. But as in all professions, the necessity of earning a living can lead to unanticipated career paths. In his excellent study of Hollywood studio musicians, Robert R. Faulkner notes, "These realities often conflict with the ideals that first encouraged the player to undergo the rigors of discipline and practice, as well as the values on which his aspirations are based."[41]

Aside from the financial rewards, job stability, and the relatively predictable hours of network orchestra employment, the music itself presented a challenge. Musicians derived a great deal of satisfaction from being able to play anything put before them, often under pressure and with little or no rehearsal. Wilder regularly played everything from classical music to jazz and pop music of every conceivable type. "You did whatever shows they had coming in," he said. "There was so much variety in the number of shows and the kind of music we played that it was like spending several years in a conservatory. You would work six or eight hours a day but not necessarily every day. You got a good salary and could survive by just doing that." Much of the music had to be sight-read, adding to the pressure of studio work. "Sometimes you rehearsed, but other times the music was passed out, you got a downbeat from the conductor, and you played it live on the air," Wilder said. "In the beginning, having to come in every day and face new music, I was a little apprehensive. I would ask myself, 'What's going to happen tomorrow?' But then you came to realize, this is what you do every day, and nobody else in the band has seen this music before either. You began to look forward to it like a challenge, and any nervousness you felt when you started would dissipate, and you began to feel this is where you wanted to be every day. It was a joy."

The music itself ranged from pedestrian to inspiring, depending on the arranger or composer. "Whenever you got a call and somebody said it's for Neal Hefti, you would stop whatever you were doing and got yourself ready to do that date because you knew it was going to be musically enjoyable," Wilder said. "And there were many others who were like that." And even if the music was less than stimulating or in a genre outside their forte, the musicians challenged themselves to play it as well as possible. "We prided ourselves on being able to play anything as well or better than the people who played that particular style all the time," Wilder said. Studio life created a sense of camaraderie. Wilder was working with the same musicians day after day, in a variety of contexts. "We grew close and covered for one another," Wilder said. Many of his colleagues at ABC became lifelong friends.

A sense of humor helped relieve some of the tension of the pressure-packed studio environment. Wilder was often the perpetrator of the gags, but he was the object of one particular prank that has become legendary in studio lore. Like his bandmates in Lionel Hampton's group in the 1940s, Wilder's colleagues at ABC were determined to force him to break his prohibition against swearing. As Wilder recounted:

> We were doing a Christmas television show with the ABC Symphony and the Salvation Army band. The producer, instead of writing out the whole script, decided to wing it. We started at nine o'clock in the morning, and by four in in the afternoon, the Salvation Army segment wasn't even done yet, and we were still trying this and that. Now it gets to be, like, eight or nine o'clock at night, and [bassist] Arnold Fishkin came over to me and said, "If we go to midnight, can I have your word that you'll say 's-h-i-t'?" I figured we'd been at this for twelve hours—there's no way it can go on till midnight, so I agreed.

Saxophonist Leon Cohen, Wilder's colleague at ABC for two decades, recalled what happened next:

> Arnold let Frank Vagnoni, the contractor, in on it, telling him, "Joe Wilder's gonna swear!" So at two o'clock in the morning, we're still going, and Frank walks in, stops everything, and says, "Okay, let's have a tympani roll." So the tympanist lets it fly and ends with a crash of the cymbal, and Mr. Vagnoni looks at Joe and says, "Okay, Mr. Wilder, don't you have something to say?" Joe answers, "No, Frank, you can't do that to me!" And Frank said, "Joe, you either say what you promised you were going to say, or you're fired!" For Joe, that was a "gol-darn," "golly-gee" moment, which was the extent of his cursing.[42]

"I never said it," Wilder admitted. "Arnold Fishkin was brokenhearted. 'You gave me your word!' he told me." Wilder himself mocked his refusal to swear by saying that he even used to refer to Art Van Damme, the popular accordion player, as "Art Van Darn."

Trumpeter Ray Crisara also recalled teasing Wilder at a session: "We were playing, and something was not exactly right. I reached over and picked up

Joe's trumpet part, and underneath this one wrong note, I wrote out the fingering for him! We had such a good relationship that we could kid each other like that. Joe has a great sense of humor, and his improvisation included some of the humor that was in his conversation. If you heard Joe play, you could not stop yourself from smiling."[43]

One of the earliest ABC programs on which Wilder played was Ernie Kovacs's radio show, billed as "Mayhem in the Morning." Wilder probably worked with Kovacs in 1956, before becoming a regular ABC staff musician. The program aired live from six to nine in the morning, six days a week, requiring the musicians to arrive before five to rehearse. He was part of a sextet led by pianist Buddy Weed, and Wilder remembered the music called for a fair amount of improvisation. "Kovacs was great to work with," Wilder said. "He loved musicians, and he featured the band on one or two tunes every morning. He was always pulling pranks on us. We did one show on the Fourth of July, so he had the band playing a feature, and he came over with a firecracker, put it in the middle of the group, and lit it. We're trying to play while looking at this thing and waiting for it to explode. It turned out to be a dummy."

Wilder also worked with another comedic genius, Sid Caesar. After Caesar's iconic *Your Show of Shows* ended at NBC in 1957, he moved to ABC with a new program, *Sid Caesar Invites You*, which reunited him with regulars Imogene Coca and Carl Reiner. Wilder played trumpet in a small group conducted by Mike Colicchio that accompanied the sketches. The half-hour program, which aired Sunday nights, lasted only five months. Wilder found Caesar, who was a saxophonist himself, "very friendly to the musicians." This was not the case with another legend with whom he worked at ABC—Jack Paar. Wilder had subbed occasionally on the *Tonight Show* on NBC, and in 1973, when Paar hosted the short-lived *Jack Paar Tonight* as part of *ABC's Wide World of Entertainment*, Wilder was assigned to play in the band. He found Paar to be an "egomaniac" and "not particularly friendly to the musicians."

Wilder also played on the *ABC Dancing Party*, a three-hour radio show that aired on Saturday nights. The band played original arrangements of a wide variety of bands, including Glenn Miller, Benny Goodman, Duke Ellington, Fletcher Henderson, Jimmie Lunceford, and Xavier Cugat, among others. The *ABC Dancing Party* program was discontinued in 1956, so Wilder's participation probably predated his joining ABC as a regular staff musician.

ABC's *Voice of Firestone* television show afforded Wilder extensive opportunities to play classical music. The program, which began as a radio show in 1928, moved to television in the late 1940s and switched to ABC in 1954. In 1959, ABC replaced it with *Music for a Summer Night* (later *Music for a Spring Night*), a similar program but without the sponsorship of Firestone.

The show was resurrected as *Voice of Firestone* in 1962 but was terminated in 1963 for low ratings. *Voice of Firestone* was an institution, bringing culture to the masses for nearly thirty-five years. It featured many leading opera stars, performances of standard classical repertoire by the ABC Symphony, and some popular performers in a "Boston Pops" type of musical setting. In lamenting its demise, *New York Times* critic Alan Rich, called it "a fascinating lesson in tightrope walking," concluding, "'The Voice of Firestone' may not be mourned much in the upper circles of musicology but, like the departure of a lovable country cousin whose table manners were just on the verge of respectability, one feels the pang."[44]

When Frank Vagnoni learned of Wilder's abilities as a classical soloist, he asked him to play Haydn's *Trumpet Concerto* under Canadian conductor Wilfrid Pelletier. It was for an August 10, 1960, broadcast of *Music for a Summer Night*, hosted by Margaret Truman, daughter of the former president.[45] "Now they'll know why you're here," Vagnoni told Wilder. Leon Cohen described his performance as "one of the most impressive things I ever heard. It was fantastic."[46] Wilder reprised his performance of the Haydn concerto in 1963, in a live WABC-FM radio concert conducted by Glenn Osser.[47]

Another important showcase for Wilder's classical abilities was the ABC Brass Quintet. Wilder played second trumpet to Ray Crisara's first, with Charlie Small on trombone, Tommy Mitchell on bass trombone, and Jim Buffington on French horn. The Quintet performed an hour-long "live chamber concert" on WABC-FM in the mid-1960s, alternating with a woodwind quintet and string quartet.[48] Ray Crisara recalled the group's great camaraderie: "We would rehearse at somebody's house, and we all enjoyed each other's company very much. Joe was a big part of the group's success. I think it meant a lot to him to have the opportunity to play in that area [classical music], in which he was well versed."[49]

Wilder, in turn, was inspired by the group, and especially by Crisara, who remained a lifelong friend: "When I listen to recordings of our performances, I realize his playing lifted me to do things I never thought I was capable of doing. It was like I was a race car driver following along at high speed in the draft of the lead car."[50]

Concurrent with these classical programs, Wilder regularly played in a small group on the *Jimmy Dean Show*, hosted by the country music legend. Wilder was often featured as a soloist on the one-hour weekly variety program, which ran for three seasons, from 1963 to 1966, and included appearances by most of the leading country-and-western stars of the day.

Wilder was clearly thriving at ABC. He was earning a good living and was able to spend time with his growing family. Also, he was playing a wide variety of music—often challenging—with colleagues whom he respected and who respected him. Occasionally, however, he was reminded that segregation was not very far from the surface, even in the 1960s. He recalled one of the *Voice of Firestone* shows, which was to feature opera stars Leontyne Price and Robert Merrill. "They were supposed to sing a duet, but after they had rehearsed, somebody decided that the show's Southern viewers wouldn't be happy seeing this African American woman and white man singing together," he said. "She was annoyed but agreed to leave it out. Then they discovered they didn't have enough music to fill out the program, so they asked her to reinstate the duet. She said, 'I'm sorry, you didn't want it then, and I'm not doing it now.'"[51]

Wilder himself had a similar experience involving the *Voice of Firestone*:

We were doing Leroy Anderson's "Bugler's Holiday" with four trumpets, and I was the only African American in the group. When they set it up, I was on the end closest to the camera, and they used my arms to frame the other three guys. I didn't know it till I got home and asked my wife if she'd seen the program. She told me that she did, but she didn't see me—just my arms. I was friendly with a couple of the camera guys because we were all interested in photography. When I asked one of them about it, he said, "Firestone didn't want us to show you because they were afraid it would offend the Southern clientele."

Thanks to Frank Vagnoni, ABC had a fairly liberal policy about allowing its staff musicians to accept outside work as long as it did not conflict with their network commitments. "I used to get calls from other contractors, like Lou Shoobe at CBS, asking if I could do the *Jackie Gleason* or *Ed Sullivan* shows," Wilder said. "Mr. Vagnoni was proud of the fact that they would come to our network if they needed somebody." The vastly popular Gleason contributed to the integration of the studios by using black musicians on his television show, as well as on his record dates. He loved jazz and jazz musicians, featuring them on his extensive series of "easy listening" dates for Capitol. Between 1952 and 1969, Gleason made nearly three dozen albums for the label, almost all of which incorporated solos by well-known jazz artists, white and black. The trumpet soloists alone included Bobby Hackett (Gleason's favorite), Buck Clayton, Yank Lawson, Pee Wee Erwin, Ruby Braff, Charlie Shavers, and Wilder. Bassist Milt Hinton credits Gleason with helping him gain entry into the studios when he used him on *Music for Lovers Only*, the 1952 Capitol album that launched the series.[52] Wilder, who had subbed on the famous 1950s *Honeymooners* television show at CBS, remembered that show as having an integrated orchestra. He also performed on one of Gleason's albums, the 1967 *Doublin' in Brass* (Capitol SW2880), playing solos on "Ti-Pi-Tin" and "Cabaret." Wilder said, "We did the album with two full orchestras for a stereophonic effect. Gleason loved Bobby Hackett, Charlie Shavers, and Billy Butterfield, but they weren't available, so that's how I was hired to improvise a couple of things." Although unable to read music, Gleason nonetheless "conducted" at his dates. "He had good musical instincts, and he knew what was good and what was bad," Wilder recalled. "And he loved musicians—especially those who drank! When I'd go there to sub, every time we'd get a fifteen- or twenty-minute break during rehearsals, all the guys would run next door to a Chinese restaurant that had a bar. I'd wonder how we were going to get through the theme, but they played it every time—no flaws!"

Much of the work that Wilder performed outside of his staff commitments at ABC involved commercial jingles. New York's jingle industry represented another lucrative source of income for a pool of musicians, some of whom were members of network orchestras and some freelancers. The musicians were typically hired by a contractor for an advertising company to provide soundtrack music for commercials hawking products of all types. The requirement was similar to that of the studio orchestras: the ability to sight-read and play in a variety of styles was paramount. "On these jingle dates, there wasn't a lot of ad-libbing," Wilder said. "Everything was written out."

The jingle contractors would try to accommodate the schedules of the network musicians they wanted to use. In the heyday of the jingle industry in the 1960s, the volume of work was almost limitless for those qualified to perform it. "There had to be a hundred guys doing these jingle dates both from the networks and outside," Wilder said. "Sessions were going on all day long." Wilder was so busy during this period that he began to feel overextended to the point of exhaustion. A full-time staffer at ABC while subbing frequently for Broadway shows, he was also doing as many as four or five jingle dates a day. "I knew what my physical capabilities were," he said. "I got to the point where I limited it to three in one day. Sometimes it would end up being something so simple that you could have played six of them with no problem physically. But you could get three that were longer and more involved, and at the end of the day, you were just worn out. There was so much work, and the number of guys who could do it was more or less limited, so there was more than enough to keep everyone busy."

Wilder recalled that there were a number of other black musicians who worked regularly on jingle dates, including trumpeters Jimmy Nottingham and Thad Jones, pianist Hank Jones, and bassists George Duvivier and Milt Hinton. Trumpeter Clark Terry, who was also extremely active in the studio scene, remembered the pressure of these jingle dates:

Those contractors had to be confident about whomever they called because some of the dates were very short. Had to be completed in twenty minutes. You couldn't be doing multiple takes. It was blap, bup, thap, bam! . . . When we were called for dates for cola, beer, candy, cigarette, or soap commercials, we came in expecting almost anything as far as personnel or material was concerned.[53]

One television commercial that Wilder played on featured Louis Armstrong in a 1964 ad for Suzy Cute dolls. Wilder can be heard playing Dixieland-style trumpet on the soundtrack, which was clearly an attempt to capitalize on the astonishing success of Armstrong's recent recording of "Hello Dolly." Wilder recalled:

The fellow who owned the doll company was a big Louis Armstrong fan. After Louis ran through it, the guy said, "Mr. Armstrong, when you get to the end, could you sing, 'Oh Yeaaaahh!'"? So Louis said, "Okay, Pops." We did around three more takes, and each time Louis just forgot to do it, so the guy comes out very perturbed and says, "Mr. Armstrong, you promised me that you'd sing, 'Oh, Yeaaaahh!'" and each time he said it, he sang it just like Louis did. Finally, Louis says, "You know, this cat thinks he's me!"

Wilder had his camera with him in the studio and captured an evocative series of candid portraits of Armstrong, several of which were published in a Wilder photo folio in the *Annual Review of Jazz Studies*.[54]

The Urban League: Integrating the Network Orchestras

In 1958, the year after Wilder came on staff at ABC, the Urban League of Greater New York issued its wide-ranging report, *Job Status of the Negro Professional Musician in the New York Metropolitan Area*, prepared by G. Douglas Pugh. The report's findings about black musicians in Broadway pit orchestras, as cited previously, has them woefully underrepresented. The report also deals with the network radio and television staff orchestras. As previously noted, John Hammond's crusade in 1942 first called attention to the dearth of African Americans in the network orchestras and led to the hiring of several black musicians. By the mid-1950s, the situation had regressed, as the Urban League's report makes clear:

It is generally thought by the community that the medium of Television and Radio provides the Negro commercial and jazz musicians with ample work. This belief is probably due to the fact that some Negro performers and musicians are frequently featured as special guests on regular Television shows. A casual look at the regular staff musicians working on Television and Radio networks will show that Negro musicians are obviously excluded even though they are colloquially referred to as the "greatest" in the commercial and jazz field.[55]

The report notes that the approximately sixty-five staff musicians employed by each network individually earned from $220 to $600 a week. (Using consumer price index inflation adjustments, this represents a yearly salary in 2011 of $90,000 to $245,000.) The report briefly summarizes the status of black musicians at the three major networks as follows:

- In 1942, NBC and its subsidiary Blue Network, had "engaged two Negro musicians for the first time as staff men.[56] Their [*sic*] have been no Negro musicians on the staff of NBC since 1943 even though many qualified Negro musicians have applied for staff positions."[57]
- In 1943, ABC bought the Blue Network from NBC and continued to employ the two aforementioned black musicians until 1946, when they were dismissed because of retrenchment, along with twenty-five white musicians. Most of the whites were subsequently rehired, but "the Negroes were told that 'things are slow' in the words of one of the musicians not rehired." Subsequently, "in the period from 1947 to September 1957, no Negroes were employed by ABC. They presently employ one Negro trumpet player [Joe Wilder]."[58]
- In 1958, CBS employed "five Negro staff musicians,"[59] likely drawn from the group previously cited in the 1954 *New York Amsterdam News* series on African Americans in the entertainment industry: Teddy Wilson, Milt Hinton, Specs Powell, Tyree Glenn, Jimmy Nottingham, Averill Snow [Arvell Shaw], and Joe Marshall.[60]

Urban League president Sophia Yarnell Jacobs, in her 1959 year-end report, was able to announce that thirty-three orchestras had opened their ranks to black musicians, thanks to the organization's survey. Joining Jacobs in her praise of the music industry for these breakthroughs was none other than John Hammond, chairman of the Urban League's music committee. The report, which was widely covered in the African American press, listed specific musicians who had been hired in the various types of orchestras as a result of "conferences held with leading musical organizations in the city."[61] Several black musicians were cited in the articles as having been hired for Broadway shows, including oboist Harry Smyles (*Once upon a Mattress* and *Fiorello*), guitarist Kenny Burrell and bassist Joe Benjamin (*West Side Story*), trombonist Benny Morton and violist Al Brown (*Whoop-Up*), and drummer Jimmy Crawford and bassist Wendell Marshall (*Gypsy*).

The Urban League was also successful in furthering integration in the radio and television orchestras. Many of these hires, however, were for specific series or even individual shows, and not for the more lucrative and coveted permanent staff orchestra positions. For example, African Americans hired at ABC included flutist Antoinette Handy for *Voice of Firestone* and violist Al Brown for *The Pat Boone* Show, *The Joe Franklin Show*, *The Patti Page Show*, and *Music for a Summer Night*.[62] The only artists identified as hired for staff positions were bassist Milt Hinton and drummer Osie Johnson, who "were engaged as staff musicians for NBC-TV for several weeks during the month of April, 1959"—hardly regular positions—and pianist Hank Jones for CBS-TV in July 1959.[63]

The absence of black staff musicians at NBC remained an embarrassment for network head David Sarnoff, who claimed to be unaware of the situation. The ubiquitous Milt Hinton, in fact, turned down a regular NBC staff offer because he found freelancing to be more lucrative.[64] "A few years earlier we would have been delighted because the studios paid $220 a week for five days, three or four hours a day," he said.[65] Hinton, in his place, recommended two qualified African American bass players, Al Hall and Arvell Shaw. "Instead they hired George Shaw, a fine bass player and a good guy. But he was white, and the Urban League still hadn't gotten any blacks in."[66]

Wilder, of course, had already been hired as a regular staff musician at ABC in 1957, the year before the Urban League's survey. He is listed in the press coverage of the organization's achievements as having been "engaged for the Bell Telephone Hour program, 'Adventure in Music' on January 12 [1959]" and NBC's December 7, 1959, *Sid Caesar Show* (along with Milt Hinton), assignments he fulfilled outside of his regular ABC commitments.[67] (I examine progress announced by the Urban League in the integration of classical orchestras, as well as Wilder's testimony at the league's hearings, in Chapter 9.)

Just as Hammond's 1942 campaign had brought about immediate but merely temporary breakthroughs, the 1958 Urban League effort succeeded in expanding opportunities for African Americans not only in the networks but in classical and Broadway orchestras as well. Like Hammond's effort, however, when the spotlight was removed, many of the gains evaporated. As we shall see, a decade later, the New York Commission on Human Rights would conduct even more comprehensive and higher profile hearings into discrimination in all aspects of the music industry.

Record Dates: Sideman and Leader

The late 1950s was an extremely busy time for Wilder. On staff full time at ABC and on call for frequent assignments at other networks and in the flourishing jingle industry, he was also in constant demand for record dates by a wide range of artists. Between 1957 and 1959, Wilder played on some sixty-five albums, including jazz dates under such diverse leaders as Quincy Jones, Don Redman, Neal Hefti, John Lewis, Michel Legrand, George Russell, Herbie Mann, Cab Calloway, and Steve Allen. Wilder continued to be a favorite of vocalists, who found his sympathetic obbligatos complemented their work, no matter what the style. During the same three-year period, Wilder played on sessions with singers Harry Belafonte, Perry Como, Bobby Short, Diahann Carroll, Tony Bennett, Pearl Bailey, and Billie Holiday. Among the more esoteric albums on which Wilder found himself was a 1956 LP by Jean Shepherd, which featured the humorist's recitations interspersed with modern jazz tracks arranged by Mitch Leigh and Art Harris and played by an excellent small ensemble, including trombonist Sonny Russo and drummer Bobby Rosengarden. A copy of the album, released on the obscure Abbott label, sold for $1,995 on eBay in 2003.

Preceding his solos on Jackie Gleason's *Doublin' in Brass* (1967), Wilder was featured on several other pop/jazz instrumental albums in the late 1950s and early 1960s, under leaders Henry Jerome, Marty Gold, George Siravo, and Kenyon Hopkins. Although frequently marketed as "easy listening," many of these dates were in essence straight-ahead jazz recordings with solos by leading jazz players. One example is the 1957 *Sound and Fury* LP by arranger-conductor Sid Bass (Vik LX1084), which features Wilder on "Pickin' a Fight," a trumpet battle with one of his idols, Charlie Shavers. "It wasn't really a cutting contest," Wilder recalled. "During the trades, Charlie would take what I played and play it up an octave, as if to say, 'I like what you did!' It was more a sign of respect because he and I were good friends."

Wilder also had his first chance to record as a leader since the 1956 *Wilder 'n' Wilder* date for Savoy. In 1959, no fewer than two Wilder albums were released: *Jazz from Peter Gunn* and *The Pretty Sound*. And even more remarkable was the fact that they appeared on a major label: Columbia. Although Wilder was achieving some critical acclaim through his work as a sideman, he was still laboring anonymously in the studios for the most part—and not even playing jazz for much of the time. By 1959, Wilder was well respected by musicians, critics, and serious jazz fans alike, but his name recognition among the general public was hardly on a par with other Columbia jazz artists of the day. He did not have the profile of a Dave Brubeck, Miles Davis, Erroll Garner,

Duke Ellington, or even Teddy Wilson or Buck Clayton. Wilder's signing by Columbia was undoubtedly the work of Nat Shapiro, the label's A&R director and a veteran jazz writer, who coauthored the often-cited *Hear Me Talkin' to Ya* (with Nat Hentoff) and other important works. Shapiro produced the two Wilder albums, which were vastly different in concept.

The Pretty Sound (Columbia CL1372) was intended as a showcase for Wilder's lyrical and melodic side. Two sessions took place in December 1958, but the album was put on hold to complete the second project, *Jazz from Peter Gunn* (Columbia CL1319), featuring music from the television detective series, which ran three seasons, from 1958 to 1961. To capitalize on the popularity of Henry Mancini's hit score, Wilder and his quartet recorded the entire album in one day, January 18, 1959, and Columbia rushed it out in March of that year. Mancini's music was a far bigger hit than the series itself. As film and television music historian Jon Burlingame has pointed out, "Prior to 1958, jazz was rarely heard in a television score except as source music from an occasional radio, record player, or jukebox."[68] Every episode of *Peter Gunn* featured an original jazz score, with music often filling as much as half of each thirty-minute episode.[69] The catchy themes, striking instrumentation, and dramatic voicings created a sensation. Mancini's *Peter Gunn* soundtrack album, recorded for RCA, reached number one on the *Billboard* pop charts in 1959 and won two Grammys, including Album of the Year. It also spawned a spate of "covers," by both jazz and pop artists. Clearly, Columbia hoped that the popularity of Mancini's *Peter Gunn* music would help compensate for the fact that Wilder was relatively unknown to the public. The instrumentation—trumpet with rhythm section—was spare and somewhat unusual, although identical to that of Wilder's debut album three years earlier for the more budget-conscious Savoy. Because the Wilder album was a pet project of Nat Shapiro's with uncertain sales potential, it is likely that the producer might have wanted to keep the costs down. Wilder recalled that the quartet format was chosen not for budgetary reasons alone but because a small-group interpretation, emphasizing improvisation, would set the album apart. "Most of the other *Peter Gunn* albums were arranged with larger orchestras, so we thought it would be novel to play those things the way we did," he said. "When they asked me to do it, I took the tunes home to practice and see what I could come up with, so I came in with some ideas. We talked it over in the studio, and everyone made suggestions, but we were essentially improvising all that stuff."

The indispensable Hank Jones was once again on piano, with Wilder's friends Milt Hinton on bass and John Cresci Jr. on drums. As on his 1956 Savoy album, Wilder credits Jones's knack for on-the-spot arranging with much of the success of *Jazz from Peter Gunn*. "There was something about

him and me—I guess because we were so close in age and experience," Wilder
said. "I could start playing something, and he would pick it up immediately.
Then he'd do something, and I'd pick up on it. We could almost read each
other's minds."

The varied moods of Mancini's themes as well as the resourceful, if impromptu, arrangements give the tracks a diversity that belies the limited instrumentation. In addition, Wilder's masterful use of mutes greatly enhances
the tonal variety of the set.

The literate but unsigned liner notes to *Jazz from Peter Gunn* were undoubtedly by Shapiro and, in addition to an accurate biography of Wilder,
contain some insightful comments on his playing: "The most refreshing thing
that one becomes aware of while listening to Joe Wilder is that this is a musician with the rare ability to be both modern and uncomplicated at the same
time—a seeming contradiction in terms in an era in which hyper-tension and
introversion have become accepted as characteristics of contemporary music,
both 'classical' and jazz." Shapiro added that Wilder "is blessed with impeccable taste, penetrating intelligence and the most beautiful horn tone since the
great Joe Smith blew his heavenly sounds in Fletcher Henderson's band."[70]
Billboard gave Wilder's *Peter Gunn* three stars, noting, "There are other pack-
ages available on the same [theme], but the quartet's rhythmic and direct style
under Joe Wilder's lead makes the LP a strong contender for sales."[71] And the
usually phlegmatic John S. Wilson wrote in *High Fidelity*:

> Month by month, the music from *Peter Gunn* receives better and better
> jazz performances. Henry Mancini's sound track from the show was
> impressive, considering its television origins. Shelly Manne's version
> on Contemporary gave the tunes a stronger jazz treatment. And now
> trumpeter Joe Wilder . . . has produced a relaxed and strongly rhyth-
> mic set that is even more warmly jazz-oriented.[72]

Also, Wilson delivered a backhanded compliment to Hank Jones, noting that
his piano solos "have more vitality than he has shown recently."[73]

After the release of *Peter Gunn*, Wilder returned to the studio in May 1959
for the final session of *The Pretty Sound*, which was released in November of
that year. While *Peter Gunn* was essentially a jazz date, *The Pretty Sound*, as
the title implies, was intended to highlight Wilder's melodic side and to display his "lyrical improvisatory powers," as the liner notes (again uncredited
but probably by Nat Shapiro) state.[74] The album sought to counter the "dis-
tressing absence of humor, warmth, grace and good, old-fashioned romanti-
cism" in the "new jazz."[75] As such, ballads predominate, and the arrangements

by Mike Colicchio and Teo Macero were designed to set off Wilder's "pretty sound." For most of the tracks, three horns, including multiple doublings by woodwind specialists Phil Bodner and Jerry Sanfino, were used in addition to the leader's trumpet to create a surprisingly lush backdrop. A clear departure from the impromptu jamming of his Savoy date and the tight small-group format of *Peter Gunn*, *The Pretty Sound* was the album Wilder had yearned to make. "This was the first time when I had almost complete control over what I wanted to play," he said. Wilder worked especially closely with Mike Colicchio, who did the bulk of the arrangements. "I discussed it with him, and he would get an idea of what I wanted, and he would add his creative talents to it," Wilder said. "You can hear what a good job he did with the instrumentation." The repertoire comprised an intriguing cross-section of standards ("Blue Moon," "Autumn in New York"), show tunes ("Guys and Dolls," "I Hear Music"), Alec Wilder's "It's So Peaceful in the Country," the pop hit "Harbor Lights," the traditional "Greensleeves," Juan Tizol's "Caravan" (one of only three medium or up-tempo pieces), and Hugh Blane and Ralph Martin's "The Boy Next Door," popularized by Judy Garland. The album concludes with a moving reading of "Brahms's Lullaby," which Wilder included "because I wanted to play something for my mother-in-law, who had no particular interest in jazz." Surrounded by musicians who were also friends, including Hank Jones on piano, and George Duvivier and Milt Hinton, who shared the bass duties, Wilder was able to achieve the relaxed approach called for by the album's concept.

The reviews of *The Pretty Sound* were uniformly positive, with most critics able to distinguish the album's lush and lyrical yet creative concept from the nondescript "easy-listening" genre albums that proliferated during the period. As Leonard Feather wrote in his three-and-a-half-star review in *Down Beat*, "Don't dismiss this as just another mood music set. . . . True, it's commercially designed but in generally faultless taste and with several virtues above and beyond the estimable leader." Feather continued, "The title is ideal; I can't think of a trumpet player who has a prettier or more individual sound than Wilder," although Feather felt he "should have indulged in more ad libbing on the changes." On the one real up-tempo piece, "Caravan," he found Wilder to be "brilliant, both muted and open; his release on the first chorus is a model of constructive, integrated spontaneous creation." Feather concluded his review, noting, "Not recommended to hard boppers, experimentalists, or advocates of *le cool*; this package is strictly for trumpet players, students of Emerson. ('Beauty is its own excuse for being . . .') and people who just dig dignity."[76] Feather's aside about "strictly for trumpet players" proved perspicacious; until it was reissued on CD in 2003, *The Pretty Sound* became something of a cult classic among trumpet players of several generations, who would share tapes of the long out-of-print LP.

Billboard was equally enthusiastic, calling Wilder "one of the best and perhaps least publicized of modern trumpet men," adding that "he has rarely been heard on records to better advantage."[77] Despite the critical acclaim and the promotion of a major label, sales did not justify Columbia extending Wilder's contract beyond the two 1959 releases. As was common practice, artists would begin receiving royalties after studio and production costs of an album had been recouped. For years, Wilder's statements from Columbia indicated that sales had not yet exceeded costs, so no royalty payments were forthcoming. Wilder had no regrets, however. "It gave me a chance to play something I wanted to play," he said. "I didn't expect to get rich from any royalties." Columbia wanted to arrange a tour for Wilder in support of the albums, but he demurred. I couldn't just walk away from my commitments at ABC," he said. In addition, he was reluctant to go back on the road, even for a short time.

Wilder was as happy with *The Pretty Sound* as he was about any recording he ever made. It almost turned out to be his swan song as a leader, however; it would be more than three decades before he recorded again as the sole leader of a date.

"The Sound of Jazz"

In December 1957, shortly after joining ABC, Wilder took part in perhaps the most celebrated and effective presentation of jazz on television, "The Sound of Jazz." Part of the CBS-TV series *The Seven Lively Arts*, the star-studded yet unpretentious one-hour live show presented a galaxy of jazz luminaries of all musical styles in a setting notable for its informality. With cameras visible and musicians free to wander around the set and enjoy the performances of their peers, the show elicited the sort of relaxed and intimate performances rarely captured on television. "When they called me to do it, I had no idea who was involved," Wilder said. "We got there, and there were all these guys, some of whom you'd never expected to play with. It was such a happy gathering, and everyone was in such good spirits. It wasn't a cutthroat kind of thing, where everyone was trying to outplay everyone else." Wilder, of course, brought his camera. "It was all very relaxed. They let me take pictures—I had my Rolleiflex with me." Wilder managed to capture some extraordinary images of Coleman Hawkins, Lester Young, Pee Wee Russell, Jo Jones and others. "Billie Holiday wasn't drinking any more, and I took a picture of her leaning on the piano, and next to her was a bottle of 7UP," he said.

Produced by Robert Herridge, and with writers Nat Hentoff and Whitney Balliett providing the jazz expertise, "The Sound of Jazz" is filled with poignant moments, perhaps the most touching of which was the reunion of Billie Holiday and Lester Young on "Fine and Mellow." According to Hentoff, Holiday's very presence was challenged by a sponsor who sent a note to Herridge saying that "he did not want a woman coming into the homes of America on a Sunday afternoon who had been in prison on a drug charge." Herridge sent a note back saying that if Holiday was not on the show, he, Balliett, and Hentoff were leaving. "That was the end of that," Hentoff said.[78]

Wilder played on a Count Basie All Stars segment, featuring a big band made up of Basie alumni and other jazz stars. Looking intense and highly focused, Wilder solos on "Dickie's Dream," one of the two pieces played by the band. Other soloists included Count Basie, Ben Webster, and Benny Morton, who preceded Wilder, as well as Gerry Mulligan, Vic Dickenson, Roy Eldridge, Emmett Berry, Coleman Hawkins, Dickie Wells, and Joe Newman, who followed him. The playing of drummer Jo Jones made a particular impression on Wilder: "He was just unbelievable; whatever he did, the tempo remained constant."

By 2014, Wilder was the only survivor of the historic show. "Everybody who was involved knew it was something special," he said. "It was such a joyful thing to do."

Benny Goodman: USSR Tour

Although Wilder's musical activities in the 1960s centered around his studio work at ABC as well as the growing demands for his talents as a classical player, in 1962, he took time off from these endeavors to tour for six weeks with an all-star jazz orchestra led by Benny Goodman. Wilder had long shunned the road and had not traveled with a band since leaving Count Basie in 1954, but this was a historic event: the first U.S. State Department–sponsored visit to the Soviet Union by an American jazz group.

The U.S. government had discovered the potential of jazz as a tool of diplomacy (or propaganda) as early as 1956, when it sent Dizzy Gillespie on two tours: to the Middle East and South America. Later that year, Benny Goodman traveled to Asia on his first State Department tour. Dave Brubeck followed two years later with an extensive itinerary that included East Berlin and Poland—the first official foray by a jazz group behind the Iron Curtain. And in 1960, Louis Armstrong, America's most celebrated musical "ambassador," led his All Stars on a triumphant visit to Africa.

Occurring at the height of the Cold War, the Goodman Russian tour received a great deal of publicity as one would expect because of its groundbreaking nature. It drew additional attention because of dissension within the orchestra caused by the erratic actions of its leader. Even before it began, the Goodman tour was shrouded in controversy. Many questioned why Goodman, who was identified with an older style of jazz, and not Duke Ellington, one of the music's originators and a bandleader whose work was more eclectic and "modern," had been chosen for this historic mission. Jazz had a long history in Russia, despite a regime that, at worst, attempted to repress jazz as a symbol of Western decadence and, at best, tried to control it and even, occasionally, claim it as its own. The jazz audience in the USSR of the 1960s was composed predominantly of young people who tended to embrace the music's more progressive forms, along with rock, blue jeans, and other manifestations of Western culture. In addition, some critics and musicians felt that it would have been more appropriate for a black bandleader, like Ellington, to have been chosen.

To Soviet officials, Benny Goodman seemed less "subversive" than some of the more contemporary jazz groups. As Penny Von Eschen observes:

> Goodman's traditional jazz and his facility with classical music were more palatable to the Soviets and less threatening than the torrid, hyperkinetic blues of jazz. The latter was more improvisational and, perhaps, more explosive. Goodman's swing—"sweet" music, in 1930s jazz parlance—was seen as smoother and safer. The very style of jazz that had been officially proscribed during the 1930s now became acceptable a generation later.[79]

Although one might question Von Eschen's broad characterization of Goodman's music—after all, Goodman himself ignited something of a youth cultural revolution in the 1930s and was certainly considered to be on the "hot" side of the "hot" versus "sweet" divide—by the 1960s, the "King of Swing" was no longer cutting edge.

Wilder, who had never worked with Goodman before the State Department tour, does not recall how he himself was selected. His abilities as a classical player probably played a role because Goodman was planning to perform some classical repertoire during the tour. The Soviet composer Aram Khachaturian (1903–1978) was set to write a piece for trumpet and clarinet to feature Wilder with Goodman, but after the trumpeter fell out of favor, the idea was dropped. Wilder also recalled that, at a rehearsal, Goodman was impressed that he could play Ziggy Elman's famous "fralich" trumpet solo on "And the

Angels Sing" and told him they would do it on the tour, but that chart was never played. Wilder was regularly featured on Tadd Dameron's "Swift as the Wind," one of the few "modern" charts Goodman consented to play, as well as with the rhythm section on Ellington's evocative ballad "I Got It Bad (and That Ain't Good)"; both titles were included on the live LP *Benny Goodman in Moscow* (RCA LOC-6008).

The six-week tour began in Moscow on May 28, 1962, and encompassed thirty-two concerts in six cities. Musician-writer Bill Crow, the bassist in the Goodman orchestra, published a detailed account of the tour. Aptly titled "From Russia without Love," Crow's work chronicles many of the grievances that, from the musicians' perspective, detracted from the success of the trip.[80] Their discontent stemmed from three general sources: (1) the repertoire, (2) Goodman's attitude and behavior toward them, and (3) alleged nonpayment of negotiated wages. Crow succinctly summed up his feelings about Goodman: "During my brief time with him, I watched him completely demoralize an excellent band."[81] Regarding the repertoire, the main complaint was that, although Goodman had commissioned more modern arrangements by such writers as Bob Brookmeyer, Tadd Dameron, Oliver Nelson, and others, very few of them were incorporated into the band's program. Instead, Goodman emphasized the classic swing arrangements, which had helped propel his orchestra to glory some twenty-five years earlier—music with which he felt far more comfortable. As Wilder put it, "This band doesn't think big; it thinks back."[82]

Of course, as leader—and an eminent one at that—Goodman had the prerogative to play whatever he wanted. But given the groundbreaking nature of that particular tour and the broader diplomatic function of the band as representatives of the United States and its culture, the leader had obligations that transcended his own personal tastes. Many felt that the program should have reflected a more complete picture of the diversity of jazz as it then existed in the United States. Moreover, despite the Soviet Union's best efforts, it had been unable to suppress the Russian people's rabid interest in American music, and there existed a sizable younger audience that avidly followed Willis Conover's jazz programming on Voice of America. These sophisticated young fans, while appreciative of earlier jazz styles, were also interested in more contemporary sounds. As *Newsweek* reported, "In Sochi, Russian young people knew all the Goodman soloists by their first names, shouting 'Phil!' for Phil Woods and 'Zoot!' for Zoot Sims."[83] In Goodman's defense, tickets were expensive, and the audiences tended to be older and in some places included many Communist Party functionaries, whose appreciation for any jazz, let alone modern jazz, was minimal. The noted jazz writer Leonard Feather, who was on the Russian trip, wrote, "Older members of the audience seemed pleased with Goodman's music, but the younger element of fans and musicians are saying Art Blakey, Miles Davis, John Coltrane, the Modern Jazz Quartet or some other combo representing present-day jazz would have been a suitable choice for a USSR tour."[84] Goodman defended his choice of material, contending that modern jazz "would fall on its face."[85] The leader also addressed criticism of his frequent and seemingly arbitrary changes in the programs from concert to concert: "I always change them to suit myself, anyhow, to keep from getting bored."[86] In response to some of the musicians' charges that Goodman capriciously cut off (or in some cases, cut out) their solos, he said, "I'm not a devotee of playing eighteen choruses on a solo. . . . I call that practicing on the job. You should be able to say what you have to say in two or three choruses."[87]

Goodman's personal idiosyncrasies are legend among musicians of several generations. While capable of supremely generous acts, his often boorish behavior, aloofness, and parsimony received far more attention. The pressure of worldwide scrutiny and the grind of a demanding schedule seemed to have exacerbated the leader's faults. Unfortunately, Joe Wilder's experience while on tour with Goodman was far from unique yet particularly unpleasant. Although he was certainly aware of Goodman's reputation, unlike most of the other band members, Wilder had never worked with him before. "I don't like to condemn the man for some personal things that went on," Wilder said. "Playing with him added to whatever credits I had as a musician. But he was kind of hard to deal with." In retrospect, Wilder felt he might have gotten off on the wrong foot with Goodman, even before the band left the United States: "After I had heard all these stories from the guys in the band who had worked with him before, I said something like, 'Gee, Benny, it's really nice being a member of your band, because I'd heard a lot of bad things about you as a band leader.' It didn't come out the way I'd intended!"

On the tour, Wilder resented the fact that Goodman distanced himself from his musicians: "He would have nothing to do with us. During meals, the orchestra all sat together at tables, but Benny had a table all by himself over in the corner with a little American flag on it. One of our purposes was to show how well we got along, but it never quite got through to him."

Dan Morgenstern was one of the few writers who came to Goodman's defense: "Almost without exception critics, musicians and journalists revealed with embarrassing clarity the provincialism and immaturity of precisely that segment of American opinion which should have been most vocal in acclaiming a major victory for jazz—and incidentally, for the cause of freedom."[88] On Goodman's alleged mistreatment of his musicians, Morgenstern wrote, "Sure, Benny is a tough man to work for. Is that jazz news? Part of the trouble might be that there are too many 'leaders' and not enough sidemen in jazz today. Goodman has long since earned the right to be bossy, eccentric and opinionated."[89] Finally, Morgenstern defended Goodman's refusal to play some of the more modern arrangements: "Does he not have the right to consider the music he represents in the history of jazz the music he wishes to present to the public? . . . Is he obliged to follow fashionable opinion and consider himself outmoded when thousands of people still love—and buy—his stuff?"[90]

But Wilder's major disagreement with Goodman was not so much personal or musical but financial. Each musician had made a separate agreement with Goodman regarding salary. "Then, three or four days before we left, he called us together and said the State Department wouldn't pay that much, and everybody would have to take a $100 cut," Wilder said. "That started a lot of dissension. I refused to sign the contract. As soon as we arrived in Moscow, we were invited to the embassy, and to a man, everyone asked the State Department representative why they had to cut the salaries. He told us they had nothing to do with it—that they paid Benny Goodman a lump sum, and he determined what to pay the band!"

Goodman kept pressuring Wilder to sign his contract. "His road manager kept telling me, 'If you don't sign, he's not going to pay your per diem or your transportation back home,' Wilder said. "I told him, 'I'm here. I can't get out of Russia until the tour is over. If he doesn't want to pay me, he doesn't have to, but if he doesn't pay me, I'm not going to play.'" As Bill Crow noted, many others in the band refused to sign as well:

> There were restrictions on our deportment and rules about our behavior toward Benny. We were to agree to obey all of his instructions and be under his command 24 hours a day. . . . The one we balked at was an agreement to options on our services, a week at a time, for a couple of months *after we got back to the States*, tying up our ability to book any other work, but giving Benny no obligation to hire us![91]

The final straw for Wilder came when Goodman threatened to charge him for excess luggage if he did not sign his contract. Wilder had sent his wife and daughters to Sweden to stay with Solveig's family. He planned to fly there directly from Russia to join them for a few weeks and therefore had to pack for a longer trip. "My luggage was overweight at the beginning of the tour—in the States but not in Russia," Wilder said. "But when we got to Seattle, I put some things that totaled the excess in a carton and mailed it from the post office, registered; I had the receipt to prove it. So by the time we got to Russia, it wasn't an issue."

Things reached a boiling point in Moscow on the last day of the tour, when the musicians were given an ultimatum: no contracts, no paychecks. As Bill Crow reported, "We talked it over and decided that the only remedy was to refuse to play the last concert until we got paid."[92] At the last minute, a compromise was reached. The musicians agreed to sign the first page of the contract, pertaining to wages, eliminating the more objectionable clauses. The checks were passed out, and the musicians filed onto the stage to begin the concert, albeit twenty minutes late. Wilder glanced at his check and discovered that $300 had been deducted for excess baggage. He refused to play the final concert, and as the *Baltimore Sun* reported, "His chair stood empty."[93] Wilder's refusal to play was mentioned in several other papers, but most of the articles failed to accurately report the reason.[94]

Wilder had already had a few incidents with Goodman earlier in the tour. As an avid photographer, Wilder had naturally brought all of his camera equipment. Goodman approached him and asked whether he was "working for someone." When Wilder asked what he meant, Goodman explained that if Wilder were shooting for a magazine, he, Goodman, was entitled to a cut. There were musical issues as well. "If I had a trumpet solo, I'd stand up to play, and Benny would call out, 'Bar 39!' skipping two choruses after my solo. After he'd done this to me three times, the next time he pointed at me to play, and I said, 'Yeah, Benny,' and I just sat there."

For Wilder, the consummate professional, to have refused to play the final concert is ample testimony to how egregiously he felt he had been treated. As Bill Crow wrote, "As well as being a flawless musician, Joe Wilder is courteous, cooperative, and sweet-natured. He was delighted to be in the band and was prepared to do a professional job, and he couldn't believe the way Benny was treating us."[95] Going back to his earliest days in Philadelphia, Wilder had always scrupulously fulfilled his obligations as a professional musician, adhering to the highest standards of deportment, punctuality, and performance. But as a professional, he also felt that he should be treated fairly by his employers. As he had already demonstrated, Wilder had confronted previous leaders, such as Lionel Hampton and even his good friend Dizzy Gillespie, when he felt they were wrong—and at a point in his career when he was far more vulnerable. And unlike some members of the Goodman State Department band, he was not beholden to the leader in any way for his livelihood beyond the tour.

Wilder cited one example of Goodman's often mercurial behavior: "One night he called me into his dressing room before a concert and said, 'I just want to let you know I think you're a fine musician and how nice it is to have you in the band.' I just looked at him and said, 'Benny, I can't believe you asked me down here to tell me this after you've treated me like dirt through the whole tour!' And I turned around and walked back on the bandstand."

As African Americans, there were added pressures on Wilder, fellow trumpeter Joe Newman, pianist Teddy Wilson, and Joya Sherrill, the band's vocalist. The Soviets had traditionally tried to capitalize on America's race problem, and the State Department and the musicians themselves were concerned about what approach they should take when questioned about the situation. Wilder raised the issue at a State Department briefing. "They just said, 'Well, just answer the way you feel.' I did run into a couple of occasions where some people would try to goad me into saying something offensive," Wilder said. "I just told them, 'I'm a musician, not a politician, and I'm not here to push politics, yours or ours. If you want to ask me about music, go ahead.'" Wilder recalled one incident in Sochi:

> Sochi was like a summer resort, and you had people from all the different provinces. There were a lot of Armenians and people from Uzbekistan, who are more Asian-looking, many of whom were dark complexioned. So this one guy on the beach was saying, "Ah, here in Russia, all people are together—not like in the United States," and so on. I wasn't a State Department representative, but I'm an American. I was born here, and I resent a lot of things that happen here. But at the same time, I wasn't going to stand by and have somebody denigrate my country and try to promote his at my expense.

So Wilder interrupted him and said, "Wait a minute! There's no denying that we have discrimination in the States, but we're working hard to eliminate it." A *Life* reporter who was covering the tour happened to be listening and mentioned the encounter in a fairly extensive piece on the Goodman trip. Wilder was dismayed that *Life* quoted only the first part of his response—"There's no denying it [segregation] exists"—but conveniently omitted the second part.[96] The Associated Press (AP) also carried a report of the incident: "Half the band members went to the beach Sunday and Joe Wilder, Negro trumpeter, was immediately surrounded by Russian bathers asking questions about segregation in the United States." The AP dispatch also included a somewhat more complete version of Wilder's response: "Wilder said he told the Russians segregation exists but that "things are getting better now.""[97]

Many of the Russians they met had no political agenda—they were simply fascinated by the sight of black people. As Wilder related to George Avakian in his essay for the RCA double-LP recordings from the tour, "I went to the beach to take some pictures and in no time people were taking pictures of *me* and asking me to pose with them. One lady asked me to wait while she went to get her little boy—she didn't want him to miss what might be his only chance to see a Negro. I told her I'd be happy to wait—I didn't want him to miss it either!"[98]

Wilder also reported that he witnessed some "reverse discrimination" at the concerts. Some fans applauded wildly whenever he or one of his fellow African American bandmates played anything:

> If [white trumpeter] Johnny Frosk stood up and played a solo that could have been a hundred times better than what I played, they would applaud more for me because I was an African American. It was like, "We'll show them that we treat them better than they do in their own country." Joya Sherrill was a very attractive African American woman, and they had never seen someone like that up close. She'd come out and didn't even have to sing, and they'd be screaming!

The African American press followed the tour, highlighting the exploits of the black musicians. *Jet* reported that "Negro performers Joya Sherrill, Joe Newman and Teddy Wilson proved to be the big hits of the tour," and that "the crowds also went wild whenever Newman and Wilson opened Count Basie's *One O'Clock Jump* or Joe Wilder was featured on Duke's *I Got It Bad And That Ain't Good*."[99] *Jet* also noted incidents of discrimination reported by the black musicians during the tour: "Featured singer Joya Sherrill and 40-year-old Negro trumpeter Joe Wilder . . . said they were shocked at the racial problems existing in Russia through which they toured. Wilder complained of taxi drivers unwilling to pick him up and Miss Sherrill spoke of various 'unofficial' acts of segregation she witnessed."[100]

After the tour ended, Wilder lodged a complaint against Goodman with the American Federation of Musicians (AFM) for the money that had been deducted for the alleged overweight baggage. As Bill Crow reported:

> The day before the hearing was scheduled, Joe got a call from a secretary at the AFM. She said, 'Mr. Goodman is willing to forget the whole thing.' Joe reminded her that he was the one making the complaint, and insisted on seeing it through as a matter of principle. At the hearing Joe produced a receipt from the post office in Seattle proving he had sent home everything over his allotted forty-four pounds when Jay [Feingold, Goodman's manager] had first complained that his baggage was overweight. Nothing had been weighed after Seattle. Goodman

and his staff had just assumed he was still overweight, and had used it as a pretext to harass him.[101]

The union reprimanded Wilder for refusing to play the last concert and did not require Goodman to repay the overweight baggage money he had wrongly deducted. But Wilder got some measure of satisfaction when, at the hearing, Goodman told him, "In all the years I've been a bandleader, nobody has ever brought me up on charges." Wilder responded, "Benny, that's because I don't depend on you for a living. I'm not afraid of you."

Apart from the unpleasantness with Goodman, Wilder enjoyed the trip and was overwhelmed by the warmth with which the musicians were greeted. "They really were very receptive, and the fans really respected our music." And he told *Life* magazine after participating in a jam session with local musicians in Tiflis, "I can't get over it, it's amazing, this common knowledge. I just can't get over it."[102]

Years later, Wilder found himself playing in the orchestra for an ABC show with Merv Griffin, on which Goodman was the featured artist. "When he saw me in the band, Benny sort of waved at me, but we kept our distance," Wilder recalled.

Miss America Pageant

After Wilder returned from the State Department tour, arranger-conductor Glenn Osser, with whom Wilder had worked frequently at ABC, invited him to play in the orchestra for the Miss America pageant in Atlantic City. "He told me they were getting a lot of contestants who came in with operatic arias, and the guys in the trumpet section weren't familiar with that kind of music," Wilder said. This began a yearly engagement that would last until 1987. Osser, who had served as musical director for the pageant since 1955, called on Wilder's symphonic experience as well as his solo abilities: "I had four trumpets, and if I had any kind of a solo, whether it was a swing or ballad thing, I always had a mike in front of Joe and told the engineer, 'If there's a trumpet solo, he's going to play it.'"[103] Although the pageant was hard work for the musicians, Wilder enjoyed the excitement of the competition and the challenge of a live television production:

> It used to be awfully hard in the beginning, because we used [to] arrive on Tuesday. On Tuesday evening we'd start rehearsing. We'd rehearse all night and get up early the next morning and rehearse, and do the first performance, the elimination performance, on Wednesday,

Thursday, Friday. Then Saturday we did the show live on the air. It was a lot of work.[104]

Over time, there was more prerecording, which made it easier for the orchestra. Eventually, as more contestants began to provide their own prerecorded accompaniment, the twenty-nine-piece orchestra became superfluous and was phased out.

During the early years with the pageant orchestra, Wilder's positive experience was marred by occasional but ultimately predictable incidents involving the production staff and the local police, who were not noted for their tolerance. During the 1960s, Atlantic City was the site of many protests against segregation and police brutality, and the pageant, itself, had come under attack. As Bryant Simon noted, "Like the city itself, the competition practiced racial exclusion. When the original organizers of the beauty contest wrote the bylaws for the competition, they barred African American women from participating. After World War II, they scratched this section from the rule book, but still no black woman made it to the finals in the years that followed."[105] And in 1987, "local civil rights activist Edgar Harris demanded that city leaders keep the contest out of the municipally owned Convention Hall, complaining, 'We should not be calling it the Miss America Pageant because it won't be that until we find some Negroes representing some of these United States.'"[106] Wilder too was troubled by the lack of black contestants: "It was discriminatory at the beginning, but then they got a producer from California, and he's the one that talked them into having some black contestants." When African Americans began to compete, Wilder noticed that they never approached him, even though he was the only black member of the orchestra. "But both the white and black contestants had an aloofness, almost as if they didn't want to be associated with people in the orchestra," he said. Nevertheless, Wilder was gratified to be present on September 17, 1983, when Vanessa Williams became the first African American to be named Miss America: "Even people who heretofore had almost resented the fact that they had begun having black contestants had a feeling like, I think something is going to happen here. It was . . . was just so heartwarming to see it."[107]

Family Life

One advantage of Wilder's decision to leave the road was the opportunity to spend more time with his family. Joe and Solveig's first daughter, Elin, was born in 1958, followed by Solveig (who shared her mother's name but became known as "Little Solveig") in 1960 and then Inga, the youngest. Growing up, the three girls were very close to their father, and they remain a close-knit family. Although none of them became musicians, all three were profoundly influenced by their father's background and career, as well as their mother's Swedish heritage.

Elin has had multiple careers in art and design, publishing, and radio. A graduate of New York's High School of Art and Design, in the late 1970s, she served as associate publisher of *Punk*, the underground music magazine. In the 1980s, she moved to NBC radio, working as an assistant to Don Imus, as well as with Howard Stern, and later helped shape the station's classic rock and talk radio formats. After the birth of her sons, Dylan and Samuel, influenced by her father's "obsession" with photography, she worked in the photo industry and has been active in community organizing and children's advocacy groups.

"Little Solveig" has amassed four master's degrees in fields ranging from community organizing to urban studies and American history. She has been a lifelong political activist, noting, "At five, I was already organizing and yelling about politics. Ironically, that came more from the people I met in Sweden than from Harlem."[108]

Inga did her undergraduate work at Upsala College, where she majored in German translation and multinational corporate studies. She is a graduate of Yale Law School and has her own practice specializing in corporate transactional law and intellectual property.

The sisters' lives were profoundly affected by their shared experiences growing up in a bicultural, biracial environment. "We grew up speaking Swedish at home and basically learned English from the TV and radio," Elin said. "When I was growing up, there weren't that many interracial marriages. If I saw another kid on the subway who looked like me, we would practically embrace!"[109] Being biracial also subjected the girls to bullying. "We would get beat up, not even knowing why," Inga recalled. "It's so different now, but then, nobody would even know about it."[110] Even in Sweden, Inga recalled being "ostracized by other children. I didn't understand it at the time. As a kid, you just know that people are being mean to you." On the other hand, Solveig said, "I love Harlem, but I preferred the small town in Sweden. Without that peaceful foundation of rural small-town life I would have snapped. It gave me the foundation I needed."

Despite the challenges, the sisters have positive memories of their bicultural upbringing. Inga observed:

It's been extremely rewarding. It gives you a much broader perspective that you would never have looking in from the outside at other people's

lives. I think that the fact that Barack Obama had a cross-cultural experience made him more acceptable to the American public; he knows
what the other side is like. It makes you more able to sympathize, em-
pathize, and understand other people.

When his daughters were growing up in the 1960s and 1970s, Joe was working long hours at ABC and doing freelance studio work; nevertheless, he tried
to take an active role in the girls' daily lives. "When we were in school, he
would be working at night, and when he came home, we were already in bed,
but every chance he had to take us to school in the morning he would," Elin
said. And when he couldn't see them in the morning, all three daughters recalled their father writing down some of his infamous puns and leaving them
on the table for the girls to read upon awakening. He also took his daughters to
work with him whenever possible. "He would take each one of us to a different
work event," Inga recalled. "It made us feel pretty special." Elin explained, "I
was 'the quiet one,' so he would take me to the studios because I could sit there
for two hours and not make a sound." Elin also remembered stopping by the
Dick Cavett Show "every day on my way home from school to hang out with
my dad and do my homework. [Bandleader] Bobby Rosengarden used to ask
me, 'Elin, you got any requests?' and I'd always ask for 'Shaft' which would
make my father angry because it wasn't a song he particularly liked to play!"

Although they met many musical celebrities while accompanying their father, the girls did not always fully appreciate the significance of these encounters. "I met Tony Bennett and Lena Horne, but a lot of the people I met I didn't
understand at the time who they were," Elin said. She remembered Harry
Belafonte attending her high school graduation: "It took place near Carnegie
Hall, and he happened to be in the area and stopped by." Solveig noted, "Just
walking with my father on the street, so many people would stop him." Henny
Youngman made a strong impression on the youngster: "He talked nonstop
and just threw out those one-liners. I was in awe of these people!" Meeting
Dizzy Gillespie was a memorable event for Solveig and Elin. "He was wearing
a dashiki, which was pretty cutting edge at the time. He was absolutely charming," said Elin.

But Wilder's daughters were even more impressed when they learned of
his associations with some of the pop stars more in tune with their own generation. Inga recalled:

When we were starting to get excited about rock music, Dad would
say, "Well, I did a recording with a big rock group," but he wouldn't
tell us who they were, so we would check the mail for the checks for

the jobs. They would have the band's logo on the outside, so we would find out that way. We also got to go to the dress rehearsal of Howard Cosell's variety show. My best friend and I were very excited because we got to see the Bay City Rollers perform before everybody else in America! Then we began to think Dad was important!

Elin was similarly impressed when she met actor Larry Storch with her father: "I was a huge fan of *F Troop,* so that was one of the few times I could put into perspective one of these encounters with people my father knew."

Joe's popularity in the music and entertainment industry did have some disadvantages from his daughters' perspective, however. "With my dad, we never made it to a movie on time," said Elin. "Dad was 'Mr. Social.' You could not get down a city block without him running into somebody he knew. In those days, they would run the movie all day, so we always came in half an hour late and then stayed for the beginning. You can imagine coming into *Lawrence of Arabia* a third of the way through and not knowing what the hell was going on!"

Although he never pushed his daughters to go into music, they do recall that he taught them to sing in three-part harmony. "We ran with it, and probably much to my parents' dismay, we would constantly be singing Andrews Sisters tunes in the back of the car," Inga said. But much of what they learned from their father came from simply being around him and seeing how he conducted himself. Elin noted, "Whenever we would pass musicians on the street with their hats on the ground playing for money, my father always gave them something. He would tell us how fortunate he was to be working at something he loved and point out how he had an obligation to help out musicians who weren't working steadily." Solveig summed up her father's influence in this way:

He had a profound impact on everything I say and do. Just having my father there and knowing he was so prominent [in the music business] and being exposed to all these people he knew gave me a different take on things as far as black people in the arts is concerned. There were no lectures, like "Let's sit down and talk about racism," but passing remarks he or his friends would make stuck with me.

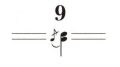

A Dream Realized

Return to Classical Music (1964–1974)

J oe Wilder's original musical training had been almost exclusively classical, and as we have seen, during his early years in Philadelphia, he was far more inspired by Herbert Clarke and Del Staigers (through his teacher Frederick D. Griffin) than by Louis Armstrong. His brief stay at Mastbaum was also devoted to classical training. His first experiences in playing jazz or dance music occurred when he tagged along on his father's gigs, and later, as he progressed, playing in many local dance bands in Philadelphia. Wilder readily admits that in those early years, he was in demand for his sight-reading and lead trumpet skills and not for his improvisational ability, which would develop later. As with many teenagers, he did not formulate a "career plan" but took what playing opportunities came along to help support his family. Of his

---

Members of the Symphony of the New World, ca. 1968.
From left to right: Leonard Goines (trumpet), unknown, Paul Ingraham (French horn),
Jack Holland (trumpet), Joe Wilder, unknown. *(Photo by Joe Wilder.)*

classical studies at Mastbaum, Wilder recalled, "That's all I knew. People say that I knew I couldn't make a living as a classical player. I wasn't even thinking about making a living. I was just being a trumpet player with whatever resources were available to me. I was just trying to learn to play the trumpet as well as I could."

At some point, however, probably toward the end of his year at Mastbaum, the youngster began to come to grips with the realities of the barriers he faced: "I realized pretty early on that as a black musician, I wasn't going to get an opportunity to do much classical playing." Wilder pointed out other factors preventing African American children from receiving classical training: "One reason why there were so few black string players or bassoonists or oboe players was because their parents couldn't afford to pay thousands of dollars for an instrument during the Depression." Those who persevered faced nearly insurmountable obstacles: "My father had friends who were fine [classical] players—they played violin and viola—and one of the musicians auditioned for the Philadelphia Orchestra and was told that he played exceptionally well, but [they said], 'Don't call us, we'll call you.' Philadelphia was bountiful with [African American] players like that, but they never got an opportunity, and of course, from those experiences, my father let me know that there was no future in that [classical music] for me." So in 1939, the seventeen-year-old left Mastbaum after his freshman year, and after a period working with local bands in Philadelphia, in 1941, he joined Les Hite's orchestra, beginning a big-band odyssey that would last a decade.

Drummer and arranger Shep Shepherd, with whom Wilder had grown up in Philadelphia and who preceded him at Mastbaum, also aspired to a classical career but eventually shifted course:

> Unbeknownst to me, my teacher, Mr. Bill Cole, was actually grooming me for the Philadelphia Orchestra. The things he was teaching me, such as the great staff, I couldn't understand what all that had to do with drumming. But I paid attention, and by the time he got around to teaching me bells and marimba and things like that, even though I couldn't afford to buy the instruments at the time, he gave me a basic understanding of them. And since I came from a family that was raised in the West Indies on solfège [a method of sight-reading], that gave me a leg up. Mr. Cole died early—while I was going to Mastbaum, and Ross Wyre introduced me to Benjamin Podemski, the chief percussionist of the Philadelphia Orchestra. I took snare drum and specialized on tympani with him. But I could see the writing on the wall—I was not ignorant of it [discrimination in symphony orchestras], and

when I got to hear Ellington, Basie, and Lunceford, I started to change my mind. So when Benny Carter opened me up to his knowledge and talent, I saw many more possibilities and didn't even think about the Philadelphia Orchestra any more. I wanted to be like Benny Carter![1]

In contrast, some of the musicians Wilder would later encounter during his tenure with the integrated Symphony of the New World, governed either by choice of instrument or by artistic preference, did not seek refuge in the world of jazz or dance music but steadfastly pursued their dreams of classical careers. Their reminiscences about their educations and early experiences as African Americans aspiring to classical careers follow.

ALFRED BROWN (VIOLA)

I went to [the High School of] Music and Art [in New York City], and also I got a couple of scholarships, so I was able to study with some pretty good teachers. I went to the Eastman School, but I was not very happy. I'd had a few incidents that turned me against the school. I had seen a group of musicians from Curtis [Institute in Philadelphia]. When I heard the students from Curtis, I was overwhelmed. I thought they were magnificent players. I had wanted to go there for a long time, but that just did it for me. So I got in touch with Curtis, and I went down and auditioned. William Primrose [1904–1982], my teacher-to-be, was away on tour, so I auditioned for his assistant, Karen Tuttle [1920–2010]. I studied with him and his assistant. I never thought it would be possible, but it happened. That was a fabulous experience. I wasn't the first [black student] at Curtis, but there were none when I arrived there except for singers. Now there are quite a few. I never played in the philharmonic or other orchestras, and I ended up playing wherever there was work—freelancing. I ended up on staff at ABC; Joe Wilder was on staff there already. I think that's where I first met Joe.[2]

HAROLD JONES (FLUTE)

I was drawn to classical music. I'm from the Chicago ghetto, and the family who lived above us was outstanding in a way because the father had a steady job. The two sons and the cousin studied music with a violinist down the block, and since they were my best friends, I thought I'd do the same. When I switched from violin to flute, I remember my violin teacher telling me, "Oh, flute's a higher-class instrument." I was in the DuSable High School band. Walter Dyett was the director, and he was very strong. You pursued what you wanted to do, and I wanted to be a flute player. I played in the concert band, and I knew that I didn't see any [black classical musicians], except James Mack, who went to Roosevelt College in Chicago. He played beautiful flute, and my teacher, David

Underwood, was also a black man. They played nothing but classical music. So my inspiration and aspiration was classical right from the get-go, so to speak. All my friends and colleagues in high school were jazz persons. My family was very religious Baptists, so playing jazz was not accepted. I went to the Sherwood Music School for a couple of years, and then there was an audition for the Civic Orchestra. I took it, and I got in and was there for two or three years. When my teacher, Lois Baker, left Chicago for New York, I said I'm going to go also. I took the audition for Juilliard, and my new life began. I was a scholarship student and stayed there four years.[3]

KERMIT MOORE (CELLO)

From the very beginning, it was my dream to become a classical musician. When I was five years old, my mother began to teach me piano. I was the third child, so I was following in the footsteps of my brother and my sister. They had been studying with my mother also. The paucity of black people [in orchestras] didn't occur to me very much; neither did it seem to me that that was going to be an obstacle. And it wasn't. When I started studying as a teenager in New York, I played with the philharmonic as a guest musician. I traveled with them as a guest. So I never worried about the obstacles. I bumped into them and I fought them, but it never occurred to me, "Oh, that's not going to work." It did work. I became first cellist at the Hartford Symphony, and then I became a faculty member at the University of Hartford, and I conducted them a few times as well. So it didn't occur to me until I really grew up that this is a bad world and that there are people whose profession it is just to be obstinate about race—and that annoyed me very much.[4]

WILMER WISE (TRUMPET)

There are many parallels between Wilder and Wilmer Wise, a trumpeter of a younger generation (born in 1936). Wise, a native Philadelphian, has played jazz but was drawn to classical music from an early age.

I grew up in a neighborhood that was like a who's who of jazz, but I didn't go in that direction. I was the "long-hair" player of that time. My junior high school classmates were Bobby Timmons, Tootie Heath, Ted Curson. We had a band that played bebop. When I was about fifteen or sixteen, I met Joe's dad, Curtis Sr., at the Musicians Union, where we used to practice. Joe's father came into the room one day and said, "Oh, you kids sound good! Do you know my son?" I didn't know Joe. I think at that point, Joe had just gotten into the studios in New York City—this was the mid-1950s. When I was a kid, I was told that black people couldn't play white classical music, by, of all people, a fellow who

*was one of the directors at Mastbaum, the school in Philadelphia that Joe at-
tended. He grabbed my lip and said it was too thick! And my teacher said, "Oh,
really?" and asked me to play a two-and-a-half octave scale from the lowest note
of the trumpet to a note well above high C, which I did. I was about ten at the
time. I had played through the Arban book, the trumpeter's bible. I was a stubborn little kid. Having no role models, I was just doing it pretty much on my
own. And then I discovered Mr. Wilder. It was a wonderful thing.*

*[When I was coming up,] I don't think there was a black player in any sym-
phony orchestra in America. I graduated high school in 1955, and I think the
first black player in any major orchestra was in 1957. I was one of the first when
I joined the Baltimore Symphony on 1965. Before that, I had played with the
Philadelphia Orchestra as a soloist in 1963, which was the first time a black
player—certainly a black trumpet player—had performed with the Philadelphia Orchestra. I just wanted to be the very best trumpeter I could be, and I had
been lucky enough to study with several members of the Philadelphia Orchestra,
which I guess wasn't viable when Joe was a kid.*[5]

During his decade-long peregrination through the big bands in the 1940s
and early 1950s, Wilder never abandoned his dream of playing classical music. When he settled in New York and began to make inroads in the studios
and the Broadway orchestras, the dream became a reality. As we have seen,
Wilder was able to enroll at the Manhattan School of Music, hoping to have
the chance to play more classical music, in addition to furthering his overall
musical skills. And as a staff musician at ABC, Wilder had the opportunity
to play regularly in a number of classical settings, notably with the ABC Symphony on the *Voice of Firestone* and other programs and as a member of the
ABC Brass Quintet.

African Americans in Symphony Orchestras:
The Beginnings of Change

In the opening chapter of her definitive *Black Women in American Bands
and Orchestras*, D. Antoinette Handy presents a historical overview of African Americans in classical orchestras. She notes that "the black presence in
the business of 'elite art' instrumental ensemble music dates back to the early
1800s," when "four 'colored' musicians were observed in an otherwise all-
white orchestra playing in Philadelphia in 1826."[6] There were other isolated
instances of integrated orchestras, including the 1872 Peace Jubilee Orchestra
in Boston, which had two black violinists who were "subjected to severe musical tests prior to their acceptance."[7]

The nineteenth century saw the birth of a long tradition of black classical orchestras, beginning with the Société Philharmonique in New Orleans, which flourished from as early as the 1840s. In his comprehensive program notes for a 2011 re-creation concert of the Société, Alfred E. Lemmon cites *Music and Some Highly Musical People*, the pioneering 1878 survey of African American musicians, by James M. Trotter, an amateur historian born into slavery, as "the first book devoted solely to American musicians." Trotter noted that, although the Société Philharmonique was made up of black musicians, "liberal-minded native and foreign gentlemen of the other race were always glad to come and play with them."[8]

A similar organization was founded in New York in 1876, and black orchestras and musical societies followed around the turn of the century in Washington, DC, and Philadelphia; in Chicago and Baltimore in the 1920s; and in Pittsburgh and St. Louis in the 1930s.[9] In the 1940s, black conductors Dean Dixon and Everett Lee founded orchestras in New York, and the same period saw the rise of Chicago ensembles under the leadership of Charles A. Elgar, Owen Lawson, and E. J. Robinson.[10]

There was no dearth of qualified African American musicians to fill the chairs in these orchestras. Despite the popularity of jazz, swing, and its derivatives, musical training at most black institutions of higher learning was strictly classical; jazz or dance music was not deemed an acceptable area of study. There are many testimonials by aspiring jazz and even gospel artists to the fact that, as late as the 1960s, their music was banned from the practice rooms of prestigious black institutions.[11] In February 1968, students staged a protest at Howard University, accusing the institution of "desperately trying to remain an imitation white school turning out imitation white people."[12] A month later, they closed the university down, protesting the absence of African American history and culture in the curriculum.[13]

Furthermore, in many black homes—especially deeply religious ones— jazz was often viewed as "the devil's music," and youngsters were discouraged from playing or listening to it. Consequently, despite the allure of jazz and popular music, many African American youngsters were traditionally channeled into formal classical study.

By the late 1950s, as the civil rights movement was moving into a much more activist phase, new efforts were launched to address the nearly total segregation among the nation's symphony orchestras. In 1956, *New York Times* music critic Howard Taubman wrote an article titled "An Even Break," calling attention to discrimination in the classical world. Taubman, one of the few classical critics with an appreciation for jazz and the cultural contributions of African Americans, made the case for fair treatment of black musicians, mentioning the background of three who had contacted him seeking a voice: timpanist Elayne Jones, oboist Harry Smyles, and violist Alfred Brown, all of whom would play central roles in the formation of the groundbreaking integrated Symphony of the New World six years later. "Music, which knows no barriers of language, should lead the way in striking down those based on color," Taubman concluded.[14]

In 1957, *Life* magazine ran an extensive illustrated essay on de facto segregation in the North, a follow-up to a similar piece on the South, which had appeared the year before. The article looked at a wide range of professions and the barriers still faced by African Americans despite what the legislative progress had achieved. "From artists to day laborers, Negroes in the North find themselves excluded from work which white men may do," *Life* declared.[15] In a brief section on discrimination in music, the article profiled African American oboist Harry Smyles, a friend of Joe Wilder's who would later become a founding member and the personnel manager of the Symphony of the New World. *Life* called Smyles "one of the best classical oboists in the country," and quoted the late Serge Koussevitzky, longtime conductor of the Boston Symphony, who wrote that Smyles was "perfectly qualified to take a position in any orchestral organization in America."[16] *Life* continued, "Yet Smyles has never found a symphony that would hire him. He [Smyles] has strongly and vocally attacked such exclusion and has in turn been accused of left-wing activity. This is not what keeps him out. No top American symphony orchestra employs any Negro instrumentalist."[17] The article also mentioned the black conductor Dean Dixon, who was unable to find a permanent position in the United States and eventually moved to Sweden, where he became conductor of the Gothenburg Symphony. Such a direct and unequivocal indictment in the nation's premier general-interest magazine undoubtedly helped bring wider attention to the problem of discrimination in the classical world.

A year later, in May 1958, the Urban League of Greater New York published its report *Job Status of the Negro Professional Musician in the New York Metropolitan Area*, the findings of which have been cited with regard to the Broadway and network staff orchestras. In its survey of the five major classical orchestras in New York, the Urban League found:

1. The Philharmonic Symphony Society of New York [New York Philharmonic] has never employed a Negro professional musician.

2. The Metropolitan Opera Orchestra has never employed a Negro professional musician.

3. The Little Orchestra Society employed a Negro woman (violinist) of extreme fair complexion during the 1955–56–57 season.

4. The City Center New York Ballet Orchestra and the City Center New York Opera Orchestra has only employed one Negro musician [Elayne Jones] in its entire history. The musician, a Negro woman tympanist was engaged during the 1949 season.

5. The Symphony of the Air engaged three Negro musicians during the 1956 season for one concert. This was accomplished by a number of newspaper articles written by Howard Taubman, New York Times music critic which pointed out the availability of competent Negro musicians in New York.[18]

The report briefly addressed the hiring process in an orchestra: "Generally speaking, musical ability and the policy of the Board of Directors are major factors involved in the employment of musicians. These considerations vary with each musical organization especially when employment involves women, controversial figures and Negroes."[19] (This is one of very few occasions when the issue of discrimination against women was raised in contemporaneous discussions of discrimination in the music industry.) The report identified the major decision makers in hiring: (1) board of directors, (2) conductor, (3) personnel manager (or contractor), and (4) first chair player.[20] It also pointed out that notice of auditions was primarily by word of mouth and rarely by public announcement, which presented another obstacle for prospective minority candidates.

There were some positive aspects to the Urban League's survey, such as a listing of some eight symphony orchestras in which African American musicians were currently playing or had played. These included the Boston Symphony (Ortiz Walton, bass), the Cleveland Orchestra (Donald White, cello), and the Los Angeles Philharmonic (Henry Lewis, bass).[21]

The Urban League also criticized New York's Local 802 for its "hands off" policy in the breaking down of music industry racial barriers. While the Musicians Union itself was fully integrated, with African Americans making up one-sixth of its more than thirty thousand members, the report noted that the union should incorporate a nondiscrimination clause in its standard contracts with employers, adding "the act of omission is as significant and harmful as an act of commission."[22] The report concluded, "Competent, qualified Negro professionals have had to contend hopelessly with an iron curtain of discrimination, barring them from any opportunity to build a career in their chosen field. This is true in every branch of the music industry—orchestral musicians, conductors, composers, arrangers, contractors, managers, etc."[23]

To answer those who questioned the availability of African American musicians qualified to play in symphony orchestras, the report included an appendix of ten short biographies—musicians with extensive classical training and experience, ranging in age from nineteen to forty-four. In addition to Joe Wilder, those listed are Harry Smyles (oboe), Antoinette Handy (flute), Alfred Brown (viola), Harold Jones (flute), Richard Davis (bass), Frank Fields (composer, conductor, pianist), Julius Watkins (French horn), Sanford Allen (violin), and Warren Petty (double bass). Wilder is described as "an example of a trained classical musician who found it necessary to alter his symphonic sights in order to make a living," adding, "Mr. Wilder has the reputation of being one of the best trumpeters in the country today."[24]

In November 1958, five months after the Urban League issued its report, the *New York Times* ran an article on the charges of discrimination leveled by the Urban League against the New York musical establishment that included responses from representatives of the orchestras and networks named. A spokesman for the New York Philharmonic asserted that it had notified Local 802 of any vacancies, but "in the last ten years, not one Negro has shown up to audition."[25] The spokesman also stated that the orchestra's personnel manager, Peter De Angelis, had asked the Urban League for the names of "any qualified Negroes." De Angelis claimed that during the previous summer, they did have a trumpet vacancy and he had contacted Wilder, who was apparently on the list, "but he was too busy each time." In response, Wilder explained to the reporter that he "vaguely recalled a summer call from De Angelis, but not for the Philharmonic."[26] According to the minutes of its November 24 meeting, the board of directors of the philharmonic heard a brief report from Managing Director Bruno Zirato on the Urban League charges. Zirato reiterated that "the claim that the New York Philharmonic has been discriminatory is not based in fact," again noting that orchestra vacancies were "posted with the local of the Musicians' Union," and that "in the past ten years not one Negro has showed up for a Philharmonic audition."[27] The minutes of the meeting also noted that the Urban League had recently informed personnel manager Peter De Angelis of potential black candidates for the philharmonic. Finally, concerning the attempt to hire Wilder, the minutes concluded somewhat snidely, "Mr. De Angelis, in engaging extra players for the Orchestra, has made an effort to engage a trumpeter, Joe Wilder, who is presumably qualified, but apparently Mr. Wilder's schedule of activities has been too crowded for him to fit in the Philharmonic."[28]

Years later Wilder explained that De Angelis called him several times for a long-running series of concerts at Lewisohn Stadium, which involved musicians from the philharmonic but not the New York Philharmonic itself. (Programs from this period bear out Wilder's contention, listing the orchestra as the "Stadium Concerts Symphony Orchestra" and later the "Stadium

Symphony Orchestra.") "Every time he called, it was for a Saturday rehearsal and a Sunday concert," Wilder said. "I was on staff at ABC, and that's when we did *Voice of Firestone* or *Music for a Summer Night*, so there was no way I could do it. But he was correct in saying he had called me." Wilder also suggested that, since De Angelis knew he was never available for those time slots, he may have continued to call him simply to be able to report that the philharmonic had attempted to hire an African American musician but was turned down each time. Wilder would later repeat this charge when he appeared as a witness in a highly publicized 1969 New York Commission on Human Rights case against the philharmonic.

By 1964, the time was ripe for the birth of a new orchestra that would enable Joe Wilder and many other African Americans with classical aspirations to realize their dreams.

The Symphony of the New World

The Symphony of the New World was the brainchild of conductor Benjamin Steinberg, who had long championed the cause of integration in symphony orchestras and for decades had tried to open doors for minority musicians and conductors. As early as 1940, Steinberg, who once played first violin with Arturo Toscanini's NBC Symphony, had attempted to form an orchestra with noted African American conductors Dean Dixon and Everett Lee, both of whom felt it necessary to move to Europe to pursue their careers.[29] Dixon had the distinction of being the first African American to conduct the New York Philharmonic, when in August 1941 at age twenty-six, he led the orchestra at a concert at Lewisohn Stadium. In its review, the *New York Times* noted that Dixon "made an excellent impression," and that "the 5,600 members of the audience recalled him twice before the intermission and four times at the end of the concert," adding that the orchestra members "joined with the audience in applauding him."[30]

By 1964, the idealistic Steinberg felt the time was right, and in May of that year, a committee was formed to establish a new, fully integrated orchestra. The original committee consisted of Steinberg and thirteen prominent musicians, twelve of whom were African American, including Joe Wilder.[31] Flutist Harold Jones recalled the enthusiasm of the early meetings: "Ben [Steinberg] had his proposal of what he wanted to do—to get us together to make sure that an integrated orchestra could happen and that there were black talents out there that could do it. Emotions were very high. When you had a situation where you weren't given the opportunity to play and to find someone who wanted to do this, to get the group going, that's why everyone was so 'up.'"[32]

Cellist Kermit Moore remembered Wilder's participation at the initial meetings: "Joe certainly spoke up, but he was never pushy and was always a gentleman. But he was never shy about giving his opinion."[33] Early on, Wilder was named principal trumpet and seemed to be treated as something of an elder statesman by other orchestra members, although he was only forty-two when the orchestra was formed. "His leadership came through in the way he played," said Harold Jones. "He was admired and looked up to. He was very outspoken in the way he thought things should be and about blacks in orchestras like the philharmonic. He was one of those people who gave—if you didn't have, he would assist. If you didn't know, he would tell you."[34]

Steinberg's appointment as musical director and principal conductor of the new orchestra seemed natural, given the fact that it was his idea, and there is no indication that there was any initial objection to having a white conductor. Furthermore, Steinberg regularly brought in prominent African American guest conductors, including Everett Lee and James DePriest. But the seeds of discontent were sown at those early meetings, which would lead to a rift a few years later that threatened to tear the orchestra apart.

From the beginning, there seemed to be a divergence of opinion as to the very purpose of the new orchestra. Was it to be a professional orchestra in its own right on a par with other major symphonies or was it to function as a training ground for minority musicians to gain experience and eventually move on to other orchestras? "We all saw something a little bit different," Kermit Moore recalled. "We never all saw eye to eye. One [fundamental] question was whether the orchestra should be an established symphony or a feeding vehicle for other orchestras. That was the main issue."[35] If the early press releases and articles about the Symphony of the New World are any indication, this issue was never resolved.[36]

In addition to providing a classical outlet for minority musicians, a common goal from the beginning was the desire to include women in the new enterprise. Kermit Moore recalled, "That was very much a goal. There wasn't one woman in the New York Philharmonic at the time—even the harpist was a man. Lucille Dixon and Elayne Jones [members of the original Symphony of the New World committee] didn't have to tell us that we were going to involve as many women as possible."[37] The inclusion of a significant number of women musicians was an important achievement that was often eclipsed by the attention accorded the groundbreaking interracial aspect of the orchestra.

Steinberg undertook the daunting task of finding financial support, and a fund-raising campaign was begun, probably in late 1964. A fund-raising mailer from that time lists many luminaries as "Sponsors from the Art World," including Leonard Bernstein, Theodore Bikel, Aaron Copland, Duke

Ellington, Ruby Dee, Langston Hughes, and Zero Mostel. (Mostel conducted the orchestra in 1969 for a benefit concert celebrating its fourth anniversary; Marian Anderson was mistress of ceremonies.) The elaborate mailer contained biographies of the members of the founding committee. It is interesting to note that the short paragraph on Joe Wilder omits any reference to his jazz career. For example, it states that in 1962, Wilder "toured the Soviet Union for the United States State Department" but fails to mention that the tour was with Benny Goodman's orchestra.

Steinberg had many connections and enjoyed some success through the years in obtaining grants from the Ford Foundation, the Martha Baird Rockefeller Fund, the National Endowment for the Arts, Exxon, and other organizations and patrons of the arts. One of those who wrote on his behalf to the Rockefeller Fund was Leonard Bernstein, music director of the New York Philharmonic. After calling Steinberg "extremely able and gifted," Bernstein endorsed the basic concept of the new orchestra:

> Most important of all, of course, is the sociological impetus behind the project—a truly integrated symphony orchestra. The success of this project will certainly stimulate more of the same, and may provide us with our first big step out of the unfair and illogical situation in which we now find ourselves with the Negro musician.[38]

Only four years later, Bernstein and the rest of the New York Philharmonic leadership would become the target of a bitter lawsuit charging discriminatory hiring practices on the part of the orchestra.

Finally, on May 6, 1965, a pioneering integrated Symphony of the New World took to the stage of Carnegie Hall for its premiere concert. In his review for the *New York Times*, Howard Klein described the orchestra as being made up of "about 52 white musicians, 36 Negroes and 7 Orientals," adding, "What makes it even more integrated is its feminine complement of 30."[39] Klein's assessment of the actual performance was mixed: "The group played well, following the economical but clear beating of its conductor, Benjamin Steinberg, with energetic playing. But the sound was crude, balances were off, and the level was mezzoforte in the softest passages and noisy in the loudest."[40] Klein found the "high point" to be the appearance of Philippine soprano Evelyn Mandac and described the concert's finale, Stravinsky's *Petrushka*, as "serviceable."[41] Joe Wilder played the famous trumpet solo in the "Dance of the Ballerina" segment of the work. Although not mentioned in the review, Wilder's electric performance is still remembered by his fellow musicians. Flutist Harold Jones explained, "You never heard anything like it! There were some very seasoned players behind me; to hear what came out of Joe was a magical moment. One player said, 'My God, Heifetz couldn't have played it any better on the fiddle!' It was one of those moments in life—it was just incredible."[42] And Wilmer Wise, Wilder's colleague in the trumpet section that night, simply said, "Joe played the hell out of it!"[43]

The *Times* review ended on an encouraging note: "Experience and rehearsal will tighten the ensemble, and when the members learn to listen to one another the balances will improve. If it can survive its initial struggle, the city may have an important and valuable new orchestra."[44] For many members of the audience and for the musicians themselves, the significance of the event transcended the performance. Some forty-five years later, trumpeter Wilmer Wise still remembered the emotion that swept through the hall that evening: "Some people were crying because it was something we had dreamt about, and it had finally come to fruition."[45]

One of the original goals of the symphony was "to give concerts of the highest artistic and professional standards in communities of low-income, such as Bedford-Stuyvesant and [the] Harlem areas of New York City,"[46] and three days after its inaugural concert, the orchestra repeated its program at the High School of Music and Art in Harlem. Over the next decade, the symphony continued its work in the community, sending numerous ensembles throughout the Metropolitan area for performances and workshops.

After the initial Carnegie Hall concert, the symphony moved to Philharmonic Hall at Lincoln Center, where on May 8, 1966, it celebrated its first anniversary. A limited-edition LP of the concert lists the "Mayor and Mrs. John V. Lindsay" as honorary patrons. The orchestra had clearly improved over the year, with *New York Times* critic Allen Hughes calling it "a very capable music ensemble," adding, "It's playing under the direction of its founder-conductor, Benjamin Steinberg, was precise, of good sonority and flexible in expression."[47] In addition to performing the standard classical repertory, Steinberg featured works by noted African American composers, including Hale Smith's *Contours* in 1966 (with Everett Lee as guest conductor) and Smith's *Music for Harp and Orchestra*, commissioned by the Symphony of the New World in 1967. A year later, the symphony performed another commissioned work, *Address for Orchestra*, by prominent African American composer George Walker. The orchestra also collaborated in performances with such jazz notables as John Lewis and the Modern Jazz Quartet (1968) and Duke Ellington and his orchestra (1973).

Joan Peyser, writing in the *New York Times*, noted the interracial makeup of the Philharmonic Hall audience, estimated (by Steinberg) at 60 percent African American for the October 22, 1967, concert: "The first floor of

Philharmonic Hall appeared to be dominated by white people while Negroes filled the less expensive seats in the balcony." Peyser contrasted the demeanor of the Symphony of the New World audience with that of the hall's regular clientele: "All who came to Philharmonic Hall—even those with children and infants—responded enthusiastically and behaved impeccably." She added that the audience remained for the entire performance, "in contrast to the early mass exodus of white matrons every Friday afternoon, when the New York Philharmonic subscription audience rushes for taxi cabs and suburban trains while the concert is still in progress."[48]

Although the orchestra was making progress artistically and garnered much positive press attention, it was never able to build the financial base to fund a sufficient number of performances per season to offer the type of full-time employment and benefits that the New York Philharmonic and other top-rank orchestras provided their members. Moreover, toward the end of the 1960s, internal disagreements began to surface that would eventually threaten the orchestra's very existence. Some of the points of contention revolved around the purpose and goals of the orchestra, issues that had never really been resolved during its founding. Once again, the question of whether the orchestra was to serve primarily a training ground for other professional symphonies or compete on their level was central. Several members grew increasingly disturbed by some interviews in which Benjamin Steinberg seemed to espouse the former position. They found one article, a 1967 *New York Post* piece titled "Negro Minor League of Note," particularly offensive. It claimed that Steinberg "is the last maestro to complain that his Symphony of the New World is constantly being raided by the major symphonies" and that the "prime purpose of his [Steinberg's] highly-rated and sprightly orchestra is to give Negro classical musicians the experience they need to play in the symphonic big leagues."[49] Around the same time, Steinberg told *Newsweek*, "For the time being, the chief purpose of the Symphony of the New World is to be a farm team."[50] Cellist Kermit Moore was one of those who objected to these minor league baseball analogies: "Well, that wasn't the idea. The New York Philharmonic isn't a fine feeding device; it's an established orchestra. Some of us felt insulted."[51] Nevertheless, Steinberg continued to enjoy support both within and outside the orchestra. For example, violinist Sanford Allen, the first African American member of the New York Philharmonic, praised Steinberg's efforts "to create an atmosphere of receptivity to any and all qualified players."[52]

Over the following two or three years, a faction of the orchestra grew increasingly dissatisfied with other aspects of Steinberg's conduct as music director, and by 1971, several founding members, including Kermit Moore,

Lucille Dixon, and Harry Smyles, began a serious effort to remove him. The disgruntled musicians formed a committee and drew up list of grievances. They accused Steinberg of "blatant disregard" and "open contempt" in his treatment of "both the musicians and the premises which were the basis for the creation of the Symphony." Other allegations included the mishandling of funds, an "inability to rehearse [the orchestra] to achieve a professional standard performance," and nepotism in hiring. The dissidents concluded by once again raising the old "minor league" issue: "In addition Ben Steinberg has attempted to remake the image of the Symphony of the New World into a training orchestra."[53]

Despite Steinberg's frequent use of black guest conductors and the orchestra's regular performances of the works of black composers, there was an underlying if not explicitly articulated feeling that the conductor of the Symphony of the New World should be an African American. By the late 1960s and early 1970s, the civil rights struggle had turned in a more militant direction, and the prevailing calls for "black power" undoubtedly influenced the attitudes of some of the orchestra members. Kermit Moore, one of the members of the committee seeking Steinberg's ouster, denied that the color of the conductor was at issue: "If somebody felt that way, I didn't hear it. If I had heard it, I'd have been furious."[54]

The situation erupted on October 5, 1971, when a list of demands was presented to Steinberg at the orchestra's rehearsal for its October 10 concert. The rehearsal went on, and the orchestra manager, Benjamin Patterson, carried out negotiations with the dissidents over the next few days. On the following Sunday, however, just before the concert was scheduled to begin, several members refused to play unless certain demands were met, among them the reinstatement of Kermit Moore as principal cellist. Apparently, Moore had agreed to allow a young black cellist, Ronald Lipscomb, to gain experience as first chair—a common symphony practice. Other first chair players had acquiesced to these requests, including the well-known white bassist Homer Mensch, who moved to second chair behind the black bassist Arthur Davis. In the case of Moore and Lipscomb, however, race would not appear to be an issue, since both Moore and his younger replacement were African American.[55] So that the concert might proceed, Steinberg agreed to resign, and the performance continued under his baton. *New York Times* critic Donal Henahan did not mention the preconcert drama but observed, ironically, that the orchestra "seems to get blacker and better each year. In past seasons, about one-third of the members were black; on this occasion, the proportion appeared to have risen considerably, to about half."[56] Amazingly, the performance seemed unaffected by the near-mutiny that had preceded it. As Henahan wrote, "In spite of a few instrumental flaws, notably in the woodwinds, the level of performance stayed quite high."[57]

After Steinberg's resignation, a struggle ensued over what constituted the legitimate leadership of the symphony. On October 18, 1971, symphony board president John Hammond, the Columbia Records executive and ardent talent scout, called a special meeting of the board. Representatives of the dissident musicians' committee, accompanied by their attorney, reiterated their grievances and called for a new board and a new conductor. Following the meeting, the committee contacted the symphony's funding sources and requested that future payments be channeled through them. As a result, funding was held up pending a resolution of the dispute. In a letter to subscribers dated February 1, 1972, Steinberg announced the cancellation of the rest of the 1971–72 season "due to an internal controversy as well as unforeseen financial difficulties." He then appealed to subscribers to consider designating their payments for tickets to the three canceled concerts as a contribution to the symphony.[58]

Meanwhile, the dissident musicians decided to proceed on their own with a scheduled February 27 concert, using the Symphony of the New World name. In his mostly negative review in the *New York Times*, Donal Henahan noted that the orchestra had been "recently shaken by an internal power dispute," and found its performance under conductor Denis Montague de Coteau underrehearsed, "possibly owing in part to its internal difficulties." He added, "As its new leaders undoubtedly realize, the Symphony of the New World is in the position now of having to make decisions that will determine its life or death." In a final swipe at the guest conductor, Henahan concluded, "There are a number of extraordinary conductors around, many of them black, and only by resolutely avoiding the ordinary ones will the orchestra fulfill its real potential."[59]

Henahan addressed the dissension within the symphony again a year later, stating, "Although the dispute was not entirely a black-and-white issue, a strong movement did develop among the younger and more militant blacks to force the white players and board members to resign."[60] This statement fundamentally misrepresented the dissidents' position, as there is no evidence that they ever wanted to get rid of the white members of the orchestra—only Steinberg—and, they would claim, that was not racially motivated. Orchestra personnel manager Harry Smyles responded in a letter to the *Times*: "The fight was between the majority of the orchestra members, white and black, against the former music director and his regime. . . . The present orchestra and board of directors are as integrated as ever."[61]

It is not clear whether a majority of the orchestra or even a majority of its black members supported the effort to replace Steinberg. Founding member and violist Alfred Brown recalled, "There were some people—not the majority—who had a problem with him. Some of them felt the conductor should be black. I was not one of them. I liked him very much. He was very idealistic."[62] Brown remembered an early encounter with Steinberg, when the violist was a student at the Curtis Institute: "He came to conduct a show, and he put me in the orchestra, which had never been done before, and he was very encouraging to me."[63]

Joe Wilder remained a staunch supporter of the beleaguered conductor. Although he had his own misgivings about the direction of the symphony, he tried to resolve them by appealing directly to Steinberg: "He had us playing repertoire that was more advanced than the orchestra could handle because it hadn't played together that long. I tried to tell him to play some of the less difficult things until we became accustomed to playing together. But he was stubborn. We got through them, but they could have been at a higher level if we had played together longer. In a way, Benny [Steinberg] was his own worst enemy. He thought he was as good a conductor as Bernstein, and because it was his orchestra, it could do anything any other orchestra could do." Wilder also noted that there were some ego problems, and some musicians—black and white—who were habitually late for rehearsals: "I told Benny, 'These prima donnas are acting like they're doing you a favor coming to rehearsals.' Benny was a little timid about doing anything about it because he didn't want to be accused of being antiblack." Wilder left the orchestra in 1971, around the time of the upheaval. Because of his expanding studio commitments, he had already been cutting back on his work with the Symphony of the New World. But the unpleasantness surrounding Steinberg's resignation certainly hastened his departure: "I had been very proud to be a member of the orchestra, but I was annoyed at some of the racial overtones to Ben Steinberg's resigning."

In 1972, after an arbitration process, the symphony regrouped under a new board of directors and new acting music director Coleridge-Taylor Perkinson, who had been one of the African American guest conductors brought in by Steinberg.[64]

Benjamin Steinberg died on January 29, 1974, at the age of fifty-eight. Although the cause of death was pancreatic cancer, his daughter, Barbara, is convinced that he died of a broken heart. Whatever his failings, Steinberg had a vision and devoted his life to the ideals of integration and breaking down the barriers facing minority musicians in the classical world. After years of struggle, he realized his dream with the founding of the Symphony of the New World, and when that dream was taken from him, he never recovered.

Over the following few years, the orchestra persevered with an ambitious series of concerts, returning to Carnegie Hall as its home base in October 1975. Funding remained a perennial problem, and in February 1975, the orchestra was forced to cancel a scheduled concert for financial reasons. Conductor George Byrd, who led the symphony in an October 29, 1972, concert, remarked, "It seems to me macabre that the Black Panthers find it easier to raise money than the Symphony of the New World."[65] The 1977–78 season seems to have been the symphony's swan song. The *New York Times* Arts and Leisure section lists a Symphony of the New World concert for Sunday, April 9, 1978, and no dates beyond that.[66] The groundbreaking orchestra seems to have dissolved without fanfare or even an announcement.

Despite the shortage of funding, the internal strife and upheaval, and the struggle to find its niche in the insular world of classical music, the orchestra's alumni look back with pride on the achievements of the Symphony of the New World and feel it made a difference. "It built hope where there was very little," said flutist Harold Jones. "It showed that, as black people, we had paid our dues, and we could do it as well as anyone else. It was such a moment in life that I'm overwhelmed with it. I just wish it could have lasted. The inspiration that this could be done [remains] in all of us."[67]

Violinist Gayle Dixon (1947–2008) was one of the younger musicians who benefited from the orchestra's training programs. Dixon, who went on to a distinguished career as a musician, educator, and Musicians Union official and activist, noted, "One of my finest musical experiences as a young musician was playing in the first chair octet of the Symphony of the New World, and in the octet for young players, which was funded by a Ford Foundation grant. . . . [W]hat could be better than earning a living playing chamber music?"[68]

As Jones, Dixon, and many other orchestra alumni make clear, the Symphony of the New World offered hope to a generation of African American musicians who aspired to classical careers at a time when other avenues were virtually closed to them. But musicians like Joe Wilder still yearned for the day when they could compete on equal ground with their white colleagues for positions in the nation's major orchestras. Similarly, African American composers resented the fact that their works were frequently relegated to black music retrospectives or festivals, and they hoped for the opportunity to present their music on the nation's major stages. The distinguished composer Hale Smith wrote:

> We *must* be part of the mainstream in this country or all of the black programs are a sham. Place our music not on all-black programs. We can do that ourselves, for the benefit of our own people. Place our work on programs with Beethoven, Mozart, Schoenberg, Copland, and— if they can stand the heat—the current avant-gardists. We don't even have to be called black. When we stand for our bows, that fact will become clear when it should—*after* the work has made its own impact.[69]

The 1969 Human Rights Commission Hearings

A decade after the Urban League's report and five years after the founding of the Symphony of the New World brought about a new public awareness of their symphonic abilities and aspirations, many African American musicians still felt largely excluded from the nation's major classical orchestras. In 1969, two black musicians with extensive classical credentials, double bassist Arthur Davis and cellist Earl Madison, formally charged the New York Philharmonic with discriminatory hiring practices, lodging their complaints with the New York City Commission on Human Rights. Madison filed first, in January 1969, followed by Davis, in March.[70] The case was heard by the commission in a series of ten sessions that took place over a three-month period, from July 30 to October 20, 1969. The more than two thousand pages of testimony ranged far beyond the immediate charges, as the commission called dozens of witnesses, including such celebrities as pianist André Watts and New York Philharmonic conductor Leonard Bernstein, as well as orchestra administrators and other prominent musicians—both white and black and on both sides of the issue. Originally, Bernstein had been named along with the New York Philharmonic Society in Earl Madison's complaint, but his name was dropped at the cellist's behest before the hearings began. Nevertheless, the maestro was in attendance for the opening session, looking "obviously a bit peeved."[71] Although no longer a "defendant," Bernstein was called as a witness at a later session, on September 29, 1969.

The complainants had different backgrounds, but both felt they had been refused employment by the New York Philharmonic "solely because of their race."[72] In addition to his classical work, Arthur Davis (1934–2007) was a prominent jazz bassist, whose extensive discography includes recordings with such seminal artists as Max Roach, Dizzy Gillespie, John Coltrane, Count Basie, and Rahsaan Roland Kirk. As early as 1951, while still a teenager, Davis was involved in an incident that presaged his 1969 suit against the New York Philharmonic. A native of Harrisburg, Pennsylvania, Davis auditioned for a spot in the Harrisburg Symphony but was initially rejected. Davis claimed he was unfairly treated because of his race, and the orchestra's conductor, Edwin McArthur, concurred, telling the audition committee, "If you don't want him, then you don't want me."[73] A founding member of the Symphony of the New World, Davis was outspoken and supremely self-confident; on his website, he later billed himself as "the world's greatest bassist."[74] After the Human Rights Commission hearings, Davis claimed to have been blacklisted by the music industry for a decade in the 1970s. He went back to school, earned a doctorate in psychology from New York University in 1981, and spent several years in private practice and teaching. He eventually returned to music, continuing to perform in both jazz and classical settings.

Earl Madison (born in 1945), only twenty-three when the case was brought before the commission, was raised in Chicago, where he studied with several noted teachers. He became first cello of the Youth Orchestra of Chicago and made seven solo recordings with the NBC Symphony Orchestra for the television program *Artists' Showcase*, performing the concertos of Dvořák, Saint-Saëns, Lalo, Haydn's D Major, Schumann, and Tchaikovsky's Rococo Variations, and as guest soloist with the Chicago Symphony. He joined the Pittsburgh Symphony Orchestra at age twenty and later played with the Chicago-based Renoir Trio. He played principal cello for visiting ballet companies, including the American Ballet and the Joffrey. After performing solo recitals in Europe, he joined the faculty of the Wisconsin Conservatory of Music. Ultimately, he moved to Los Angeles and has had a prolific career in the film studios, playing on hundreds of soundtracks under leading composers.[75]

From the outset, the Human Rights Commission hearings were marked by acrimony, with witnesses on both sides finding themselves in extremely awkward positions dictated by the very nature of the case. In essence, to defend the "respondent" (the New York Philharmonic) against the charges of discrimination, the witnesses for the philharmonic had to show that the "complainants," Davis and Madison, were rejected not because of their race but because they were not as qualified as those hired for the orchestra. Musicians were called on to denigrate the abilities of fellow musicians, and supposedly enlightened members of the arts community, often ardent supporters of the civil rights movement, were forced to examine their own attitudes toward race. The tone was set in an opening statement by Robert Weitz, deputy general counsel for the Commission on Human Rights:

> Although some may think it inconceivable that symphony orchestras and symphonic musicians, practitioners of the arts, may be guilty of racial discrimination, unfortunately, musicians not only are . . . as illiberal as the rest of us, but the symphony orchestras, we'll show by the evidence, are perpetuating a grotesque state of affairs which find the five leading American orchestras with a total of two—that's t-w-o—black musicians. That's a total out of about 500 musicians over all. One of these musicians is in the New York Philharmonic and the other in the Cleveland Orchestra. I think it has been very well said that Cleveland has as many black mayors as it has black classical musicians.[76]

On the second day of hearings, Carlos Mosely, managing director of the New York Philharmonic, discussed the audition process—key to establishing whether Davis and Madison had received fair treatment. Double bassist Ortiz Walton testified for the complainants, endorsing the qualifications of Davis and Madison as symphony musicians.[77] Walton laid claim to being the first African American to join a major symphony orchestra when he became a member of the Boston Symphony in 1957, at age twenty-three.[78] He also testified about his alleged harassment during his five-year tenure with that orchestra.

The hearings resumed on September 24, 1969, with Earl Madison himself testifying about his treatment at his first philharmonic audition in 1967: "When I first walked in, it was a very strange atmosphere existing. The personnel manager and several people, whom I don't know as far as names are concerned, looked at me as if . . . I have no business here. . . . They stared at me as if I was some kind of subhuman."[79] Five days later, during his testimony, Leonard Bernstein addressed the question of Madison's perception of hostility at the audition: "I can understand any candidate feeling that way. In the case of a black candidate, I can understand this feeling doubly or triply or a hundred fold."[80]

It was at the September 24 hearing that Joe Wilder's name surfaced for the first time, during the testimony of John Hammond, who appeared as a witness for the complainants. After testifying that Arthur Davis was qualified to play for the philharmonic, Hammond, who was identified as vice president of the Symphony of the New World, was asked about other black musicians, and specifically about Wilder. Hammond answered with his customary enthusiasm and a bit of hyperbole:

Joe Wilder went to the Manhattan School of Music. He was a completely qualified musician in every which way. There was a time, of course, when there was discrimination in music schools, but fortunately that has gone by the boards. But Joe Wilder had a job as a first trumpet with Count Basie's orchestra, and Count Basie took a trip to Europe, something like 11 years ago, and when Joe Wilder was with the orchestra the Stockholm Symphony offered him the chair of first trumpet. But I think, he, being an American, wanted to stay in America. Now Mr. Wilder is employed at the American Broadcasting Company as a staff musician, and is also . . . our first trumpeter at the Symphony of the New World, and he is just wonderfully great.

Q: You feel he is qualified to play for the respondent [the New York Philharmonic]?
A: Absolutely. They would be lucky to have him.[81]

Upon reading Hammond's testimony decades later, Wilder was flattered but quick to point out its exaggerations.

> First of all, I wasn't the first trumpet with Basie; I played some first trumpet parts. When we were in Stockholm, the black conductor, Dean Dixon, who was conducting the Stockholm Symphony, invited the Basie orchestra to come to one of the rehearsals. I was the only guy who showed up! He talked to me and asked, "How would you like to audition for the symphony?" I said I'd be very flattered, and he asked me to send him some of the classical things I'd done. So when we got back, I sent him some things, but he never responded.

Hammond's testimony ended with the following exchange:

> Q: Just offhand, can you think of the names of any other black musicians, other than those you have testified to, whom you would consider qualified to play with the Philharmonic?
> A: I can name you 40.[82]

Because of its historic role as an integrated orchestra, the Symphony of the New World surfaced often in the testimony as evidence of the availability of qualified African American symphonic players. Symphony of the New World founder and conductor Ben Steinberg also testified at the September 24 hearing, recounting his and early attempts by others at forming integrated orchestras, as well as the plight of black conductors, such as the aforementioned Dean Dixon:

> He is the most famous of Negro conductors. He has conducted all over the world, except here in the United States, because he refuses to come back here just for a guest appointment. He said he would come back if they offered him a major symphony. He is now the conductor of the Frankfurt Symphony, in Germany. He has conducted in every other country in the world. We invited him to conduct our opening concert, but he would not come.[83]

The Symphony of the New World was also prominently mentioned when the hearings continued the next day, September 25. The orchestra's personnel manager and oboist, Harry Smyles, testified that Arthur Davis had been the principal bassist with the symphony, while Homer Mensch, a noted white bassist and member of the philharmonic, played second chair. This attempt to show that Davis was at least the equal of—if not superior to—Mensch was disingenuous, since, as previously noted, in accordance with the mission of the Symphony of the New World, conductor Steinberg on occasion would prevail on white principal players to defer to African Americans to allow them to gain experience in the first chair. This point was not brought out in the cross-examination by Martin Oppenheimer, attorney for the New York Philharmonic, who chose instead to question Smyles about the audition practices of the Symphony of the New World.

One of the key charges against the philharmonic was its lack of "blind" auditions—that is, auditions conducted behind a screen, which would presumably remove the race of the candidate as a factor. Smyles admitted that even the Symphony of the New World did not use a screen in its auditions. When Oppenheim asked why, Smyles responded, "Because we're two of the—our reasons for being, first of all, is to the black musicians, to give them a showcase; and, secondly, to give women a showcase, because we feel that there has been discrimination against women in the major symphony orchestras; and to give young players a chance. So we don't feel we discriminate; we don't feel the need for it [a screen]."[84]

On September 26, the commission heard from several prominent African American musicians, some of whom had auditioned for the philharmonic, and one who had substituted in the orchestra. Cellist Kermit Moore addressed the inherent problems of trying to assess a candidate on the basis of a single audition, even if fairly administered: "You would know only how he responded to that given situation. You would know better how he really played if you allowed him to play in the orchestra for a week or two, observed him, let his colleagues observe him. Then you would have a better way of appraising his musicianship."[85]

Flutist Hubert Laws, another musician who attained prominence in the jazz world, testified that he had played as a sub for the philharmonic for a series of concerts dedicated to Martin Luther King Jr., but he was never called again. When asked, "Do you wish to play with the New York Philharmonic?" Laws responded, "It is another job."[86]

Violinist Sanford Allen, as the first and at the time of the hearings, still the only African American member of the philharmonic, was in a unique position to offer insights into its practices. He told the commission that he had auditioned and advanced to the finals on two occasions but was not hired originally. After subbing extensively, Allen was finally admitted in 1962. Allen, in his eighth season and still playing second violin, was blunt about his treatment, stating that musicians with less seniority had been promoted ahead of him. He claimed to have asked Leonard Bernstein whether he was being "disciplined," and whether those who had moved ahead of him were superior players, but Allen was told that this was not the case. "I then ventured the opinion that perhaps there was some other extra-musical considerations which had led to this," he said. "I was again told no. That was pretty much how the conversation ended."[87]

The cross-examination of Allen became personal as the philharmonic's attorney, Martin Oppenheimer, raised questions about Allen's alleged "aloofness" toward fellow orchestra members, some of whom had lodged a complaint against him. Allen responded:

> My observation was that there are now and always have been in the orchestra people who do not speak to me. This has happened since the first day I came in there. My position simply was that if there is someone there whom I feel should speak to me and doesn't, I will take it up as a personal matter. I don't quite understand going upstairs to the management about something that a person feels I am not giving him. It is difficult for me to comprehend this. . . . I interpreted that it [the complaint] may have possibly meant that I did not go out of my way to say good morning to each member of the orchestra. Since each member of the orchestra does not say good morning to me, I can't see any reason why I should.[88]

While the case against the philharmonic was still pending, Allen was also quite candid to critic Donal Henahan, who wrote an extensive and often critical essay on the orchestra for the *New York Times Magazine*. The violinist told Henahan that, in general, the American symphony orchestra was "definitely segregationist by instinct" and that he was tired of being singled out as a "glorious example of the Philharmonic's enlightenment."[89] In the same article, Allen also alluded to the tension between himself and fellow orchestra members. Noting that he had formed close relationships with only three of his colleagues, he joked that his relations with the others were "nonviolent."[90]

Two years earlier, Allen had published his own measured yet powerful *New York Times* piece on the injustices he had encountered in pursuit of a classical career. In "Why Hasn't the Negro Found a Place in the Symphony?" he wrote:

> There is obviously the need to create a climate in which everyone believes that the admission of a member of any minority into any organization is something that occurs simply in the normal course of events. The majority must understand that members of a minority group

cannot humanly be expected to show gratitude for that which should be a logical consequence of application and basic qualification, rather than the result of some divine right which befits a more feudal society.[91]

Leonard Bernstein, who had stepped down as philharmonic music director in May 1969, appeared at the opening hearing on July 30. However, he was not called as a witness until September 29. The entire Human Rights Commission inquiry was particularly galling to Bernstein, who had long championed liberal causes, especially civil rights. Bernstein biographer Joan Peyser writes:

> In the 1930s and 1940s, Bernstein was involved in all kinds of left-wing political activities that would have been compatible with a strongly pro-black position. But in 1958, when he took over the Philharmonic, he became an employee of an elitist organization where policies were firmly controlled by George E. Judd, associate managing director, and Joseph De Angelis, orchestra manager, neither of whom was a compassionate man. So Bernstein's humanitarian impulses were muzzled for the next ten years.[92]

As early as 1947, Bernstein had written a piece in the *New York Times* titled "The Negro in Music: Problems He Has to Face in Getting a Start," in which he made some of the same points that during the commission hearings, some twenty years later, were being used to call into question his and the philharmonic's practices. For example, Bernstein wrote, "There is not a single Negro musician employed in any of the major symphony orchestras, and that goes right down the list." The thrust of Bernstein's piece, however, was to call attention to the lack of musical training opportunities for black musicians:

> I became interested in the problem of the Negro in music some years back, but at no time was it made more graphic to me than when I was auditioning musicians for the New York City Symphony three years ago. I must have heard about 400 musicians, but of this number only three were Negroes. To each of the three I listened eagerly, hoping they would meet the required standards; but in each case they failed. And I don't think it was a lack of talent, but something more serious, a lack of the opportunity for proper training.[93]

In calling for more scholarships for black students at Juilliard, Curtis, and Eastman so that young musicians might be heard "when they are in the growing stage by someone who knows what to do with them, instead of having to wait until it is too late," Bernstein concluded: "This is a social, not a musical problem. And that is why everything we can do to fight discrimination—in any form or field—will ultimately work toward ameliorating the musical situation."[94] This statement presaged the argument used in the Human Rights Commission hearings to defend the philharmonic against charges of discrimination in hiring—that the dearth of black musicians was symptomatic of a greater societal failure and not the result of any discriminatory practices on the part of the philharmonic itself.

In his opening statement to the commission, Bernstein stressed his long history of commitment to the struggle for equal rights: "If you look . . . at the letterhead of any Civil Rights organization, on most of them you will find my name or you will find some record of my having supported it in one way or another."[95] Much of the questioning of Bernstein concerned the audition process. Oddly, Bernstein stated that it was his policy that black candidates, no matter how they performed at the audition, should automatically advance to the finals, so he could personally hear them. Also, he defended the philharmonic's rejection of blind auditions, contending that use of a screen "cuts off a certain human contact which may be of great advantage to the candidate as well as to the judge, which may help to put the candidate at his ease. . . . [T]here is a kind of human relation which a screen would simply obliterate."[96]

Ironically, on January 14, 1970, less than four months after defending himself and the philharmonic against discrimination charges before the Human Rights Commission, Bernstein hosted his controversial fund-raiser for the radical Black Panther party, inspiring Tom Wolfe's iconic *New York* magazine piece "Radical Chic."[97]

The final four days of testimony were largely devoted to witnesses for the philharmonic. On September 30, 1969, African American piano prodigy André Watts, then twenty-three, stated that he had experienced no discrimination during his regular appearances as guest soloist with the orchestra. He was also asked by Human Rights Commissioner Jerome M. Kay, "Now, have you in your experience at the Philharmonic felt or seen or known of any discrimination toward your race to others beside yourself?" Watts simply replied, "No."[98]

The hearings resumed on October 17, with the testimony of several philharmonic administrators and orchestra members, including double bassists Robert Brennand (principal), Orin O'Brien, and John A. Schaeffer, all of whom testified that Arthur Davis's playing was not up to philharmonic standards. The testimony of James Chambers, philharmonic personnel manager, who had attended Davis's audition, was particularly supercilious. After describing Davis's playing as "weak in general," he was asked to assess the quality of performance of the Symphony of the New World, which was cited throughout the hearings by the plaintiffs' witnesses as evidence of the availability of qualified African American musicians. When asked, "Would you say that they were of a caliber equal to any of the twenty-eight major orchestras?" Chambers answered, "Of course not." And when asked if he would characterize it as a "training orchestra," he responded, "Yes, of that quality and merely for that purpose."[99] This pronouncement was made on the basis of a half-hour visit to a Symphony of the New World rehearsal the day before. On cross-examination, however, Chambers did concede that there might be some outstanding individual musicians in the symphony.

The next day, the attacks continued, with philharmonic bassist Homer Mensch, who, as mentioned, had voluntarily moved to the second bass chair when Arthur Davis assumed the principal chair in the Symphony of the New World. Mensch said of Davis, his erstwhile colleague, "I thought that he wasn't qualified to play not only [with] the Philharmonic, but [with] any major orchestra."[100] Like Chambers, Mensch admitted that some members of the Symphony of the New World were qualified to play with the philharmonic.

Joe Wilder's testimony took place on October 20, 1969, the last day of the hearings.[101] Unfortunately, the transcripts from that session seem to have been lost, so the account of Wilder's participation comes from his memory of the event, corroborated by plaintiff Earl Madison.[102] Wilder was called as a witness for the defense, but his testimony turned out to be far from supportive of the philharmonic's position. In a press statement at the time of the Urban League report in 1958, a philharmonic spokesman had contended that the orchestra had called Wilder to play on several occasions, but each time he was unavailable. At the 1969 hearings, the philharmonic asked Wilder to verify this claim as evidence that it had, in fact, tried to hire black musicians. As Wilder had previously explained, he had been called to play with the Lewisohn Stadium orchestra—not the philharmonic, per se—and that he had told them that, as an ABC staff musician, he was regularly committed for that time slot to the *Voice of Firestone* television broadcast. "The Philharmonic tried to rebuff the charges of discrimination by saying they tried to hire me but I was never available," Wilder said. "But when I tried to explain why and suggested that they were calling me for a time for which they *knew* I wasn't available and never for anything else, their lawyer said, 'Strike that!' At that point, I got angry," Wilder recalled. "I told them, 'I'm an American musician and just want the same opportunity as anyone else!'" drawing another objection from the philharmonic's attorney, even though Wilder was a witness for the defense.

On November 5, 1969, Amyas Ames, president of the New York Philharmonic, issued a "Report to Subscribers," defending the philharmonic's position in an attempt to refute some of the negative publicity it had received as a result of the hearings. Affirming that "the Philharmonic is not a racist institution," and describing its former music director, Leonard Bernstein, as "one who has worked and fought with courage in the cause of black people throughout his life," the report synthesized many of the arguments presented in defense of the philharmonic during the hearings.[103] One of Ames's explanations for the dearth of black applicants was that "qualified black instrumentalists are offered so many opportunities on television, in recording studios, etc., that they do not come to our auditions or accept permanent positions with symphonic orchestras."[104] This argument is patently ridiculous given the statistics presented earlier by the Urban League study on African Americans in the network orchestras. Ames then repeats the "societal failure" explanation posited by Bernstein in his testimony but in a far more condescending manner:

> The cause is, undoubtedly, a societal one. First, and at the source, is the blacks' heritage of discouragement in a society where they have been discriminated against for so long—a sense of defeatism in the face of the long, hard years of technical study required for performing in our foremost orchestras. There are also the environmental deprivations which have kept black children from being exposed at a young enough age to the satisfactions of playing a musical instrument.[105]

Of course, such patronizing speculation fails to acknowledge the long tradition of musical training in black families, the countless stories of parents of modest means (like Joe Wilder's) scrimping to pay for music lessons for their children, the customary presence of a piano in homes where food was often scarce, and the technical virtuosity of black instrumentalists in virtually every other area of music. By essentially placing the blame on the victims, Ames's disingenuous statement ignores the most obvious cause for the lack of African American candidates—that young black musicians just might have been dissuaded from pursuing classical careers because for decades, no matter what their abilities or achievements, no orchestra would admit them. Ames's report concludes with a self-serving statement about "standards," from which African Americans might infer that their exclusion was in their own interest:

> So it is the policy of the New York Philharmonic to maintain the highest standards of quality among our musicians. At the same time it has been and will be our policy to do everything in our power to search for and find qualified black musicians; we will check and double check our procedures, which we believe have been fair and right, to see that they remain so and, if possible, improved. But in the interests of the

arts, we must fight for excellence. In the long run, it is in the interests of the black people, as of all people, that we do so.[106]

A month after the hearings ended, the Human Rights Commission issued a restraining order that barred the philharmonic from filling two vacant positions, cello and double bass, until the commission completed its investigation. Commission chair Simeon Golar called the philharmonic "particularly arrogant and contemptuous of this commission" for scheduling auditions for the disputed positions while the case was pending.[107]

After a year of deliberations—the longest in the history of the Human Rights Commission—on November 16, 1970, the commission delivered a mixed verdict.[108] It found that the philharmonic had "engaged in a pattern and practice of discrimination with respect to the hiring of substitute and extra musicians, and that the complainants [Davis and Madison] were within the class affected by this pattern and practice." But it found "no discrimination on the part of the respondent against these complainants with respect to their applications for permanent employment," adding, "We do not hold that the complainants are not well-qualified symphonic musicians," only that they "have not shown that the respondent unlawfully discriminated against them with respect to permanent employment." The key issue was "not their qualifications standing alone, but the quality of musicianship as heard by respondent's auditioners compared with their competitors at the time of their auditions."[109]

The decision absolving the philharmonic of discrimination in the hiring of permanent members hinged on the orchestra's right to "artistic discretion," a "fundamental civil liberty" that "must be preserved." While the commission acknowledged that "the complainants have raised serious questions as to the Philharmonic's audition procedures," they "have fallen short of the quantum of proof necessary to find that the respondent abused its artistic discretion."[110]

In the matter of the hiring of substitutes, however, the commissioners found the evidence to be irrefutable, noting that during the 1960s, the philharmonic "hired at least 277 different substitutes or extras who played a total of 1,773 weeks during that period. Of these, *one* was black and he played for one week."[111] The decision pointed out that a high percentage of the substitutes hired were students of the philharmonic section heads, stating, "We are not persuaded by the respondent's contention that there was good and sufficient reason for the use of these students rather than experienced, talented and available black musicians."[112] The decision noted that "the Symphony of the New World, an integrated orchestra based at Lincoln Center (as is the respondent), was a readily available source of musical talent which the respondent did not see fit to use," and cited evidence that "substitutes and extras were also hired on the basis of friendship."[113]

The commission expressed its admiration for the complainants, Davis and Madison, "whom we judge to be sincerely-motivated, public spirited men who came to this forum as much in the interest of their fellows as in their own," as well as praising them "for their courage in coming forward despite possible risk to their musical careers."[114]

The day after the verdict was announced, Arthur Davis and Earl Madison held a news conference at the New York Civil Liberties Union at which they challenged the philharmonic to allow them to play man to man, behind a screen, against any or all of the of the orchestra's bassists or cellists. "They say they are the greatest, so let them prove it," said Madison.[115]

Following the decision, Nat Hentoff attacked both the philharmonic's practices and the commission's findings in a *Village Voice* piece titled "Un-Chic Racism at the Philharmonic." With his customary passion, Hentoff railed:

Does it seem logical to you that a pervasive pattern of discrimination against Black substitutes and extras suddenly stops when it comes to hiring permanent Philharmonic musicians? And what of the fact that in the 128 years of its existence, the Philharmonic has had just *one* permanent Black instrumentalist? . . . They got that rhythm, but they can't cut Bach? Bullshit! (Or rather, musical Jensenism).[116]

Hentoff pointed out the disparity between the *New York Times* coverage of the decision and that of the *New York Law Journal* as embodied in their respective headlines: "Rights Unit Clears Philharmonic but Finds Bias in Some Hiring" (*New York Times*) and "Philharmonic Ordered to End Racial Bias" (*New York Law Journal*).[117]

Hentoff also discussed the consequences of the case for the careers of the two complainants. He noted that Arthur Davis, "having been severed from his job on the Merv Griffin show, is now unemployed." Davis told Hentoff that he had been regularly featured on the show but, after the hearings began, he was "put in his place." Hentoff reported that Earl Madison, "formerly third cellist with the Pittsburgh Symphony (before he tried to move on up in the time-honored American way), is living in Chicago with his parents and taking whatever gigs he can get."[118]

In the ensuing years, the outspoken Davis often discussed the case and its effect on his career. In a 1982 interview, he recalled writing a letter with Max Roach to Leonard Bernstein, when Lincoln Center was being built, saying "that those funds were black peoples' funds as well, but that in fact there were no blacks in the orchestra."[119] In 1986, he told *Cadence* that, as a result of the philharmonic case, he had been "whitelisted."[120] Regarding his tenure in *The Merv Griffin Show* band, he said, "I was supposed to be the good little boy since I had a job working; I'm supposed to keep my nose clean."[121] And in a 2002, he told *Double Bassist* magazine, "I went up against the big power people and lost 10 years of my life. . . . I feel vindicated, and I wouldn't be a Dr. Art Davis if it hadn't happened."[122]

Earl Madison's Reflections

In sharp contrast, although it deeply affected him personally and professionally, cellist Earl Madison, Davis's co-complainant in the philharmonic suit, has tried to distance himself from the case, rarely, if ever, mentioning it in the ensuing forty-three years. "It made me unemployable," he simply stated.[123] In 2012, however, Madison, a thoughtful, articulate, and extremely frank man, graciously agreed to provide some insights into that turbulent era and to correct some of the factual errors and misrepresentations that he believes have been promulgated concerning the philharmonic case in general and his own role in it.

After earning a string of awards and honors while still in his teens, in 1965, at age twenty, Madison successfully auditioned for the Pittsburgh Symphony and became a regular member of the orchestra under music director William Steinberg. Among major U.S. symphonies, Pittsburgh had a comparatively progressive record in hiring African Americans. In 1966, Patricia Prattis Jennings became the first African American woman to be awarded a full contact by a major U.S. symphony when, after two years as a substitute with the orchestra, she was hired as the Pittsburgh Symphony's regular principal keyboardist.[124] Another African American musician, violinist Paul Ross, had joined the orchestra in 1965.

Unlike Sanford Allen's testimony about his alleged mistreatment by the New York Philharmonic and Ortiz Walton's claims of harassment while a member of the Boston Symphony, Madison remembered his experience in Pittsburgh as extremely positive. "The Symphony was my oasis," he said. "My colleagues on the whole could not have been friendlier to me. We used to go out together after the concerts, and on Thanksgiving and Christmas, I went to their homes." Nevertheless, Madison wanted to return to his hometown of Chicago and play for the prestigious Chicago Symphony. As he pointed out, the seeds of his involvement in the 1969 New York Philharmonic case were sown during a 1966 Chicago Symphony audition.

Madison's first audition for the Chicago Symphony took place in 1964, when he was only eighteen, and it came at the invitation of Frank Miller, the symphony's principal cellist, who along with the other string principals, had recently heard him play at a musical event. After the audition, Madison was told by conductor Jean Martinon that he thought he was too young. In December 1965, Madison auditioned again. This time he was told by a first violinist in the orchestra that he had won the audition but that "they were not hiring Negroes." His teacher advised him to ignore this and continue to practice and study, which he did.

In October 1966, he was urged to audition for a third time. By then, Madison was already a regular member of the Pittsburgh Symphony. Since the orchestra's schedule conflicted with the Chicago audition date, Pittsburgh conductor William Steinberg informed Madison that he would have to engage a substitute cellist for the week at his own expense. Steinberg also asked him, "Does this job mean so much to you?" When Madison answered yes, "the maestro flinched," Madison recalled. "He seemed so offended, but he said he would not stand in my way. I will never forget this meeting and his reaction to my tactless answer. He was so offended that I would leave Pittsburgh to audition in Chicago, when he knew I had just auditioned there. In retrospect, maybe he knew something about what was going on in Chicago."

Madison went ahead with the Chicago audition and performed well. He later learned that he had been unanimously accepted by the audition committee, but in an unprecedented action, his appointment had been vetoed by the symphony's board of trustees, who Madison was told, "didn't want the image of a Negro in the orchestra." Madison's father, Earl W. Madison (1917–2009), also a cellist and supervisor of music education for the Chicago public schools, attempted unsuccessfully to get the decision overturned, as did several Chicago city aldermen, who wrote, "The Chicago Symphony Orchestra is too valuable a Chicago asset and too great a musical resource to permit its integrity to be jeopardized by its lily-white policy."[125] With the same position still vacant in 1967, Frank Miller once again encouraged Madison to audition. This time the cellist refused. The Pittsburgh Symphony was on tour, and Madison did not wish to risk further insult to conductor Steinberg by yet again requesting time off to audition in Chicago. Also, as he told his father, "Why should I audition again? I already won the audition! The problem has nothing to do with my playing!" Miller felt so bad about the younger Madison's treatment that whenever he ran into Earl's father at Ravinia, home of the Chicago Symphony, he would make a point of apologizing to him, saying, "I know Earl should be in this orchestra, and I wanted him. I wish he were here." Understandably, the young cellist was profoundly disappointed with the outcome of his Chicago audition. "It weighed on me very badly during my years at Pittsburgh, and I didn't handle it well," he said.

Although Madison refused to audition again for the Chicago Symphony, he saw an ad for an opening in the New York Philharmonic and sent in an application. "I had not thought about New York—my focus had been on the Chicago Symphony," Madison said. "But, to me, New York was a more interesting place than Pittsburgh."

The audition took place in January 1967, on a Saturday, when Madison had a day off from his Pittsburgh Symphony commitments. Ten cellists appeared that day before a committee that included Leonard Bernstein. "On paper, I was the most qualified person because I was the only one playing in a major orchestra," Madison said. The young cellist was pleased with his twenty-minute performance. A friend, who was also one of the candidates, told Madison after hearing all the performers, "Well, you definitely won this one!" (When Madison later asked him whether he would testify to that effect during the hearings, the musician told him, "You know I can't, Earl. That would ruin my career.")

Shortly thereafter, Madison received a letter from the philharmonic thanking him for auditioning but informing him that someone else had been selected. "So I let it go until I met Art [Davis]," he said. Madison auditioned twice more for the philharmonic, in January and October 1968. Both auditions came as a result of advertisements he had seen, not by invitation. "I bothered them; they didn't bother me!" Madison joked. Madison admitted he did not play at his peak on either occasion, noting, "My best audition was the first one for Bernstein. I did a good deal of what I wanted to do on that day."

Based on his own audition experience, Madison questioned the testimony that emerged at the hearings about the philharmonic's policy of advancing all black candidates to the finals so they could be heard by the music director. For his 1967 audition, at which Bernstein was present, there were no preliminaries. "Everyone there was playing for the first time," he recalled. "And how would they know in advance that I was black? My sole contact with them had been a one-minute phone call to set up a workable audition time." Madison believed that policy may have been instituted *after* the suit in an attempt to increase the opportunities for black musicians. In his testimony at the hearings, he stated that he believed he was advanced to the finals because he had already had experience in a major orchestra (Pittsburgh), not because he was black. When Bernstein himself was asked how he knew that Madison was black and should be advanced, he responded, "I don't remember, but I must have been told. I had this arrangement."[126]

No matter how well meaning the intent, Madison thought the policy of automatically advancing black players was misguided: "It's very condescending.

No one wants to advance like that. There have been some people I've known who have gotten jobs through connections, and it was known that they didn't win the auditions. Believe me, they have paid for it every day they're on the job, with guilt and insecurity."

It was in 1968, during his tenure with the Pittsburgh Symphony, that Madison first came in contact with Arthur Davis. The bassist was deeply committed to breaking down the racial barriers in the symphony, and he sent a telegram apprising Madison of an opening in the cello section of the Philadelphia Orchestra. During a visit to New York, Madison met Davis at the Musicians Union. He remembered seeing the bassist in his customary sunglasses on *The Merv Griffin Show*. Around the same time, Madison was undergoing a transformation in his own racial consciousness, aided by such cataclysmic events as the assassination of Martin Luther King and the tumultuous Democratic National Convention in Chicago, which the cellist had witnessed firsthand as a member of the convention orchestra. "All you think about is music and the cello," he told himself. "You're asleep! You don't know what's going on!" He read *Black Rage* and *Soul on Ice* and adopted the prevailing Afro hair style. "My awareness was in the early stages of evolvement. At that time, if you weren't angry, you weren't really black. And as a classical musician, there was always the question as to whether you were black or not. So I was going to show them how black I was."

Madison decided to follow Davis's advice and prepared for two months for his audition for the Philadelphia Orchestra:

It was probably the best audition I ever played in my life. [Musical Director Eugene] Ormandy commented that I played the solo well but that the sight-reading wasn't good. To this day, I don't know what he was talking about. I might have missed a note in one of the excerpts, because there was no list—you didn't know exactly what they were going to ask you to play. But when you think about it, if I played in public, what are people going to hear me play? A solo! You're not going to play an excerpt anywhere.

Madison was not hired, and he reported what had happened to Arthur Davis.[127] "I thought I had been badly misled and was angry," he said. Davis stoked that anger by telling the younger musician, "They're making a fool out of you!" Madison recalled, "When he told me that, I said, 'That's enough!' That was just unacceptable to my psyche. I began to think maybe there's a systemic problem here, and something else needs to be done." It was at that point that Madison went with Davis and lodged their complaint with the Human Rights Commission.

Initially, they were met with great skepticism. "They weren't even going to have a hearing," Madison said. "They were just going to throw out the complaint, thinking I was a crackpot. They said, 'Suing Leonard Bernstein? Are you crazy?'" Before they began to take him seriously, the commission looked into Madison's background: "They called all over to see if I was who I said I was, if I was legitimate. I had to get letters of recommendation saying I was as good as I said I was."

In May 1969, between the opening of the case and the beginning of the hearings, Madison resigned from the Pittsburgh Symphony. "It had nothing to do with the suit—I had always wanted to pursue a solo career," he explained. In retrospect, he called it "the dumbest thing I ever did." He returned to Chicago, where he freelanced at Chess Records. "I took that option, not thinking it could be a precarious existence," he said. "I didn't think that Chess would go out of business or that work would be dependent upon what styles of music were popular." After seeing an account of the Human Rights Commission case in *Newsweek*,[128] Madison's father told him, "Okay, you've ruined your career. Do you think you can call Pittsburgh and get them to take you back without an audition?" Madison recalled, "He was so angry and afraid for me, but I told him I wanted to pursue my solo career. I was bullheaded, and he wasn't going to change my mind." After a year, Chess Records folded, and Madison decided to go to Europe, thinking, "No one is going to hire me here after what I've done!" He soon returned to the United States and, in September 1972, auditioned successfully for the Milwaukee Symphony, remaining with that orchestra for five years.

Madison pointed out several common misconceptions concerning the coverage of the case: "Some people thought I was suing the philharmonic to get a job. Remember, I already had a job! I had a tenured job, and if I had stayed in Pittsburgh, this would have been my forty-seventh year. I still visit there from time to time, and people ask me, 'Why did you leave?' And I still can't answer that question." Even after the suit was launched, the Pittsburgh Symphony attempted on several occasions to convince Madison to remain with the orchestra.

Despite Nat Hentoff's fervent support of the two black musicians in his *Village Voice* article, Madison resented his implication that he was somehow forced out of the Pittsburgh Symphony as a result of the hearings. The cellist also takes issue with Hentoff's portrayal of him as the victim, "living in Chicago with his parents and taking whatever gigs he can get." Madison explained, "Art [Davis] told him that. Nat Hentoff never interviewed me." He stressed that he was not forced to move in with his parents but did so because it would enable him to pursue a solo career: "The goal was to have sufficient capital reserves to fund my solo endeavors. The commercial recording way of life allowed me to earn at least as much as I had been making in Pittsburgh and was more favorable to the eight-hours-a-day practice I needed to prepare for my solo commitments. My parents also had a soundproof practice room in their home."

From Madison's perspective, the most damaging coverage of the case was probably the most prominent: the nearly two-column article (with a photo of Davis and Madison) in *Newsweek* that Madison's father found so disturbing. The piece was generally sympathetic to the philharmonic's position, asserting that "there is evidence that the Philharmonic itself has been actively looking for qualified blacks," and concluding with an excerpt from Leonard Bernstein's "societal failure" testimony at the hearings: "They [remedies to the situation] have to come in ghettos and they have to come in youth and in schools and in our whole approach to our black brothers in our society."[129] By also quoting Sanford Allen's criticisms of the philharmonic, as well as a brief observation by Benjamin Steinberg on the lack of effort to recruit minorities by symphony orchestras, *Newsweek* attempted to maintain at least the appearance of objectivity. But the article's depiction of Madison, by an unidentified writer who never contacted the cellist, bordered on vendetta. After reporting that an unnamed "orchestra official" of the Pittsburgh Orchestra had stated that the cellist "failed to show up for many performances and rehearsals," the piece quoted Seymour Rosen, Pittsburgh's managing director, who said Madison had "capitalized on the struggle of the Negro people to his own advantage."[130] Rosen did not elaborate on this curious statement. At the hearings, Rosen made similar charges about Madison's alleged absences, despite the fact that they would have occurred before Rosen became orchestra manager. On the other hand, he also stated that when the cellist had attempted to resign from the Pittsburgh Symphony, "We would not have asked him to leave and we would have been happy to have him there."[131] And later Rosen said, "We had no intention of getting rid of Mr. Madison because of poor artistic standards. As a matter of fact, the reverse: We tried to keep him, and he tried to break his contract."[132]

In retrospect, Madison regretted many of the things he said during and immediately after the hearings. Even though he was in many ways goaded by the more experienced and politically savvy Arthur Davis, he made no excuses for his statements. For example, of his testimony that he was viewed with hostility during his first audition with the philharmonic, he now acknowledged that "it could have just been surprise on their part," adding, "When I walked out, people were looking at me, wondering, 'Who the hell is this?' It can be a great misperception to assume that people are racist because you think they're looking at you in a strange manner." Of his challenging members of the philharmonic to a face-off, he said, "I'm really sorry about that comment. That was absurd arrogance, and shortly after making that statement, I knew it." Finally, on the key issue of "artistic preference," Madison had arrived at a position far removed from the one he espoused some four decades ago. He explained, "Bernstein had testified at the hearing that I played well—he simply chose someone else. A conductor certainly has the right to prefer someone else without being called a racist."

Many of the decisions that Madison now regretted were certainly attributable to his youth and inexperience in issues beyond music. The cellist was twenty-three when the case was first opened and twenty-four during the hearings. He had no idea what he was about to subject himself to. For an accomplished musician, who had to that point enjoyed success at every stage of his young career, perhaps the most devastating experience was having to sit through days of testimony devoted to proving that his playing was in some way deficient:

> It was the height of profound humiliation. It affected my self-esteem tremendously, and it affected my playing. I could play freely in Europe, but I noticed when I came back to the United States, and I auditioned for Milwaukee, it was very hard for me. I could still feel the weight of what everyone had said. What else could they say except that your playing is lacking? There was nothing else for them to say in order to prove that they weren't racist. And this was publicly, not behind closed doors. That's what I opened myself up to.

There were some positive outcomes from the Human Rights Commission hearings. As part of its ruling, the commission ordered the philharmonic to submit, within sixty days, "an affirmative action personnel program which will afford black and other minority instrumentalists an equal opportunity to work as substitutes or extras and which will more effectively encourage the application of black and other minority instrumentalists for permanent employment."[133] It also stipulated that the philharmonic offer Davis and Madison work as substitutes "at the first opportunity."[134] The *New York Times* reported, "Both musicians said they doubted such an offer would be made to them because of their role in publicizing the situation, though other blacks might benefit."[135]

The philharmonic management claimed that, before the hearings, they had already changed some of their policies and had instituted training programs to increase the pool of minority musicians. In 1970, the philharmonic named Leon Thompson, an African American conductor, to the post of Director of Educational Projects, a position he held for a decade. Thompson, who organized the philharmonic's 1977 *Celebration of Black Composers*, engaged in outreach to the black community and established closer ties with the Symphony of the New World. In a memo dated December 7, 1970, Thompson summarized a meeting he had had with Benjamin Steinberg, Symphony of the New World music director, detailing ways in which the philharmonic could assist the symphony. The memo, which was sent to philharmonic manager Helen Thompson, included a list of African American players that the symphony identified as "ready to be used as substitutes" in the philharmonic. Among the sixteen musicians named were Joe Wilder and Earl Madison but not Arthur Davis.[136] Davis nevertheless did substitute with the philharmonic under conductor Karl Böhm. Madison was also offered work as a sub with the orchestra but declined. Had he accepted, Madison thought that his motivation for the suit itself might be construed as self-interest.

Joe Wilder played with the philharmonic on two occasions in the early 1970s—once under Pierre Boulez and once under André Kostelanetz. Ironically, with Kostelanetz, he was one of three added trumpet players who were positioned offstage for several performances of *Pines of Rome*. Wilder pointed out that placement of the trumpets offstage, however, was by no means some new manifestation of prejudice on the part of the philharmonic but the regular format for performances of Respighi's piece, adding, "We came out and took a bow at the end." Under Boulez, he was seated in the orchestra. Wilder had no problems during his appearances with the philharmonic: "Everyone was very friendly. I knew some of the guys, like Homer Mensch, because we used to do a lot of jingle dates together. And I had played with the principal trumpet player, Gerard Schwartz, in the Municipal Concerts Orchestra. He was awfully nice to me."

The Human Rights Commission case also raised awareness of discrimination in hiring in other musical areas, including Broadway show orchestras. As trumpeter Wilmer Wise recalled:

> When I came to New York, I was known by quite a few musicians but not by the contractors, so I called Morris Stonzek, the biggest contractor in town. I recited my complete résumé, and at the end, when I told him I had played with the Symphony of the New World, he said, "Wait! Are you black?" I said yes, and he said, "I have a show for you!" All it took was mentioning that I was black! This was during the time of Art Davis's and Earl Madison's suit, so everyone was a little sensitive about the complexion of their orchestras.[137]

But apart from the hiring of more minority substitutes, the Human Rights Commission edict and the philharmonic's rhetoric had little immediate or long-range effect on the hiring of African Americans as regular members of the philharmonic itself. In 1972, the philharmonic boasted of a plan, agreed to by the Human Rights Commission, to increase minority membership, touting it as "the first of its kind in the history of American symphony orchestras" and one that would "serve as a model for such antidiscrimination plans throughout the country."[138] Shortly thereafter, Donal Henahan noted, "It is not unusual nowadays to look up and see black instrumentalists working in the Philharmonic." At the same time, he acknowledged, "So far, progress has been limited to engaging substitutes and extras." Henahan was optimistic, however, that the philharmonic's newly installed training programs would eventually lead to the hiring of minority musicians as permanent members: "As so often happens in such cases, once action was obligatory the Philharmonic started pushing ahead under its own newly developed head of moral steam."[139]

While several black musicians had been hired as substitutes and some African Americans had been added to the philharmonic staff, two years after the conclusion of the case, Sanford Allen remained the only black regular member of the philharmonic. As one of the African American substitute players told Henahan, whose reporting throughout the entire Human Rights case was thorough and fair, "The Philharmonic players can put up with substitutes, but regular players—that's family."[140]

Women, however, had made some headway during that time. Bassist Lucille Dixon, an experienced jazz player as well as a founding member of the Symphony of the New World, wrote in a *New York Times* essay in 1971:

> As a woman musician, I must say that it's rather nice that the New York Philharmonic is hiring members of my sex these days. Since 1966, the Philharmonic has judged four women competent enough to be employed as permanent members of the ensemble, and a fifth will start this fall. I think that's fine. But as a *black* woman musician, I'd like to ask a question: How come the Philharmonic could find five qualified women musicians in such a short period of time when in the entire 129 years of its history it has found only *one* qualified black musician, irrespective of sex?[141]

Three years later, a prominent African American woman musician brought charges against another major symphony orchestra. In June 1974, timpanist Elayne Jones sued the San Francisco Symphony after she was denied tenure. A founding member of the Symphony of the New World and longtime campaigner for equality for minorities and women in orchestras, Jones had also testified at the 1969 Human Rights Commission hearings. Her case against the San Francisco Symphony dragged on for three years before it was eventually dismissed in 1977.[142]

In April 1974, Dick Campbell, who had extensive experience as a concert manager, undertook a new survey to determine what progress, if any, had been achieved in integrating the nation's symphony orchestras over the preceding decade. With the participation of the National Urban League affiliates, Campbell surveyed orchestras in sixty cities, dividing the respondents into (a) major symphonies, (b) metropolitan symphonies, (c) small-town, urban orchestras, and (d) colleges or music schools. Of the approximately 2,400 musicians employed by the twenty-eight "major" symphonies, some 42 were black (approximately 1.75 percent). Expanding the survey to all the major and metropolitan orchestras, it found there were nearly 9,000 musicians receiving salaries, of which some 70 were black (less than 1 percent).[143] And at the time of the survey—five years after the Human Rights Commission hearings—the New York Philharmonic still had only one black musician: Sanford Allen.

By 2012, more than four decades after the hearings, the makeup of the philharmonic had changed drastically. Nearly half of its 106 regular members were women, with many Asian players on the roster. The number of African Americans had also changed: now there were none.

Other Classical Activities

In addition to his symphonic work at ABC and his tenure as principal trumpet of the Symphony of the New World, during the 1960s and 1970s, Wilder played with several other classical groups, notably the Municipal Concerts Orchestra and the Manhattan Brass Quintet. Both groups were dedicated to bringing classical music to wider audiences.

The Municipal Concerts Orchestra was founded in 1960 by Julius Grossman, who in addition to his work as a conductor, established the music department at New York's celebrated High School for the Performing Arts, where he taught for more than two decades.[144] The orchestra performed a full schedule of free concerts in parks, community centers, and other public spaces throughout the five boroughs and Long Island. The orchestra was committed to integration and included African American musicians from its inception. It also hired Selwart Clarke, a violist, as contractor—the first African American to occupy that important position for any New York–based classical music organization.[145] Wilder played with the orchestra from 1963 to 1966, often as a featured soloist. In 1963, he played Haydn's *Trumpet Concerto* with the orchestra on a WNYC radio broadcast.[146] Despite these frequent appearances, the notion of an African American playing classical music was still a novelty to many New Yorkers. Wilder recalled one incident during a Municipal Concerts Orchestra performance on Long Island. He arrived in a white dinner jacket, the standard dress for a soloist. "This cop saw me and said, 'We're going to have some hot jazz tonight!' I said, 'If Haydn is hot jazz, that's what you're going to get!'"

In the early 1970s, as a member of the Manhattan Brass Quintet, Wilder made regular appearances under the auspices of New Audiences, which had been bringing music of all kinds to schools since the early 1950s. Wilder played second trumpet with Bunny Barron (first trumpet), Dick Berg (French horn), Bill Stanley (tuba) and Arnold Fromme (trombone). "We would teach the kids about the instruments and then show them how they were used," Wilder said. "The kids related to us because every time they saw a concert group, everyone had on tuxedos, and everything was so stiff. We were much more casual and relaxed." Occasionally, they were a bit too relaxed, as Wilder recalled:

> At one concert, we were playing "The Stars and Stripes Forever," and in the middle, there's a bugle call. Bunny Barron and I would alternate playing it at each performance. At one concert, we couldn't remember who had done it the day before, and Bill Stanley announced, "And the bugle call goes like this . . ." I picked up my horn, and then I saw Bunny pick up his, so I put mine down. Each of us thought the other was going to play. We did this three times, and Bill Stanley is getting annoyed and repeats, "And the bugle call goes like this! . . ." But by then, each time we tried to play it, we started laughing so hard that neither of us could do it. It was a shambles. Even the teachers started laughing.

Wilder was especially gratified to be able to serve as a role model for the minority students for whom they played: "We would go to schools in Harlem and the Bronx, and the black kids would start pointing me out to each other. You could see that it meant something to them to see a black musician playing that kind of music."

Wilder and Wilder: Joe and Alec

A highlight of Wilder's increased classical activity during this period was his opportunity to record a classical album as a featured soloist in 1964. The focus of that recording was the premiere of "Sonata for Trumpet and Piano,"[147] written especially for him by composer Alec Wilder, whose music was indefinable and cut a broad swath through the American musical landscape, encompassing classical, jazz, film writing, and popular song. The warm relationship between the unrelated—other than musically—Wilders began in the mid-1950s. Alec Wilder biographer Desmond Stone notes that unlike his other favored jazz players, whom the hard-drinking composer had met in various musician hangouts, "this Wilder [Joe] did not drink."[148] Rather, he was first introduced to Joe's trumpet sound on a record played for him by John Barrows, the noted French horn player and teacher—and one of the composer's closest friends. Alec recalled, "It was a record of no great consequence except for the trumpet sound I heard. It was the sound I always dreamed of hearing and never had. From then to this moment I am lost without his [Joe Wilder's] sound whenever I write for trumpets."[149] Tuba virtuoso Harvey Phillips was also a close mutual friend, and probably played a role in bringing the two Wilders together.

Their first recorded collaboration took place in June 1956, when Joe played on the album *New Music of Alec Wilder* (Riverside RLP12-219), led by guitarist Mundell Lowe and supervised by the composer himself. In the 1930s, Alec Wilder had written some pioneering octets that combine jazz and classical elements—foreshadowing the Third Stream of the 1950s—and the Lowe album was an extension of that genre and well suited to the talents of Joe Wilder, who, of course, was experienced in both areas. Although the relatively few solos on the album are short, Wilder's trumpet is a key color on the composer's palette, frequently emerging from the ensemble to assume the melodic lead, as well as adding a distinctively warm voice to the subtle harmonic blend.

The musical empathy that developed between the two Wilders, however, transcended the mere fact that Joe could play classical music and Alec had an appreciation for jazz. It soon became apparent to both that they shared an overall musical aesthetic and a respect for melody. In *Alec Wilder and His Friends*, Whitney Balliett quotes music historian James T. Maher, who said, Alec was "primarily a melodist, a composer who thinks in terms of timbres and coloristic things."[150] Of course, Joe Wilder, the player, is also a melodist; even as an improviser—particularly on ballads—he is devoted to enhancing and embellishing a composer's work rather than transfiguring it. Balliett, a friend and admirer of both Wilders, describes Alec's writing in a way that also uncannily fits Joe's playing:

His songs have an airy, elusive quality quite unlike that of any other American songwriter. The melodic lines flicker and turn unexpectedly, moving through surprising intervals and using rhythm in a purposeful, agile, jazz-based manner. The songs have a sequestered, intense gentleness, a subtle longing for what was and what might have been that eludes most ears.[151]

These shared qualities were not lost on the composer, who as early as his *The New Music of Alec Wilder* album, already considered Joe's trumpet an indispensable element of his musical vision. Mundell Lowe recalled, "We were putting the band together, and I was leaning on Alec to pick the players because I wanted him to be happy. When we got to the trumpets, he immediately asked, 'What about my namesake?' I said, 'I thought he was your brother!' and that cracked Alec up!" Lowe added, "Joe's playing just seemed to fit in with Alec's writing style. Alec had a certain soft approach to music, and Joe knew how to do that. A lot of other players would just blast away and screw up the balance. And Alec recognized that quality in Joe."[152]

Orrin Keepnews, the album's producer, recalled how essential Joe's sound was to Alec's conception on the *New Music* album: "Alec apparently felt that Joe was the only trumpet player capable of dealing with this music."[153] Joe, however, was unavailable for one of the sessions, so they were forced to replace him with the highly respected studio and jazz trumpeter Jimmy Nottingham. As Keepnews wrote:

> But it wasn't Joe Wilder. Alec suffered in silence, but as soon as the session was over, approached me with what was obviously a carefully thought-out solution. Although nothing was demonstrably wrong, the entire session just didn't feel right to him, simply because it lacked that other Wilder. So if we would agree to completely scrap the session— just throw away, without discussion or attempts to salvage anything, everything that had just been recorded . . . and reschedule for the earliest time Joe could make it, he would reimburse us for the entire cost of the evening! It was a monumental offer (in the ensuing almost-42 years, I have never had another experience to match it), and it made abundantly clear how strongly he felt.[154]

"That's exactly right," Mundell Lowe agreed. "We ended up killing that whole session. Nottingham was a wonderful trumpet player, but he was not Joe Wilder. He didn't have that romantic sound that Joe gets."[155]

Alec Wilder's music was difficult, and there was no rehearsal. "In those days, the union wouldn't allow it unless you were paid for a record date, and the company didn't want to do that," Lowe recalled. "Everything was written, and the guys in the band read like hawks, so there was no problem at all." The composer deferred to Lowe and his musicians, making no attempt to impose his own interpretations on the music. "Alec stood off to the side," said Lowe. "He wouldn't interfere—he loved every note we played!"[156] The guitarist also noted the personal rapport between the composer and the trumpeter on that date:

> Joe was full of puns, and Alec had a great sense of humor, but he was very quiet. He would laugh behind his hand. But every time Joe said something, it would break him up. It was contagious—the rest of the band would hear it and start laughing. I would interrupt and say, "Wait a minute, guys! We have to record this thing now. The clock's running!"[157]

When the album was reissued in 1963 on the Offbeat label, Frank Sinatra, another admirer of Alec Wilder, wrote the insightful liner notes.[158]

After the 1956 Mundell Lowe recording, Alec Wilder used his namesake on a series of projects, from film scores and television shows to commercials. Apart from their musical compatibility, a personal friendship emerged. Alec got to know Joe's family, and Joe's wife, Solveig, still recalls his kindness toward her. Joe also appreciated Alec's respect for musicians and his insistence that they be treated fairly. In November 1960, Joe led a jazz group for an NBC television special featuring host Dave Garroway.[159] Alec Wilder, who served as musical director, insisted that the musicians receive proper screen credit, a rare occurrence then (as now). "He wrote a special piece to be used as the trailer listed every musician's name," Joe recalled. "Alec was so proud of the musicians who worked for him that he always wanted to make sure that they got their due." Joe also recalled that the composer stood up for his musicians financially: "Alec hired some of us from the Garroway show to do a commercial. The advertising agency decided at the last minute to cancel without paying us. Alec lit into them. 'You don't have to pay me,' he said, 'but you have to pay the musicians.' So they paid us for a session. That's the kind of person he was."

In 1961, Alec Wilder was commissioned by *Life* magazine to write the music for a film about fashion titled *Since Life Began*, and again chose Joe to participate. The composer agreed to accept a lump sum for the project, regardless of the instrumentation. "Had I written for a small combo I'd have made a fair amount of money," Alec recalled. "But I kept thinking of all those great players I had come to meet through John Barrows. So before I knew it I was scoring a twenty-minute movie for seventeen musicians. So of course I wound up with very little money, but a great deal of joy and beautiful playing."[160] Joe also played on the soundtrack of two films scored by Alec Wilder for filmmaker

Jerome Hill: *The Sand Castle* (1960) and *Open the Door and See All the People* (1964).

The musical relationship between the two Wilders culminated in the recording of Alec's "Sonata for Trumpet and Piano." Written specifically for Joe in 1963, the piece was recorded in 1964 on the trumpeter's only classical album, his eponymous LP on the Golden Crest label (RE7007). In addition to the premiere of "Sonata for Trumpet and Piano," the album included selections by Haydn (Andante from the *Trumpet Concerto*), Brandt ("First Concert Piece"), Saint-Saëns ("The Swan"), Fiocco ("Allegro"), and Leroy Anderson ("A Trumpeter's Lullaby"). Joe picked the repertoire himself, choosing some of the pieces he had played more than a decade earlier at his graduation recital at the Manhattan School of Music.

Golden Crest was a small independent label founded by Clark Galehouse Jr., a musician who became a record company owner. Galehouse had his own studio in Huntington Station, Long Island, about forty miles from New York City. Golden Crest also had its own pressing plant and print shop at the same location. The label recorded a wide variety of music from doo-wop to chamber groups and school orchestras, as well as a surprisingly eclectic array of jazz artists, ranging from Don Redman and Joe Venuti to Ran Blake. Galehouse was a friend and admirer of Alec Wilder, and over the years, Golden Crest issued albums of Alec's music played by Harvey Phillips (tuba), Barry Snyder (piano), Paul Brodie (saxophone), John Barrows (French horn), Robert Levy (trumpet), David Soyer (cello), and others.

When Alec first proposed that Joe record the trumpet sonata, the composer sent him a telegram. Joe remembered that the message said, "I've decided us Wilders have to stick together." The trumpeter was apprehensive at first, especially after seeing the music: "My first reaction was, 'Oh, my God, there's no way in the world I can play this!'" When he expressed his concerns to the composer, Alec told him, "I don't see how it could be over your head. After all, I wrote these things because I've heard you play them!" Indeed, as music historian James T. Maher, a friend of both men, wrote in his highly literate album annotation, "The piece clearly reflects the composer's admiration for the player—the performance movingly declares the player's affection for the music and his high regard for the composer."[161] Maher also points out the sonata's "rediscovery of the truly gorgeous sound of the middle and lower register of the trumpet," a particular strength of Joe's, explicitly tapped by the composer. The first three movements of the "Sonata for Trumpet" showcase the lyrical side of Joe's playing. It was probably the fourth movement, "Rhythmic," with its challenging intervals, range, and double- and triple-tongued passages that prompted the trumpeter's initial trepidation. Joe executed the piece with aplomb, as he did the even more demanding "First Concert Piece," by Brandt, with its spectacular finale.

Alec Wilder took an active role in the recordings of his music and usually attended the sessions, as was the case for the Golden Crest Joe Wilder recording. "Alec was there for the recording of the sonata, and was very encouraging," Joe said. "After everything I played, he would give that smile and say, 'That's really fine.' He was a very compassionate kind of guy. He never made you feel uncomfortable. He might make little suggestions, changing the nuances, but you had freedom."

Perhaps Alec's feelings for Joe were best summed up by radio host Willis Conover, who reported that the composer was growing "a bit weary of disclaiming kinship with Thornton Wilder, Billy Wilder and Honeychile Wilder," but quoted him as saying, "I'd like to be related to Joe."[162]

Joe also credits his accompanists, pianists Milton Kaye (1909–2006) and Harriett Wingreen (born in 1925), with "helping me through it." Kaye, who played on "Sonata for Trumpet," was a versatile performer. His long and eclectic career included work as a musical director for all three major networks, as well as stints as Jascha Heifetz's accompanist and as a member of Toscanini's NBC Symphony of the Air. Wingreen, who played on the rest of the Golden Crest album pieces, began an association with the New York Philharmonic in 1965 that continued into 2011. "Had it not been for her," Joe said, "it never would have come off as well as it did." Some forty-seven years later, the pianist also had fond memories of her collaboration with Joe: "I liked him very much and enjoyed the session immensely. I liked everything about his playing, and he was such a nice person. We got along great."[163]

Although Joe Wilder had done an extensive amount of classical playing in the 1950s and 1960s, most of it was for live performance or in conjunction with his work on staff at ABC. The relatively rare Golden Crest LP is essentially the sole recorded evidence of what he sounded like as a classical artist. Despite the different demands of classical and jazz playing, one is struck by how much of his musical persona carries across the genres. Wilder's singular tone and phrasing is unmistakable, whether the context is jazz, commercial, or classical music. While his classical background and formal repertory study equipped him to "play the notes," his life experience and overall artistic sensibility imbues each piece with a poignancy not always present in the playing of highly accomplished trumpet soloists with more traditional classical backgrounds. Indeed, it is that elusive quality that attracted Alec Wilder to Joe's playing in the first place.

James T. Maher also discussed the problems faced by a musician like Wilder, who enters the classical arena from a "nontraditional" background:

If he turns to the performance of formal ("classical") music, jazz apologists are apt to use his work, however inept it may be, to "prove" that jazz players can "play anything." The tolerant music lover is, on the other hand, likely to applaud him simply for performing a formal work without making a shambles of it. As Samuel Johnson long ago remarked about lady preachers, one is not concerned that they preach well but that they preach at all. The serious player is not served by the attitude of the jazz apologist, or the tolerant formalist. To put it simply, what Joseph Wilder wanted was for his performance to be weighed solely on its musical merits.[164]

The reviews of the album, although few, were highly complimentary. *New York Times* critic Theodore Strongin wrote, "In superb fashion, Joe Wilder, an ex-jazz man, makes his way through Alec Wilder's *Sonata for Trumpet and Piano* and miscellaneous conservatory showpieces, among them Vassily Brandt's *Concert Piece No. 1*, and Leroy Anderson's *A Trumpeter's Lullaby*. Joe Wilder makes the 'Lullaby' almost sound like a lullaby, a technical and musical feat practically unheard of in band clinics, where the piece is a standard test of skill."[165] And an unsigned review in the *Instrumentalist*, although brief, alluded to Wilder's sound: "In both tonal beauty and phenomenal technique this is an extraordinary display of trumpeting. . . . If you have forgotten how gorgeous is the sound of the trumpet's middle and lower register, 'The Swan' will remind you."[166]

In June 1982, some sixteen months after Alec Wilder's death, Joe was one of many artists who paid tribute to his friend at a Carnegie Hall concert, part of the Kool (formerly Newport) Jazz Festival. As he often did, Whitney Balliett singled out the trumpeter's contribution, "stately, handsome readings, one muted and one open-horn, of 'Trouble Is a Man' and 'Blackberry Winter,'" for praise.[167]

Joe Wilder's making of a classical album has inevitably led to comparisons with Wynton Marsalis, who twenty years later, made his stunning classical recording debut with a Grammy-winning collection of trumpet concertos with the National Philharmonic Orchestra, under Raymond Leppard. As Whitney Balliett wrote in his extensive *New Yorker* profile of Wilder, "Wilder was one of the earliest musicians to move easily between the world of straight music and the world of jazz, and he was certainly the first black musician to do so. He paved the way for Wynton Marsalis before Marsalis was born."[168] And Richard Williams, writing in the *Times* of London, noted that "Marsalis's tone is now approaching the sort of lustrous perfection previously the sole property of the unsung Joe Wilder who—rather than [Miles] Davis—is Marsalis's true forbear." Williams then posed the rhetorical question, "Why the laurels for Marsalis, then, and never for Wilder, who has made fewer recordings in his own right in 30 years than Marsalis has made in three?"[169]

Wilder, a great admirer of Marsalis (as is Marsalis of Wilder), is uncomfortable with the parallels frequently drawn between their careers and quickly downplays any suggestion that he "paved the way" for the younger trumpet star. "I might have been playing classical music before Wynton Marsalis, but I was *here* before Wynton Marsalis!" Wilder said. "I never played on the level that Wynton plays on. Wynton is in a class with people like [Timofei] Dokschitzer, the Russian trumpet player, and Maurice André. I wish people would stop saying that I did it first. It has no meaning in this case."

In fact, Wilder is quick to deflect any credit for being "the first" at anything—even when a convincing case may be made for it. Yet he is scrupulous in acknowledging the contributions of others who preceded him. "I was well aware that if I played classical music well, it might take the onus off the jazz players to some extent," he explained. "But I was certainly not the first black trumpet player to play classical music. For example, Billy Horner [1921–1997] played with Leopold Stokowski's All-American Youth Symphony Orchestra. A lot of people don't even know who he was. To my knowledge, he was the first black player to play classical music in an established symphony orchestra."

There is certainly no comparison between the impact of the major label (CBS/Sony) classical debut of Marsalis, at twenty-one already perhaps jazz's most visible—and at times, controversial—figure, and Wilder's little-publicized release two decades earlier on the relatively obscure Golden Crest label. There were also vast differences in the preparation of each artist for their recordings. In 1983, Marsalis had the luxury of taking time off from his jazz playing to condition his embouchure for the classical project. In 1964, Wilder, forty-two and with a family to support, had to fit the Golden Crest recording into his normal busy schedule of staff assignments at ABC, freelance recordings, and commercial jingles. "I didn't take any time off, but I did have a chance in between to practice and get these things together, so I felt comfortable doing them," Wilder said, adding, "I think Wynton did it the right way. In order to really do it well, I think you have to sever yourself from one or the other and then devote your attention to the particular thing that you're doing. You want to get into that frame of mind, whether for jazz or classical. They both require a little different technique." Wilder elaborated on the different requirements of jazz and classical playing:

> It's both mental and physical. In classical music, you don't have the liberty to do some of the things that you can do in jazz. If you're playing

jazz, and you feel all of a sudden there's something you would like to attempt, you can. Also, in jazz, if you make a mistake or fluff a note, you can turn it into something creative. In classical music, if it's there, you're required to play it, and you have to play it in a particular way. You can't suddenly decide to bend a note in Tchaikovsky. You can't just take those liberties. You can in your cadenzas and maybe in your phrasing, but basically, you have to play those notes. There are some things, like the half-valve effect, that we do in jazz that you wouldn't do in classical music. You're more or less bound to a stricter routine.

Wilder recalled one embarrassing incident when he played a major piece for the first time with a classical orchestra:

> We were doing the *New World Symphony*. It was the first time I'd seen it, and it's such a beautiful piece of music. I saw these thirty-second notes, and I figured they had to be played really fast: ya-bum-bum-bum, bah-bee-bip-bee-bee! I had just charged into this thing, and they're all looking at me like, "Where in the world did this guy come from?" There's no hole deep enough to dig and bury yourself![170]

Wilder did acknowledge there is room in classical music for individual expression, however. "When you have a trumpet solo, you can put your own feeling into it and play it with your own sound, even as you adhere to what's on the paper," he said.

Despite these differences, Wilder feels there is an overriding spirit that pervades all music. No matter what the genre, when conditions are right and everything is in balance, he finds the effect to be magical: "In both classical music and jazz music, sometimes you can play something, and it just touches your heart. You have no idea when this is going to happen. The music is so beautiful that it seems to come from just someplace unknown to you, but at the moment it happens, you just feel so happy about it."

Although his classical career was in a sense "a dream deferred," he was grateful for the opportunities that eventually opened up for him in the 1960s and 1970s. He also reflected on some of his friends and colleagues who never lived to see those opportunities. "I think a lot of fellows would have gone into classical music if they could have," he said. "When he was with the John Kirby band, Charlie Shavers used to tell me, 'Well, they won't let us in the symphony orchestra, but I can do this!' And he'd imitate something that the philharmonic or the Philadelphia Orchestra had played, and he'd play it as well as they did. He'd just laugh about it! Later on, he would incorporate excerpts from a classical piece in his solos. He was more or less telling the audience, 'Look, I never got a chance, but I'm capable of doing it.'"

1960s Recordings

In the middle of his increased classical work as a member of the Symphony of the New World and other ensembles and his full schedule at ABC, Wilder still found time to freelance in the recording studios, playing on more than seventy-five albums during the 1960s. These dates included sessions with such jazz creators as Dizzy Gillespie, John Lewis, J. J. Johnson, Gene Krupa, Oliver Nelson, Gil Evans, and Tadd Dameron and singers of all types, including Ray Charles, Johnny Mathis, Leontyne Price, Oscar Brown Jr., Della Reese, Tony Bennett, and Harry Belafonte. Also, during this time, he made motion picture soundtrack albums, such as *The Hustler*. Unlike during the previous decade, however, the trumpeter's solo work was rather sparse, consisting primarily of obbligatos behind singers or some melody statements or brief solos on borderline jazz/easy-listening albums led by Marty Gold, Ray Martin, Burt Bacharach, Jackie Gleason, and Henry Jerome. Wilder's two stellar solos on Tadd Dameron's 1962 *Magic Touch* (Riverside RLP419), "Dial B for Beauty" and "Bevan's Birthday," were rare opportunities during the decade for Wilder to shine on pure jazz dates.

Among the odder places Wilder turned up was on a 1962 LP by an Israeli folk group, the Four Ayalons, on which he plays a convincingly idiomatic solo on "Hava Nagilah."[171] Wilder also played the trumpet heard in the background of Staff Sergeant Barry Sadler's hit record, "Ballad of the Green Berets," a patriotic Vietnam-war anthem that topped the *Billboard* charts for several weeks in 1966. Five years earlier, Wilder had made another recording with a military theme: an album of Army and Navy bugle calls for Choice Records, a Savoy subsidiary.[172] The recording was intended for use by military posts without the services of a live bugler. All in a day's work for a freelance studio musician in New York in the 1960s.

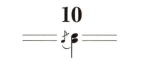

Freelance (1974–1990)

The End of the Staff Orchestras

By the early 1970s, the golden era of the network orchestras was coming to a close, and abundant freelance studio work in New York was waning. Changes in popular taste, the pervasive influence of rock, and the use of "canned" music for films and television—as well as the diffusion of the recording industry to such cities as Nashville, Detroit, and Los Angeles—all contributed to the end of a way of life for the select group of players that had dominated the New York studio scene since the 1940s. Changes in technology also played a major role, especially the advent of synthesizers, which could produce at least the semblance of an orchestral sound at a fraction of the cost. "Synthesizers were the bane of the network orchestras," Wilder said. "One keyboard player could supplant twenty other musicians. Musically, it wasn't the same, but to the public it didn't make any difference." In the early 1970s, the networks began phasing out their regular orchestras, as their programming budgets could no longer sustain sixty-five or seventy-five musicians on staff.

Wilder with Benny Carter, Concord recording session, Coast Recorders, San Francisco, August 1985. *(Photo by Ed Berger.)*

The last bastion of the staff orchestra was the late-night talk-show house band. The major shows each had its own orchestra: there was NBC's *Tonight Show* band, led by Doc Severinson (the show moved from New York to Los Angeles in 1972); *The Merv Griffin Show* band, led by Mort Lindsey (the show originated in New York only from 1969 to 1970); ABC's *Dick Cavett Show* band, led by drummer Bobby Rosengarden; and *The David Frost Show* band, with musical director Billy Taylor.

Wilder was a member of *The Dick Cavett Show* orchestra at ABC from 1969 until its termination in 1974. After a few months in prime time, the program switched to the late night time slot in direct competition with NBC's *Tonight Show*, hosted by Johnny Carson, and *The Merv Griffin Show* on CBS. Cavett did not feature the band as prominently as Carson did *The Tonight Show*'s orchestra, with its flamboyant leader, trumpet star Doc Severinson. "He didn't usually show the band, unless we were accompanying a guest," Wilder recalled. "Dick Cavett was very nice to the musicians, but he wasn't into the band like Johnny Carson was. He was more of an intellectual." Saxophonist Leon Cohen agreed:

> It was a marvelous orchestra—the cream of the crop at ABC. There was some rivalry between us and *The Tonight Show* band before Carson moved to California. But it wasn't a musical show. Cavett preferred ninety minutes of talk and would be having such a good time doing an interview with someone like Katharine Hepburn that he would get carried away. The producer would be off camera signaling frantically to end a segment, and Cavett would get incensed and say, "We're not going off the air until we're finished!"[1]

Soon after the show went off the air in 1974, Wilder ran into Cavett at a telethon. "He told me he regretted that he hadn't featured the band more because he felt our band was as good as Johnny Carson's," Wilder said.

The trumpeter was present on October 13, 1970, when a group of black musicians disrupted taping of the Cavett show to protest the "dearth of black jazz musicians on television."[2] The incident was the latest salvo in a campaign by a group calling itself the Jazz and People's Movement, which had recently launched demonstrations against *The Tonight Show*. The group's leader, saxophonist Rahsaan Roland Kirk, was out of town, so Lee Morgan, Billy Harper, and Andrew Cyrille led the action.[3] "There were some nice guys involved," Wilder said, "guys who could play, but they never stopped to think of the effect of what they were doing. It was just tactless." The Cavett show band had several black musicians who became targets of the protesters. "At one point, some of them called me, Milt Hinton, and Ernie Royal 'Uncle Toms,'" Wilder recalled. "I told them, 'If you call me that again, you'll find out I'm one of the thugs from the street just like you!'" The demonstration led to an invitation for the protesters to appear on the Cavett show on October 22, 1970. Edith Kirk (wife of Rahsaan Roland Kirk), Cecil Taylor, Freddie Hubbard, Billy Harper, and Andrew Cyrille took part in a half-hour discussion with Cavett.[4] Dan Morgenstern, then editor of *Down Beat*, supported the goals of the Jazz and People's Movement but grew increasingly disillusioned with the political rhetoric of the group and its promotion of avant-garde jazz to the exclusion of other forms. He felt that the organization's representatives had failed to make a compelling case on the Cavett show:

> On the evidence of the discussion . . . jazz is a music almost exclusively made by musicians who are black, are never seen on TV, play to please themselves rather than their audience, reject all entertainment values, are deprived of recognition, and speak in the language of contemporary political radicalism. In addition, the impression was created (even if perhaps not intended) that the only truly valid jazz today is made by the musicians on the panel and those who think and play like them.[5]

The movement achieved its greatest exposure when, as the networks sought to stave off another demonstration, the group was given a five-minute slot on *The Ed Sullivan Show*, the nation's most renowned variety program.[6] A nine-piece ensemble, which included Kirk, Charles Mingus, Archie Shepp, and Roy Haynes, appeared live on January 24, 1971. Reaction to the surreal segment was mixed, with supporters praising the music as "uncompromising" and detractors, including Morgenstern, finding it unfocused and chaotic. Morgenstern writes, "The ad hoc group's single number, which showed no signs of being rehearsed, was a musical and visual shambles, perplexing even seasoned jazz listeners and viewers. An opportunity to strike a blow for the cause of jazz on commercial TV dissolved into hot air."[7] Of course, jazz—especially the more progressive or experimental forms advocated by the Jazz and People's Movement representatives—was not the only type of music rarely if ever seen on commercial television. The music of John Cage and other classical avant-gardists would have as little chance of major network exposure as did progressive jazz, although in the case of the former, the explosive issue of race was not a factor.

Wilder and his fellow musicians in the Cavett show band were luckier than most of their colleagues at the network. As Leon Cohen recalled, "At ABC, they gradually let people go until there were only the sixteen or eighteen members of the Cavett show orchestra left. When that ended, we were all gone."[8] The official termination date for the staff orchestras of all three networks was January 31, 1974. One immediate consequence was what the American Federation of Musicians (AFM) termed a "withholding of services"—essentially a strike—against the networks. The union had been granting the networks more favorable terms in their contracts because they maintained full-time staff orchestras employing a substantial number of musicians. Now that the networks had eliminated this avenue of employment, the union sought to end the preferential treatment. Another point of contention was the use of music recorded outside of the United States for American programs.[9] The contract was finally agreed to by the networks in July 1974.[10]

Although the musicians were entitled to severance pay, Wilder recalled one method by which the networks tried to reduce the amount:

> There was an agreement between the networks and the AF of M based on the number of years you had been with the network and your salary. But the networks would get around that by saying, "Well, we don't use violins on all these daytime soap operas," so they started reducing the number of days a week the string players worked and then based the severance pay on that number of days. They had all kinds of gimmicks.

Just as many of the veterans of the swing era big bands had sought refuge in the studios in the 1940s and 1950s, now these studio musicians had to find other avenues of employment. During the 1970s, there was still some freelance work in the New York recording studios, but that began to drop off too, as did the lucrative jingle industry. "The ad agencies like Young and Rubicam began to be staffed by younger people," Wilder said. "They wanted their colleagues to get the jobs and began easing a lot of the older fellows out."

Some of the former staff musicians found work in the Broadway pit orchestras, others moved to the West Coast studios, and still others went into teaching. "It was difficult for them because the networks had been their main source of income," Wilder said. "Some of them were reduced to doing club dates or whatever else they could get. But they had no connections with that world because they had been with the networks for so long." "Club date" is a blanket term referring to a wide range of musical employment, encompassing private parties, weddings, bar mitzvahs, charity fund-raisers, and other functions. Ensembles fulfilling the most exclusive of these engagements were generally known as "society orchestras." Wilder himself began to take some of these jobs, primarily with Peter Duchin, whose orchestra represented the pinnacle of this curious musical genre.

Peter Duchin and the Society Orchestra Phenomenon

Beginning in the 1970s and continuing into the late 1990s, Wilder worked fairly often for Peter Duchin, pianist and leader of one of the most prestigious society orchestras. The son of bandleader Eddy Duchin, Peter became a musical institution, fulfilling as many as a thousand engagements a year—often simultaneously supplying several musical groups under his name. His clientele included nearly every celebrity, as well as U.S. presidents and European royalty. This type of playing required some very specific musical skills. Because of the need to be able to play a huge repertoire of tunes—a 2009 article about Duchin claimed his band members each knew three thousand songs[11]—without preparation and without music, musicians needed to be able to "fake," or play pieces with which they were unfamiliar. "You had to think on your feet," Wilder said. "A lot of times, you'd run into tunes you'd never heard before, and that would put your harmonic abilities to the test." As Duchin himself wrote, "Unlike jazz or concert bands, successful dance bands play mostly without music, since they don't want to break the flow of the evening by fumbling for the arrangements. Dance band musicians have to carry around thousands of tunes in their heads, along with the fundamental four-part harmonies of each song."[12] Bruce A. MacLeod, in his comprehensive study of the club date phenomenon, describes the central role of faking within that industry:

> The absence of written music during performance, which you noticed at your nephew's wedding reception, *is* completely standard practice throughout the club date business, regardless of the size of the band. Of course, there are musicians playing private parties or nightclubs outside of New York who have large memorized repertoires, but in New York memorized repertoire has become a prerequisite for getting any work in the club date field. Brass, woodwind, and violin players must also be able to play harmony parts for most of the songs if they hope to work in any bands that use more than a single melody instrument.[13]

MacLeod also points out that written arrangements were not practical because the size of the ensemble could vary greatly from night to night and that a large portion of the repertoire consisted of requests.

In 2012, Duchin elaborated on the process: "The guys would know the tunes and the type of harmonies we expected. They would know that their instrument fit into, say, a third alto position and should be playing the third alto notes. The more talented people can add more harmonically because they understand the full graph of the chord or the harmonic structure of the piece."[14]

Singer-pianist-educator Nancy Marano, who worked with the orchestra for about a decade early in her career, also witnessed firsthand the extemporaneous process of music making in the Duchin organization:

> It was all off the cuff—nobody had a stitch of music. People would come up with requests, and everyone would just go right into it. The musicians had to come up with instant arrangements. The lead players of the sections would come up with something, and the second and third players would have to make up their parts as if they had an orchestration. You would do this from four to six hours. It was amazing that the band sounded as good as it did. There was a select group of players in New York who could step in and do that very well.[15]

As a singer, Marano's contribution was closely dictated by the format: "Every once in a while, Peter would insert a vocal. I would call my key and have to figure out a song that would fit the tempo they were in. It was all about dancing, and I came to hate a lot of songs because I would have to fit them into tempos that they weren't made to play in. Years later I found out that 'Just in Time' is a nice song when I heard it at the right tempo!" With Duchin, Marano also greatly expanded her repertoire: "It was great practice because you had to learn all of the great Gershwin and Rodgers and Hart songs. Of course, everybody also had to learn all of the latest tunes from every hit record. If a new show came out, we knew there would be requests for it. And of course we had to learn the horrific 'Strangers in the Night' and 'Feelings'—some of those were just torture!"[16]

Duchin, who was born in 1937, was a serious jazz fan. He had played in a Dixieland group in junior high school and recalled dissecting classic recordings with fellow student Maitland Edey. "We'd sit glued to the phonograph, quizzing each other about who was playing what instrument," he writes. "Our taste expanded from Armstrong and Bix to Teddy Wilson, Billie Holiday, and Benny Goodman, and eventually to Thelonious Monk, Charlie Parker, Dizzy Gillespie, and Miles Davis."[17] So the leader could fully appreciate Joe Wilder's skills as a jazz player as well as his ability to fit in with the primary "society" music function of the orchestra. "I thought that with his musical knowledge, it might be kind of interesting if he came and played with the band and added an element of jazz to what we were playing," Duchin said. "He had such wonderful taste. When it was time for Joe to take a solo, it was always a pleasure to listen to him. And I can't say that about everybody!"[18]

"Joe would add that extra jazz element that Peter really liked," Marano said. "Peter loved jazz, and while he himself wasn't a jazz player by any stretch of the imagination, he respected jazz players in general, and he loved Joe's playing." Although much of the time, Duchin's music provided ambience for parties or the backdrop for dancers, Marano noted that "when Joe would play, everybody would just listen. He's just such a beautiful player."[19]

During his heyday, Duchin might be called on to supply several orchestras at once for different events. "Peter would work the best-paying date himself," Marano recalled, "and then he'd send out his second band, which could do pretty much as well as the first band. The third band might be a little less skilled. One good thing about Peter Duchin was that he always paid the union benefits and pensions; a lot of those guys never did that."[20]

Beginning in the 1970s, as popular tastes evolved, both the demand for sophisticated society orchestras and the pool of musicians able to staff them declined.[21] As of 2009, there was still enough work, however, for Duchin to maintain fifteen tuxedos and command up to $25,000 for a performance.[22] "The business has changed primarily in the area of deejays," Duchin noted. "People are hiring deejays because they're cheaper than a big band and also because younger people are used to that kind of deafening sound. One of our musicians said, 'Let's put the band on stun—just play as loud as we possibly can!' But I think there's still a demand for the American songbook and the big band stuff."[23]

Duchin also pointed out that it became increasing difficult to find musicians with the requisite skills to produce the on-the-spot arrangements needed for club dates: "There used to be the Borscht Belt, Grossinger's and the other resorts in the Catskills, and each one of them had a live band. Many of the musicians in town would go there and spend the summer, and that's where they learned the business. That doesn't exist anymore."[24] Duchin, who serves on the board of the Manhattan School of Music, is helping to establish formal courses in club-date playing at both the Manhattan School and Juilliard to increase the pool of musicians. While club-date work is not usually among the career ambitions of students at these prestigious conservatories, it is a practical means of earning a living in the increasingly economically challenged world of the performing arts.

Wilder enjoyed working with Duchin and appreciated the musicianship of his fellow band members but, ultimately, found the genre limiting, as did Marano. "The people that Peter hires are very nice and very good players, but there's a certain routine," Wilder said. "Nobody's going to really get a chance to do any real improvising. You just move from one tune to the next. But that's the nature of that kind of playing, and you accept it. It's another aspect of the music business."

Sometimes the musicians would turn to humor to break up the monotony of the club-date life. Wilder recalled that at one function, to amuse themselves, the musicians conspired to play the bridge to "Dinah" on every tune. The dancers never noticed and continued to applaud enthusiastically after each number. Marano sang occasionally with Lester Lanin, another legendary society orchestra leader, whose career began in the early 1930s. "The musicians would pull stunts on him, like playing 'Strangers in the Night' in 5/4 [time]," she said. "He knew something was odd. He'd turn around hoping to catch somebody, but everybody had such straight faces. Lester Lanin was a big target because no one had any respect for him."[25]

Wilder once used his sense of humor to liven up a recording date with Lanin. After the band ran through "Sweet Leilani," Wilder overheard Lanin asking guitarist Everett Barksdale to follow the melody with a guitar figure that would enhance the Hawaiian ambience of the tune. When Lanin returned to the control booth, Wilder got on his mike and "innocently" suggested the same thing to the leader. "He couldn't believe it," Wilder, said. "He told me, 'I just said the same thing!'" A few minutes later, while the band was playing "Lassus Trombone," Lanin came into the studio and this time suggested that trombonist Eddie Bert play some more prominent smears. Again, Wilder overheard him and made the same suggestion to the leader, who was utterly amazed by this coincidence. Wilder continued with his "helpful" suggestions while his fellow musicians laughed so hard they could barely play. Finally, after a run-through on "Hello, Dolly," in which the band members sang a less-than-successful chorus, Wilder again had the answer. "Lester, we really need you to come out and lead us when we sing." The leader did and was very pleased with the results, after which he pronounced, "I wish I had musicians as helpful as Joe Wilder on every date!"

In an acerbic piece in *Down Beat*, bassist Whitey Mitchell noted the long-standing "curious relationship between jazzmen and society music," which he described as "a hodgepodge of warmed-over music of the '20s, Broadway show tunes, movie themes, naughty French or Italian songs, and standards, all superimposed on a cut-time kickbeat rhythm called 'businessman's bounce' in an incongruous medley that lasts all evening."[26]

As studio work diminished, many former network musicians with jazz credentials, such as Milt Hinton, George Duvivier, Hank Jones, Clark Terry, and Joe Wilder, simply shifted their focus back to jazz, which in the 1970s, was experiencing something of a revival. The expanding markets for jazz included a burgeoning interest in Japan, an expanded festival scene in the United States and Europe, the advent of the "jazz party," and the birth of the jazz repertory orchestra movement, as well as the rapid growth of jazz education in the academy.

In addition to increased jazz activity, Wilder was able to return to Broadway orchestra work, which he had had to forgo while on staff at ABC. And unlike some of his colleagues, Wilder had been careful to save his money during the halcyon years. "I grew up during the Depression, and I knew what it was like to not have food," he said. "I would always put aside any extra income outside the network salary in the bank. That gave me some financial security, so that when things dropped off altogether, I still had a source of income from savings."

Return to Broadway

Apart from a four-month stint as first trumpet on *Man of La Mancha* in 1972, Wilder had not been a regular member of a Broadway orchestra since the closing of *The Most Happy Fella* in 1957. The demands of his work as a full-time staff musician at ABC precluded the type of long-range commitment a Broadway show required. But with the phasing out of the network orchestras in the early 1970s and their final demise in January 1974, Wilder was free to add this musical outlet to his other activities, which filled the void. He was immediately hired for *Lorelei*, which starred Carol Channing, and soon afterward became principal trumpet for *Shenandoah*, which opened in January 1975 and ran until August 1977.

Wilder was dismayed to find the situation for minority musicians virtually unchanged since his initial Broadway breakthroughs in the 1950s. After the 1958 Urban League report, *Job Status of the Negro Professional Musician in the New York Metropolitan Area*, prepared by G. Douglas Pugh, there had been several efforts to increase minority representation in the Broadway pit orchestras. In 1970, Robert Magnum, Commissioner of the New York State Division of Human Rights, met with theater owners, producers, contractors, and musicians in an attempt to effect change. On November 18, 1976, the New York City Commission on Human Rights conducted a hearing devoted specifically to discrimination in the Broadway orchestras and issued a new report: "Hiring Practices for Broadway Musical Orchestras: The Exclusionary Effect on Minority Musicians."[27] Some twenty witnesses testified, including producers, contractors, and musicians. Commissioner Eleanor Holmes Norton, who chaired the meeting, pointed out in her opening statement that "the pits of the average show are as white as they were decades ago," and "the bulk of the black musicians have had to depend upon the black shows to find work."[28] Trombonist Jack Jeffers, a veteran of many Broadway shows, attested to the short-term nature of gains made after the Urban League's efforts in 1958 and the New York State Division of Human Rights initiative in 1970, noting that after a year or two, the number of black musicians returned to previous levels.[29]

The event that brought the issue of discrimination on Broadway to a head was the Houston Grand Opera's revival of *Porgy and Bess*, which opened in

New York in September 1976 at the Uris Theatre. Despite its depiction of what purported to be African American life in Charleston in the 1920s, only four members of the forty-three-member orchestra were black, a fact that Commissioner Norton termed "an especially dramatic example of an industry-wide pattern of severely restricted opportunities for minority musicians in Broadway musicals."[30] In attempting to explain the difficulty of finding qualified minority musicians, Virginia Hymes, a representative of the company coproducing the show, fanned the flames by saying, "The score, as Gershwin wrote it, requires highly trained classical musicians," adding that "many blacks were contacted by the orchestra contractor, but they were unavailable."[31]

Actor Ossie Davis, the first witness at the 1976 hearings, in an emotional statement, criticized not only the paucity of black musicians in the orchestra of *Porgy and Bess* but also the content of Gershwin's opera, which many African American critics had found offensive as early as 1935, when it was first staged: "The hero on his knees singing that he has plenty of nothing, that he wants nothing. No protest, no argument, no petitions to any Commission of Human Rights. Plenty of nothing and nothing is plenty for me."[32] Around the same time as the hearing, Harold C. Schonberg, the *New York Times* music critic, expressed a similar point of view, citing the libretto's "crap-shooting, watermelon toting black stereotypes who in moments of stress fall on their knees and start shouting spirituals." He also noted, "In the past, blacks have been disturbed by this libretto, and many still are. It is true that by now 'Porgy and Bess' can be regarded as a period piece. Still, there is something distasteful about the condescension of librettist and composer—two white men slumming in Charleston."[33]

In January 1978, as a result of the hearings, an agreement was signed by the League of New York Theaters and Producers and the New York City Commission on Human Rights to increase the number of black and Hispanic musicians in Broadway show orchestras to a minimum of 20 percent and to expand minority participation in all Broadway shows, not just the black productions.[34] The agreement called for the maintenance of a list of qualified minority musicians and required producers to report on their progress in minority hiring. The *New York Times* announcement of the pact also reported that at the time of the hearings (November 1976), "there were 18 musicals using 366 musicians, of whom 62 were black and two were Hispanic. At that time there were five 'black' shows on Broadway."[35] As in previous integration efforts, the 1976 Human Rights Commission hearings resulted in some short-term gains, but as time passed and the pressure to hire black musicians lessened, the situation regressed. Interviewed in 2000, violinist Gayle Dixon said, "When I started working, there were two Black people, at best, in a pit—and there still are, if there are two. At

Phantom [of the Opera], I am the only one. We haven't made much progress on Broadway, and the situation is worse in the symphonic field."[36]

Joe Wilder, of course, had already worked on Broadway as early as 1950, in *Alive and Kicking*, a quarter century before the 1976 Human Rights Commission hearings. He was already well known to producers and contractors, so it is unlikely that his return to Broadway orchestra work was prompted by this latest antidiscrimination effort. In 1978, however, Wilder was offered his first opportunity as a contractor for a Broadway show, an invitation that may well have been motivated by the hearings. During his testimony, Jack Jeffers had addressed the issue of African American contractors: "There are many musicals that are based on black themes. There are many black musicians playing on Broadway. There is one black house contractor. As far as I know, in the entire history of the Broadway theatre, there have been a total of four. There has never been more than one at a time."[37]

Wilder both served as contractor and played first trumpet for *Angel*, which opened at the Minskoff Theatre on May 10, 1978, and closed on May 13, after only five performances. The musical coordinator was Earl Shendell, a leading contractor who had hired Wilder for many previous engagements, including *Shenandoah*. "Whatever his faults, Earl Shendell was one of the first Broadway contractors who consistently hired black musicians for most of the pit bands for whom he contracted," Wilder said. Shendell had also testified at the Human Rights Commission hearings.

Contracting presented some problems for Wilder. Having spent his entire career as a player, his sympathies lay with his fellow musicians, many of whom were also longtime friends. As a contractor, however, he was in a sense part of management. His allegiances were further clouded by the fact that he was also playing first trumpet in the orchestra. "The musicians respected me because they knew I wasn't a flunky for the management," Wilder said. "I went by the rules, but I wanted to make sure that the guys were treated fairly." Because *Angel* closed after only five performances, management attempted to avoid paying the musicians for their rehearsal time. "As the contractor, I threatened to take them to the union," Wilder recalled. "They reluctantly paid, but they would not make out separate checks—they just paid me a lump sum, and I had to make out all the individual checks."

For the first time, Wilder also had to deal with personnel issues, some rather sensitive. "We had one guy who was a fine violinist, but he was an alcoholic and was always making obscene remarks to the women in the orchestra," Wilder recalled. "Every time he passed them, he'd pat one of them on the behind. They complained to me about it, so I took him aside and told him, 'Look, you and I are the two oldest guys in the orchestra. I don't want to fire anyone, but if you keep doing what you're doing, I'll have no choice.' He took me at my word and stopped bothering them."

Wilder's next stint as contractor was for *Reggae*, which ran only from March 27 to April 13, 1980, at the Biltmore Theatre. The show featured a nearly all-black cast headed by Philip Michael Thomas of *Miami Vice* fame. It was directed by Glenda Dickerson (1945–2012), one of the first African American women to direct a Broadway show. (For some unknown reason, Gui Andrisano was added as codirector between the previews and the opening.) The story line, which Robert Palmer described as "a kind of Third World 'Hair,'"[38] was set in Jamaica and involved a Jamaican pop singer who returns to her homeland and is reunited with her childhood sweetheart, a marijuana farmer. Reggae music, Rastafarianism, and pot were leitmotifs. Apparently, the band took the plot to heart. "All these guys would be back there smoking 'ganja,' as they called it," Wilder recalled. "When the curtain opened up, it looked like the Resurrection! You couldn't see the audience from the stage, and the audience couldn't see the performers because of the smoke. I think they made me the contractor because I was the only one who wasn't smoking pot!"

The band was not the typical Broadway pit orchestra. The nine-piece ensemble, led by Jamaican keyboard legend Jackie Mittoo, included only two horns: Wilder and trombonist-flutist Art Baron.[39] As contractor, Wilder again found himself in the unpleasant position of having to discipline musicians: "We had a West Indian bass player who was constantly showing up late. I told him, 'Look, this is Broadway. It's not a club date. You can't just come in whenever you decide to.' I said I'd have to replace him if he kept it up. He came on time, but that didn't win me any friends." In his review, *New York Times* critic Mel Gussow was more enthusiastic about the music than the musical, concluding that *Reggae* "might have been happier as a concert than as an overbooked flight of a musical."[40]

Around the time *Reggae* closed in April 1980, Wilder was approached to serve as contractor for another show: the revival of *The Music Man* at the New York City Center. Once again, the offer came from Earl Shendell, who was the show's music supervisor. "They told me they were thinking about me but not to say anything yet," Wilder said. Although he had not divulged anything about the show or his role as contractor, Wilder soon began receiving calls from musicians lobbying him for spots in *Music Man*. He was also given a list of musicians whom management did not want him to hire for the orchestra. "These were fine musicians and guys with whom I was working on a daily basis," he recalled. "I had no idea why they shouldn't be hired, but it would have put me in a bad position, so I just told them to forget it." This marked the end of Wilder's brief career as a contractor.

In June 1980, Wilder was hired for the revival of *Camelot* at the New York State Theatre (now the David H. Koch Theater). Wilder was to play first trumpet in the production, which starred Richard Burton in the role he had filled to great acclaim in the original production that ran from 1960 to 1963. But Wilder left the show during rehearsals. "It was the only time I can remember being fired," he said. Wilder had clashed with noted European-born conductor Franz Allers, the show's musical director:

> He was a real taskmaster. The music was so old that he had us recopying the parts at rehearsal. This was against union regulations, and all the guys were grumbling, but no one said anything. At one point, he had given some instructions to the brass section. As I was trying to explain to one of the other guys what he had said, he yelled, "Hey, Wilder! I'm talking." I said, "Maestro, I'm just trying to explain to him what you told us to do."

Wilder also brought up the issue of the illegible music, telling the conductor, "We're not supposed to be copying these parts. You're supposed to be paying a copyist." In addition, Wilder knew that Allers was not satisfied with his handling of the lead chair: "I didn't have the stamina for what they required, and he was upset about that." Two days later, the conductor called Wilder and asked him whether he would be willing to switch to second trumpet. "He told me he had a fellow who'd been playing first trumpet with him, and he'd like to have him on lead," Wilder said. "But somebody's going to have to be fired if you're bringing in someone else," Wilder told him, adding, "I don't want someone else to be fired because you're not happy with what I'm doing, so you can just fire me." Wilder asked for four weeks' pay, to which Allers agreed, and he left the show before it opened. Although it might be argued that he had not technically been fired, it was certainly a rare instance of Wilder's not measuring up to the demands of an assignment.

In August 1980, Wilder joined the orchestra of what was to become his final and longest-lasting Broadway pit engagement, *42nd Street*, which ran until January 1989, encompassing some 3,400 performances. The show was based on the 1933 film of the same name, with many added musical numbers. Reviewer Frank Rich found the musical numbers "so good and plentiful that they make the story seem an unwanted intrusion into the action."[41] Wilder, who played second trumpet, remembered *42nd Street* as "a joy to play." He explained, "David Merrick, the producer, was a very nice man. He felt so proud of the show that he decided that all the musicians in the orchestra should have the chance to see it, so he paid for a sub to come in for each of us. It was a wonderful gesture." Merrick, who had been unable to find backers for the production, ended up financing it himself. The opening night triumph was marred by the tragic death earlier that day of the show's director and choreographer, Gower Champion, the news of which Merrick announced onstage at the closing curtain.

Bassist Bill Crow was in the orchestra, which had a rather unorthodox instrumentation. Crow said, "John Lesco was the conductor, and he decided he didn't want a string section. Since there was a twenty-four-musician minimum in the theater, they had a huge sax section with lots of doublers, so the arranger could have all that color availability."[42] According to Crow, Lesco also insisted that there be some black musicians in the orchestra; in addition to Wilder, multi-reed specialist George Barrow was hired. Wilder, Bernie Glow, Dick Perry, and John Frosk formed a potent trumpet section. "Joe was one of the pleasures of that eight-year run," said Crow. "A lovely man to hang out with, and his musicianship of course was always first class." The bassist was also able to observe Wilder's humor on a regular basis. "Joe gives the appearance of being such a straight-life guy, but when you get to know him, you discover that he's got this wicked sense of humor," Crow noted. "The guys would be sitting around in the band room warming up, and Joe had a way of warming up that sounded just like a kid who was just starting to play. He'd play a note with semi-confidence and then play very softly all of the chromatic notes up to the next note he wanted to play and then play that with great confidence. It was a very funny bit that he did."[43] When tuning up, Wilder would often perform a variant of this routine. He would ask the pianist for an A, play a glaring off-pitch clinker on the trumpet, and then nod sagely, indicating that he was ready to go.

Wilder appreciated the predictability of a long-term engagement in a top show like *42nd Street*. It allowed him to make a good living while remaining at home with his family. "Of course with any Broadway show, there's a certain monotony because you're playing the same music every day," Wilder said. He cautioned against complacency, however, especially when playing the same music day after day for more than eight years:

> You'd commit most of it to memory, and unless there was a problem onstage, you wouldn't have to look at the music. But if there was a mix-up, and the conductor suddenly said, "Bar 22!" and you're sitting there with your book closed, it could be a disaster. I learned to keep the book open and follow it as the show was going on, even though I'd memorized the music.

In 1986, while still playing in the *42nd Street* orchestra, Wilder received wide popular exposure through an acting and playing role on television's award-winning *Cosby Show*. In the episode "Play It Again, Russell,"[44] Russell "Slide" Huxtable (played by Earle Hyman) comes out of retirement to play one last gig in memory of an old friend. He reunites with his old group, the Jazz Caravan, at a Harlem nightclub, the Baby Grand. Wilder plays trumpet and leads the band, which consists of an all-star jazz contingent that both appears onstage and plays on the soundtrack: Bootsie Barnes, Jimmy Heath, and Jimmy Oliver (tenor sax); Tommy Flanagan (piano); Eric Gale (guitar); Percy Heath (bass); Art Blakey (drums); Tito Puente (timbales); and Carlos "Patato" Valdés (congas). Actor Earle Hyman does a credible job of pretending to play the trombone solos, which were actually performed by Slide Hampton. Cosby chose the musicians, and true to his Philadelphia roots, no less than five of them—Wilder, Jimmy and Percy Heath, Barnes, and Oliver—were from his hometown.

Jimmy Heath, Tito Puente, and Patato Valdés all have brief lines, but Wilder as the bandleader, has the most prominent speaking role. As the band is about to launch into a blues number, he announces, "Before we start playing, I'd like you all to take a good look because standing here is about a thousand years of jazz." Wilder delivers his lines with great sincerity and polish, seeming much more at ease than on those rare occasions when he actually found himself to be the leader of a group. "Cosby insisted that the cast commit everything to memory so it would look natural on camera," Wilder said.

The program has been aired countless times over the years and was released on DVD.[45] "Every time Cosby saw me and Jimmy Heath, he'd say, 'You guys are gonna be making a whole lot of money! You've got speaking lines, and you're playing solos!'" Wilder recalled. As it turned out, Wilder had a hard time collecting residuals for his widely distributed appearance: "When I went to the union and told them that I wasn't getting any residuals, they looked it up and told me my name wasn't on the contract. The contractor had put his own name down as the trumpet player."

Wilder had another brush with stardom when he was asked to participate in a photo shoot with pop star Madonna. Wilder arrived at a Manhattan studio with his horn, not knowing what to expect. He found the singer dressed in a somewhat revealing outfit for the photo, which was to be used to promote her 1991 documentary film *Truth or Dare*. When Wilder asked what they wanted him to do, the producer replied, "Just look down her breasts." Wilder replied, "Wait a minute. Who's going to give me a letter explaining this to my wife?" He was told, "Just tell her you're working." Wilder went ahead with the shoot but refused to ogle the superstar. Several versions of the photo, taken by the iconic fashion photographer Steven Meisel, were released. Although a few show the scantily clad Madonna draped over a piano next to Wilder and saxophonists George Coleman and Benny Golson, there is a more tasteful rendering designed to evoke the 1930s swing era, which Solveig allowed to be displayed in the Wilders' home.

1980s Recordings

During the 1980s, Wilder's freelance recording activity was certainly not as prolific as in previous decades, reflecting both changes in the music industry and the demands of his work in the orchestra for *42nd Street*. He also found that an extended commitment in the pit made it more difficult to respond to the varied demands of studio recording work. "It was a mental thing," Wilder said. "You'd get so comfortable playing the show, where nothing deviated one iota, that when you're called for a record date, you weren't really up to snuff. It took a couple of weeks to get back the flexibility to play other things." Nevertheless, in addition to performing in the section on some significant recordings, he also was heard to good effect playing solos on several sessions during the decade. And singers like Johnny Hartman, Helen Humes, Teresa Brewer, and Anita O'Day continued to feature his solos and accompaniment on their albums.

A 1980 Johnny Hartman date, for the small Beehive label (*Once in Every Life*, Beehive 7012), was a welcome event for Wilder, who greatly admired the singer's style and approach to melody. Some tracks from the album were later used most effectively on the soundtrack to Clint Eastwood's film *The Bridges of Madison County*; Wilder's full chorus on flügelhorn on "Easy Living" is a highlight,[46] although, as Gregg Akkerman points out in his biography of Hartman, tracks from the Beehive LP were slowed down to lengthen them for use on the film soundtrack, detracting from the performance.[47]

Wilder was also heard to great advantage as a "special guest artist" on four CDs by opera luminary Eileen Farrell. Farrell, known as the queen of crossover, was one of the first classical singers to embrace popular music. At the 1959 Spoleto Festival, the diva was pressed into service to perform "On the Sunny Side of the Street" with Louis Armstrong's band, replacing the ailing trumpeter. The segment, which was included on *The Ed Sullivan Show*, was Farrell's first major exposure as a popular singer:

> I had a fabulous time, and the band paid me its ultimate tribute in jazz lingo, by calling me "solid." Both audiences and the press went wild over my "transformation" from classical soprano to pop singer. I didn't

realize it yet, but I had taken the first step in a major new phase of my career, and I had Ed Sullivan to thank for it.[48]

In July 1988, Wilder traveled to Charlotte, South Carolina, at the invitation of pianist Loonis McGlohon, a good friend, to record the first two projects with Farrell: songbooks devoted to composers Rodgers and Hart[49] and Harold Arlen.[50] McGlohon did the arrangements and led the small group backing the singer. A highlight of the Arlen album is an impromptu version of "Happiness Is a Thing Called Joe," which opens with an exquisite full-chorus melody statement by Wilder's plunger-muted trumpet. As Farrell described it, "While we were cutting the Arlen album, I fell in love with the trumpet playing of Joe Wilder. We decided on the spur of the moment to add 'Happiness Is Just a Thing Called Joe,' which hadn't been on the original list of Arlen songs we were set to record. We didn't have an arrangement; Joe and I just winged it, and we got the song down in one take."[51]

Wilder was equally enthusiastic about working with Farrell. "She knew how good she was, but there was no ego involved at all," he said. "She was as down to earth as you could be." Wilder recalled an appearance Farrell had made on *The Patti Page Show* in the late 1950s, when he played in the ABC orchestra: "She was always doing something to entertain the band. At dress rehearsal, while she's singing "Climb Every Mountain," we looked up, and she's down on her hands and knees, climbing. The band just cracked up!"

A year later, Wilder returned to Charlotte to record two more albums with the singer: *Eileen Farrell Sings Torch Songs*[52] and *Eileen Farrell Sings Alec Wilder*.[53] On the former, reviewer Jerry Shinn described Wilder as "a laid-back but nonetheless awesome presence," praising his "elegant obbligatos and mellow, lyrical solos."[54]

Instrumental showcases for Wilder during the decade included a 1982 reunion for the Pablo label with pianist-composer Michel Legrand, on whose historic 1958 album *Legrand Jazz* the trumpeter had played. Wilder is particularly effective on the title track, "After the Rain," as well as on "Pieces of Dreams," with saxophonists Phil Woods and Zoot Sims. In his review, *Washington Post* critic Richard Harrington wrote, "The album's surprise is Wilder, whose pretty, introspective solos recall Clark Terry."[55]

In 1984, Wilder teamed with fellow trumpeter Joe Newman for *Hangin' Out*, a Concord date also featuring pianist Hank Jones. The album was Wilder's first as leader (actually, coleader with Newman) since his 1959 Columbia releases. Wilder and Newman were longtime colleagues, having played together with Lionel Hampton in the 1940s and Count Basie in the 1950s. Their contrasting styles fit well together and the varied repertoire provided ample opportunities for each to shine, as well as for much interaction; there are several witty dialogues displaying the trumpeters' skill with mutes. Arrangements by the "two Franks"—Foster and Wess, colleagues from the Basie band—give the set structure. A highlight is "Battle Hymn of the Republic," a piece Wilder often played at concerts but had never recorded. Although Wilder was satisfied with the track, it did not turn out exactly the way he had envisioned it. "My idea was that we should play like two jackleg preachers," he said, "but instead of talking, we would answer each other back and forth on our horns and make it kind of humorous. But every time Joe [Newman] came in, he played everything he could! It worked out okay, but it didn't have the effect I had in mind. I should have written out the music the way I wanted it to be, instead of trying to explain it at the session." Newman, a naturally more aggressive player and personality, took over to such an extent that Bennett Rubin, the album's producer and a fan of Wilder, approached him and asked, "Joe, why don't you say something? I intended for *you* to be in charge!" According to Wilder, "Joe [Newman] and I were good friends, but he could be a little obnoxious." Nevertheless, Wilder enjoyed the date: "We had a good time with the plunger because we'd both been playing with it for so many years." Wilder was also the session photographer, contributing several photos of his colleagues on the back of the album, as well as the warm cover self-portrait of himself and Newman.

Another session that was particularly meaningful to Wilder was his first recorded collaboration with Benny Carter, on the alto saxophonist's 1985 Concord album, *A Gentleman and His Music*. Wilder had been influenced by Carter's ability to "tell a story" on his instruments, and over the years, they had developed a friendship. Although they shared many similar musical and personal qualities and had played together from time to time at jazz parties and festivals, until producer Carl Jefferson brought them into the studio in August 1985, they had never made an album together. Shortly afterward, Wilder told his father, then eighty-four years old, about the Carter date:

> My father was a great admirer of Benny Carter and used to always talk about him and play his music for us. When I mentioned that I had made an album with Benny, he stopped and said, "Wait a minute! You know Benny Carter?" I said, "Yeah, he's a friend of mine." And he said, "Benny Carter is a friend of yours?" We started talking about something else, and every so often he would stop and say, "You know Benny Carter?" Nothing I had done up to that point impressed him that much. So when I saw Benny, I told him about my father's reaction, and Benny said, "Oh, come on, Joe!" He thought I was putting him on!

One track on the Carter album had special significance for Wilder. His close friend George Duvivier, who had been scheduled to play on the recording, died a month before the date, and Carter dedicated "Blues for George" to the universally respected bassist. "Playing that piece was a very moving experience for me," Wilder said. "It gave me a chance to express my feelings for George musically. I wasn't even conscious of what I was going to play; it just came out. I know I had tears in my eyes when we recorded it."[56]

New Outlets

Jazz Repertory and Jazz Parties (1990–2000)

The 1960s and 1970s saw the beginnings of a true jazz repertory movement that paralleled the rise of jazz within the academy. Previously, the province of dedicated amateur scholars, collectors, and journalists, jazz was now becoming accepted as a legitimate field of study in higher education, with professional scholars emerging in musicology, history, sociology, African American studies, and other disciplines that examined the music from their own perspectives. It became fashionable to view jazz as "America's classical music," reinforcing the notion that like classical music, jazz should have orchestras capable of playing its newly recognized body of work from all periods. Unlike classical orchestras, however, jazz repertory ensembles had to deal with the issue of improvisation. Some chose the path of exact replication

Wilder solos with the Smithsonian Jazz Masterworks Orchestra at the NEA Jazz Masters induction concert, Toronto, January 2008; fellow inductee Candido Camero and NEA Jazz Master Paquito D'Rivera are at left. *(Photo by Ed Berger.)*

of recordings, including note-for-note transcriptions of solos. Others played the original arrangements but allowed their soloists the freedom to create their own improvisations, albeit within the stylistic parameters of the piece. And still others chose a more radical approach, deconstructing the original arrangement and transforming it into what was essentially a new work. A few orchestras used all three of these methods. As bassist George Duvivier noted about the difficulty of attempting to reproduce the music of Duke Ellington, "The notes are there but the voices are gone."[1]

The two major orchestras with which Wilder played in the 1990s, the Lincoln Center Jazz Orchestra (LCJO) and the Smithsonian Jazz Masterworks Orchestra, espoused two different approaches to soloing within a repertory context. The Smithsonian opted to re-create the solos as recorded, while the LCJO soloists were encouraged to improvise within the stylistic framework of the piece. David Berger, conductor of the LCJO and noted transcriber of historic jazz orchestral works, stated, "I never want to re-create the records . . . because it comes out stilted, lacks energy and conviction, and doesn't do anything for the players—they can't be themselves."[2] It should be noted, however, that neither orchestra used these approaches exclusively. Furthermore, improvised solos and riffs, transcribed from the original recordings for repertory performance, are often "codified" in newly published arrangements, which themselves may become the standard sources for playing particular pieces. This process is the musical equivalent of Walter Ong's theory of secondary orality, which describes the relationship between spoken and written language.

Finally, there is a fine line between repertory and nostalgia. Repertory orchestras are known for performing classic works from the full spectrum of jazz history. But groups that try to appeal to the nostalgia market tend to limit themselves to one time period—usually the swing era. The latter type would include the "ghost bands," whose function is to perpetuate the memory and music of long-deceased popular leaders, like Glenn Miller, Tommy Dorsey, and other big-band icons.

Jeffrey Sultanof, in his comprehensive survey of jazz repertory ensembles,[3] traces the beginnings of the movement back to the late 1930s, when the Original Dixieland Jazz Band, Sidney Bechet, Bob Crosby's big band, and other groups began revisiting older jazz idioms. But the credit for the first true "jazz repertory orchestra," as the term is now understood, probably belongs to bassist Chuck Israels, who founded his National Jazz Ensemble in 1973. In 1978, Wilder made a live recording with Israels's group, and his extended solo on Fats Waller's "Jitterbug Waltz," expertly arranged by saxophonist Kenny Berger, is a highlight of the trumpeter's work of the period.[4]

Mention must also be made of Ron Roullier, a British pianist and composer who moved to New York in 1959 and founded his New York Jazz Repertory Orchestra in the late 1960s. Roullier described his aim: "The idea was to present a cross section of the repertory: Basie, Ellington, Dizzy Gillespie, Johnny Carisi's chart on 'Israel,' plus some new works, some of my things, and others."[5] In 1973, George Wein formed the New York Jazz Repertory Ensemble, which presented several notable concerts covering a wide range of styles during its two-year existence.

The 1980s and 1990s might be viewed as the golden era of jazz repertory, with the creation of the American Jazz Orchestra by Gary Giddins and John Lewis in 1986, the Lincoln Center Jazz Orchestra (directed by Wynton Marsalis) in 1988, the Smithsonian Jazz Masterworks Orchestra (conducted by David Baker and Gunther Schuller) in 1990, the Carnegie Hall Jazz Band (directed by Jon Faddis) in 1991, as well as orchestras in several other cities and abroad.[6] In addition to permanent orchestras, many ad hoc ensembles were formed for jazz repertory performances as part of festivals and concert series.

Joe Wilder had a close association with two of the major jazz repertory organizations: the Lincoln Center Jazz Orchestra, with which he toured in 1992, and the Smithsonian Jazz Masterworks Orchestra, of which he was a charter member, remaining with the group from its inaugural season in 1991 until 2002. Just as Wilder's musical abilities ideally suited him for the Third Stream experiments of the 1950s and 1960s, he became equally in demand for the burgeoning jazz repertory movement. Half a century after his big band odyssey of the 1940s and 1950s, Wilder now found himself in the singular position of revisiting classic arrangements he had played when they were new.

Lincoln Center Jazz Orchestra

Wilder joined the Lincoln Center Jazz Orchestra in 1992 when he was asked by Wynton Marsalis to fill in as a last-minute replacement for trumpeter Umar Sharif, who had suffered a heart attack just before the orchestra was to begin an extensive five-week, twenty-five-concert cross-country tour. The tour ran from September 12 to October 19 and included stops in some fifteen states from the Northeast to the West Coast. At age seventy, Wilder was not the oldest member of the orchestra; saxophonist Norris Turney was seventy-one, and trombonist Britt Woodman, Wilder's friend and colleague from the 1942 Les Hite band, was seventy-two.

Apart from the 1962 Benny Goodman State Department tour to the USSR, Wilder had not traveled with a big band since his tenure with Count

Basie from 1953 to 1954, and the trumpeter found himself struggling at first to play the demanding Ellington-based LCJO book: "It took some adjusting because this was far removed from playing in the pit, which I'd been doing. It was kind of rough at the beginning because I wasn't physically up to playing at their level, but it got better after a while." Wilder played fourth trumpet in a section that included Lew Soloff, Marcus Belgrave, and Marsalis. Wilder sat next to Marsalis and was impressed that the leader chose to sit in the trumpet section rather than stand in front of the orchestra. "Morale-wise, it was good for the other guys because it showed he had a great deal of respect for them," Wilder said. He also marveled at Marsalis's playing: "It was a joy sitting next to him and listening to him. He is a flawless trumpet player, and every night he played things I found interesting." The younger trumpeter also sought to avail himself of Wilder's knowledge. Wilder said, "He wanted to learn everything and would ask me particularly about playing with the plunger. After we'd finish work, we'd stand around like a couple of kids playing things for each other."[7]

Wilder was also impressed with the orchestra, and playing Ellington's works night after night transported him back to his youth, when he had heard the band in person in Philadelphia: "They play the music so well and so authentically that you could almost imagine yourself sitting in the middle of Duke Ellington's orchestra. I remembered hearing Duke play some of these things. They had the same feeling. I could just drift back and remember, when I was a kid, how impressed and how thrilled I was that here was Duke Ellington's orchestra, and I could hear them."[8]

The tour attracted near-capacity audiences, including a segment of younger fans drawn by the charisma of Marsalis, whose fame had transcended the narrow jazz market.[9] Wilder was not featured extensively, but he did attract some notice. Bill Eichenberger, reviewing the band's Columbus, Ohio, appearance, wrote, "An intense incidental pleasure last night was the sight, on the bandstand, of one of the truly great trumpet players in the history of jazz: Joe Wilder. His solos were few and brief and his manner subdued; he is, after all, 70 years old. But age has not diminished the purity and luster of his tone."[10] Wilder later joked about his age and the rigors of returning to the road: "When I went out I guess I was seventy-some years old . . . and [when] I came back I was about ninety."[11]

Wilder left the band after the tour and was not involved in the controversy that erupted in May 1993, when Jazz at Lincoln Center director Rob Gibson sent a letter dismissing members of the orchestra older than thirty years of age. Because of the resultant public outcry, not to mention the possible legal ramifications of such an edict, Gibson quickly rescinded the letter.

Smithsonian Jazz Masterworks Orchestra

Wilder enjoyed a far longer tenure with the Smithsonian Jazz Masterworks Orchestra (SJMO), which was established by an act of Congress in 1990. John Hasse, orchestra founder and executive director, hired David Baker and Gunther Schuller as conductors. Wilder joined as a charter member in 1991, remaining until 2002. During his decade with the band, Wilder played a wide variety of music and toured extensively throughout the United States and Europe. During his first few years with the orchestra, despite his senior status and, more important, the fact that he had had firsthand experience in many of the bands whose music was being featured, Wilder was rarely called on for his insight or expertise. As Loren Schoenberg, SJMO member and later conductor, noted:

> It was a lost opportunity. At that stage of his career, Joe was no longer a lead trumpet player, but the band would have been better off if they had let Joe almost take charge of the brass section—definitely the trumpet section—and organize it in terms of who plays lead, who plays solos, blend, phrasing—everything. It was ironic to be sitting in a band with Joe Wilder and being told how to phrase things by various conductors who didn't know as much about the music in a practical sense as he did. We all knew we were around a legend—one of the great musicians of all time. For example, I don't think anyone ever said, "Let's ask Joe, he played in the Lunceford band."[12]

Pianist Michael Weiss, who played with Smithsonian orchestra during its early years, concurred:

> Joe was the consummate musician, and he always maintained a very high professional demeanor, but like many of us, he would show his frustration at times to the other musicians. He was by far the most experienced musician with that music. There were a number of other "elder statesmen" in the band, such as Britt Woodman, Buster Cooper, and Joe Temperley, who had lived that music, but the conductors had their own way of doing things.[13]

Nevertheless, the mere presence of Wilder, a direct link to the era and creators of the music being performed, had a salutary effect that did not go unnoticed by the critics. In an extended review of the SJMO's Duke Ellington concert at the Apollo Theater in October 1993, Whitney Balliett raised some of the essential questions that always surface in any discussion of jazz repertory: "How do you reproduce the timbres and attacks of musicians who were often inimitable and had sometimes worked together for decades . . . ? Do you copy, however wanly, the original recorded solos, or let your soloists step out on their own and risk making a different music?" Of the Smithsonian orchestra's performance, Balliett wrote, "None of the questions were answered. Some of the tempos were off, and the ensembles were pallid without Harry Carney's massive bottom tones. Of all the solos—some copied, some original—only Joe Wilder's open-horn and plunger work was beautiful."[14] In his review of the same concert, George Kanzler wrote that "the plaintive vocalized wails of Joe Wilder's plunger-muted trumpet on 'Echoes of Harlem' [1936] transported the audience back to a lost era."[15] And Clive Davis noted in a review of a Smithsonian orchestra performance in London in 1999: "A living link with yesteryear came in the burnished trumpet and flugelhorn playing of Joe Wilder, who made the most of an elegant solo spot on I Got It Bad And That Ain't Good." Davis also endorsed the value of hearing historic charts performed live and "free of the period fog that accompanies any recording, however well remastered."[16]

Ken Kimery, executive producer of the SJMO, agreed that, early on, Wilder's talents were not fully employed, particularly during the era of dual conductors: "Gunther's [Schuller's] approach was more dictatorial and didn't necessarily elicit input from the musicians. So Joe might impart some insight outside of the rehearsal or performance setting—not necessarily to Gunther but more to the guys in the band."[17] When David Baker assumed sole conductorship, Wilder's role began to change somewhat. "As a player himself, David had a more democratic nature, and he elicited more insights from Joe," Kimery said. Both Schoenberg and Kimery agreed that it was counter to Wilder's nature to force himself or his opinions, no matter how relevant, on anyone. "Joe would never say, 'Hey, you guys are playing it wrong!' But when asked, Joe was very eloquent in providing some insight," Kimery said. "The trumpets were very honored to have Joe in the section and were very anxious to know what his thoughts were on a particular piece."[18] The Smithsonian publicly recognized Wilder on several occasions. In 1996, Wilder was chosen to play Dizzy Gillespie's trumpet at a gala celebrating the one hundred fiftieth anniversary of the Smithsonian's founding. In March 2002, Wilder was honored at a concert celebrating his eightieth birthday. Featured with the Smithsonian Jazz Masterworks Quintet, the trumpeter "dazzled and delighted a standing room-only crowd in the Carmichael Auditorium."[19]

On a personal level, Wilder formed close friendships with many band members, most of whom were decades younger than he. "Despite the age difference, Joe's integration into the band was seamless," Kimery said. "A lot of it had to do with the fact that his ears were so wide open. He continued to enjoy the work of the younger musicians, like [trumpeters] Tom Williams and Greg Gisbert. Joe loved Larry Wiseman [1943–2002], our lead trumpet player. For all of us, it wasn't just the honor of being around Joe but the ease of friendship with him."[20] Schoenberg added, "He never made us feel that we were in the presence of an august elder. I think he enjoyed hanging out with young people."[21]

On the road, no matter how arduous the travel schedule, Wilder never sought any special accommodation. "If we were lifting bags and moving stuff, Joe would always step up and say, 'Let me give you a hand,'" Kimery recalled. "Although he was senior in age, the majority of us did not match up to his physical strength."[22] Schoenberg remembered an incident at the Duke Ellington School for the Arts in Washington, DC: "Somehow the topic of health and exercise came up, and Joe, who would have been well into his seventies at the time, all of a sudden put his hands on the table and straightened his body out parallel and held that position. We couldn't believe it!"[23]

When Schoenberg had the opportunity to conduct the orchestra, he made it a point to feature Wilder in contexts where the trumpeter could be himself:

> There was a total change of atmosphere when he would come down and play a solo with the rhythm section. All of a sudden, we would go from being a good band playing jazz repertory music to having one of the giants of the era coming down and doing his thing. You could just sense the feeling and the emotion that Joe transmitted and the audience reaction. It was an incredible moment.[24]

Schoenberg also described the effect when Wilder would play a piece from an era in which he had been an active participant:

> We would do an extended version of "Roll 'Em." I would come down front to play a tenor solo, build up to a climax, and then hand it over to Joe—like passing a baton. The band would work up a head of steam, and Joe would use a green plastic water cup as a mute to "preach" over the band. We were hearing somebody speak the language that he had a role in creating. It was one of the most treasured moments of my playing career.

Schoenberg pointed out the vocal quality of Wilder's solos: "There's a point where music becomes like speech. I've always felt that with Joe. When I think of Joe playing one of those ballads, the way he scoops into the notes, the phrasing, it has the same effect that Tricky Sam Nanton or Rex Stewart or Ben Webster had. He's talking to us with the same phrasing and meaning as when he speaks. It's outstanding."[25]

Revisiting music he had first played decades earlier gave Wilder a new appreciation for the difficulty of charts he might have taken for granted in his youth: "When I look at some of these arrangements, especially some of the Gillespie things, I ask myself, 'I played this at some point in my life?' Now I find myself really laboring to play some of those things that at the time we just accepted as a way of life. But I can reflect on them and appreciate them a lot more than I did then."

While one might argue about their approach, SJMO conductors Gunther Schuller and David Baker had a vision and understood the need for classic jazz pieces to be played live. As Schuller put it, "It's very nice to have the masterful recordings of . . . the past, but a music cannot live forever in archives or in museums or on recordings. It has to be played by living, breathing human beings."[26] And Baker, in defending his philosophy of using detailed transcriptions of recordings in addition to consulting all extant scores to determine the most authentic version of a piece for performance, stated, "It would never have occurred to us to go after something that was approximately right when we're getting ready to do the Bartok 'Concerto for Orchestra.' We think enough of the music and realize it's important enough that it's necessary that we give to the student, to the listener, the most faithful manifestation of that composer's intention."[27]

Schuller and Baker also had the knowledge to seek out a wide-ranging repertoire for the orchestra. Some pieces would elicit a deep emotional response in Wilder, triggering fond memories of events and friends long gone: "Whenever I would play Rex Stewart's solo on 'Dusk' with the Smithsonian, I would get tears in my eyes, because I remembered as a little kid in the Lincoln Theatre in Philadelphia hearing him play it. He had such a wonderful way of expressing himself. It touched me so much that I would rush home, grab my horn, and try to play what I'd heard him play. I could recall every note! It was so pretty that when I played it, I would try not to change anything."[28]

Wilder noted that, although "on occasion, you might want to improvise something of your own," he had no problem with re-creating classic solos of others: "That's what a repertory orchestra is supposed to be doing. You play it the way they played it, even if they might not have played the correct chord changes or you hear it differently." When given the freedom to improvise within the repertory orchestra context, Wilder stressed the need to play within the apposite stylistic context: "I try to play something that is still in that idiom, rather than playing a bebop thing in the middle of a Dixieland tune or something like that." Other band members felt that being asked to play note-for-note solo re-creations relegated the music to the status of a museum relic. "Having the freedom to improvise within the idiom rather than being asked to play a solo transcription breathes life into the music," said pianist Michael Weiss.[29]

Wilder also acknowledged that live performances or new recordings of classic jazz arrangements can illuminate aspects of the pieces obscured by the limitations in the recording technology of the period and even, at times, by the technical shortcomings of the early bands: "I think men like Ellington and [Fletcher] Henderson sometimes wrote over the heads of their musicians. I think we can give a piece like 'Stampede' or 'Diminuendo And Crescendo In Blue' a precision and accuracy that they couldn't achieve in the originals."[30] On the other hand, Wilder criticized the tendency of some repertory orchestra leaders to overconduct, noting, "Following the baton can tend to stiffen you up a bit, at least for me." Apparently, his annoyance at the superfluous gesturing was such that he was even moved to praise Benny Goodman's leadership: "When we played the same thing with Benny Goodman, he counted off and you just played."[31]

While touring with the Smithsonian orchestra, Wilder could not help but notice the changes in the makeup of both the orchestra and the audience from his big band travels in the 1940s when, as a young musician, he faced the indignities of life on the road in segregated America. In a sense, he had come full circle, now performing with a diverse orchestra to integrated audiences worldwide who respected jazz not only as entertainment but as high art. Wilder noted:

> The Smithsonian concerts were rewarding because they gave people, especially younger people, who never did hear a big band live, a chance to hear what it sounded like in a concert setting. And for the people in the audience closer to my age who do remember that era, they come and they reminisce, and it just brings them right out of the doldrums. This was an integrated orchestra, which is another good point about it. People who remember the era when segregation was at its peak, see the joy we musicians get out of playing together, and it makes them happy, too.

Wilder continued to play in jazz repertory settings fairly frequently throughout the 1980s and 1990s, and even into the new millennium at various jazz festivals and concert series, like the long-running Jazz in July series directed by pianist Dick Hyman at the 92nd Street Y in New York. "He brought an authenticity," Hyman said. "While many of us were re-creating what we had learned from recordings, Joe had actually been there. He could play a growl trumpet solo or some other stylistic thing out of the past with perfect authenticity."[32] In addition to Wilder's musical prowess, Hyman also appreciated Wilder's personality. The pianist was well aware of the obstacles Wilder had faced, both within the music business and society at large, and noted, "The fact that he was not at all embittered says a lot about his character and strength." Hyman's only criticism of his friend was that "he always dressed a bit more formally than he needed to."[33]

In addition to the 92nd Street Y series, Wilder collaborated with the pianist on other repertory projects. Hyman served as composer, arranger, and conductor for many of Woody Allen's films, and he used Wilder on the soundtrack of *Stardust Memories* (1980), *Mighty Aphrodite* (1995), and *Everyone Says I Love You* (1996).[34] "That was Joe being a perfect section man," said Hyman. Wilder also played on Hyman's 1973 RCA recording of Jelly Roll Morton pieces, *Ferdinand "Jelly Roll" Morton: Some Rags, Some Stomps and a Little Blues* (Columbia MQ32587). In his review of that album, John S. Wilson singled out Wilder's "masterfully growling trumpet solo" on "The Crave," describing the trumpeter as "a great jazz musician of long standing who has been sadly overlooked on recordings."[35] Although he could be laconic and sometimes acerbic, the longtime *New York Times* critic was a consistent champion of Wilder's work, often describing it in uncharacteristically effusive terms. That same year, Wilder played the "old-timey" trumpet solo on "Pine Apple Rag," from Marvin Hamlisch's soundtrack for *The Sting*, the film that made Scott Joplin a household name some five decades after the composer's death.[36]

While he enjoyed bringing classic pieces to life before new audiences, because of dental problems and deteriorating vision, he was less comfortable reading transcribed solos in later years. Despite the fact that Wilder was by now recognized as a distinctive jazz soloist with a unique style and a contemporary of many of the artists whose work he was asked to replicate, producers still expected him to be someone else. In his seventies and even into his eighties, Wilder was called on to "channel" everyone from Rex Stewart and Cootie Williams to Bix Beiderbecke and Miles Davis. Simply allowing him to play something of his own choosing with a good rhythm section would have yielded far more meaningful results. But Wilder took it in stride. After struggling through Rex Stewart's solo on "Boy Meets Horn" at a 92nd Street Y concert, Wilder joked that he had sounded more like "Wreck" Stewart. When given the freedom to play what he wanted, Wilder, even into his seventies and eighties, could still enthrall an audience by merely stating a melody. Relying on the beauty of his sound and the lyricism and subtlety of his improvisation, Wilder could deeply affect listeners and hold their attention without resorting to empty pyrotechnics and bombast. Whitney Balliett described one such moment at a 1986 concert at the 92nd Street Y. He wrote, "Then there was a resounding event: Joe Wilder, on flugelhorn, played two a-cappella choruses of 'Willow Weep for Me.' It was a flawless demonstration of how to make a melody, through close embellishment, so concentrated that it doubles in intensity."[37]

Garrison Keillor and *A Prairie Home Companion*

In 1989, humorist Garrison Keillor added Wilder to the cast of his popular *A Prairie Home Companion* public radio show. Keillor was in the process of expanding his "Coffee Club Orchestra," and Wilder joined as second trumpet (his friend John Frosk played first). Although not technically a jazz repertory orchestra, much of the music Wilder was called on to play during his tenure with the show was of a historical nature, including a wide range of jazz, blues, popular, country, and folk tunes. Wilder found re-creating some of the 1920s and 1930s pieces "depressing" because they reminded him of his family's struggle during the Depression.[38] Although he hired Wilder to play trumpet, when Keillor discovered that Wilder was fluent in Swedish, the host assigned him an occasional speaking role in some of the skits for which the show was famous.

A Prairie Home Companion is a throwback to an earlier era of radio: it is performed live every Saturday night. "The music was often very difficult," Wilder said, "and there was the added pressure of playing it each week in front of a live audience." In addition, the music is integrated into Keillor's skits and monologues without much time to rehearse. "Garrison did all the writing himself, and many of the things he came up with were brilliant," Wilder said. Violinist Andy Stein, who worked on the show for more than two decades, described the process:

> We didn't do anything until Friday, the day before the show. We would all get together on Friday afternoon. We would bring stuff, throw it against the wall, and whatever stuck we worked on. We had Russell Warner, an amazing arranger, sitting at a table in the wings, furiously turning out music cues. There were some stressful moments, because it was difficult trying to put together two hours' of brand-new material every week. On Broadway, it would be like first-night previews every Saturday.[39]

Keillor expected all the cast members, including the musicians, to contribute to the creative process. "Garrison wasn't that happy with some of the New York freelancers in the Coffee Club Orchestra," Stein said. "It was like, 'Give me the arrangements, and we'll read it down,' and they would bury their noses in the music and wouldn't participate in the rest of it."[40]

Wilder remained with the program for three years, until 1993, when Keillor decided to pare down the orchestra. "He wanted a smaller ensemble so things could be more spur of the moment," Stein recalled. "The band kind of dribbled off. It went from the Coffee Club Orchestra to the Demitasse, to the Dregs."[41] Wilder did a fair amount of traveling with the show, and he felt that one mishap may have contributed to his termination. The show was booked for consecutive weeks in Cincinnati and Chicago, and Wilder had both tickets with him when he arrived at New York's LaGuardia Airport. He mistakenly flew to Chicago instead of Cincinnati. When he realized his error, Wilder was able to book a flight to Cincinnati, arriving in time for the program but missing the rehearsal. "I wasn't exactly fired, but he just stopped calling me," Wilder said.

The Jazz Party Phenomenon

Beginning in the early 1970s, Wilder became a frequent participant in the jazz party scene, which represented a new avenue of employment for musicians. The line between a jazz party and a jazz festival is sometimes blurred, but in general, a jazz party is staged by an individual jazz fan, who invites fellow aficionados to attend for a fee that may or may not cover the expenses. It is usually held over a weekend in a single location, typically a hotel ballroom. A festival is a more ambitious undertaking, often involving city or corporate sponsorship, and held over several days, sometimes in multiple venues.

The man credited with founding the jazz party movement was Dick Gibson, an investment banker and jazz lover. After relocating from New York to Denver, he found himself missing the vibrant jazz scene, and in 1963, he rented a hotel ballroom in Aspen, hired ten of his favorite musicians, and invited some two hundred guests, who paid fifty dollars each for a weekend of nearly continuous music.[42] Over the following thirty years, the Gibson Jazz Party changed locations several times and expanded to include more than sixty musicians and some six hundred paying guests. Beginning in the early 1970s, Wilder became a regular at the Gibson event and at other concerts sponsored by Dick Gibson in the Denver area.

Gibson brought together the cream of "mainstream" jazz artists, with some more traditional and modern players included seamlessly in the mix.

As in fantasy baseball, one of the prerogatives of a jazz party producer is the power to assemble one's dream combinations. Unlike fantasy sports leagues, however, the jazz party host can actually see his players take, in this case, the stage. Dick Gibson relished the opportunity to mix and match at his parties. Sometimes his concoctions failed to coalesce, but many of the party's most memorable moments were provided by the mixing of styles or generations. For example, there was the 1976 pairing of Eubie Blake, then ninety-three, with the twenty-three-year-old trumpeter Jon Faddis, or the annual meetings between Phil Woods and his first inspiration on alto, Benny Carter. In 1992, the last year of the party, Carter also shared the bandstand with the twenty-two-year-old trumpet star Roy Hargrove, who was sixty-three years his junior.[43] Carter once remarked that Gibson "has a wonderful, dramatic feeling for what will work musically. The audience and the players always come away with a sense of musical history—the continuum."[44] Wilder relished the opportunity to play with some of the previous generation of musicians, fondly remembering musical encounters at the Gibson party with violinist Joe Venuti, whom he recalled hearing on the radio as a youngster in Philadelphia, and with drummer Ray McKinley at the Conneaut Lake jazz party in Pennsylvania. Apart from deciding who would play with whom, some jazz party hosts also dictated what should or should not be played. Wilder recalled one party impresario who regularly circulated lists of songs to be avoided, including most of the popular jazz standards, because he felt they were overplayed.

For the musicians, the lure was not primarily financial; most of the jazz parties paid a modest honorarium plus expenses. "The real reason was social," wrote Milt Hinton, a ubiquitous presence on the jazz party circuit. "It was Colorado, so musicians from both coasts were there and we all got to spend a long weekend together. What made it even better were the guests. They loved jazz, of course, but they also seemed to appreciate us outside of what we could do on the bandstand."[45] Hinton also credited Gibson with changing the way jazz was presented—in a nonconcert setting:

> You used to have to play in clubs that were noisy and smoky and filled with people who were there for every other reason but to listen to music. And not just black, but white musicians weren't treated with much dignity. He changed all that. He wanted to hear the music, and in a civilized, comfortable place.[46]

Like Hinton, Wilder forged some lasting friendships with fans whom he saw year after year on the jazz party circuit. He was particularly gratified by the changes he witnessed in the South and in the attitudes toward black musicians on the part of the many Southern jazz fans he encountered. "They were so nice to me that, just as in the Marine Corps, I had to remember not to judge people by where they were from or by the depth of their drawls," he said.

The Gibson party was also fertile ground for Wilder's photographic pursuits. When not onstage, Wilder and his friend and fellow camera buff, Milt Hinton, spent much of the weekend photographing their colleagues, as well as audience members.

The Gibson party spawned many other similar gatherings across the country and abroad. By 1992, Leonard Feather counted sixty-six "spin-off" jazz parties, including one in Cape Town, South Africa.[47] Wilder became a regular at many of these affairs, including the Odessa-Midland Jazz Party in Texas, the Sarasota Jazz Festival in Florida, Jazz Charlotte, the North Carolina Jazz Festival, the Allegheny Jazz Society's party (produced by Joe Boughton in Conneaut Lake, Pennsylvania, and later in Chautauqua, New York), the Swinging Jazz Party in Blackpool, England, and the San Diego Jazz Party, which honored him in 2006. As the popularity of the concept grew, jazz parties became another viable outlet for musicians, many of whom had been overlooked by the larger, more commercial jazz festivals. "The Gibsons should be given a gold medal for what they did because they opened up avenues of work for everybody," Wilder said. "The jazz parties brought attention to a lot of people who had been in the big name bands but had no place to play. Some of these musicians would basically make their living doing jazz parties—after a while, that's all they did!"

Over the years, the roster of the jazz party performers gradually changed from a mix of white and black musicians to predominantly white. In later years, at Joe Boughton's Chautauqua event, for example, Wilder often found himself the only African American musician present. The venerable writer Stanley Dance alluded to this phenomenon in his review of Eric Nisenson's *Blue: The Murder of Jazz*.[48] To rebut Nisenson's criticism of the absence of white musicians in the programming of Jazz at Lincoln Center, Dance wrote, "The arguments about the over-emphasis on black musicians at Lincoln Center are rehashed and shamefully, because none of the pro-white critics has so far, to my knowledge, had a word to say about the virtually lilywhite groups that play to largely white audiences at jazz parties throughout the country."[49] Equating the "whitening" of the jazz party scene with Lincoln Center's conscious decision during its early seasons to focus on black creators—whether true or not—was somewhat disingenuous on Dance's part. The shift in the racial makeup of the jazz parties was more the result of demographics than of some subtle—or not so subtle—form of racism. Although in its very earliest incarnation, Dick

Gibson's party featured the nucleus of what would become the primarily white World's Greatest Jazz Band, that event and its offshoots soon focused on the original musicians who had come to prominence during the swing era, many if not most of whom were black. In time, these swing era musicians began to die off. Gibson humorously acknowledged the aging of these veterans by ending the 1989 party with a set performed by the Great American Youth Movement Jazz Band; it consisted of Doc Cheatham, Benny Carter, Milt Hinton, Marshal Royal, Flip Phillips, Jay McShann, George Chisholm, Harry Edison, Johnny Frigo, Panama Francis, and Snooky Young. They all were in their seventies and eighties. By the end of the next decade, their ranks had thinned considerably.

The predominantly white jazz party audiences, on the other hand, did not change very much as time went on. Over three decades, the same faces could be spotted year after year, and musicians and guests alike began to joke about the number of canes and walkers in evidence at the typical event. The musical tastes of this aging audience remained constant as well: traditional and swing styles, with occasional forays into bop. The musicians working in these older idioms tended to be white, so with the exception of a few survivors like Wilder, Milt Hinton, and drummer Jackie Williams, younger white players began to dominate the jazz party scene. And while there were certainly contemporary black artists well versed in the music favored by jazz party audiences—trumpeters Wynton Marsalis and Nicholas Payton and pianist Eric Reed among them—most of these artists were leading their own groups, playing their own music, and frankly, earning far more than the typical event could afford to pay. One exception was trombonist Wycliffe Gordon, who made fairly regular jazz party appearances.

Over the years, Wilder noticed a change in the ambience of the jazz parties, which made him feel less enthusiastic about playing them. "Some of them got to be very cliquish," he said. "A couple of musicians would ingratiate themselves with the sponsors and end up dictating what everyone should be playing." Wilder also resented being frequently enlisted to play repertory-type material, which he felt was counter to the spirit of these gatherings. "I guess they assumed that at my age, I should know all these obscure tunes from the 1920s, so I'd end up struggling to improvise something," he said. "I couldn't just relax and just play something I felt comfortable with."

By the mid- to late 1990s, many of the traditional jazz parties seemed frozen in time. While the music remained at a high level, the narrow repertoire and fairly limited pool of musicians failed to reach a sizable segment of the jazz audience. As a result, other parties began to arise, featuring a more diverse roster of performers, playing a broader range of music, and catering to a somewhat younger audience. One example is the Vail Jazz Party, founded in 1995 by Howard Stone, a retired real estate attorney and jazz fan who had been a regular at the Gibson parties over the years. The Vail party grew into the Vail Jazz Foundation, which added an educational component and jazz festival to its mission.

Passing It On

Teaching, Awards, and Honors (2000–)

Juilliard

A lthough Wilder had occasionally worked with students privately over the years and had conducted workshops at schools and universities, he had no regular academic affiliation until joining the faculty at Juilliard in 2002. This worked to his advantage, as he brought no preconceived notions to his new career as an educator; his approach to teaching was simply an extension of his overall personality and character. Wilder had been deeply affected by teachers who helped him at all stages of his career, from early lessons in Philadelphia with cornet virtuoso Frederick D. Griffin and his junior high school teacher Alberta Lewis, to later studies with Joseph Alessi Sr. and William Vacchiano at the Manhattan School of Music (where Wilder himself

---

Wilder leading a workshop at Hartt School of Music, University of Hartford, West Hartford, CT, 1999; program chair Jackie McLean is seated at far left.
(Photo by Ed Berger.)

did some student teaching as part of his degree requirements). He remembered the crucial roles these mentors played in shaping his future, and Wilder drew from his experiences with them: "I try to remember some of the things that helped me as a student when I was coming up. You don't browbeat anybody. You try to help the students as much as possible." His concern for his students transcended music: "If they have social problems, you try to help them. That contributes to their growing up and becoming better people."

The jazz program at Juilliard, founded in 2001, was closely allied with Jazz at Lincoln Center (JALC), and several of its faculty were drawn from the Lincoln Center Jazz Orchestra, including its first director, saxophonist-educator Victor Goines. The program was able to take advantage of the extensive outreach activities of Wynton Marsalis and JALC to recruit students. In establishing the new program, Goines envisioned a curriculum that drew on both the musical and broader life experiences of established jazz professionals like Joe Wilder:

> I've always believed that in music or in anything else, you should spend time with people who do what you want to do. That's where Mr. Wilder and people like him became very important. To study with Joe Wilder was to study the history of jazz in real time because he lived that music. He was able to pull from the experiences he had throughout his life in each of his lessons. Every time he picks up his horn, he brings that experience to every bandstand or educational situation, or just to a conversation. So it was really important to me to have someone like him participate in the program. It gave students the opportunity to understand what it was that they were hoping to embark upon as a life endeavor.[1]

Goines had met Wilder through the trumpeter's association with the Lincoln Center Jazz Orchestra, but he had no direct knowledge of Wilder's ability to teach. "I knew of his performance abilities but didn't know him as a teacher," Goines said. "But life is a great educator, and considering the experiences he's had and the things that people who really knew him had to say about him, I knew he would be a great teacher. And all the feedback that came back about him was very positive."[2]

When Wilder was hired at Juilliard, the trumpeter was eighty, an age at which most faculty have long retired and moved to emeritus status. But Wilder's age did not deter Goines. "To me it was a plus," he said. "It's an American myth that when people reach a certain age, we need to retire them. In other parts of the world, they're actually celebrated. And I wanted to have that in my program—to celebrate a man like that in a situation where students could sit down and study with him."

Goines found that Wilder had much to add to the program as a colleague, both in and outside of the classroom. "Having the opportunity to work with him was a dual educational opportunity, not just for the students but for all of us faculty members," Goines said. "He taught us in ways that were non-traditional to the academic situation so that we wouldn't get so caught up in academia that we would forget what the music was all about."[3]

Goines also noted that Wilder regularly attended student concerts at Juilliard. By observing his students in performance, Wilder was able to better tailor his private lessons to a student's strengths and weaknesses. "Having him care enough to attend was also a great support factor," Goines added.[4]

Goines, who left Juilliard in 2007 to direct the jazz program at Northwestern University, still refers to Wilder as "Mr. Wilder." About which, Wilder commented, "At Juilliard, they all did, I guess because of my age. I would tell them, 'Why don't you call me Joe? Everybody calls me Joe!' And they'd say, 'Okay, we'll try, Mr. Wilder.'"

Although Wilder was technically a member of the jazz department at Juilliard and primarily worked one on one with aspiring jazz trumpeters, he drew on his experience outside of jazz in his work with his students:

> I stress that it's a good idea to be able to play jazz and classical and commercial music because not only does it give you a wider field to operate in, but it also makes you a better musician. There are a lot of things that you can gain from playing classical music that work in jazz, and a lot of jazz things that you might be able to play a lot better because of your technical training in classical. This applies to intonation and your understanding of harmonic structures. When you improvise, you listen to the original theme and try to play something in the same mold without destroying it. When you're just walking down the street, you can be thinking about what you can play that will enhance the piece. It helps you become more proficient at improvisation. You don't even need an instrument!

Wilder also stressed the need for teamwork in making music, no matter what the genre, and would often play duets from the Arban book with his students: "They have folk songs, and I'd have them play these with me. We'd each take one of the parts. This gives them some experience in playing in relationship to a section, whether a big band or a small group. You learn how your part relates to the lead and how to blend."

Once again, Wilder's message to students transcended mere technique and stressed the importance of personal as well as musical harmony within an ensemble, whether jazz or classical:

> One of the things I try to impart is not to envy the person in the prin-
> cipal chair but to listen and emulate what he's doing. One trumpet
> player can't play the three or four parts you have in the symphony, and
> if you're playing the fourth chair, you want to play it as well as the prin-
> cipal trumpet plays his part. You're making a contribution and are an
> important part of that orchestra and that piece of music. . . . Also, I try
> to stress that when you're playing with other players, you want to try
> to have some rapport with them and establish some relationship with
> them as friends.[5]

Finally, recalling his own fascination with other instruments as a youngster, Wilder would encourage his students to listen to other players, thereby enhancing their own techniques:

> As wind players or whatever instrument you play, you can learn to play
> better on your own instrument if you listen to the things being played on
> other instruments. Like we were talking about the violin; if you think
> in terms of the pizzicatos that the string players play, it's a clean kind of
> thing. Rhythmically, you try to remember how they did it. You listen to
> piano concerti and you hear these beautiful phrases almost as if they're
> playing a wind instrument. If you listen to these and apply them to your
> own instrument, all of a sudden you're playing with a little more artistry.
> And if you have difficulty playing in the higher range, listen to the flau-
> tists and the clarinet players and how smoothly they get into this.[6]

One of Wilder's first students at Juilliard was Dominick Farinacci, who has since emerged as a major new figure on the jazz scene. Farinacci, who was born in 1983, was discovered at the age of seventeen by Wynton Marsalis, who encouraged the young trumpeter to move to New York from his native Cleveland and enroll in the newly established Juilliard jazz program. In 2001, he became a member of the inaugural class and initially studied with Warren Vaché, who, Farinacci recalled, "was always talking about Joe Wilder."[7] When Wilder joined the faculty in 2002, Farinacci began taking lessons with him.

Farinacci was familiar with Wilder's work well before meeting him at Juilliard: "When I was growing up in Cleveland, I was studying trumpet players of his generation. *Wilder 'n' Wilder* was my first exposure to him. He had such a beautiful, brilliant sound, and his feel was unique—much different from many of the guys who I checked out from his generation." As with so many other players over the years, Farinacci was captivated by Wilder's singular interpretation of "Cherokee" from that album: "I transcribed part of his solo, which was very difficult. I gained so much by learning how he phrases and his melodic choices and his feel."[8]

Another member of that inaugural class at Juilliard was trumpeter Brandon Lee, who has since achieved much success as both a performer and educator. Lee, who earned bachelor's and master's degrees at the school, studied with Wilder for four years. He joined the Juilliard faculty in 2008.

Both former students felt that the fact that Wilder was relatively new at teaching made him more adaptable to the students' needs and goals. As Farinacci noted:

> One reason it was so wonderful was that he didn't come in with a set agenda. The first thing I did was play for him, and he cited some of the influences that he heard and asked me what I was looking to do. He tailor-made the lesson around what I wanted to get out of it and what my strengths and weaknesses were, so it was a very personal lesson, not a preconceived curriculum.[9]

Lee still recalled his first lesson with Wilder and his new instructor's somewhat unorthodox approach:

> We basically sat there and talked—he asked me about myself. He had so much information to share. He talked about the people he'd played with—Count Basie, Dizzy Gillespie—not just as musicians but as friends. It was really cool to get that experience from somebody who had been there and was talking about it not just as a scholar but as someone who witnessed it. I got a history lesson at every lesson; it didn't necessarily have to do with the trumpet, but it was unlike anything else I had had before. I would leave the lessons knowing a lot more.[10]

The jazz trumpet students benefited from the classical elements that Wilder incorporated into the lessons. "I hadn't played classical music at all," Farinacci said. "Joe would bring in a lot of different trumpet etudes, and hearing him play them was much different than listening to the other great teachers and players at Juilliard. He has such a distinct, personal sound, and he made them come alive for me."[11]

Lee also recalled playing classical duets with Wilder and his instructor's insistence on treating the etudes as music and not simply exercises:

> When we sight-read through things, that's when he would get on me. Obviously, playing in the studio orchestras for all of those years, he was reading all the time, and that was a lot different from the background of a lot of the jazz trumpet players. He never did anything in a mean-spirited or negative way, but he did point out what I was doing wrong. If I was playing an etude out of the Arban book, he would talk to me a lot about articulation, about being very musical in everything that I played. I had always approached playing technical exercises as just that—not as music; he always talked about bringing the music out of those exercises.[12]

During his two years of study with Wilder, Farinacci credits him with helping to correct his embouchure:

> The physicality of playing the trumpet is so demanding. You look at Joe Wilder and Clark Terry, who are playing so beautifully at that [mature] age. Joe's embouchure is perfect. When he plays, you can see that he isn't using much pressure at all, so he has all of the little muscles working correctly. At that time I was going through an embouchure change, because I had learned to play incorrectly. Wynton initially helped me, and so did Warren [Vaché], and Joe helped me with some little tweaks that really made a world of difference in terms of developing sound and execution. One thing I love about Joe's playing is that, even when he's playing very softly, he can fill an entire room with his sound. It's not necessarily about the volume but the substance. His sound goes right into my heart.[13]

Lee also noted the high level of Wilder's own playing, despite his age:

> When Joe would take the horn out of its case, there was no warm-up—it took him about one minute, and then everything would sync up. Most of what I got from him was from playing together. Even into his eighties, the clarity of his ideas, and his swing, all of that was very clear. I got so much out of playing with him—about pacing, telling a story. His playing, like his speech, was very concise, and when we were trading back and forth, everything he did was very organic—it was coming

from inside of him. It was just amazing to be able to experience, and I learned a lot from it.[14]

As Wynton Marsalis had done a decade earlier while touring with Wilder, Lee and other trumpet students at Juilliard sought out his guidance in the use of the plunger. "Being in the big band at Juilliard, we had to play with the plunger a lot," he said. "I'd figured out as much as I could about it on my own, but sitting next to Joe Wilder, a master at it, brought a lost art form to life."[15]

Farinacci felt that some of the most valuable lessons he learned during his study with Wilder had nothing to do with technique. "It went well beyond just learning to play the trumpet. He would talk to me about life in general, about all the things he had experienced and the people he had known. I recorded some of the lessons and listened to them over the years."[16]

In summing up his experience with Wilder, Farinacci emphasized Wilder's respect for his students, his ability to make them feel he was on their side, and his concern for them as human beings as well as musicians:

> He has a way of making the younger musicians feel really special. I remember the first time I was hanging out in the front area of Juilliard. Joe was walking by with his camera, and he took a couple of photos of me. I remember thinking, "What the hell is he taking photos of me for?" It made me feel really special, like he really takes me seriously. He has a way of bringing people in and making them feel like family.[17]

Lee also stressed Wilder's concern for his students outside the classroom:

> He would always ask me about how school in general was going. He was always encouraging me to keep writing, and he came to all the concerts, so he heard my pieces, and we would talk about them at the next lesson. He met my parents and always asked about my family. The lessons I had with him encouraged me as a teacher to take that approach with my own students, especially the advanced ones—to not get so much into talking about technical aspects but to really lead by example.[18]

On February 27, 2007, five days after his eighty-fifth birthday, Wilder was honored with Juilliard's President's Medal, as was Frank Wess, James Moody, Dr. Billy Taylor, and Clark Terry.

Wilder was equally effective in communicating with younger students. In the 1970s, as a member of the Manhattan Brass Quintet, he had visited many elementary and high schools through New Audiences, and in the 1990s, Wilder continued this outreach activity through his connection with the Smithsonian Jazz Masterworks Orchestra, as well as with the National Jazz Museum in Harlem. Loren Schoenberg, who helped found the Museum in 1995 and serves as its artistic director, was also on the Juilliard faculty during Wilder's early years there. "His students had immense respect for him," Schoenberg said. "I heard through the grapevine that one student who was to study with Joe hadn't shown up for a lesson, and while that wasn't uncommon for kids in college, the fact that it was Joe was regarded as a real sin!"[19] Schoenberg invited Wilder to participate in some of the early education outreach programs of the Jazz Museum:

> We brought him in to the Frederick Douglass Academy and had the students interview him. I don't think I've ever seen a more exemplary performance by an educator in that role. As always, he showed up dressed to the nines and gave the most balanced, challenging, and honest interview about his life and career that I've ever seen. It was remarkable because these kids were born around 1990, and Joe could have been their great-grandfather. I don't think they had come into contact with many people like him, but the sheer force of his personality reached them. He had obviously given a lot of thought to what he wanted to say, and he said it in a way that wasn't preaching. I liken it to his playing. His playing is not bravura, but it reaches people on a more profound level than people who are shouting at you or playing in capital letters.[20]

Wilder was always completely natural in approaching young people, and his honesty, sincerity, and humor would invariably win them over. Often imparting an antidrug message, he did so without moralizing or condescension. He simply spoke of the great musicians who were his friends and how substance abuse affected their lives and careers.

Monk Rowe, director of the Hamilton College Jazz Archive, formed a close friendship with Wilder, and since the late 1990s, has invited him to participate in several educational initiatives, both at Hamilton and local public schools. Rowe, a saxophonist and pianist, would put together a compatible group to accompany Wilder in performances, which were combined with discussions and question-and-answer sessions with the students. "He was speaking to third, fourth, and fifth graders, and he was very articulate, and kids recognized that right away," Rowe said. "He didn't change the way he spoke to them because they were kids. They really paid attention to what he had to say."[21]

Rowe, who also served as artistic director of the Utica Arts and Education Institute, was able to lay the groundwork by meeting the teachers and students in advance and preparing them for Wilder's visits. He recalled that Wilder particularly enjoyed his time in the Greene, New York, school district, which had made a serious commitment to incorporating jazz into the broader curriculum:

> The teachers were really into it, and they would devote months of study to jazz and were interested in Joe's story. They found a way to use jazz and photography in the classroom, so that was another connection. Of course, Joe brought his camera, and he took pictures of the kids, and they took pictures of him. I had made several visits beforehand and prepared the students, so they knew who he was. It wasn't like school concerts often are: "Come into the gym and be quiet because we think this is good for you."[22]

Also, Wilder played with the student group in Greene. "At the concert, we had some of the student trumpet players standing next to Joe." Rowe recalled. "I would turn to him and ask, 'What would be an answering riff that would work?' and—bam!—Joe would play something so perfect that I couldn't have even conceived of it!"[23]

Rowe found Wilder to be equally effective in working with college students at Hamilton. Once again, Wilder's openness, sincerity, and lack of condescension made an immediate impression. "He didn't try to be hip or cool," Rowe said. "There was none of the current jazz 'lingo.' Over the years, I've been amazed at the inability of some very well-known jazz people of different generations to relate to students. But Joe had no problem at all." Once again, photography helped to break the ice, with Wilder photographing the students as usual. "About a week after he did his Hamilton residency, he sent a big bunch of photos," Rowe said. "He had counted the students in the group picture, and he sent a copy for every one of them!"[24]

Rowe also had the opportunity to play with Wilder in a variety of settings, and as many other musicians have pointed out over the years, to Joe Wilder, music was always a cooperative venture, not a competition. "I never felt intimidated because he would say what he had to say in a chorus, and then he would pass it on," Rowe said. "Even though he had so many years of experience and could have blown me off the stage if he wanted, he would never do that." Rowe also noted that, despite his age, Wilder never sought any special treatment: "Not only wouldn't he let you help carry his bags, but after a concert, I would turn around and see him carrying speakers and loading the car with our equipment!"[25]

In addition to his regular teaching position at Juilliard and his association with Hamilton College, during the 1990s and 2000s, Wilder conducted workshops and seminars at the Hartt School (University of Hartford), William Paterson University, Princeton University, Indiana University, and Temple University, among other institutions. Sometimes, Wilder's lessons were not limited to music. At Princeton, for example, after bringing in one of his famous homemade cheesecakes to Phil Schaap's jazz history class, students besieged him for the recipe, which he graciously provided.

Awards and Honors

Monk Rowe was largely responsible for Wilder's receiving an honorary degree from Hamilton College in 2004. Wilder was the last of a group of jazz artists so honored by the college. Previous recipients were Kenny Davern, Harry "Sweets" Edison, Milt Hinton, Dick Hyman, Marian McPartland, Bucky Pizzarelli, Bobby Rosengarden, George Shearing, Ralph Sutton, Clark Terry, Bob Wilber, and Joe Williams. While all these honorees had made major contributions and were highly respected among their peers and jazz fans, most did not have the household name status of jazz performers typically singled out for such an award, and for many, like Wilder, it was his only honorary degree.

The honorary jazz degrees and the Hamilton Jazz Archive were the visions of wealthy Hamilton alumnus Milton Fillius Jr. (class of 1944), who was a trustee of the college and a jazz fan. Fillius, who was particularly close to Milt Hinton and Joe Williams, felt it was important to capture the stories of these and other musicians and, in 1995, launched the Hamilton Jazz Oral History Project, which, under Rowe's direction, has grown to encompass more than three hundred videotaped interviews with jazz artists of many generations and styles.[26] Fillius proposed that Joe Williams receive an honorary degree, which was awarded in 1988, followed by one for Milt Hinton in 1991, and Fillius handpicked the subsequent recipients.

After Fillius's death in 2002, the attitude toward the honorary degrees changed. "It was like, 'Okay, we've done enough of these jazz people,'" Rowe said. But before leaving office, Hamilton's outgoing president, Gene Tobin, who had been a confidant of Fillius's and a supporter of the jazz program, solicited one final degree recommendation from Rowe, who proposed Wilder. "I'm sure Milt [Fillius] would have been happy, because he got to know Joe from his visits and liked him a lot," Rowe said.[27] So on May 23, 2004, Wilder stood onstage in his academic robe and received the degree of Doctor of Music, with his wife, Solveig, in attendance. The citation praised Wilder's professional achievements, but the most meaningful paragraph dealt with his personal qualities and the impression he had made while on campus:

> But beyond your remarkable versatility and technical command, you are enormously and universally admired for your professionalism and for your personal qualities that combine warmth and good humor with caring. Indeed, your engagement with our students when you were an artist in residence at Hamilton some years ago is well and fondly remembered.[28]

One of the most prestigious honors accorded Wilder was his selection in 2008 as a National Endowment for the Arts (NEA) Jazz Master. Considered the Nation's highest jazz honor, the awards began in 1982, with honorees Roy Eldridge, Dizzy Gillespie, and Sun Ra, and each year for the following two decades, the program chose three living jazz contributors to receive the coveted medal. Beginning in 2004, the number of yearly awards increased to as many as eight. The award has also carried a cash prize, which in recent years, has reached $25,000. During the Jazz Masters program's early years, such seminal figures as Count Basie, Ella Fitzgerald, Lionel Hampton, Miles Davis, and Sarah Vaughan were still living and were obvious choices. Nevertheless, during the program's first decade, some lesser-known figures were also honored alongside these legends, including Melba Liston, Cleo Brown, George Russell, and Andy Kirk. By the new millennium, the selections became more problematic, as the number of indisputable candidates dwindled, and those still living had, for the most part, already been honored. This thinning of the ranks resulted in several controversial selections. Critics of the program felt some of the honorees had spent too much of their careers outside of jazz (Tony Bennett, Ramsey Lewis, Johnny Mandel), or were too young. The Marsalis family, for example, received the first and only group award in 2011, when each member, with the exception of patriarch Ellis, was fifty years of age or younger. In questioning the Marsalis family's precedent-setting selection, Nate Chinen raised important questions about process:

> There's an unspoken seniority clause built into the Jazz Masters process, since the award goes to living artists, with no provision for estates or heirs. Given the demographics of jazz—all those important figures now approaching, or well past, mile marker 80—this is a morbid but practical consideration. . . . The salient truth is that every honoree

occupies a spot that could have gone to someone else, perhaps some-one in the burnished twilight of his or her career.[29]

While Chinen makes the case for tenor saxophonist Fred Anderson as one of those "in the burnished twilight" of a career who were overlooked (Anderson died in June 2010), he acknowledges that "dozens of similar cases could be made—and no doubt have been, behind the [NEA] panels' closed doors."[30] Chinen also called for more transparency in the selection process: "The NEA should post interviews not only with this year's recipients but also with the panelists. What went into this decision? What were the motivating factors? A little bit of context would go a long way."[31]

Given the historical background of the NEA award, the 2008 selection of someone like Joe Wilder, with little name recognition beyond the circle of mu-sicians and serious jazz fans, was surprising but not unprecedented. As Will Friedwald wrote in the *New York Sun*, "Of all the living legends of jazz certi-fied by the National Endowment for the Arts, Joe Wilder is at once among the least known to the general public . . . and the most prized by musicians, espe-cially his fellow trumpeters."[32] Friedwald's assertion was a bit of well-meaning hyperbole designed to call attention to what the writer felt was Wilder's un-warranted lack of public recognition. One might argue that Wilder was not even the least-known Jazz Master of his fellow class of 2008 honorees, which included trombonist-composer-arranger Tom McIntosh and pianist-composer Andrew Hill—certainly not well-known figures outside of jazz. (The others chosen were Quincy Jones, Candido Camero, and Gunther Schuller, who was selected in the special Jazz Advocacy category.) In any case, Wilder himself was as surprised as anyone at his selection.

Joe and Solveig flew to Toronto for the January 11, 2008, award ceremony and concert, held in conjunction with the annual International Association for Jazz Education conference. During the afternoon, Wilder participated in a panel discussion with his fellow honorees, moderated by A. B. Spellman, for-mer NEA deputy chair and the man for whom the NEA Jazz Advocacy award was named. Unfortunately, Spellman chose to open the discussion by asking Wilder for a "Lionel Hampton story," unaware of Wilder's less-than-warm memories of his former bandleader. Wilder did not mince words:

> In a sense he was a giant—at the same time, a midget. . . . He had a good band and everything, but unfortunately, he treated most of us like, "Well, if you weren't here, you wouldn't have a job at all." No mat-ter how much you tried to contribute . . . to the betterment of the band, it was just like, "So what?"[33]

Wilder then, wisely, took a lighter tack, relating a funny story about a mythical character named Barracuda, who, during the trumpeter's years on the road with Hampton, would be blamed for the disappearance of everything from an arrangement that the band didn't like to the leader's new hat, which somehow found its way out of the window of the band's bus. Wilder was asked a follow-up question about whether the young musicians of today were at a disadvantage by not having the widespread opportunities to play in the many big bands that were prevalent when Wilder was learning his craft. While he agreed with that premise, he also praised the talents of today's musicians and the jazz education system that produced them. He also took the opportunity to comment on the elevated status of jazz today in contrast to the commonly held notion when he was a youngster that it was the "devil's music." He noted that "jazz, in this era, is contributing more to the understanding and cooperation and affection for people. . . . It's raised the level of social understanding in this country and others."[34]

At the evening concert and ceremony, Wilder received his award from A. B. Spellman and, in his brief acceptance speech, eloquently expounded on some of the themes he had touched on during the afternoon Jazz Masters panel. He noted that the NEA awards were indicative of how far jazz had come in the eyes of the nation and the world and how, in turn, jazz had helped promote racial understanding and bring people together. "I hadn't prepared—it was just spontaneous," Wilder said. "I just thought about Jack Teagarden and Louis Armstrong and all the other African Americans and whites who played together because they admired each other's work and how that led to the sense of community that developed among musicians."

Wilder was equally eloquent when he picked up his flügelhorn that night and joined fellow Jazz Masters Candido Camero and Paquito D'Rivera in a version of "Walkin'," backed, appropriately, by the Smithsonian Jazz Masterworks Orchestra under David Baker.[35] One could see the affection for Wilder on the orchestra members' faces—people with whom he had spent more than a decade—and Wilder responded with seven inventive choruses that brought the house down. His remarkable solo was filled with warmth and humor, and it neatly encapsulated his musical essence. Characteristically, after the concert, Wilder remained sitting on the edge of the stage long after the other performers had gone, signing autographs, talking with fans, and having his picture taken with them.

There were several other major tributes during the 1990s and 2000s, as Wilder began to garner some of the public recognition that had eluded him during his decades in the studios and on Broadway, when he was largely out of the public view. In March 1998, he was honored by the New York Brass

Conference at its annual gathering. Fellow trumpeters Jimmy Owens and Donald Byrd performed in his honor, and many other musician friends were in attendance, including John Glasel, Ray Crisara, Joe Ferrante, Jerry Dodgion, and Barry Harris. In his remarks, Donald Byrd noted that Wilder "was known as a trumpet player who never made a mistake." Byrd also pointed out Wilder's pioneering role in integrating the studios.[36] Also present was New York State Supreme Court justice Bruce Wright, a good friend of Wilder's. Wright was the activist judge who earned the nickname "Let 'Em Loose Bruce" for setting low bail in cases involving minorities and the poor as a weapon to combat racism in the criminal justice system. During his gracious acceptance speech, Wilder injected some humor by reciting a few of his original and elaborate puns, drawing laughs from the audience and groans from his family. He also quipped, "I have so many friends here, it might be a nice time to have my funeral."[37]

On June 17, 1998, Wilder and fellow veteran trumpeters Harry "Sweets" Edison and Snooky Young were saluted by three younger players, Byron Stripling, Darryl Shaw, and Warren Vaché, at a JVC Jazz Festival concert. The format of the event, produced by Vaché, had each of the younger trumpeters play for and then introduce a short set by one of the honorees. *New York Times* reviewer Peter Watrous wrote:

> Usually the cross-generational aspect of these shows brings surprises, with the younger musicians being forced to confront the masters and often doing well, in a Freudian sort of way. But Mr. Edison and Mr. Wilder turned in the better performances of the night, in completely different styles.[38]

Watrous went on to praise Wilder's "perfectly articulated lines," and noted that the power of his improvisations "did not come from his volume or extremity but from the sheer pleasure Mr. Wilder took in thinking aloud and clearly, and from the literate and wide variety of ideas."[39] George Kanzler emphasized Wilder's "pearly, burnished sound, a tonal mix of suede and bronze" and noted his transformation of "Battle Hymn of the Republic" into "a soulful, hand-clapping, gospel romp."[40]

On August 21, 2001, Wilder was honored at New York's annual Charlie Parker Festival in Tomkins Square Park. Wilder kicked off the proceedings, leading a group with Bucky Pizzarelli on guitar, Rufus Reid on bass, and Jackie Williams on drums. Ira Gitler noted that, "because of his success as a studio and Broadway theater musician, [Wilder] is not as appreciated as a jazzman as he should be. After the opening set, an inspired piece of booking, I know that a lot more people are now aware of the trumpeter/flugelhornist."[41]

When Wilder turned eighty in 2002, several events marked the occasion. The Arbors Records March of Jazz honored him, along with pianist John Bunch (eighty) and saxophonist Jerry Jerome (ninety), at its annual jazz party in Clearwater, Florida, held March 15 to 17. A highlight of the weekend was a duo set featuring Wilder with Bunch, one of his favorite pianists. The lavish concert program booklet included an extensive selection of previously unpublished photos of and by Wilder, as well as some memorabilia from his personal collection. On August 16, Lincoln Center Out of Doors feted Wilder with a concert featuring him with old friends Bucky Pizzarelli, Tommy Newsom, and classical violinist Elliot Magaziner.

On June 17, 2003, the first major concert of the JVC Festival was a salute to Wilder and fellow octogenarian Frank Wess. It was an appropriate pairing, as the two horn men had been friends since the early 1940s, colleagues in the Basie band in the 1950s, and frequent collaborators in the studios and at countless jazz events over the years. During the past decade, Wilder was a regular guest for jam sessions at Wess's Manhattan studio, often playing with younger musicians that the tenor saxophonist was mentoring. Both men had turned eighty-one within a few weeks of each other. Among the evening's many encomiums to Wilder was Warren Vaché's remark, "He's the only man in the music business I'd let hold my wallet!" and Jimmy Heath's observation that Wilder and Hank Jones "are the only jazz musicians I know who would wear a tie to the supermarket."[42] The multigenerational assemblage included trumpeters Jon Faddis, Roy Hargrove, and Vaché, as well as saxophonists Antonio Hart, Phil Woods, and Jimmy Heath. A duet between Wilder and Vaché on "It's You or No One" was a high point. "The two brassmen engaged in one ingeniously contrapuntal chorus after another," wrote Will Friedwald,[43] with Ben Ratliff citing Wilder's "beautifully disciplined solo, basically long-tones connected by elegant little three- and four-note patterns."[44]

In April 2006, Wilder returned to his native Philadelphia to receive Temple University's Jazz Masters Hall of Fame award, along with fellow trumpeter Clark Terry. Wilder and Terry each conducted master classes and performed with the university's jazz ensemble at the ceremony. Temple jazz program director Terrell Stafford, himself a leading contemporary trumpet player, emphasized the importance of having his students interact with musicians like Terry and Wilder, both on- and offstage: "It does wonders for the students' music, motivating them to play at an even higher level," he said. "And getting to know who these people are away from their music, and their commitment to education gives them an important message."[45]

The Reluctant Leader

On January 31, 2006, three weeks before his eighty-fourth birthday, Joe Wilder stepped onto the bandstand of New York's legendary Village Vanguard to begin a weeklong stint as leader of his own quartet. So rare were the trumpeter's appearances as a leader that the engagement was greeted by much fanfare in the press; in his *New York Times* preview, Nate Chinen called it "a sort of landmark event."[46] A full house eagerly awaited the start of the opening set on that Tuesday night. In his review, Ben Ratliff perfectly captured Wilder's self-effacing demeanor even before the trumpeter took the stand for this momentous occasion: "He was in the corridor, scrutinizing the pictures on the walls, rather than waiting in the back room for his dramatic entrance." Ratliff pointed out that when he did take the stage to tumultuous applause, "he looked ill at ease, like a guest waiting to be placed at the dinner table. But when he sat down, confident logic poured out of his trumpet."[47]

Many believed the Vanguard date to be Wilder's first club appearance in New York as a leader. The trumpeter himself confirmed that fact when asked by writers, not remembering a couple of other engagements that had preceded it. In March 1990, Wilder led a group at Carlos I, a club on Sixth Avenue in Greenwich Village that presented many name jazz artists from the mid-1980s, until its demise shortly after Wilder's appearance. In addition, there were several occasions when Wilder led groups at colleges, including a 1986 appearance at William Paterson University and a 1988 concert at Rutgers, where Wilder led a group that included Frank Wess and Barry Harris. He returned to William Paterson in February 2004 to speak with students and play a concert with pianist James Williams, who directed the jazz program at the school. "I admired him," Wilder said. "He was a fantastic musician and a very compassionate guy who was so concerned with not just helping the students musically but how they conducted themselves. He was always trying to set an example."

The seeds for the Vanguard appearance were planted a year earlier, when Wilder led a group at the Kitano Hotel for one night in February 2005. That engagement was arranged by pianist Michael Weiss, who had played with the trumpeter during the early years of the Smithsonian orchestra: "When I first got to meet him and heard him play with the orchestra, I thought, 'How come he isn't being featured? Wouldn't it be great to play in a small group with him? He's such a creative soloist.'"[48] Weiss had appeared at the Kitano as a leader and as a sideman with Frank Wess and others, so he contacted the club's booker and set up the engagement.

Weiss also had a hand in arranging for Wilder's Vanguard appearance. Max Gordon (1903–1989), founder of the legendary club, had tried to book

Wilder over the years. "I had gone there and sat in a couple of times, and he'd asked me if I'd like to go in there with my own group," Wilder said, "but I didn't think I had enough going for me to sit there all night playing and keep the people interested. Finally, I thought, 'Well, with all my years of playing, there must be something I can do!'" Weiss, who had worked at the Vanguard, let Lorraine Gordon, Max's widow and now manager of the club, know that Wilder was interested, and she was quick to issue an invitation.

Weiss recruited bassist John Webber and drummer Lewis Nash to round out the highly compatible trio to back the trumpeter. From opening night, it became clear that after nearly seventy years as a sideman, the protocols of leading a band did not come naturally to Wilder. As Ratliff noted, "Joe Wilder doesn't seem used to making announcements."[49] Wilder rarely spoke to the audience, with one exception. In the middle of each set, he would take the mike and launch into a monologue consisting of several of his original puns. Some of these were quite elaborate and clever, while others were so contrived that they were even funnier. In any case, the audience found this interlude amusing, and it provided a short break for Wilder and the trio. One night, however, Wilder's spoken interlude apparently went on too long, prompting a patron to call out good-naturedly, "Play, Joe, play!" It was probably Wilder's nightly comedy routine that led critic Zan Stewart to call him "an affable, witty emcee."[50] Stewart also described Wilder as "an understated instrumental troubadour, softly singing heartfelt melodies that touched a listener."[51]

The trumpeter's reluctance to make announcements was not because of stage fright. Time and again, he had proven to be an extremely articulate and eloquent speaker at many events when he was honored, called on to eulogize a departed colleague, or stood up to address students in classes or at workshops. But there is a difference between functioning as a bandleader and public speaking.

Because of the leader's reticence, Weiss found himself assuming some of the duties normally handled by the leader. "I tried to move things along and deal with the procedural aspects—getting on and off the stage in the allotted time and maintaining some communication with the audience," the pianist said, adding, "The music took care of itself."[52] After decades in the role of sideman, Wilder's natural inclination was to look to the leader for decisions about what would be played as well as to establish the routine of a piece. It was hard to change that mind-set now that he himself was the leader. There was another reason for Wilder's diffidence. Having played for his share of capricious and domineering leaders, he vowed to act differently if ever placed in that position: "I always try to avoid what I see in some musicians who, when they're the leader, act like they're superior to everybody else." Wilder's shyness onstage also extended to his response to applause after a solo. He looked embarrassed by the attention, often turning away from the audience after only a fleeting acknowledgement.

Weiss is a sensitive accompanist and, together with bassist John Webber and drummer Lewis Nash, provided the type of backing that complemented Wilder's style and made him feel comfortable. This was a crucial component in eliciting an inspired performance from the trumpeter. Some jazz players seem unfazed by mediocre or stylistically inappropriate backing. Louis Armstrong, for example, could transcend pedestrian accompaniment through the sheer force of his musical personality, often dragging the other musicians along with him. In contrast, Wilder is a reactive player, deeply affected by the musical environment surrounding him. A pianist or a bassist who is not in tune with him harmonically, an overly busy drummer, or anyone who simply plays too loudly, can upset the delicate equilibrium Wilder needs to perform at his peak. Weiss was aware of the nuances of Wilder's style, which enabled him to provide accompaniment that was both subtle and stimulating:

> Joe was playing most of the time in the lower register of the horn. You're always conscious of where the soloist is playing range-wise, and you try not to clutter up the works. You want to leave the appropriate amount of space so that the soloist's "voice" can be heard clearly. His sense of melody is so strong, so there was rarely a time I couldn't follow where he was going or what he was doing harmonically. He wasn't using a lot of "modern" substitutions and taking liberties with the harmony as so many younger players do.[53]

Wilder's playing during the Vanguard engagement was extraordinary. Despite the fact that he was experiencing ongoing dental problems, he played with abandon, unleashing a seemingly endless flow of ideas. And even when embouchure difficulties frustrated him, he refused to play it safe. Weiss felt that the weeklong Vanguard engagement had a liberating effect on the trumpeter:

> All of a sudden the gates were opened, and he was allowed to roam free. He could play as long as he wanted—not just eight or sixteen bars. I thought his playing for someone of his age, on his instrument, remarkably consistent, and he seemed very inspired. And perhaps because he was not an established soloist-bandleader, he hadn't fallen into playing certain clichés. Everything he played was pure improvisation at its best—completely spontaneous and fresh.[54]

The pianist appreciated the significance of playing with musicians like Wilder, who are among the last links to an important era in the history of the music and to many of its forebears. Weiss also realized that future generations will not have that chance: "It's a gift and an honor for me to play with someone like Joe and get to know him. Those opportunities are so few and far between these days. I do a fair amount of teaching, and I just don't know what to say sometimes to young players who want to have a career as a jazz musician. There are so few musicians left from that time or even later that they can have the experience of having a direct, personal relationship with."[55]

One up-and-coming younger trumpet star who came to the Vanguard that week to hear Wilder was Jeremy Pelt. He said, "Young players need to know about Joe Wilder. He's a very humble person and very much a gentleman. He's one of those players that keeps a good concept of time and rhythm and harmony. I cherish those nights going to the Vanguard to see what he's got to play. Joe's sound is always warm but it also has openness."[56]

Wilder's Vanguard debut was so successful that he returned with the same trio for another weeklong engagement six months later, in July.

In 2007, Wilder turned eighty-five, an extraordinary age for a trumpet player. Of his contemporaries, only Clark Terry and Snooky Young continued to perform at such a high level. Indeed, throughout jazz history, only a handful of trumpeters that age continued to lead active performing careers, with Doc Cheatham heading the list. Despite his rigorous practice regimen and active lifestyle, age inevitably began to take a toll on his technique. For several years, he had battled dental problems, the scourge of trumpet players. Wilder had consulted a series of dentists, who, after charging tens of thousands of dollars for new bridges and implants, had failed to completely resolve the situation. As a result, Wilder's upper-register ability—never his forte—became somewhat erratic. In addition, as his eyesight deteriorated, reading music became increasingly problematic. Although a source of frustration for a musician known for his impeccable technique and his ability to sight-read anything put before him, these impediments did not deter him. "You learn to adjust," Wilder said. "At some point, you just have to forget about it and just play. If you keep thinking about it, you can't play at all." Wilder recalled an incident that occurred earlier in his career, when he was doing *The Patti Page Show* at ABC:

We were doing a commercial, which had us playing "In My Merry Oldsmobile." This thing had a high D in it, and even though Ernie Royal and the other trumpet player on the date could play two octaves above me, they gave it to me to play every time the commercial came up. I'd be sitting there, thinking, "Am I going to be able to make this thing?" Finally, I just said, "If I make it, I make it, and if I don't, I don't," and I was able to play it.

Using the same philosophy, Wilder persevered. Despite his limitations, Wilder's wondrous sound remained largely intact and his musical imagination undiminished. Drawing on a lifetime of experience, Wilder picked his spots and proved time and again that under the proper conditions, he could still deliver a commanding performance. About Wilder's appearance at the Chautauqua jazz party in September 2008, Michael Steinman wrote, "Wilder continues to amaze: it's not the simple matter of age—playing a brass instrument is difficult for anyone—but the surprises he unfurls as he plays, his dancing, leaping phrases never going in predictable ways."[57]

Another such occasion was the "All Nite Soul" tribute to Wilder at New York's Saint Peter's Church on October 11, 2009. The evening featured a galaxy of performers, including Warren Vaché, Ingrid Jensen, Jimmy Owens, Frank Wess, Wycliffe Gordon, Benny Powell, Daryl Sherman, Bucky Pizzarelli, Gene Bertoncini, Bill Charlap, and many others. After several sets by others, Wilder finally took center stage, backed by old friends John Bunch on piano and Jackie Williams on drums, with Chip Jackson on bass. Looking characteristically embarrassed by the ovation that greeted him, Wilder picked up his flügelhorn and launched into Ellington's "I Got It Bad." The audience quickly grew silent as Wilder's dulcet tones filled the church. As he so often demonstrated, Wilder could captivate an audience by delivering a melody "softly, with feeling." It was a magical moment—an artist playing from the heart—and the audience responded. Wilder was undoubtedly buoyed by the accompaniment of his friend, pianist John Bunch; it would be their last performance together, as the pianist died six months later. Most of the audience was unaware of the history behind that performance of "I Got It Bad," which was not a random selection. Bunch and Wilder had first played the Ellington piece together in 1962 on the Benny Goodman State Department–sponsored tour of the Soviet Union. Some forty years later, they reprised it in a duo version at the 2002 Arbors Records March of Jazz event. Wilder described what happened:

John seemed to anticipate everything I played. I couldn't believe that two people could be so attuned to each other. When we got through, the people were standing up and applauding. John and I were hugging each other, and I just couldn't stop the tears coming out of my eyes. It was such an emotional moment I couldn't even turn around and look at the audience.

Wilder and Bunch both remembered that wondrous performance and were able to recapture the magic seven years later at the Saint Peter's tribute.

On December 2, 2009, Wilder was asked to participate in the 150th anniversary of the hanging of celebrated abolitionist John Brown, who on October 16, 1859, had led a group of slaves in a raid against the U.S. armory at Harpers Ferry. Local officials; civil rights leaders, such as Dick Gregory; and descendants of the abolitionist gathered at Harpers Ferry National Historical Park in West Virginia to reenact the events of the fateful day in 1859, when Brown was hanged. An actor portraying Brown was transported atop a coffin by a horse-drawn carriage to the mock gallows that had been erected.[58] "It was very moving for everyone involved," Wilder recalled. "It was so realistic that you really felt you were there." Wilder closed the program with a solo trumpet rendition of the "Battle Hymn of the Republic." After his performance, Wilder returned to New York via Amtrak. Emerging from Penn Station with a Red Cap (Amtrak porter), who assisted with his luggage, Wilder was unable to get a taxi to take him uptown to his home on 141 Street and Riverside Drive. "We stood out there on the corner of Eighth Avenue and Thirty-Fourth Street," Wilder said. "Nine or ten cabs slowed down, looked at me, and then sped by. The drivers were black, white, Hispanic—it didn't matter. The Red Cap, who was white, stayed with me the whole time and kept flagging them down, until one finally agreed to take me." The irony of the situation was not lost on Wilder. "It was a little disappointing to face that after having taken part in an event commemorating a milestone in the civil rights struggle," he said.

Wilder had participated in two earlier events at Harpers Ferry. In 2002, he and trombonist Benny Powell performed at the park, and each received the Don Redman Heritage Award, named for the saxophonist and pioneering arranger who was a West Virginia native. In August 2006, Wilder returned to participate in the centennial celebration of the Niagara Movement, the civil rights group founded by W.E.B. Du Bois and William Monroe Trotter, which was a precursor to the NAACP (National Association for the Advancement of Colored People). Wilder was part of a panel discussion devoted to the theme "Breaking Barriers in America." He was selected because of his role in integrating the Broadway show orchestras and appeared with Juanita Abernathy, widow of civil rights leader Reverend Ralph Abernathy; the Reverend Walter Fauntroy, the first U.S. delegate from the District of Columbia to the U.S. House of Representatives; Dr. Eddie Henderson, the first African American to compete in the U.S. Figure Skating Championships; Monte Irvin, one of the first players to break the color barrier in major league baseball; and Cheryl White, the first African American female professional jockey. The event took a dramatic twist when twenty Ku Klux Klan members showed up at the panel discussion. The local press reported that the "audience members stiffened when the black-clad KKK members arrived. But the audience then returned its attention to a panel discussion that included Eddie Henderson . . . and Joseph Wilder, a musician who helped integrate Broadway."[59] Wilder remembered the event vividly:

> The Klan had heard about this celebration and sent a letter announcing they were coming. The law enforcement agencies—the park rangers, state police, the FBI—brought all of us who were speaking together for a meeting at the courthouse. They explained to us that they couldn't keep them from coming, but they could stop them from wearing the hoods and sheets. They said we should go ahead with the program and not to be intimidated. They would put them in a separate section, where they would be surrounded by officers, so they couldn't disrupt anything.

As Wilder recalled, at one point during the panel discussion, the Klan members did attempt to disrupt the proceedings:

> Before I spoke, the other panelists were talking about the things that had happened in this country, the breaking down of slavery and about those who had contributed to the breaking down of barriers. The Klan members couldn't stand hearing all this, and they stood up, but the police were right there with rifles and made them sit. They stopped it from becoming a disaster.

The panelists and audience continued unfazed, and the Klan members were eventually escorted out by federal officers after Juanita Abernathy's presentation. The Reverend Otis C. James, of Mount Zion United Methodist Church in West Virginia, said after the conclusion of the panel:

> This is America, and this is an open event for this town, this state and the nation at large. They have a right to come here as long as they are peaceful and non-destructive. I hope—I pray—that they leave having learned something from this discussion. But truthfully, I don't think they learned anything from what took place today, or enlarged their insight on humanity.[60]

Shortly after its appearance at the Niagara Movement event, the Klan was granted a permit to hold a rally on October 14, 2006, at Harpers Ferry, focusing on the theme, "Black Crimes in White America."[61] Gussie Wilder, Joe's mother, had told him that as a child, she remembered seeing the Klan burn a cross in Yeadon, Pennsylvania, not far from the family's home in Paschall. And after Wilder was discharged from the Marine Corps in 1946, the Klan drove down Greenwood Avenue in Paschall, where several homes had been sold to black families. To have the Klan resurface at an event in 2006 was, at the very least, disconcerting.

There were other significant moments during the decade. In February 2000, Wilder performed with Kenneth Klein's New York Virtuosi Chamber Symphony at the Kaye Playhouse in a program celebrating black composers. *New York Times* critic Allan Kozinn noted "some spectacular trumpet playing by Joe Wilder" on several Ellington pieces.[62] In November 2007, Wilder was in excellent form for a Three Generations of Jazz Trumpet concert at Symphony Space. The three generations were represented by Wilder (eighty-five), Jon Faddis (fifty-five), who produced the event, and Max Darche (twenty-five), one of Faddis's students at the State University of New York at Purchase. A year later, another talented trumpeter, Byron Stripling, invited Wilder to appear as a guest with the Columbus Jazz Orchestra for a "Roaring '20s" show. In keeping with the theme, Stripling asked Wilder what it was like growing up in Philadelphia during the Depression. "It was similar to what's going on now, but we had a lot less money," Wilder replied.[63]

Reunions with Hank Jones always resulted in some sublime music. Jones, who had played such an essential role in the success of Wilder's 1956 Savoy and 1959 Columbia albums, was almost four years the trumpeter's senior and continued to perform regularly until his death in May 2010. Wilder took part in a JVC Festival salute to Jones in June 2006, and it was clear that the musical and personal empathy between the two men was still intact, with *New York Times* critic Ben Ratliff observing that Wilder was "as fresh-minded about his craft as Mr. Jones is."[64] The pianist invited Wilder to join him as a special guest for several club engagements, the last of which took place on August 27, 2009, during the pianist's weeklong stint at Birdland; once again the bond was evident.

On June 13, 2011, Wilder returned to Birdland as a special guest for an evening celebrating the famous Ronnie Scott's Jazz Club. It was unclear to Wilder why he was invited, since he had never played at the celebrated London establishment. Nevertheless, he joined saxophonist Houston Person and a group of British musicians, turning in a sparkling performance using his patented plastic cup as a mute.

Inexorably, as time passed, Wilder was saddened by the loss of so many of his close friends, some of whom he had known for nearly eight decades.

Wilder tended to keep friends for life, and as he himself approached ninety, it seemed that hardly a week went by without his attending a funeral or memorial service. He was particularly affected by the deaths of his childhood friends and bandmates Rosario Pino (2004), Dizzy Gillespie (1993), and Percy Heath (2005). Wilder was often called on to speak and play at tributes for his musical colleagues, emotional experiences that were sometimes painful for him. Visibly moved, he seemed to channel his feelings through his horn, producing some heartrending musical statements. Thinking back to the memorial for his brother, Percy, held at the Abyssinian Baptist Church in Harlem on June 10, 2005, Jimmy Heath wrote, "The most touching performance at the memorial was by trumpeter Joe Wilder, Percy's childhood buddy. He played 'It's Easy to Remember (But So Hard to Forget)' with Michael Weiss on piano. It's so hard for me to forget that moment."[65]

A similar magical moment took place in 2007, at a memorial for Tommy Newsom at Dizzy's Club, part of Jazz at Lincoln Center. Best known as Johnny Carson's poker-faced foil on *The Tonight Show*, Newsom was a supremely gifted jazz saxophonist and arranger and a favorite of Wilder, both personally and musically. Jim Czak, of Nola studios, described Wilder's performance at the memorial, saying, "Joe came on last and played a solo version of 'Secret Love' that just stopped the show. Every note meant something; he played it with such feeling that people had tears in their eyes. After he finished, there was silence for a few seconds before the applause broke out."[66]

Recordings in the New Millennium: Evening Star

In the 1980s and 1990s, I served as producer for several recordings by Benny Carter for the MusicMasters label. In August 1991, we had scheduled a small-group session for Carter in New York, which would pair him with Joe Wilder. The two had always enjoyed playing together but had collaborated on only one record: Carter's 1985 Concord album, *A Gentleman and His Music*. In addition to Joe, the group was to include several musicians with whom Carter had frequently worked: James Williams on piano, Remo Palmier on guitar, and Benny's regular West Coast drummer, Sherman Ferguson, who came East especially for the session. Jay Leonhart was selected to play bass. Three or four days before the session, Benny fell ill and decided he was not up to doing the recording. Rather than cancel, I thought this would be an ideal opportunity to showcase Joe Wilder, who had not recorded as sole leader of his own album since *Peter Gunn* and *The Pretty Sound* for Columbia in 1959. I ran the idea by Joe, who was agreeable with both the concept and the personnel. I also discussed the idea with Benny Carter and, with his encouragement, approached MusicMasters about turning the session into a Joe Wilder date.

I pitched the idea that the release of the first album in thirty years by a highly respected legend of the trumpet would be treated as an event in the jazz world and would result in a salable product, which, of course, is of primary concern to any record company. I agreed to cover the recording costs, and I thought I had a commitment from MusicMasters to issue the album. After the date was completed, the label decided that it was not a project it saw as marketable, and since we had no written agreement, I was left with a master and no label to release it.[67] I contacted a couple of other companies that liked the music but, like MusicMasters, did not feel that Joe Wilder was sufficiently known to the public to sell enough "product" to recoup the costs. I began to consider the possibility of releasing the recording myself. By the early 1990s, there was a precedent for self-released albums by musicians, a phenomenon that would grow exponentially over the following two decades as the recording technology, digital distribution, and Internet marketing evolved. I discussed the situation with Benny Carter, who encouraged me to move forward and provided some financial support as well. In June 1992, Evening Star Records—named for Carter's ballad originally known as "Blue Star"—was born. Although we had no immediate plans for further releases, we left that possibility open.

Because it had been a Benny Carter project, we had only a few days to switch the focus to Joe Wilder. Ideally, Joe should have been given the opportunity to choose the musicians for the sessions, but fortunately, he had played with almost all the artists contracted for the Carter dates and was happy to proceed. Guitarist Remo Palmier was an old friend and a favorite. "He was a very compassionate kind of musician," Joe said. "I always liked playing with people that you could listen to and get ideas from and who would in turn listen to what you were doing and react. Remo was like that—he inspired you, and you could really build on what he did." Joe had often played with Jay Leonhart, who combined solid accompaniment with imaginative solos. James Williams turned out to be a pleasant surprise. Although of a younger generation and associated with the Art Blakey school, Williams was thoroughly grounded in the tradition and was nothing less than inspirational on the session. "He could hear what you were doing and would play things that made it so comfortable for you," Joe said. The trumpeter was so taken with Williams's creativity and relentless swing that he insisted on "letting him loose" for extended solos on several tracks. Joe had never met drummer Sherman Ferguson before the session but quickly took to his ebullient personality and exuberant playing. Also, Joe was delighted to learn that, as a teenager in Philadelphia, Ferguson had played with a group led by Joe's father.

The repertoire had to be completely revised from that originally selected for the Carter date. I asked Joe to come up with some tunes he always wanted to record but had never had the opportunity to do so, and the next few days were spent in hunting up lead sheets. Joe also devised several ingenious arrangements, including an attractive countermelody for Michel Legrand's "I Will Wait for You," a tongue-in-cheek country-and-western take on "Far Away Places," and an original blues line that we named "Joe's Blues," for lack of a more inspired title. In deference to Benny Carter, he played Carter's lovely "The Courtship," and in memory of George Duvivier, he premiered a previously unrecorded ballad composed by the bassist. "Alone with Just My Dreams," which became the title track, took on added meaning because Jay Leonhart had acquired Duvivier's bass and used it for the session. Remo Palmier and Joe played "What a Wonderful World" as a duet in tribute to Louis Armstrong. The piece had great significance for Joe, who had played in the orchestra on Armstrong's original 1967 recording of the song, which became a hit when originally released and again years later, when it resurfaced on the soundtrack of the film *Good Morning, Vietnam*:

> I was impressed by the song itself—both the melody and the lyrics. Of course, Louis added things that enhanced it as he always did. But it was his sincerity that made it. Even if he was singing a song that seemed like a real nonentity, as he went along, he'd start developing something that made it better than the original. That's what he did with "Hello, Dolly."

When Joe began playing the piece at concerts in the 1980s, he was often deeply affected. "I'd sometimes have trouble playing it because I would get tears in my eyes because it reminded me of Louis and what a nice man he was," he said. Joe preferred to play "What a Wonderful World" backed only by guitar. But until teaming with Palmier, he had not found a guitarist who was able to capture the prayer-like feeling that he was trying to evoke. "Remo understood right away that it was like a hymn, and everything he played enhanced that feeling," Joe said.

Joe Wilder's first Evening Star release was well received by critics, and although it had not sold enough to recoup expenses, we felt that there was enough interest to justify another Wilder project a year later, in 1993. Since we were starting from scratch, for *No Greater Love*, Wilder had a free hand in choosing his fellow musicians, and he selected three veterans with whom he felt comfortable and inspired. Milt Hinton was one of Wilder's oldest friends and had collaborated with him on countless studio dates, as well as live performances. The bassist had played on Joe's 1959 *Jazz from Peter Gunn*. In April 2000, only seven months before Hinton's death, Joe sent a letter to the bassist and his wife, Mona, that showed his deep affection for them:

> It seems that age is creeping up on all of us, yet we have much to be thankful for. One of the things for which I'm most thankful is my relationship with you two for so many of the best years of my musical career. My sincere thanks to you for contributing so meaningfully to it.[68]

Joe chose another longtime friend and colleague, saxophonist-flutist Seldon Powell, to join him as a second horn. Powell was a versatile and swinging player whose gifts as a jazz improviser were to some extent eclipsed by his extensive work in the commercial studios. Wilder had a long and close friendship with pianist Bobby Tucker, but the two had never recorded together. Tucker, who began as an Art Tatum–inspired jazz player, forsook his solo career to become a premier accompanist, most notably for Billie Holiday and Billy Eckstine. When I called him about the date, he was very flattered but apprehensive, explaining that he was not really a jazz soloist any more. I told him that Joe wanted him precisely for his accompaniment and that he could solo as much or as little as he wished. He reluctantly agreed. As it turned out, Tucker felt confident enough to contribute a few sparkling solos, and his accompaniment clearly brought out the best in Joe, especially on the duo and trio pieces. "The things we did together worked so well because he was playing the piano," Joe said. "He just fell in perfectly with the mood you were trying to convey. Whenever I listen to that album, I always concentrate on what he's doing; it was so perfect." Unfortunately, the album turned out to be the last recording for both Tucker and Powell.

To round out the group, Joe chose guitarist James Chirillo, an excellent soloist, a sensitive accompanist, and a fellow member of the Smithsonian Masterworks Jazz Orchestra. Drummer Sherman Ferguson was the only holdover from the first Evening Star release. For variety, Joe agreed to change the instrumentation from track to track—from the full sextet to duos and trios with just trumpet, guitar, and piano. He contributed three originals. "Come on Back" was based on "Won't You Come Home, Bill Bailey?"—more specifically on a 1961 recording of the song by Della Reese on which Wilder had played. "Harry Lulu" was Wilder's catchy reworking of "Hallelujah," and "Dylan" was a lullaby by Wilder dedicated to his grandson, who appears with him on the CD cover.

In 2002, we felt it would be appropriate to celebrate Joe's eightieth birthday with a third recording for Evening Star. The concept behind *Among*

Friends was to bring in some of Wilder's favorite players to collaborate with him in settings ranging from duets to a sextet. Musicians of three generations took part in the project, including contemporaries Frank Wess and Bucky Pizzarelli and younger stars Warren Vaché, Bill Charlap, Russell Malone, and the core rhythm section of Chris Neville, Steve LaSpina, and Chuck Redd. The final track recorded, "Lady Be Good," started out as a duet with Bucky Pizzarelli and Joe. As they were working out the arrangement, pianist Skitch Henderson, bassist Jerry Bruno, and drummer Joe Cocuzzo arrived at Nola studios for a later session with a singer. Pizzarelli immediately commandeered them into joining him and Joe for an impromptu jam on "Lady Be Good." As they were wrapping up the track, the singer arrived and was amazed to find her band already recording with someone else.

In 2007, Joe took part in another Evening Star recording, *The Benny Carter Centennial Project*, performing "The Blessing." The piece was part of Carter's *Peaceful Warrior Suite*, an extended work dedicated to Martin Luther King. The trumpeter had played the melody with Carter at the premiere of the work in 1996 at the Lincoln Theatre in Washington, DC.

Arbors Records and the Statesmen of Jazz

Mat and Rachel Domber founded the Arbors label in 1989, initially to document the work of their friend, the talented but then unrecorded saxophonist Rick Fay. In the ensuing two decades, the label grew to encompass a wide range of traditional and swing artists, including veterans like Flip Phillips, Bob Haggart, Ruby Braff, Dick Hyman, and Bucky Pizzarelli, as well as younger players working within those idioms. By 2012, Arbors had issued more than three hundred CDs and had become the primary outlet for artists in the traditional and swing genre, particularly with the change in focus by Concord Records with the death of founder Carl Jefferson in 1995. Mat Domber's own passing in September 2012 left a similar void and raised serious questions about future recording outlets for the artists and musical styles he championed.

Joe Wilder appeared on several Arbors projects over a fifteen-year period, including two recordings with fellow trumpeter Ruby Braff. Domber noted that "Ruby really liked Joe" and that Wilder somehow managed to avoid the conflicts that invariably arose in dealings with the brilliant but irascible trumpeter.[69] Engineer Jim Czak, owner of Nola Studios on Fifty-Seventh Street in New York, recalled a Ruby Braff–led Arbors recording date in 2000, on which Wilder participated:

Ruby was being Ruby. Somebody was playing, and he starts yelling, "What are you doing?" "I'm just warming up," the guy says. "This is a jazz date," Ruby answers. "You don't have to warm up!" At one point, he railed at Bucky [Pizzarelli] for something or other, and Bucky says, "What the hell are you yelling at me for? I'm as old as you are!" So they start to run down the next tune, and Ruby yells, "We don't need to run it down—let's just take it." So we did a take, and when it came time for his solo, Joe opens it with a quote from "A Day in the Life of a Fool." It was perfect! Everybody had their heads down trying not to crack up. Ruby liked Joe and respected him, so he let it slide.[70]

Wilder also was part of the Statesmen of Jazz, a group of veteran jazz performers assembled in 1994 by Domber and Maurice Lawrence, founder and first president of the Duke Ellington Society. The Statesmen, originally associated with the American Federation of Jazz Societies, was founded to provide performance opportunities for jazz players sixty-five and older. The group also had an educational mission, presenting jazz in schools and enabling students to interact directly with the elders of the music. It also represented the United States to great acclaim during several tours abroad. Wilder took part in the Statesmen's two recording projects. Asked to participate in the first Statesmen session in December 1994, Wilder originally declined because he had recently undergone dental surgery. "He came to the session just to see his friends and to take photos," Mat Domber recalled. "He liked what he heard, and Clark [Terry] convinced him to go back home and get his horn. He ended up playing on three tunes and sounded great."[71] At seventy-two, Wilder turned out to be one of the "youngsters" on the date, which included such venerable players as Claude "Fiddler" Williams (eighty-six), Milt Hinton (eighty-four), and the irrepressible Benny Waters (ninety-three).

In December 2003, Wilder led a session as part of an ambitious three-day recording project, which resulted in a double CD by the Statesmen. Aptly titled *A Multitude of Stars*, it brought together many of the veterans who had contributed so much to the music. Wilder was united with some of his oldest friends, among them Buddy DeFranco, whom he had known since their days at the Mastbaum school in Philadelphia. In addition to some fine music, there was much joking and storytelling, reflecting the deep ties among the participants. Sadly, the sessions turned out to be a final reunion for many; a third of the participants died over the next decade, including Louie Bellson, Keter Betts, Kenny Davern, Johnny Frigo, Red Holloway, Jane Jarvis, Eddie Locke, Earl May, Benny Powell, and Carrie Smith. Wilder presided over a loose and varied set of five tunes, marked by marvelous interplay among the horns (cornetist Warren Vaché, trombonist George Masso, and tenor saxophonist Houston Person), backed by a sympathetic rhythm section of Derek Smith on piano, Keter Betts on bass, and Eddie Locke on drums. Wilder's belief that music should be collaborative rather than competitive was fully realized by this close-knit ensemble.

In addition to his sessions for Evening Star and the Statesmen of Jazz, Wilder continued to record in a variety of other settings in the 1990s and into the new millennium. Although much of the New York commercial recording scene had faded, during this period, Wilder appeared as a sideman on more than thirty CDs. These included guest appearances on recordings by jazz artists like the Heath Brothers and Ken Peplowski, as well as on albums by singers, including Joe Williams, Marlene VerPlanck, Bob Dorough, Tony Bennett, and Anita O'Day. He occasionally still recorded in a big band setting, including a studio date with Louie Bellson and concert recordings with the Lincoln Center Jazz Orchestra and the Smithsonian Jazz Masterworks Orchestra. In addition, Wilder played on three film soundtrack albums: *Malcolm X* (1992, Terence Blanchard, musical director) and Woody Allen's *Mighty Aphrodite* (1995) and *Everyone Says I Love You* (1996), with Dick Hyman as music director for both.

There were several CDs during this later period that featured Wilder extensively and captured his playing at its peak. *Mostly Ellington* (BluePort J-017) documents a live performance by Wilder and alto saxophonist Marshal Royal at a January 27, 1990, concert sponsored by the San Diego Jazz Society, but the CD was not issued until 2008. Both Wilder and Royal, his bandmate in both the Lionel Hampton and Count Basie orchestras, are in excellent form, backed by a fine rhythm section.

Playing for Keeps, a 1992 studio session, teams Wilder with two more old friends: trombonist Britt Woodman and saxophonist John LaPorta. Wilder had known Woodman since their days together with Les Hite and had met LaPorta even earlier, when both were students at Mastbaum. Gunther Schuller, who produced the session and issued it on his GM Recordings label, undertook the project because he felt that "many fine 'elder statesmen' of jazz are being rather summarily ignored. Both in classical music and jazz, major record companies seem to be looking almost exclusively for teenage geniuses . . . as if there were some extraordinary artistic virtue in childhood precocity and technical virtuosity."[72] The three veteran horn men were joined by guitarist Jack Wilkins and Schuller's sons, Ed and George, on bass and drums, respectively, for a challenging set of originals and standards.

Wilder also shines on Dick Hyman's *From the Age of Swing* (Reference Recordings RR-59), another gathering of elder statesmen playing a more traditional but still intriguing repertoire, enhanced by the leader's arrangements. The 1994 session included some of Wilder's close associates from the studio years: saxophonist Phil Bodner, trombonist Urbie Green, guitarist Bucky Pizzarelli, and bassist Milt Hinton.

In the late 1990s, Wilder was reunited with composer-arranger Tom Talbert on two new big band projects. Wilder had played an essential role in the success of Talbert's acclaimed 1956 *Bix, Duke, Fats* album. On the 1997 *This Is Living* (Chartmaker PDP14480) and the 1999 *To a Lady* (Essential Music Group 1000), Wilder contributes several effective spots within Talbert's singularly challenging yet swinging pieces, especially on *This Is Living*. Doug Ramsey noted in *Jazz Times*, "Wilder's immense tone, fluency and use of wide intervals are one of the great pleasures in jazz. He is heard far too little these days, and he makes the most of his opportunities here."[73] And Scott Yanow wrote in a glowing review of the album, "Joe Wilder's lyrical playing consistently steals the show."[74] On *To a Lady*, Talbert reprised "Orange Bright" from the 1956 recording, with Wilder, trombonist Eddie Bert, and tenor saxophonist Aaron Sachs soloing in the same spots they had some four decades earlier; baritone saxophonist Danny Bank, another alumnus of the 1956 date, is in the section.

Charlie Byrd's 1999 Louis Armstrong tribute, *For Louis* (Concord Jazz CCD-4879), elicited some of Wilder's best playing on record during the 1990s. Wilder had never recorded with the guitarist before and recalled playing with him only once—at a concert at New York's Church of the Heavenly Rest in 1984.[75] The two musicians must have meshed because fifteen years later, Byrd remembered Wilder when it came time to record his Armstrong album. Although he was the leader, the self-effacing Byrd shared the solo space equally with Wilder and Steve Wilson, a talented saxophonist of a younger generation, who fit in beautifully. On such numbers as "A Kiss to Build a Dream On," "Tin Roof Blues," and even "Hello, Dolly," Wilder manages to evoke the spirit of Armstrong while remaining true to his own inimitable style. He also reprises his moving "What a Wonderful World," in an interpretation that differs radically from the one recorded in 1991 on his first Evening Star release. The new version substitutes a freer, more improvised approach for the hymnlike solemnity of the original. Sadly, *For Louis* turned out to be Charlie Byrd's last recording; the guitarist died less than three months after making the album.

Rebecca Kilgore with the Keith Ingham Sextet (Jump JCD12-24), recorded in February 2001, is a throwback to the "swing-song" tradition of the 1930s and features the singer's unassuming and appealing vocals, set off by Ingham's elegant, small-group arrangements and enhanced by short solos by Wilder, Ken Peplowski, Gene Bertoncini, and other sympathetic participants. In addition to his sterling section work, Wilder contributes some sparkling obbligatos and short solos to a program that includes a number of lesser-known gems. Wilder also has one instrumental feature, "Time on My Hands," and even took the photographs included in the CD booklet. Kilgore had appeared with Wilder at several jazz parties and festivals, and she was taken with his sensitive backing of singers. "I'm embarrassed to say that when I first met him, I was such a novice and hadn't done my homework," Kilgore said. "I didn't know all the great singers he'd played with. But even after I became aware of his background, I was never intimidated because he was so gracious all the time."[76] Kilgore described the qualities that drew singers to Wilder's playing:

> He plays like a singer himself. I would sing a phrase, and he'd answer it so beautifully and tastefully. Everything is so melodic and musical, and there's no ego involved. You don't want a horn player who will play over you, and he never would do that. The instrumentalist has to have kind of a sixth sense because he doesn't know where I'm going to stop singing or hold a note. He has to listen and respond instantaneously. Although Joe had so much experience at that, I prefer to think he's magic![77]

Wilder, in turn, always enjoyed playing behind singers. "There's something about singers that makes you think differently," he said, likening it to playing with a string section. "All of a sudden your thinking changes a bit. You begin to think a little more lyrically."[78]

Kilgore likes to include relatively obscure material in her repertoire and was impressed with Wilder's ability to quickly assimilate tunes that were unfamiliar to him. She explained, "At these events, you don't have a lot of time to rehearse, and I would ask him, like, five minutes before our set, 'Do you know such and such song?' He'd say, 'I don't think so, but I'll just listen.' It would take him all of one chorus to become familiar with it."[79]

In October 2000, Wilder made a felicitous appearance on Marian McPartland's radio show *Piano Jazz*.[80] The program featured Wilder on trumpet, with the hostess on piano and Rufus Reid on bass. Wilder was in a very relaxed and creative mood on a set of some of his favorite tunes, interspersed with warm reminiscences during the interview segments. "Marian was such a wonderful host and made me feel very comfortable," Wilder recalled. "She let me do whatever I wanted and was an excellent accompanist."

On February 19, 2011, the Jazz Museum in Harlem celebrated Wilder's life and career with a daylong program of panel discussions and media presentations, with old friends Frank Wess, Eddie Bert, and Henry Nowak on hand to reminisce with the honoree. Fellow trumpeters Warren Vaché, Jimmy Owens,

Wilmer Wise, and Dominick Farinacci contributed insights about Wilder's style, with many more friends and admirers in the audience.

Coda

By 2011, approaching ninety, Wilder remained in relatively good health. Although he had several ongoing medical issues, including prostate cancer, he continued to practice regularly and to play in public from time to time. He looked far younger than his age and still rode the New York subways and buses daily. In fact, just before his eighty-ninth birthday, he was standing on a corner in Manhattan when an elderly lady with a walker approached him and asked, "Young man, would you mind helping me across the street?" Toward the end of the year, however, his health began to decline, and he suffered the first of several serious urinary tract infections requiring hospitalization. While in the hospital, he contacted a staph infection. After several weeks in the hospital, Wilder seemed to have turned the corner and was sent to a rehab facility to regain his strength. He steadily improved, impressing the physical therapists with his dedication to the daily exercise regimen they put him through—a legacy of his Marine Corps training. Wilder was able to go home on February 21, 2012, the day before his ninetieth birthday, which he celebrated with his family. Less than twenty-four hours after that landmark event, however, Wilder was hit by another serious infection and had to return to the hospital. After several weeks of treatment in the hospital and another stay at a rehab facility, Wilder once again recovered enough to return home, on Friday, April 13.

During his lengthy illness, Wilder had been forced to cancel several scheduled appearances. One engagement that meant a great deal to him, and he had not canceled, was an invitation to perform and serve as honorary host for the annual Friends of Alec Wilder concert on Sunday, April 15, only two days after his discharge from the hospital. Wilder was determined to attend and speak, if not play. He had not picked up his horn since his initial hospitalization in February—an eternity for a brass player. On Saturday, the day before the event, he was reunited with his trumpet, wondering whether he would even be able to get a sound out of the instrument. To his amazement, he found that, although he had little stamina, he was able to play with at least some semblance of his former facility. The next day, accompanied by his family, he attended the event at Christ and Saint Stephen's Episcopal Church on New York's Upper West Side. He spoke about his affection for his friend Alec Wilder and, as John Biderman reported, played during the evening's finale: "The concert ended with the traditional audience sing-along of 'I'll Be Around,' the first chorus of which was played by Joe Wilder on his trumpet—his sound as round and full as ever—and ended with a coda by Joe, with finally an emotional standing ovation for the nonagenarian and all the wonderful music that preceded."[81]

In the months that followed, Wilder continued to gain strength, and by the summer of 2012, he was once again able to leave his apartment for social events, to attend occasional musical performances, and to take part in several panel discussions and public interviews. He even began riding the buses and subways by himself—against the advice of his doctors and family. He has not officially retired. His horns remain in easy reach on his coffee table, but whether their lyrical sounds will once again be heard by an audience is uncertain.

Of course, if Joe Wilder never plays a note again in public, his legacy is assured. That legacy, however, is not as neatly summarized as it would be for a musician whose contributions lay entirely in a single genre. The public prefers to identify an artist with a well-defined role or style, and the fact that Wilder worked in so many musical areas may have prevented him from achieving the popular recognition of players whose contributions are more concentrated. It is true that within jazz, Wilder forged a distinctive and immediately recognizable solo style. But he was also a lead trumpet player, especially early in his career, breaking the mold of temperamentally assertive players who concentrated on that demanding role and, typically, did not improvise. Furthermore, because Wilder recorded so infrequently as a leader, his recorded legacy, though substantial, is diffuse—scattered among hundreds of recordings, ranging from iconic jazz sessions to obscure pop dates of every conceivable genre, as his discography makes evident. Moreover, much of his career was spent in the even more anonymous settings of Broadway pits, network orchestras, and the New York studios, where his achievements were celebrated, for the most part, only by his peers. In addition, classical music was an area that, had its doors been fully open to him, might have led his career in an entirely different direction, garnering more popular recognition. Nevertheless, Wilder did eventually triumph in this area as well. His symphonic playing retained the personal sound that marked his work in all genres and was well received by a classical critical establishment usually suspicious of artists who attempted to cross over from jazz and popular music.

Apart from his purely musical achievements, the breaking down of racial barriers within all these musical areas—and in the Marine Corps, no less—is a major part of Wilder's legacy. His musical abilities may have opened doors, but his personality helped change minds. Although he displayed great courage in the face of indignity and, at times, physical danger, Wilder was never an activist. He was simply an individual who treated everyone with respect and demanded the same treatment from others. Despite his resolve in confronting injustice, Wilder is extremely self-effacing in other areas of his career, and that aspect of his personality, while appreciated by his friends and fellow musicians, certainly contributed to his lack of public recognition. From the time his father gently admonished the ten-year-old cornetist for allowing his budding celebrity as a rising child star to go to his head, Wilder has assiduously avoided any hint of ego or self-promotion. Finally, perhaps the most significant and lasting aspect of his legacy may be in the younger musicians he touched, both formally in the classrooms of Juilliard and other institutions, and informally at countless concerts and festivals worldwide. Musicians of several generations have acknowledged their debt to him, and many more were undoubtedly affected by even a fleeting encounter with this gentle and caring man. Joe Wilder met the many challenges of his multifaceted career in the same way he approached music: softly, with feeling.

Notes

Chapter 1

1. Unless otherwise noted, all quotations from Joe Wilder come from interviews by the author, conducted from 2005 to 2012.

2. Curtis C. Wilder Sr., "My Service in World War I and World War II." This reminiscence was taken by Solveig Wilder, Joe's middle daughter, and included on pp. 62–63 of a commemorative program booklet published by Arbors Records in conjunction with the March of Jazz party held in Clearwater Beach, Florida, March 15–17, 2002. Joe Wilder was one of several honorees at the event, and the booklet includes many photos of him and his family.

3. Ibid.

4. Ibid.

5. The bassist who taught Curtis Wilder was possibly Vincent Lazzaro Jr., who played with the Philadelphia Orchestra from 1921 to 1964, or Severino Siani, who played with the Orchestra from 1924 to 1947. See John Ardoin, ed., *The Philadelphia Orchestra: A Century of Music* (Philadelphia: Temple University Press, 1999), 222–227.

6. Diane Delores Turner, "Organizing and Improvising: A History of Philadelphia's Black Musicians' Protective Union Local 274, American Federation of Musicians" (Ph.D. diss., Temple University, 1993), 87.

7. Berisford "Shep" Shepherd, interview by the author, September 24, 2011.

8. "Southerners in Colwyn Have Their Own Sweet Way," *Philadelphia Tribune*, December 25, 1915, p. 1.

9. Ibid.

10. The 1920 U.S. Census, recorded in January 1920, shows the Wilder family already residing on Front Street.

11. Joe Wilder, radio interview by Rebecca Kilgore, *On the Road with Rebecca Kilgore*, KMHD-FM, Gresham, OR, recorded March 16, 2002.

12. Shepherd, interview by the author.

13. Jimmy Heath, interview by the author, June 3, 2011.

14. Buddy DeFranco, interview by the author, March 8, 2012.

15. Wilmer Wise, interview by the author, March 17, 2011.

16. Shepherd, interview by the author.

17. Heath, interview by the author.

18. "Local Teacher Gives Recital," *Philadelphia Tribune*, February 9, 1929, p. 6.

19. Daniel W. Chase, "Symphony Orchestra in Concert," *Philadelphia Tribune*, March 13, 1930, p. 7.

20. Jones-Moseley marriage announcement, *Philadelphia Tribune*, December 5, 1929, p. 5.

21. Daniel W. Chase, "Hoxter Pupils Give Superb Music Recital," *Philadelphia Tribune*, March 19, 1931, p. 6.

22. The trumpet method book, *Araban's Complete Conservatory Method of Trumpet*, by Jean-Baptiste Arban, first published in 1864, is still considered the trumpeter's bible.

23. Ed Berger, "An Interview with Trumpet Legends William Fielder and Joe Wilder," in *Early Twentieth Century Brass Idioms: Art, Jazz, and Other Popular Traditions*, ed. Howard T. Weiner (Lanham, MD: Scarecrow Press, 2009), 52.

24. "WPEN Starts Colored Kiddies' Hour Sun.," *Philadelphia Tribune*, March 24, 1932, p. 7.

25. Rick Condit, "The Heath Brothers: Giants of Jazz," *Jazz Education Journal*, March–April 2003, pp. 42–43, available at http://www.rickcondit.com/artbyrick.html.

26. Heath, interview by the author.

27. Ibid.

28. "Philly's Kiddie Radio Hour a Big Success," *Afro-American* (Baltimore), April 16, 1932, p. 2.

29. Ibid.

30. "Popularity of Colored Kiddies' Hour Evidenced by Overflow Audiences," *Philadelphia Tribune*, April 28, 1932, p. 7.

31. "Joseph Wilder," *Philadelphia Tribune*, April 28, 1932, p. 6; Joe Wilder's name is included in published lists of boys and girls selling the *Tribune* as early as the issue of November 12, 1931, p. 13.

32. William Holmes, Paschallville column, *Philadelphia Tribune*, December 27, 1934, p. 13.

33. "At the Theatres," *Philadelphia Tribune*, December 15, 1932, p. 12; "At the Theatres," *Philadelphia Tribune*, July 13, 1933, p. 12; "Lincoln Show Features Ruth Ellington Ork," *Philadelphia Tribune*, January 30, 1936, p. 10; "'Satch Mouth' and Orch. at the Lincoln," *Philadelphia Tribune*, February 20, 1936, p. 14.

34. "'Satch Mouth,'" 14.

35. "Lincoln Kiddies to Present Extensive Fall Program," *Philadelphia Tribune*, August 6, 1936, p. 14.

36. "Kiddie Hour Performers Stage Show on Atlantic City Beach," *Philadelphia Tribune*, September 3, 1936, p. 15.

37. "8,000 Storm Nixon Grand to Hear Kiddie Program," *Philadelphia Tribune*, August 27, 1936, p. 12.

38. "Slatko Resigns as Manager of Lincoln; Sleifel Succeeds," *Philadelphia Tribune*, March 5, 1936, p. 14.

39. "Kiddie Hour Performers," 15.

40. *Philadelphia Tribune*, October 20, 1938, p. 11.

41. David W., "Blanche Calloway Goes Bankrupt," *Chicago Defender*, October 29, 1938, p. 19.

42. "Girard College," *Wikipedia*, July 30, 2013, available at http://en.wikipedia.org/wiki/Girard_College.

43. Paschallville column, *Philadelphia Tribune*, September 15, 1938, p. 12.

44. Heath, interview by the author.

Chapter 2

1. Buddy DeFranco, interview by the author, March 8, 2012.

2. Ibid.

3. Ibid.

4. Leon Cohen, interview by the author, February 15, 2011.

5. DeFranco, interview by the author.

6. Ibid.

7. Ibid.

8. Ibid.

9. John LaPorta, *Playing It by Ear* (Redwood, NY: Cadence Jazz Books, 2001), 13.

10. DeFranco, interview by the author.

11. Arnold Jay Smith, "Octojazzarian Profile: Buddy DeFranco," *Jazz.com*, October 16, 2009, available at http://www.jazz.com/features-and-interviews/2009/10/16/octojazzarian-profile-buddy-defranco.

12. Berisford "Shep" Shepherd, interview by the author, September 24, 2011.

13. Diane Delores Turner, "Organizing and Improvising: A History of Philadelphia's Black Musicians' Protective Union Local 274, American Federation of Musicians" (Ph.D. diss., Temple University, 1993), 48.

14. Lou Garcia, "Influx of Sepia Stage Stars to Philly Makes Quaker City the Mecca of Negro Performers," *Philadelphia Tribune*, January 21, 1932, p. 7.

15. Ibid.

16. Shepherd, interview by the author.

17. Ibid.

18. Ibid.

19. Turner, "Organizing and Improvising," 218.

20. Shepherd, interview by the author.

21. Turner, "Organizing and Improvising," 218.

22. Ann D. Jensen, "Harlem in Annapolis," in *Annapolis, City on the Severn: A History*, by Jane W. McWilliams (Baltimore: Johns Hopkins University Press, 2011), 250.

23. "A Day with NEA Jazz Master Joe Wilder," National Jazz Museum in Harlem, February 19, 2011, panel 2 discussion, previously available at http://jazzmuseuminharlem.org/archive.php?id=766.

24. "Les Hite Taught Movieland to Swing; First Sepia Band to Crash Chatterbox," *Afro-American* (Baltimore), January 17, 1942, p. 15. This article lists the full band personnel: Floyd Turnham, Sol Moore, Roger Hurd, and Quedellis Martyn, saxophones; Walter Williams, Stumpy Whitlock, and Joe Wilder, trumpets; Britt Woodman, Allen Dunham, and Alfred Cobbs, trombones; Oscar Bradley, drums; Benny Booker, bass; Coney Woodman, piano; Frank Pasley, guitar; and Jimmy Anderson, vocals.

25. Van Alexander, interview by the author, December 13, 2011.

26. Royal played with Hite's band in 1939, before Wilder became a member.

27. Alexander, interview by the author.

28. Joe Wilder, interview by Donald Maggin, January 30, 2001, unpublished transcript, Institute of Jazz Studies, Rutgers–Newark, NJ, pp. 18–19.

29. Foster family, interview by the author and the staff of the Institute of Jazz Studies, November 18, 2010.

30. "Hite's 'Blackout' Causes Raid Scare," *Afro-American* (Baltimore), January 24, 1942, p. 15. A similar story appeared as "Les Hite's 'Blackout' Number Is a Thriller," *Chicago Defender*, January 24, 1942, p. 21.

31. The addition of Wilder to the Hampton band was reported in "Rowe's Notebook," *Pittsburgh Courier*, June 6, 1942, p. 20.

32. "Hampton's Sensational Band Rave of Pacific Coasts' Dance Fans," *Pittsburgh Courier*, October 31, 1942, p. 20.

33. Ibid.

34. Sam Abbot, "Casa Manana, Culver City, California," *Billboard*, September 12, 1942, p. 13.

35. Sam Abbot, "Orpheum, Los Angeles," *Billboard*, October 3, 1942, p. 17.

36. Leonard G. Feather, "Winner, New Champion of Swing—Lionel Hampton," *Pittsburgh Courier*, February 13, 1943, p. 20.

37. Ira Gitler, *Swing to Bop: An Oral History of the Transition in Jazz in the 1940s* (New York: Oxford, 1985), 14.

38. "Lionel Hampton's Band Threatens Strike for Pay," *Jet*, August 15, 1988, p. 58.

39. Wilder, interview by Donald Maggin, 23.

40. Ibid.

Chapter 3

1. Morris J. MacGregor Jr., *Integration of the Armed Forces, 1940–1965* (Washington, DC: Center of Military History, United States Army, 1981), 100.

2. Ibid., 101.

3. Bernard C. Nalty, *Strength for the Fight: A History of Black Americans in the Military* (New York: Free Press, 1986), 200.

4. The Montford Point Marine Association maintains an informative website about the history of African Americans in the Marine Corps, including transcripts of oral history interviews with those who served at Montford Point, at http://www.mpma28.com/intro_to_web_pages.html.

5. Gail Buckley, *American Patriots: The Story of Blacks in the Military from the Revolution to Desert Storm* (New York: Random House, 2001), 312.

6. "Lionel's Joe Wilder Leaves for the Army," Pittsburgh *Courier*, April 24, 1943, p. 21.

7. "First Marines in Training," *Afro-American* (Baltimore), September 19, 1942, pp. 1–2.

8. Bernard C. Nalty, *The Right to Fight: African-American Marines in World War II* (Washington, DC: Marine Corps Historical Center, 1995), available at http://www.nps.gov/history/history/online_books/npswapa/extContent/usmc/pcn-190-003132-00/sec3.htm.

9. Buckley, *American Patriots*, 313.

10. MacGregor, *Integration of the Armed Forces, 1940–1965*, 105.

11. Ibid., 106.

12. "First Marines in Training," 1–2.

13. L. A. Wilson, "Jejeune [*sic*] Boasts Smoothest Band," *Afro-American* (Baltimore), November 11, 1944, p. 6.

14. Janet Fisher, "Bobby Troup: Songwriter and Actor," *Goodnight Kiss Music*, March 1, 1999, available at http://www.goodnightkiss.com/bobby.html.

Chapter 4

1. "More than 15,000 Hear Hamp at Wrigley Field," *Afro-American* (Baltimore), October 26, 1946, p. 6.

2. The song was recorded September 23, 1946, and first issued on *Lionel Hampton: Rarities*, MCA 1351, LP.

3. Gunther Schuller, *The Swing Era: The Development of Jazz, 1930–1945* (New York: Oxford, 1989), 400.

4. In a dispatch from Philadelphia, *Billboard* reported, "Trumpeter Joe Wilder joins Jimmie Lunceford to become the third localite with Sir James, along with trombonists Alfred Cobbs and Al Gray [*sic*]." See "Music—As Written: Philadelphia," *Billboard*, November 30, 1946, p. 32; Wilder's move to Lunceford is also mentioned in the previous issue, in "Music—As Written: Philadelphia," *Billboard*, November 23, 1946, p. 20.

5. "Bands Busting Up Big," *Metronome*, January 1947, p. 58; "Band Woes Up and Down," *Billboard*, December 14, 1946, p. 17.

6. Eddie Determeyer, *Rhythm Is Our Business: Jimmie Lunceford and the Harlem Express* (Ann Arbor: University of Michigan Press, 2006), 222.

7. Ibid., 221.

8. Ibid.

9. Ibid.

10. Edward Berger, *Bassically Speaking: An Oral History of George Duvivier* (Metuchen, NJ: Scarecrow Press, 1993), 70.

11. Determeyer, *Rhythm Is Our Business*, 103.

12. Berger, *Bassically Speaking*, 70.

13. "Lunceford Teaching Band Members to Fly," *Philadelphia Tribune*, September 17, 1946, p. 12.

14. See Determeyer, *Rhythm Is Our Business*, 230–242, for a detailed account of Lunceford's final hours, with extensive input from Joe Wilder. Much of the information here comes from that excellent work, but the quotations, except where indicated, are from my interviews with Wilder conducted for this book.

15. "Heart Attack Fatal to Jimmie Lunceford," *Billboard*, July 19, 1947, p. 38.

16. Discrimination in Portland restaurants at that time was more widespread than one would have thought, according to a 1945 study by the City Club of Portland, a civic organization founded in 1916. See "Digest of City Club Report: The Negro in Portland, July, 1945," p. 11, available at http://arcweb.sos.state.or.us/pages/exhibits/ww2/life/pdf/race3.pdf.

17. Determeyer, *Rhythm Is Our Business*, 233.

18. Ibid., 242.

19. Ibid., 241.

20. Ibid.

21. Pat Harris, "Fields Has a Hard Time Proving Band Plays, Too," *Down Beat*, August 12, 1949, p. 4.

22. Michael Levin, "Dizzy, Bird, Ella Pack Carnegie," *Down Beat*, October 22, 1947, p. 3.

23. See Pat Harris, "Lucky Defends 'Clover,' Wants Modern Minstrels," *Down Beat*, March 24, 1948, p. 23; see also Bertrand Demeusy, Otto Fluckiger, Jorgen Grunnet-Jepsen, and Kurt Mohr, *Discography of Lucky Millinder* (Basel, Switzerland: Jazz-Publications, 1962), 23.

24. Harris, "Lucky Defends 'Clover,'" 23.

25. Ibid.

26. Ibid.

27. The entire first show, with Ella Fitzgerald as special guest with the Ray Brown Trio, may be heard at http://newstalgia.crooksandliars.com/gordonskene/newstalgia-down beat-lucky-millinder-an.

28. Sam Chase, "Swingtime at the Savoy," *Billboard*, September 4, 1948, p. 12.

29. "The News of Radio: All-Negro Variety Show, 'Swingtime at the Savoy,' Will Bow Tonight on NBC," *New York Times*, July 28, 1948, p. 46.

30. Mundell Lowe, interview by the author, June 27, 2012.

31. Richard Layman, "Civic Tourism," *Rebuilding Place in the Urban Space* blog, December 4, 2005, available at http://urbanplacesandspaces.blogspot.com/2005/12/civic -tourism.html. The obituary of Charlie Parker's friend Nap Turner by *Washington Post* writer Marc Fisher confirms that Turner was denied admission when he arrived at the club with Parker, but when Parker refused to play, Turner was allowed to sit near the kitchen for the performance. See Marc Fisher, "Nap Turner, Mixing Sunshine with the Blues," *Washington Post*, available at http://www.allmanbrothersband.com/modules.php?op=modload& name=XForum&file=print&fid=11&tid=17122.

32. Pat [Harris], "Music Bowl Is None Too Cozy for Cozy Cole," *Down Beat*, March 25, 1949, p. 13.

33. Cozy Cole, interview by Bill Kirchner, April 1980, NEA Jazz Oral History Project, Institute of Jazz Studies, Rutgers University, Newark, transcript of cassette 4, pp. 44–45.

34. "Chi Music Bowl Does a Fold-Up," *Billboard*, March 5, 1949, p. 42.

35. "Music Bowl Is None Too Cozy for Cozy Cole," 13.

36. Mettome eventually returned to the Fields band once Wilder departed.

37. Max Bennett, interview by the author, November 22, 2011.

38. Harris, "Fields Has a Hard Time," 4.

39. Bennett, interview by the author.

40. Dan Morgenstern, *Living with Jazz* (New York: Pantheon, 2006), 309.

41. *Herbie Fields Septet Live at the Flame Club, St. Paul, 1949*, 2000, IAJRC CD-1014, CD.

42. Bennett, interview by the author.

43. Johnny Soppel, Vaudeville Reviews column, *Billboard*, August 21, 1948, p. 39.

44. Bennett, interview by the author.

45. Don C. Haynes, "Herbie Fields Has Jumping Combo," *Down Beat*, October 22, 1947, p. 16.

46. Harris, "Fields Has a Hard Time," 4.

47. Bennett, interview by the author.

48. Harris, "Fields Has a Hard Time," 4.

49. Bennett, interview by the author.

50. Pat Harris, "Fields, Ventura Battle of Bands Ends as Expected," *Down Beat*, November 4, 1949, p. 4.

Chapter 5

1. "Sissle at Horse Show," *Afro-American* (Baltimore), November 26, 1938, p. 11.

2. Ruth Prigozy, *The Life of Dick Haymes: No More Little White Lies* (Jackson: University Press of Mississippi, 2006), 77.

3. "Old Timers Bring Back Minstrels," *Toledo Blade*, December 11, 1949, p. 13.

4. Maurice Zolotow, "The Fabulous Billy Rose," pt. 2, *Collier's Weekly*, February 22, 1947, p. 18.

5. Langston Hughes, "Maker of the Blues," *Negro Digest*, January 1943, pp. 37–38, reprinted in Christopher De Santis, ed., *The Collected Works of Langston Hughes*, vol. 9, *Essays on Art, Race, Politics, and World Affairs* (Columbia: University of Missouri Press, 2002), 224–225.

6. Al Hall, interview by Ira Gitler, November 1978, NEA Jazz Oral History Project, Institute of Jazz Studies, Rutgers University, Newark, transcript of cassettes 3–4, p. 70.

7. "Good Sidemen in Pit Ork," *Down Beat*, July 2, 1947, p. 11.

8. "Group Discusses Fight on Race Bias," *New York Times*, March 17, 1947, p. 16.

9. Charles Grutzner, "The Arts vs. Bias," *New York Times*, March 16, 1947, p. X3.

10. Leonard Bernstein, "The Negro in Music: Problems He Has to Face in Getting a Start," *New York Times*, November 2, 1947, p. X7.

11. Peggy Phillips letter, *New York Times*, November 9, 1947, p. X7.

12. Winston Collymore obituary, *Allegro Archives* 102, no. 7/8 (July 2002), available at http://www.local802afm.org/2002/07/requiem-36/#3.

13. Peggy Phillips letter, p. X7.

14. Harry Haun, "Producer Cy Feuer Is Recalled at Broadway Memorial," *Playbill .com*, September 25, 2006, available at http://www.playbill.com/news/article/102328 -Producer-Cy-Feuer-Is-Recalled-at-Broadway-Memorial.

15. "'Guys and Dolls' Ork Spots Many Jazzmen," *Down Beat*, November 17, 1950, p. 3.

16. *Guys and Dolls: A Decca Original Cast Album*, 1951, Decca, DL 8036, LP.

17. "Guys 'n' Dolls Here June 29," *Washington Post*, May 24, 1953, p. L2.

18. "A Day with NEA Jazz Master Joe Wilder," National Jazz Museum in Harlem, February 19, 2011, panel 2 discussion, previously available at http://jazzmuseuminharlem.org/ archive.php?id=766.

Chapter 6

1. "A Day with NEA Jazz Master Joe Wilder," National Jazz Museum in Harlem, February 19, 2011, panel 2 discussion, previously available at http://jazzmuseuminharlem.org/ archive.php?id=766.

2. Chris Sheridan, *Count Basie: A Bio-Discography* (Westport, CT: Greenwood Press, 1986), 365.

3. Carl-Erik Lindgren, "Down for the Count," *Orkester Journalen*, April 1954, p. 8.

4. "A Day with NEA Jazz Master Joe Wilder."

5. Solveig Wilder, interview by the author, February 4, 2011. All subsequent quotations by Solveig Wilder in this chapter are from this interview.

6. "Far Och Mor Lärde Mej: Gud Ser Inte Till Hudfärgen," *SE*, June 28, 1957, p. 18.

7. Rigmor Newman, interview by the author, February 18, 2013.

8. Undated clipping from *Jet*, shared by Rigmor Newman.

Chapter 7

1. Cy Feuer, interview by Suki Sandler, January 6, 1993, Theater Collection, American Jewish Committee, New York Public Library.

2. Joe Wilder, interview by the National Association of Music Merchants (NAMM), February 26, 2006, available at http://www.namm.org/library/oral-history/joe-wilder.

3. Knef was "renamed Neff for American audiences who might be resistant to a German star on Broadway." Bill Rosenfield, liner notes to CD reissue of original cast recording of *Silk Stockings*, 1989, RCA Victor, 1102-2-RG.

4. Hildegard Knef, *The Gift Horse: Report on a Life* (New York: Dell, 1972), 343.

5. Cy Feuer obituary, *New York Times*, May 18, 2006, p. A27.

6. Campbell Robertson, "A Producer's Hit Broadway Memorial," *New York Times*, September 22, 2006, p. C10.

7. G. Douglas Pugh obituary, *New York Times*, May 3, 2010, p. B11.

8. Douglas Pugh, *Job Status of the Negro Professional Musician in the New York Metropolitan Area* (New York: Urban League of Greater New York, 1958), 4.

9. Ibid., 4–5. In his autobiography, Cy Feuer suggests that one possible reason *Guys and Dolls* did not receive the Pulitzer Prize in 1951 was the refusal of Abe Burrows, the show's writer, to testify before the House Un-American Activities Committee. There is no implication that the hiring of black musicians played any role in this particular incident, however. See Cy Feuer and Ken Gross, *I Got the Show Right Here* (New York: Applause Theatre and Cinema Books, 2003), 151.

10. Pugh, *Job Status*, 5.

11. James "Woody" McBride, "Wandering with Woody," *Philadelphia Tribune*, December 11, 1954, p. 12.

12. Joe Wilder, interview by Rebecca Kilgore, *On the Road with Rebecca Kilgore*, KMHD-FM, Gresham, OR, recorded March 16, 2002.

13. Jack Tracy, ed., *Down Beat Jazz Record Reviews: A Critical Analysis of Every Jazz Record Reviewed in 1956* (Chicago: Maher, 1957), 225.

14. Hank Jones, *The Trio*, 1956, Savoy MG12053, LP.

15. Nat Hentoff, review of *Wilder 'n' Wilder*, *Down Beat*, May 30, 1956, p. 24.

16. Review of *Wilder 'n' Wilder*, *Billboard*, June 2, 1956, p. 42.

17. "A Day with NEA Jazz Master Joe Wilder," National Jazz Museum in Harlem, February 19, 2011, panel 2 discussion, previously available at http://jazzmuseuminharlem.org/archive.php?=766.

18. Warren Vaché, interview by the author, December 26, 2012.

19. Will Friedwald, "The Greatest Trumpeter You've Never Heard," *New York Sun*, November 12, 2007, available at http://www.nysun.com/arts/greatest-trumpeter-youve-never-heard/66274.

20. Ibid.

21. Ibid.

22. Nicholas Payton, interview by Ted Panken, *Musician's Show*, WKCR-FM, March 15, 1995, available at http://tedpanken.wordpress.com/2011/12/04/a-jazziz-feature-on-nicholas-payton-from-2001.

23. Larry Appelbaum, "Before and After: Jeremy Pelt," *Jazz Times*, October 2008, pp. 28–31.

24. Quoted in David Sinclair, "Take Me Back to Birdland—Arts," *The Times* (London), June 7, 1996, p. 35.

25. For a detailed account of Van Gelder's background and early years, see Dan Skea, "Rudy Van Gelder in Hackensack: Defining the Jazz Sound in the 1950s," *Current Musicology*, nos. 71–72 (Spring 2001–Spring 2002): 54–76. The article also includes a brief interview with Wilder.

26. Vaché, interview by the author.

27. Gunther Schuller, *The Swing Era: The Development of Jazz, 1930–1945* (New York: Oxford, 1989), 12n13.

28. Edward Berger, *Bassically Speaking: An Oral History of George Duvivier* (Metuchen, NJ: Scarecrow Press, 1993), 170. Duvivier was referring to Schuller's pieces "Variants on a Theme of John Lewis (Django)" and "Variants on a Theme of Thelonious Monk (Criss Cross)." *Jazz Abstractions*, recorded December 20, 1960, Atlantic SD-1365, LP.

29. "Jazz and Classical Music: To the Third Stream and Beyond," in *The Oxford Companion to Jazz*, ed. Bill Kirchner (Oxford: Oxford University Press, 2000), 350.

30. Gunther Schuller, "'Third Stream' Redefined," *Saturday Review of Literature*, May 13, 1961, p. 54, reprinted in Gunther Schuller, *Musings: The Musical Worlds of Gunther Schuller* (Oxford: Oxford, 1986), 116.

31. Schuller, *The Swing Era*, 706.

32. George Avakian and Gunther Schuller, liner notes to *Music for Brass*, 1956, Columbia CL941, LP.

33. Gunther Sculler, interview by Steve Schwartz, Smithsonian Jazz Oral History Project, June 29–30, 2008, interview transcript, p. 31.

34. Paul Sampson, "That Combination Again," *Washington Post and Times-Herald*, September 4, 1955, p. J11.

35. Patty McGovern, *Wednesday's Child*, 1956, Atlantic 1245, LP.

36. Bruce Talbot, *Tom Talbert—His Life and Times: Voices from a Vanished World of Jazz* (Lanham, MD: Scarecrow Press, 2004), 137.

37. Ibid.

38. Dom Cerulli, review of *Bix, Duke, Fats, Down Beat*, June 27, 1957, pp. 29–30.

39. Larry Appelbaum, "Before and After: Terence Blanchard," *Jazz Times*, September 2001, p. 72.

40. Max Harrison, CD booklet, *Legrand Jazz*, 1986, Philips 830-074-2, CD, p. 11.

41. Ibid., 8.

Chapter 8

1. Douglas Pugh, *Job Status of the Negro Professional Musician in the New York Metropolitan Area* (New York: Urban League of Greater New York, 1958), 6.

2. John Hammond with Irving Townsend, *John Hammond on Record: An Autobiography* (New York: Ridge Press/Summit Books, 1977), 238.

3. "Is Radio a Dead End for Negro Bands?" *Music and Rhythm*, December 1941, p. 15.

4. John Hammond, John Hammond Says column, *Music and Rhythm*, May 1942, p. 22.

5. Hammond with Townsend, *John Hammond on Record*, 239.

6. John Hammond, John Hammond Says column, *Music and Rhythm*, June 1942, p. 26.

7. Hammond with Townsend, *John Hammond on Record*, 24.

8. "Radio to Hire First Negroes in Studio: Discrimination Ends as Networks Create New Jobs," *Music and Rhythm*, July 1942, p. 3.

9. Ibid., 48.

10. Hammond with Townsend, *John Hammond on Record*, 238–239.

11. Stanley Dance, *The World of Swing: An Oral History of Big Band Jazz* (New York: DaCapo, 2001), 189; Cozy Cole, interview by Bill Kirchner, April 1980, NEA Jazz Oral History Project, Institute of Jazz Studies, Rutgers University, Newark, transcript of cassette 4, p. 27.

12. Billy Rowe, "Another Radio First—Ray Scott to CBS: Pianist-Composer to Form First Mixed Band for Broadcast," *Pittsburgh Courier*, July 18, 1942, p. 21.

13. Cole, interview by Bill Kirchner, 27.

14. Ibid., 32.

15. "Cootie Williams Signed for CBS Studio Orchestra," *New Journal and Guide* (Norfolk, VA), August 8, 1942, p. 17; Harold Jovien, "Mixed CBS Band Launched," *New Journal and Guide*, August 22, 1942, p. 16; and Delores Calvin, "Seeing Stars," *New Journal and Guide*, September 5, 1942, p. 17.

16. Jovien, "Mixed CBS Band Launched," 16; Harold Jovien, "Stars Who Made Calloway and Duke Ellington Now on Radio," *Chicago Defender*, August 22, 1942, p. 23.

17. John Hammond, "On the Air and in the Groove," *New York Times*, November 29, 1942, p. X12.

18. Jovien, "Mixed CBS Band Launched," 16.

19. *Down Beat*, April 1, 1942, p. 1.

20. "Benny Carter Is Signed to Write for Lucky Strike's Commercial," *Pittsburgh Courier*, February 7, 1942, p. 21; see also Morroe Berger, Edward Berger, and James Patrick, *Benny Carter: A Life in American Music*, 2nd ed., vol. 1 (Lanham, MD: Scarecrow Press, 2002), 197–198.

21. "Sinatra and Scott on Air with Mixed Band," *Chicago Defender*, May 29, 1943, p. 10.

22. Dolores Calvin, "Mixed CBS Band Sets Precedent," *Atlanta Daily World*, November 30, 1942, p. 2.

23. "Negro Group Seeks Break for Players," *Down Beat*, June 18, 1947, p. 14.

24. Dance, *The World of Swing*, 189.

25. Specs Powell obituary, *New York Times*, September 21, 2007, p. B7.

26. "Specs Powell, CBS Ace, Tops," *Chicago Defender*, January 3, 1953, p. 23.

27. Dan Del Fiorentino, "Rest in Peace Gordon," *Ancestry.com*, September 20, 2007, available at http://boards.ancestry.com/topics.obits/98543/mb.ashx.

28. Alvin "Chick" Webb, "Jim Crow: New York Style," *New York Amsterdam News*, July 3, 1954, p. 1.

29. Alvin "Chick" Webb, "Jim Crow in Radio and TV," *New York Amsterdam News*, November 13, 1954, p. 7.

30. Alvin "Chick" Webb, "Jim Crow: New York Style," *New York Amsterdam News*, November 27, 1954, p. 1.

31. Milt Hinton, David G. Berger, and Holly Maxson, *Playing the Changes: Milt Hinton's Life in Stories and Photographs* (Nashville: Vanderbilt University Press, 2008), 203.

32. Alvin "Chick" Webb, "Jim Crow in Radio and TV," *New York Amsterdam News*, December 4, 1954, pp. 1–2.

33. Ibid.

34. Edward Berger, *Bassically Speaking: An Oral History of George Duvivier* (Metuchen, NJ: Scarecrow Press, 1993), 118.

35. Pugh, *Job Status*, 6.

36. Glenn Osser, interview by the author, February 23, 2011.

37. Berger, *Bassically Speaking*, 121.

38. Ibid., 118.

39. Ray Crisara, interview by the author, February 14, 2011.

40. Osser, interview by the author.

41. Robert R. Faulkner, *Hollywood Studio Musicians: Their Work and Careers in the Recording Industry* (Chicago: Aldine Atherton, 1971), 10.

42. Leon Cohen, interview by the author, February 15, 2011.

43. Crisara, interview by the author.

44. Alan Rich, "'Voice of Firestone' Sounds Final Note," *New York Times*, June 16, 1963, p. 103.

45. Television listings, *New York Times*, August 10, 1960, p. 63.

46. Cohen, interview by the author.

47. Radio listings, *New York Times*, October 11, 1963, p. 59.

48. See *New York Times* radio listings, January 1, 1967, p. 70, and January 4, 1967, p. 68.

49. Crisara, interview by the author.

50. Jack Burt, "Uncommon Man, Uncommon Musician: Tributes to Ray Crisara from Colleagues and Students," *ITG Journal*, March 2000, p. 43.

51. This was most likely the program that aired on December 30, 1962. See "TV Guest Appearances," *Billboard*, December 29, 1962, p. 17.

52. Hinton, Berger, and Maxson, *Playing the Changes*, 164.

53. Clark Terry with Gwen Terry, *Clark: The Autobiography of Clark Terry* (Berkeley: University of California Press, 2011), 172.

54. "A Joe Wilder Photo Gallery," in *Annual Review of Jazz Studies 5* (Metuchen, NJ: Institute of Jazz Studies and Scarecrow Press, 1991), 181–182 and sixteen-page unnumbered insert.

55. Pugh, *Job Status*, 5–6.

56. These hirings were a result of John Hammond's campaign; the musicians in question were most likely trumpeter Bill Dillard and bassist John Simmons.

57. Pugh, *Job Status*, 6.

58. Ibid.

59. Ibid.

60. Webb, "Jim Crow: New York Style," 1. "Averill Snow" was undoubtedly a misprint for bassist Arvell Shaw.

61. "Top Orchs, Shows Engage Musicians after UL Protest," *New Journal and Guide* (Norfolk, VA), February 13, 1960, p. B23; "League Report Shows Musicians' Progress in Symphony, TV, B'way," *New York Amsterdam News*, March 7, 1959, p. 13, and February 13, 1960, p. 12; "Negro Musicians Find New Top Jobs in '60," *Chicago Defender*, February 13, 1960, p. 20.

62. "League Report Shows Musicians' Progress in Symphony, TV, B'way," *New York Amsterdam News*, February 13, 1960, p. 12.

63. Ibid.

64. Hinton, Berger, and Maxson, *Playing the Changes*, 214–215.

65. Berger, *Bassically Speaking*, 117.

66. Ibid.

67. "League Report Shows 11 Negro Musicians Hired," *New York Amsterdam News*, March 7, 1959, p. 13.

68. Jon Burlingame, *TV's Biggest Hits: The Story of Television Themes from "Dragnet" to "Friends"* (New York: Schirmer, 1996), 31.

69. Ibid.

70. Nat Shapiro, liner notes to Joe Wilder, *Jazz from Peter Gunn*, 1959, Columbia CL1319, LP.

71. Review of *Jazz from Peter Gunn*, *Billboard*, March 30, 1959, p. 45.

72. John S. Wilson, review of *Jazz from Peter Gunn*, *High Fidelity*, July 1959, p. 77.

73. Ibid.

74. Nat Shapiro, liner notes to Joe Wilder, *The Pretty Sound*, 1959, Columbia CL1372, LP.

75. Ibid.

76. Leonard Feather, *Down Beat Jazz Record Reviews*, vol. 4, ed. Eugene Lees (Chicago: Maher, 1960), 202.

77. Review of *The Pretty Sound*, *Billboard*, November 2, 1959, p. 38.

78. Nat Hentoff, interview by Loren Schoenberg, Smithsonian Jazz Oral History Project, February 17–18, 2007, p. 15.

79. Penny Von Eschen, *Satchmo Blows Up the World: Jazz Ambassadors Play the Cold War* (Cambridge: Harvard University Press, 2006), 103.

80. Bill Crow, "To Russia without Love: The Benny Goodman Tour of the USSR," published in four parts in Gene Lees, *Jazzletter* 5, no. 8 (August 1986): 1–8; 5, no. 9 (September 1986): 1–8; 5, no. 10 (October 1986): 1–8; 5, no. 11 (November 1986): 1–8. The account is also available at http://www.billcrowbass.com/billcrowbass.com/To_Russia _Without_Love.html.

81. Crow, "To Russia without Love," *Jazzletter* 5, no. 8 (August 1986): 1.

82. Leonard Feather, "With Music-Loving Russians," *Jet*, June 21, 1962, p. 60.

83. "Benny Goodman in Russia: The Band Blew Hot and Cold," *Newsweek*, July 2, 1962, p. 49.

84. Feather, "With Music-Loving Russians," 60.

85. "Strike Delays Performance," *New York Times*, July 9, 1962, p. 10.

86. John S. Wilson, "Goodman Basks in Success of Soviet Jazz Tour," *New York Times*, July 20, 1962, p. 15.

87. Ibid.

88. Dan Morgenstern, "B.G.," *Jazz* 1, no. 1 (October 1962): 13.

89. Ibid.

90. Ibid.

91. Crow, "To Russia without Love," *Jazzletter* 5, no. 9 (September 1986): 1 (emphasis in original).

92. Crow, "To Russia without Love," *Jazzletter* 5, no. 11 (November 1986): 6.

93. Ernest B. Furgurson, "Precedent-Setting Tour of Benny Goodman Ends," *Baltimore Sun*, July 9, 1962, p. 2.

94. The *New York Times* did mention that Wilder refused to play "because, he said, an airline baggage charge had been deducted from his salary," adding that "Mr. Goodman's aides said the deduction was for excess baggage carried from New York to Moscow." "Strike Delays Performance," *New York Times*, July 9, 1962, p. 10.

95. Crow, "To Russia without Love," *Jazzletter* 5, no. 11 (November 1986): 5.

96. Stan Wayman, "Stompin' It Up at the Savoy-Marx," *Life*, July 6, 1962, p. 22.

97. "Goodman's Band Plays at Black Sea Resort," *Hartford Courant*, June 4, 1962, p. 4.

98. George Avakian, liner notes to *Benny Goodman in Russia*, 1962, RCA LOC-6008, LP (emphasis in original).

99. "Negro Artists Star on Benny Goodman's Soviet Tour," *Jet*, June 14, 1962, p. 55.

100. "Singer, Trumpeter Find Bias in Moscow," *Jet*, July 26, 1962, p. 58.

101. Crow, "To Russia without Love," *Jazzletter* 5, no. 11 (November 1986): 8.

102. Wayman, "Stompin' It Up at the Savoy-Marx," 21.

103. Osser, interview by the author.

104. Joe Wilder, interview by Julie Burstein, Smithsonian Jazz Oral History Project, August 25–26, 1992, p. 91.

105. Bryant Simon, *Boardwalk of Dreams: Atlantic City and the Fate of Urban America* (New York: Oxford University Press, 2004), 117.

106. Ibid.

107. Wilder, interview by Julie Burstein, 92.

108. Solveig Wilder (daughter), interview by the author, May 12, 2013. This interview is the source of all subsequent quotes by Solveig in this chapter.

109. Elin Wilder, interview by the author, July 24, 2013. This interview is the source of all subsequent quotes by Elin in this chapter.

110. Inga Wilder, interview by the author, July 21, 2003. This interview is the source of all subsequent quotes by Inga in this chapter.

Chapter 9

1. Berisford "Shep" Shepherd, interview by the author, September 24, 2011.
2. Alfred Brown, interview by the author, April 26, 2011.
3. Harold Jones, interview by the author, April 20, 2011.
4. Kermit Moore, interview by the author, May 14, 2011.
5. Wilmer Wise, interview by the author, March 17, 2011.
6. D. Antoinette Handy, *Black Women in American Bands and Orchestras*, 2nd ed. (Lanham, MD: Scarecrow Press, 1998), 6.
7. Ibid., 7.
8. Alfred E. Lemmon, "Identity, History, Legacy: La Société Philharmonique," essay in program booklet for concerts produced by the Historic New Orleans Collection and the Louisiana Philharmonic Orchestra, February 10–11, 2011, p. 5.
9. Handy, *Black Women*, 7–8.
10. Ibid., 9.
11. For accounts of the rejection of jazz and other African American popular music forms at black institutions, see Bernice Johnson Reagon, *If You Don't Go, Don't Hinder Me: The African American Sacred Song Tradition* (Lincoln: University of Nebraska Press, 2001), 36–37; and James Hatch, *Sorrow Is the Only Faithful One: The Life of Owen Dodson* (Champagne-Urbana: University of Illinois Press, 1993), 206.
12. Willard Clopton Jr., "Flag Furled in Howard Protest," *Washington Post*, February 17, 1968, p. A1.
13. Roy Reed, "Howard University Is Closed as Students Seize Building," *New York Times*, March 21, 1968, p. 30.
14. Howard Taubman, "An Even Break: Negro Instrumentalists Ask for Chance to Earn Way into Major Ensembles," *New York Times*, April 22, 1956, p. 119.
15. "The Negro and the North: Segregation Is Illegal, yet He Encounters a Great Deal of Discrimination," *Life*, March 11, 1957, p. 156.
16. Ibid. The Koussevitzky endorsement is from a letter of recommendation for Smyles dated October 15, 1947, in Douglas Pugh, *Job Status of the Negro Professional Musician in the New York Metropolitan Area* (New York: Urban League of Greater New York, 1958), appendix 5. While Koussevitzky had no qualms about recommending an African American for a symphonic position, the report notes that the conductor "would not employ a woman musician because he believed that a woman's place was in the home" (3); this is not entirely correct. The first woman in the Boston Symphony was bassoonist Anne de Richard, who was hired in 1945 during Koussevitzky's tenure as conductor. See Kimberley A. Wooly, "Women in Music: The Experiences of Bassoonists Nancy Goeres, Judith LeClair, Isabelle Plaster, and Jane Taylor" (Ph.D. diss., Florida State University, 2003), 14.
17. "The Negro and the North." Smyles was called to testify in hearings held by the House Un-American Activities Committee regarding their investigation of alleged Communist ties in the Metropolitan Music School where he taught. Smyles's testimony appears in the transcript of the hearings, "Investigation of Communism in the Metropolitan Music School, Inc., and Related Fields," pp. 692–700, available at http://www.archive.org/stream/investigationofc5701unit/investigationofc5701unit_djvu.txt.
18. Pugh, *Job Status*, 2.
19. Ibid., 3.
20. Ibid.
21. Ibid.
22. Ibid., 8.

23. Ibid.

24. Ibid., appendix 2.

25. Peter Kihss, "Orchestras Here Accused of Bias," *New York Times*, November 18, 1958, p. 39.

26. Ibid.

27. Board of Directors minutes, November 24, 1958, New York Philharmonic Digital Archives, p. 4, available at http://archives.nyphil.org/index.php/artifact/190ed2ac-e984 -455d-b849-3ec053573a90/fullview#page/1/mode/1up.

28. Ibid., 4–5.

29. "Symphony of the New World," *Ebony*, November 1966, p. 39.

30. R.P., "Negro Conductor in Stadium Debut," *New York Times*, August 11, 1941, p. 16.

31. The rest of the founding committee included violists Alfred Brown and Selwart Clarke; bassists Arthur Davis, Richard Davis, and Lucille Dixon; flutist Harold Jones; timpanist Elayne Jones; timpanist and percussionist Frederick L. King; cellist Kermit Moore; composer Coleridge-Taylor Perkinson; violinist Ross Shub; and oboist Harry Smyles. See D. Antoinette Handy, "Conversation with . . . Lucille Dixon: Manager of a Symphony Orchestra," *Black Perspective in Music* 3, no. 3 (Fall 1975): 310n6.

32. Jones, interview by the author.

33. Moore, interview by the author.

34. Jones, interview by the author.

35. Moore, interview by the author.

36. Many of these documents are part of a collection of archival materials, business records, correspondence, photos, and memorabilia pertaining to the Symphony of the New World in the possession of Barbara Steinberg, Benjamin Steinberg's daughter, who kindly allowed me access to these materials in July 2011. In 2012, this collection was acquired by the Schomburg Center for Research in Black Culture (New York).

37. Moore, interview by the author.

38. Letter from Leonard Bernstein to Donald L. Engle, director of the Martha Baird Rockefeller Fund for Music, October 15, 1965, Barbara Steinberg collection.

39. Howard Klein, "3-Race Ensemble in Concert Debut," *New York Times*, May 7, 1965, p. 35.

40. Ibid.

41. Ibid.

42. Jones, interview by the author.

43. Wise, interview by the author.

44. Klein, "3-Race Ensemble," 35.

45. Wise, interview by the author.

46. List of goals, n.d., Barbara Steinberg collection.

47. Allen Hughes, "Symphony Celebrates Its First Anniversary," *New York Times*, May 9, 1966, p. 46.

48. Joan Peyser, "The Negro in Search of an Orchestra," *New York Times*, November 26, 1967, p. D18.

49. Sally Drummond, "Negro Minor League of Note," *New York Post*, March 21, 1967, n.p.

50. "Lesson of Experience," *Newsweek*, February 20, 1967, p. 102.

51. Moore, interview by the author.

52. Sanford Allen, "Why Hasn't the Negro Found a Place in the Symphony?" *New York Times*, June 25, 1967, p. D13.

53. Unsigned list of grievances, October 13, 1971, Barbara Steinberg collection.

54. Moore, interview by the author.

55. "Chronology of Events Pertaining to the Present Internal Problems of the Symphony of the New World," n.d., Barbara Steinberg collection. The document is undated and unsigned but was probably prepared sometime in 1972 by Steinberg and the symphony staff.

56. Donal Henahan, "Orchestra Opens 7th Season Here," *New York Times*, October 11, 1971, p. 50.

57. Ibid.

58. Benjamin Steinberg, letter to subscribers, February 1, 1972, Barbara Steinberg collection.

59. Donal Henahan, "'De Coteau' Leads the New World," *New York Times*, February 28, 1972, p. 39.

60. Donal Henahan, "Two Orchestras: Can They Live?" *New York Times*, July 15, 1973, p. 111.

61. Harry Smyles letter, *New York Times*, September 2, 1973, p. 95.

62. Brown, interview by the author.

63. Ibid.

64. Some of the programs and other historical documents of the symphony have been reprinted in Clarissa and Marion Cumbo, "In Retrospect . . . The Symphony of the New World," *Black Perspective in Music* 3, no. 3 (Fall 1975): 312–330.

65. Raymond Ericson, "More Deserving than Panthers?" *New York Times*, October 29, 1972, p. D19.

66. Concert listings, *New York Times*, April 9, 1978, p. D35.

67. Jones, interview by the author.

68. Joy Portugal, "Allegro Interviews Gayle Dixon," *Allegro* C, no. 3 (March 2000), available at http://www.jazzbows.com/gayledixon/gayledixoninterview.html.

69. Hale Smith, "Here I Stand," in *Readings in Black American Music*, ed. Eileen Southern (New York: W. W. Norton, 1971), 288 (emphasis in original).

70. Complaint of Earl Madison against New York Philharmonic, Complaint no. 3758-J, January 7, 1969, and complaint of Arthur Davis against New York Philharmonic, Complaint no. 3855-J, March 18, 1969, New York Philharmonic Digital Archives, available at http://archives.nyphil.org/index.php/artifact/7c3f977b-4d9e-4e8b-b232-696c9d26c51a/fullview#page/1/mode/1up.

71. Donal Henahan, "Philharmonic's Hiring Policy Defended," *New York Times*, July 31, 1969, p. 26.

72. "Philharmonic Facing Charge of Hiring Bias," *New York Times*, June 10, 1969, p. 50.

73. Chris Walker, "The Art of Survival," *Double Bassist*, Summer 2002, p. 59.

74. Arthur Davis obituary, *Washington Post*, August 5, 2007, p. C8.

75. See Earl Madison website at http://earlmadison.net.

76. "Transcript of CCHR Hearings," vol. 1, July 30, 1969, New York Philharmonic Digital Archives, p. 48, available at http://archives.nyphil.org/index.php/artifact/8798e775-9727-490b-80ed-221fefa7b5a6/fullview#page/1/mode/1up. Weitz's sarcastic remark about the number of black classical musicians and black mayors alludes to Carl B. Stokes, who served as mayor of Cleveland from 1968 to 1971.

77. "Transcript of CCHR Hearings," vol. 2, August 1, 1969, New York Philharmonic Digital Archives, pp. 189–223, available at http://archives.nyphil.org/index.php/artifact/3edab7d3-85da-4984-b858-426aa67c4909/fullview#page/1/mode/1up.

78. In his book, *Music: Black, White and Blue* (New York: William Morrow, 1972), Walton states that "the first Afro-American to be employed in an American symphony

orchestra was Charles Burrell, who was appointed to the Denver Colorado Symphony in 1954" (128).

79. "Transcript of CCHR Hearings," vol. 3, September 24, 1969, New York Philharmonic Digital Archives, pp. 242–243, available at http://archives.nyphil.org/index.php/artifact/eb14b7fe-b833-48da-a479-60d4d9ce9162/fullview#page/1/mode/1up.

80. "Transcript of CCHR Hearings," vol. 6, September 29, 1969, New York Philharmonic Digital Archives, p. 896, available at http://archives.nyphil.org/index.php/artifact/83b690b2-fb99-43f0-8b1a-0bfdb2572b66/fullview#page/1/mode/1up.

81. "Transcript of CCHR Hearings," vol. 3, September 24, 1969, pp. 336–336A.

82. Ibid., 350.

83. Ibid., 383–384.

84. "Transcript of CCHR Hearings," vol. 4, September 25, 1969, New York Philharmonic Digital Archives, p. 613, available at http://archives.nyphil.org/index.php/artifact/2ca2bbaa-0deb-44ae-8285-9126e3fe7121/fullview#page/1/mode/1up.

85. "Transcript of CCHR Hearings," vol. 5, September 26, 1969, New York Philharmonic Digital Archives, p. 713, available at http://archives.nyphil.org/index.php/artifact/8f42f63b-4ead-47df-a67c-b8c2d727d07a/fullview#page/1/mode/1up.

86. Ibid., 737.

87. Ibid., 757.

88. Ibid., 793.

89. Donal Henahan, "Some Sour Notes, but Not a Bad Town to Work In: Philharmonicsville (pop. 106)," *New York Times Magazine*, September 28, 1969, p. 135.

90. Ibid., 136.

91. Allen, "Why Hasn't the Negro Found a Place in the Symphony?" p. D13.

92. Joan Peyser, *Bernstein: A Biography*, rev. ed. (New York: Billboard Books, 1998), 415–416.

93. Leonard Bernstein, "The Negro in Music: Problems He Has to Face in Getting a Start," *New York Times*, November 2, 1947, p. X7.

94. Ibid.

95. "Transcript of CCHR Hearings," vol. 6, September 29, 1969, pp. 842–843.

96. Ibid., 984.

97. Tom Wolfe, "Radical Chic: That Party at Lenny's," *New York*, June 1970, pp. 27–56.

98. "Transcript of CCHR Hearings," vol. 7, September 30, 1969, New York Philharmonic Digital Archives, p. 1066, available at http://archives.nyphil.org/index.php/artifact/ee3278be-cb77-474b-9454-0e657dfde535/fullview#page/1/mode/1up.

99. "Transcript of CCHR Hearings," vol. 8, October 17, 1969, New York Philharmonic Digital Archives, p. 1436, available at http://archives.nyphil.org/index.php/artifact/2f70cf9a-2147-4230-9c24-3496a70997c7/fullview#page/1/mode/1up.

100. "Transcript of CCHR Hearings," vol. 9, October 18, 1969, New York Philharmonic Digital Archives, p. 1589, available at http://archives.nyphil.org/index.php/artifact/b65c53fe-9137-48fa-8034-697416ef832e/fullview#page/1/mode/1up.

101. Commission on Human Rights hearing notes, July 30, 1969–October 20, 1969, New York Philharmonic Digital Archive, p. 2, available at http://archives.nyphil.org/index.php/artifact/027c61e5-272e-44a9-8f0d-37ca4c919360/fullview#page/1/mode/1up. Wilder is listed as one of the witnesses at the October 20, 1969, session on these handwritten pages, presumably compiled by the philharmonic's attorneys.

102. In response to a request in April 2011, the New York City Commission on Human Rights informed me that it no longer have the hearing transcripts in its archive and suggested contacting the Municipal Archives of the City of New York. In January 2012, the

Municipal Archives reported that, although it would normally serve as the repository for legal transcripts such as these, the transcripts for this case were not among its holdings. The only archive that holds these transcripts seems to be the New York Philharmonic Archives, whose holdings are complete with the exception of the final day of hearings.

103. Amyas Ames, "Report to Subscribers," November 5, 1969, New York Philharmonic Digital Archives, p. 1, available at http://archives.nyphil.org/index.php/artifact/3c3282f5-fd00-4f22-824b-d54f642801da/fullview#page/1/mode/1up.

104. Ibid., 2.

105. Ibid.

106. Ibid., 3.

107. Donal Henahan, "Rights Unit Bars Philharmonic from Filling 2 Disputed Chairs," *New York Times*, November 27, 1969, p. 54.

108. "Rights Unit Clears Philharmonic but Finds Bias in Some Hiring," *New York Times*, November 17, 1970, p. 53.

109. City of New York, Commission on Human Rights, Complaint no. J-3758 and J-3855, Decision and Order, October 29, 1970, New York Philharmonic Digital Archives, p. 2, available at http://archives.nyphil.org/index.php/artifact/fb7b9324-6980-433d-82a3-3180bf34d989/fullview#page/1/mode/1up.

110. Ibid., 3.

111. Ibid., 4. As previously noted, the one black substitute player hired was flutist Hubert Laws.

112. Ibid.

113. Ibid., 6.

114. Ibid., 1–2.

115. "Black Musicians Issue Challenge: Losers in Rights Case Seek to Test Philharmonic Best," *New York Times*, November 18, 1970, p. 40.

116. Nat Hentoff, "Un-Chic Racism at the Philharmonic," *Village Voice*, December 17, 1970, pp. 30–31, 56 (emphasis in original). "Jensenism" refers to psychologist Arthur Jensen, whose controversial theories on IQ differentials between blacks and whites had recently been published.

117. "Rights Unit Clears Philharmonic but Finds Bias in Some Hiring," *New York Times*, November 17, 1970, p. 53; "Philharmonic Ordered to End Racial Bias," *New York Law Journal* 164, no. 97 (November 19, 1970): 1.

118. Hentoff, "Un-Chic Racism at the Philharmonic," 56.

119. Arthur Davis, interview by David Lee, *Coda*, April 1982, p. 16.

120. Arthur Davis, interview by Elliot Bratton, *Cadence*, September 1986, p. 16.

121. Ibid.

122. Walker, "The Art of Survival," 63.

123. Earl Madison, interviews by the author, May 2012. All quotes by Earl Madison, unless otherwise indicated, are from this series of interviews.

124. Handy, *Black Women*, 263–264.

125. William Cousins Jr., Leon M. Despres, and A. A. Rayner Jr., "Confidential Memorandum Re Danger to Chicago Symphony Orchestra from Its Uninterrupted 79-Year Pattern of Racial Exclusion," n.d., Earl Madison collection.

126. "Transcript of CCHR Hearings," vol. 6, September 29, 1969, p. 913.

127. The Philadelphia Orchestra hired its first black member, violist Renard Edwards, in 1969; Henahan, "The Philadelphia Gets First Black," 42.

128. See "Black and White Notes," *Newsweek*, August 18, 1969, p. 82.

129. Ibid.

130. Ibid.

131. "Transcript of CCHR Hearings," vol. 4, September 25, 1969, p. 430.

132. Ibid., 432.

133. City of New York, Commission on Human Rights, Complaint No. J-3758 and J-3855, Decision and Order, October 29, 1970, p. 8.

134. Ibid., 7.

135. "Black Musicians Issue Challenge," 40.

136. Memo from Leon Thompson to Helen Thompson, December 7, 1970, New York Philharmonic Archives, Lincoln Center, New York.

137. Wise, interview by the author.

138. Donal Henahan, "Philharmonic, City in Antibias Pact," *New York Times*, May 30, 1972, p. 42.

139. Donal Henahan, "An About Face on Black Musicians at the Philharmonic," *New York Times*, June 11, 1972, p. D15.

140. Henahan, "Philharmonic, City in Antibias Pact," 42.

141. Lucille Dixon, "Is It 'Artistic Judgment' or Is It Discrimination?" *New York Times*, August 1, 1971, p. D11 (emphasis in original).

142. Handy, *Black Women*, 210–212.

143. Dick Campbell, "Symphony Orchestras: A Bad Scene," *The Crisis*, January 1975, pp. 12–17.

144. Julius Grossman obituary, *New York Times*, November 19, 2002, p. B10.

145. "Negro Appointed Orchestra Agent: He Is First of Race to Get Hiring Job with Classical Organization in City," *New York Times*, June 29, 1959, p. 54.

146. Radio listings, *New York Times*, August 11, 1963, p. 102.

147. Alec Wilder's *Suite for Trumpet and Piano* (1972), recorded by trumpeter Robert Levy, is a different work from the one written for Joe Wilder.

148. Desmond Stone, *Alec Wilder in Spite of Himself: A Life of the Composer* (New York: Oxford, 1996), 129.

149. Ibid.

150. Whitney Balliett, *Alec Wilder and His Friends* (Boston: Houghton Mifflin, 1974), 184.

151. Ibid., 183.

152. Mundell Lowe, interview by the author, June 27, 2012.

153. Orrin Keepnews, post on Friends of Alec Wilder Listserv, previously available at http://www.cs.trinity.edu/~rprather/members.html (accessed March 30, 2011).

154. Ibid.

155. Lowe, interview by the author.

156. Ibid.

157. Ibid.

158. Mundell Lowe, *Tacet for Neurotics: The Music of Alec Wilder*, 1963, Offbeat OLP3010, LP.

159. Richard F. Shepard, "Garroway Plans TV Tour of R.C.A.: Building to Be Background for Variety Show," *New York Times*, October 12, 1960, p. 79.

160. Stone, *Alec Wilder in Spite of Himself*, 128.

161. James T. Maher, liner notes to *Joe Wilder, Trumpet*, 1964, Golden Crest RE7007, LP.

162. Willis Conover, "Alec Wilder," *BMI Journal*, December 1967, Institute of Jazz Studies, Rutgers–Newark, NJ.

163. Harriet Wingreen, interview by the author, June 13, 2011.

164. Maher, liner notes to *Joe Wilder, Trumpet*.

165. Theodore Strongin, "Haphazard Treatment," *New York Times*, November 29, 1964, p. X24.

166. "New Recordings for Instrumentalists," *The Instrumentalist*, January 1965, p. 14.

167. Whitney Balliett, "Jazz: Making Do," *New Yorker*, July 26, 1982, p. 57.

168. Whitney Balliett, "Jazz: Joe Wilder," *New Yorker*, January 6, 1986, p. 58.

169. Richard Williams, "Caught on the Hook of Holland: Review of Rock and Jazz Records," *The Times* (London), November 2, 1985.

170. Joe Wilder, interview by Rebecca Kilgore, *On the Road with Rebecca Kilgore*, KMHD-FM, Gresham, OR, recorded March 16, 2002.

171. The Four Ayalons, *Sing Along with Israel*, 1962, ATE Records (S)AC633, LP.

172. Joseph Wilder, *The Sound of the Bugle*, 1961, Choice Records MG505, LP.

Chapter 10

1. Leon Cohen, interview by the author, February 15, 2011.

2. "Taping of Cavett's Show Disrupted by Jazz Group," *New York Times*, October 14, 1970, p. 41.

3. Benjamin R. Tess, "The Jazz and People's Movement: Rahsaan Roland Kirk's Struggle to Open the American Media to Black Classical Music" (honors thesis, Boston College, 2008), 82.

4. "Jazz Protesters Do Cavett Show, Push On," *Down Beat*, November 26, 1970, p. 8.

5. Dan Morgenstern, "Afterthoughts," *Down Beat*, December 10, 1970, p. 37.

6. Tess, "The Jazz and People's Movement," 98–99.

7. Dan Morgenstern. *Living with Jazz* (New York: Pantheon, 2004), 650.

8. Cohen, interview by the author.

9. Les Brown, "TV Musicians Refuse to Work as Talks on Contract Bog Down," *New York Times*, May 9, 1974, p. 87.

10. "TV Nets, AFM Conclude 2 Yr. Contract Talks," *Billboard*, August 3, 1974, p. 48.

11. Eric Konigsberg, "His Music Still Makes Society Whirl," *New York Times*, December 3, 2009, Arts, p. 1.

12. Peter Duchin, *Ghost of a Chance: A Memoir* (New York: Random House, 1996), 239–240.

13. Bruce A. MacLeod, *Club Date Musicians: Playing the New York Party Circuit* (Urbana: University of Illinois Press, 1993), 5 (emphasis in original).

14. Peter Duchin, interview by the author, July 11, 2012.

15. Nancy Marano, interview by the author, June 23, 2012.

16. Ibid.

17. Duchin, *Ghost of a Chance*, 130.

18. Duchin, interview by the author.

19. Marano, interview by the author.

20. Ibid.

21. MacLeod, *Club Date Musicians*, 84.

22. Konigsberg, "His Music Still Makes Society Whirl," 1.

23. Duchin, interview by the author.

24. Ibid.

25. Marano, interview by the author.

26. Whitey Mitchell, "My First 50 Years with Society Bands," *Down Beat*, February 2, 1961, p. 20.

27. New York City Commission on Human Rights, "Hiring Practices for Broadway Musical Orchestras: The Exclusionary Effect on Minority Musicians," November 18, 1976, available at http://www.nyc.gov/html/cchr/pdf/hiring_practices_for_broadway_musical_orchestras-the_exclusionary_effect_on_minority_musicians.pdf.

28. Ibid., 4.

29. Ibid., 199.

30. "Discrimination in Hiring in Broadway Orchestras Charged by Mrs. Norton," *New York Times*, September 26, 1976, p. 27.

31. Ibid.

32. New York City Commission on Human Rights, "Hiring Practices for Broadway Musical Orchestras," 17.

33. Harold C. Schonberg, "A Minority Report on 'Porgy,'" *New York Times*, October 17, 1976, Section 2, pp. 1, 19.

34. C. Gerald Fraser, "Black and Hispanic Musicians to Get More Work on Broadway," *New York Times*, January 3, 1978, p. 36.

35. Ibid.

36. Joy Portugal, "Allegro Interviews Gayle Dixon," *Allegro* C, no. 3 (March 2000), available at http://www.jazzbows.com/gayledixon/gayledixoninterview.html.

37. New York City Commission on Human Rights, "Hiring Practices for Broadway Musical Orchestras," 200.

38. Robert Palmer, "The Reggae Rhythm Comes to Broadway," *New York Times*, March 16, 1980, p. D6.

39. *Playbill: Reggae*, March 1980, p. 32.

40. Mel Gussow, "Theater: 'Reggae,' Musical at Biltmore," *New York Times*, March 28, 1980, p. C3.

41. Frank Rich, "Theater: Musical '42d Street': A Backstage Story," *New York Times*, August 26, 1980, p. C7.

42. Bill Crow, interview by the author, June 22, 2012.

43. Ibid.

44. "Play It Again, Russell," *The Cosby Show*, season 2, episode 17, first aired February 13, 1986, NBC, available at http://www.youtube.com/watch?v=WiJpFti2StE.

45. *The Cosby Show: Season 2*, 2006, Carsey Werner, 25322-7, DVD.

46. For a discussion of Eastwood's use of Hartman's recording, see Krin Gabbard, *Black Magic: White Hollywood and African American Culture* (New Brunswick, NJ: Rutgers University Press, 2004), 59–61, 65–72.

47. Gregg Akkerman, *The Last Balladeer: The Johnny Hartman Story* (Lanham, MD: Scarecrow Press, 2012), 322–323. For example, on the LP, the timing of "Easy to Love" is 5:55, and the key is B flat, whereas on the soundtrack, the time has been lengthened to 6:26 and the pitch lowered to A. The original issue of the CD *Music from the Motion Picture The Bridges of Madison County* (1995, Malpaso/Warner Bros. 45949) contains the slowed-down versions, but later issues of the same CD have restored the tracks to the correct speed. The only difference between the two CD releases is that in the slowed-down version, the photo and design credits on page two of the insert appear on one line, whereas on the corrected release, they appear on two lines. Needless to say, this practice detracts from the performance and is hard to condone, especially when apparently sanctioned by a jazz devotee like Clint Eastwood. Moreover, although the soundtrack CD scrupulously credits composers, publishers, engineers, producers, and eighteen others, whose unspecified contributions fall under "Special Thanks," none of the musicians are mentioned.

48. Eileen Farrell and Brian Kellow, *Can't Help Singing: The Life of Eileen Farrell* (Boston: Northeastern University Press, 1999), 133–134.

49. Eileen Farrell, *Eileen Farrell Sings Rodgers and Hart*, 1989, Reference Recordings, RR-32, CD.

50. Eileen Farrell, *Eileen Farrell Sings Harold Arlen*, 1989, Reference Recordings, RR-30, CD.

51. Farrell and Kellow, *Can't Help Singing*, 225.

52. Eileen Farrell, *Eileen Farrell Sings Torch Songs*, 1990, Reference Recordings, RR-34, CD.

53. Eileen Farrell, *Eileen Farrell Sings Alec Wilder*, 1990, Reference Recordings, RR-36, CD.

54. Jerry Shinn, "The Great American Songs—Farrell, McGlohon Capture the Best of Popular Music," *Charlotte Observer*, May 21, 1990, p. 7A.

55. Richard Harrington, "Legrand and Co.: A Silky, Sassy Collaboration," *Washington Post*, December 9, 1983, p. 38.

56. Edward Berger, *Bassically Speaking: An Oral History of George Duvivier* (Metuchen, NJ: Scarecrow Press, 1993), 208.

Chapter 11

1. Edward Berger, *Bassically Speaking: An Oral History of George Duvivier* (Metuchen, NJ: Scarecrow Press, 1993), 76.

2. David Berger, interview by George Kanzler, *Star Ledger* (Newark, NJ), September 11, 1992.

3. Jeffrey Sultanof, "Jazz Repertory," in *The Oxford Companion to Jazz*, ed. Bill Kirchner (Oxford: Oxford University Press, 2000), 512–521.

4. Chuck Israels, *National Jazz Ensemble*, 1978, Big 3 Music, 1179, LP.

5. Alex Stewart, *Making the Scene: Contemporary New York City Big Band Jazz* (Berkeley: University of California Press, 2007), 63.

6. Sultanof, "Jazz Repertory," 518.

7. See the Foreword for Wynton Marsalis's observations about the tour and his relationship with Joe Wilder.

8. Joe Wilder, interview by Julie Burstein, Smithsonian Jazz Oral History Project, August 25–26, 1992, p. 861.

9. Peter Watrous, "How Jazz Could Become the New Rock and Roll," *New York Times*, November 14, 1992, p. C17.

10. Bill Eichenberger, "Lincoln Center Features Mostly High Notes," *Columbus Dispatch*, October 3, 1992, p. 4H.

11. Joe Wilder, interview by Monk Rowe, April 12, 1996, Hamilton College Jazz Archive, Clinton, NY, transcript p. 1, available at http://elib.hamilton.edu/cdm4/document.php?CISOROOT=/jazz&CISOPTR=1401&REC=5.

12. Loren Schoenberg, interview by the author, July 26, 2011.

13. Michael Weiss, interview by the author, July 16, 2012.

14. Whitney Balliett, "Celebrating the Duke," *New Yorker*, November 29, 1993, p. 143.

15. George Kanzler, "Ambitious Salute to Ellington Both Sharp, Flat," *Star Ledger* (Newark, NJ), October 18, 1993.

16. Clive Davis, "The Cotton Club Revue—Jazz," *The Times* (London), July 26, 1999, p. 45.

17. Ken Kimery, interview by the author, June 10, 2011.

18. Ibid.

19. Jill Kamp, "The Best Things Life Offers Can Be Free," *Washington Times*, March 13, 2002, p. B5.

20. Kimery, interview by the author.

21. Schoenberg, interview by the author.

22. Kimery, interview by the author.

23. Schoenberg, interview by the author.

24. Ibid.

25. Ibid.

26. Gunther Schuller, interview by Mark Schramm, *Morning Edition*, NPR, May 17, 1991.

27. Ibid.

28. Dick Hyman has pointed out the similarity between Rex Stewart's solo on "Old Man River," recorded with Luis Russell's orchestra for Banner, August 8, 1934, and Wilder's own style. Dick Hyman, interview by the author, September 12, 2012.

29. Weiss, interview by the author.

30. John McDonough, "Joe Wilder," *Down Beat*, February 1993, p. 14.

31. Ibid.

32. Hyman, interview by the author.

33. Ibid.

34. Adam Harvey, *The Soundtracks of Woody Allen: A Complete Guide to the Songs and Music in Every Film, 1969–2005* (Jefferson, NC: McFarland, 2007), 59, 136, 137, 142, 144.

35. John S. Wilson, "Rediscovering the Classic Swing of Jelly Roll Morton," *New York Times*, June 9, 1974, p. 142.

36. *The Sting: Original Motion Picture Soundtrack*, 1974, MCA 390, LP.

37. Whitney Balliett, "Jazz: From Joplin to Goodman, and Slightly Beyond," *New Yorker*, August 25, 1986, p. 74.

38. Wilder, interview by Monk Rowe, 1.

39. Andy Stein, interview by the author, August 17, 2012.

40. Ibid.

41. Ibid.

42. Burt A. Folkart, "Dick Gibson; Host of Jazz Concerts," *Los Angeles Times*, June 19, 1998, available at http://articles.latimes.com/1998/jun/19/local/me-61481.

43. Leonard Feather, "Jazz Review: Gibson Throws a World-Class Party," *Los Angeles Times*, September 9, 1992, available at http://articles.latimes.com/1992-09-09/entertainment/ca-44_1_jazz-parties.

44. Larry Orenstein, "The World's Greatest Jazz Party," *High Performance Review* 8, no. 4 (Winter 1991/1992): 46.

45. Milt Hinton, David G. Berger, and Holly Maxson, *Playing the Changes: Milt Hinton's Life in Stories and Photographs* (Nashville: Vanderbilt University Press, 2008), 286–287.

46. Orenstein, "The World's Greatest Jazz Party," 46.

47. Feather, "Jazz Review: Gibson Throws a World-Class Party."

48. Eric Nisenson, *Blue: The Murder of Jazz* (New York: St. Martin's Press, 1997).

49. Stanley Dance, "Ted Gioia, *The History of Jazz*; Eric Nisenson, *Blue: The Murder of Jazz*; Tom Piazza, *Blues Up and Down: Jazz in Our Time*," *JazzTimes*, March 1998, available at http://jazztimes.com/articles/21128-the-history-of-jazz-ted-gioia.

Chapter 12

1. Victor Goines, interview by the author, August 7, 2012.

2. Ibid.

3. Ibid.

4. Ibid.

5. Edward Berger, "An Interview with Trumpet Legends Williams Fielder and Joe Wilder," in *Early Twentieth-Century Brass Idioms: Art, Jazz, and Other Popular Traditions*, ed. Howard T. Weiner (Lanham, MD: Scarecrow Press, 2009), 55–56.

6. Ibid., 56.

7. Dominick Farinacci, interview by the author, July 24, 2012.

8. Ibid.

9. Ibid.

10. Brandon Lee, interview by the author, August 24, 2012.

11. Farinacci, interview by the author.

12. Lee, interview by the author.

13. Farinacci, interview by the author.

14. Lee, interview by the author.

15. Ibid.

16. Farinacci, interview by the author.

17. Ibid.

18. Lee, interview by the author.

19. Loren Schoenberg, interview by the author, July 26, 2011.

20. Ibid. For some short video excerpts of one of Wilder's discussions with students at Harlem's Frederick Douglass Academy, see http://www.youtube.com/watch?v=VgnJdgj GvL0.

21. Monk Rowe, interview by the author, July 29, 2102.

22. Ibid.

23. Ibid.

24. Ibid.

25. Ibid.

26. See the Hamilton College Jazz Archive website at http://www.hamilton.edu/ jazzarchive.

27. Rowe, interview by the author.

28. Text appears on the honorary degree plaque.

29. Nate Chinen, "NEA Jazz Masters Mistake," *JazzTimes*, October 2010, available at http://jazztimes.com/articles/26497-nea-s-jazz-masters-mistake.

30. Ibid.

31. Ibid.

32. Will Friedwald, "The Greatest Trumpeter You've Never Heard," *New York Sun*, November 12, 2007, available at http://www.nysun.com/arts/greatest-trumpeter-youve -never-heard/66274.

33. "2008 NEA Jazz Masters Panel, Part 1," June 8, 2010, available at http://www.you tube.com/watch?v=pMDmxdtgVbo.

34. Ibid.

35. The performance was posted on the WBGO blog at http://www.wbgo.org/blog/ category/16439.

36. Alan Nahigian, "Wilder Tribute Highlights NYC Brass Conference," *Down Beat*, September 1998, p. 16.

37. Ibid.

38. Peter Watrous, "3 Mentors Trumpeting Their Skills, *New York Times*, June 19, 1998, p. E31.

39. Ibid.

40. George Kanzler, "Jazz Festival Salutes Arlen, Trumpeters," *Star-Ledger* (Newark, NJ), June 20, 1998, p. 37.

41. Ira Gitler, "Charlie Parker Jazz Festival 2001," *JazzTimes*, August 28, 2001, available at http://jazztimes.com/articles/17869-charlie-parker-jazz-festival-2001.

42. Ben Ratliff, "Two Contemporaries Meet, on Trumpet and Tenor Sax," *New York Times*, June 19, 2003, p. E3.

43. Will Friedwald, "Life Begins at 80," *New York Sun*, June 20, 2003.

44. Ratliff, "Two Contemporaries Meet," E3.

45. Harriet Goodheart, "Jazz Greats Clark Terry and Joe Wilder to Perform with Temple's Jazz Band," *Temple Times*, April 6, 2006, available at http://www.temple.edu/temple_times/4-6-06/jazzband.htm.

46. Nate Chinen, Jazz listings, *New York Times*, January 27, 2006, p. E23.

47. Ben Ratliff, "Stepping Gently out of the Sideman Shadows," *New York Times*, February 3, 2006, p. E23.

48. Michael Weiss, interview by the author, July 16, 2012.

49. Ratliff, "Stepping Gently out of the Sideman Shadows," E23.

50. Zan Stewart, "Vanguard Debut Well Worth the Wait," *Star-Ledger* (Newark, NJ), February 2, 2006, p. 56.

51. Ibid.

52. Weiss, interview by the author.

53. Ibid.

54. Ibid.

55. Ibid.

56. Larry Appelbaum, "Before and After: Jeremy Pelt," *JazzTimes*, October 2008, pp. 28–31.

57. Michael Steinman, "With Dispatch and Vigor (Thursday Night at Chautauqua)," *Jazz Lives*, September 22, 2008, available at http://jazzlives.wordpress.com/tag/charles-peterson.

58. Naomi Smoot, "John Brown's Final Day Remembered," *The Journal* (Martinsburg, WV), December 3, 2009, available at http://www.journal-news.net/page/content.detail/id/528636.html.

59. "KKK Shows Up at Niagara Meeting," *Charleston Gazette*, August 21, 2006, p. 3A.

60. Kanika J. G. Georges, "Klan Presence Raises No Ripples," *The Journal* (Martinsburg, WV), August 20, 2006, available at http://vnnforum.com/archive/index.php/t-37278.html.

61. "Ku Klux Klan Plans Rally in Harpers Ferry National Park," *Charleston Daily Mail*, September 29, 2006, p. 6A.

62. Allan Kozinn, "Some Like It Straight, and Some Like It Hot," *New York Times*, February 15, 2000, p. E5.

63. Gary Budzak, "Selections from '20s Oddly Timely Today," *Columbus Dispatch*, October 16, 2008, p. 2A.

64. Ben Ratliff, "Time to Show Dexterity, but No Time for Cuteness," *New York Times*, June 15, 2006, p. E5.

65. Jimmy Heath and Joseph McLaren, *I Walked with Giants: The Autobiography of Jimmy Heath* (Philadelphia: Temple University Press, 2010), 260.

66. Jim Czak, interview by the author, August 23, 2012.

67. MusicMasters did eventually lease the Wilder recording for issue on its mail-order Jazz Heritage label.

68. Letter from Joe Wilder to Milt and Mona Hinton, April 8, 2000, private collection of David G. Berger.

69. Mat Domber, interview by the author, August 16, 2012.

70. Czak, interview by the author. Wilder's musical interpolation occurs in "Liza," on Ruby Braff, *Variety Is the Spice of Life*, recorded July 24–25, 2000, Arbors ARCD19194, CD.

71. Domber, interview by the author.

72. Gunther Schuller, liner notes to *Playing for Keeps*, recorded January 4, 1992, GM Recordings GM 3026, CD.

73. Doug Ramsey, "Tom Talbert, *This Is Living*," *JazzTimes*, May 1998, available at http://jazztimes.com/articles/8608-this-is-living-tom-talbert.

74. Scott Yanow, "Tom Talbert, *This Is Living!*" *AllMusic*, n.d., available at http://www.allmusic.com/album/this-is-living!-mw0000032362 (accessed September 12, 2013).

75. "Charlie Byrd to Appear," *New York Times*, December 7, 1984, p. C19.

76. Rebecca Kilgore, interview by the author, September 16, 2012.

77. Ibid.

78. Joe Wilder, interview by Rebecca Kilgore, *On the Road with Rebecca Kilgore*, KMHD-FM, Gresham, OR, recorded March 16, 2002.

79. Kilgore, interview by the author.

80. Joe Wilder, interview by Marian McPartland, *Piano Jazz*, NPR, aired February 13, 2001, available at http://www.npr.org/templates/story/story.php?storyId=91470414.

81. John Biderman, "Twenty-Seventh Annual Concert in New York," *Yahoo! Groups: Alec Wilder Group*, April 27, 2012, available at http://launch.groups.yahoo.com/group/awilder/message/427.

Discography/Solography

This listing attempts to document all issued sessions on which Joe Wilder participated in all areas of music and to indicate his contributions as a soloist. Given Wilder's prolific career in the studios, this list is, almost by definition, far from complete—especially in the field of popular music, where discographical data is far less available than in jazz. Although the listing is limited to released recordings, a few significant broadcasts have been included for which recordings are known to exist (in some instances, these are available online).

To save space while highlighting Joe Wilder's solo work, the format and level of detail differ from those of standard discographies. For each session, the leader's (or group's) name is given first, and the sessions are ordered chronologically. Full album credits are included only for sessions in which Wilder is leader. Only songs in which Wilder solos or is prominent as accompanist (e.g., playing fills or obbligatos behind a singer) are listed, and the length in measures of Wilder's contribution (e.g., 8b) follows each song title. If Wilder does not solo in a session, "No solos" appears in place of the song titles, indicating that I have listened to the recording(s) and verified that he does not solo. For sessions originally recorded for release on 78 or 45 rpm singles, the original recording company is listed after the leader's name, and the original issue and format appears after the song title. For sessions from the LP and CD eras, the name of the arranger-conductor (if available) appears in parentheses after the leader's name, and the original album title and issue is supplied in the heading. Reissues, mostly CDs but including some LPs, are listed below each session. Unless otherwise indicated, reissues have the same leader and title as the original. The reissue release information is not comprehensive and is intended only as a guide for those wishing to obtain these recordings. Session leaders are included in the index.

I acknowledge the standard jazz discographies of Walter Bruyninckx and Tom Lord, which proved invaluable. Other specialized sources include Steve Albin's discography of Tony Bennett, available at http://www.jazzdiscography.com/Artists/Bennett/index.php;

Charles Mingus Discography Project, available at http://www.jazzdisco.org/mingus; and Ake Holm's Harry Belafonte and Friends discography, available at http://www.akh.se/harbel/index.htm.

Most of all, I am grateful to Joe Wilder for sharing his personal collection with me and for verifying solo credits.

The list uses the following abbreviations:

ob = obbligato
tp = trumpet
JW = Joe Wilder

LES HITE (Hit)
April 1942, New York
"I Remember You," Hit 7001, 78 rpm (8b)

LIONEL HAMPTON
Unissued Armed Forces radio broadcast, AFRS Program 3
October 1942, Los Angeles
"The Great Lie" (64b)

LIONEL HAMPTON (Decca)
September 9, 1946, Los Angeles
"Playboy," Brunswick (E)04322, 78 rpm (4b)
"Cobb's Idea," *Rarities*, MCA 1351, LP (8b 2nd tp solo)

Reissue (both titles): *Lionel Hampton and His Orchestra 1946*, Classics 946, CD.

LIONEL HAMPTON (Decca)
September 17, 1946, Los Angeles
No solos

LIONEL HAMPTON (Decca)
September 23, 1946, Los Angeles
"Double Talk," *Rarities*, MCA 1351, LP (32b)

Reissue: *Lionel Hampton and His Orchestra 1946*, Classics 946, CD.

JIMMIE LUNCEFORD (Majestic)
May 1947, New York
"Call the Police," Majestic 1122, 78 rpm (8b)

Reissue: *Jimmie Lunceford and His Orchestra, 1945–1947*, Classics 1082, CD; *Jumpin' with the Big Swing Bands*, Savoy 17182, CD.

LUCKY MILLINDER
Swingtime at the Savoy, **unissued NBC radio broadcast**
July 28, 1948, New York
"Sabre Dance" (opening and closing melody)

Note: The performance is available at http://newstalgia.crooksandliars.com/gordonskene/newstalgia-downbeat-lucky-millinder-an (see Chapter 4 for details).

LUCKY MILLINDER with BILLIE HOLIDAY
Swingtime at the Savoy, **unissued NBC radio broadcast**
August 18, 1948, New York
  "Billie's Blues" (ob throughout)

Note: A performance tape exists; see Chapter 4 for details.

LUCKY MILLINDER (Victor)
January 3, 1949, New York
  "I Ain't Got Nothin' to Lose," Victor 20-3495, 78 rpm (8b)

Reissue: *Lucky Millinder and His Orchestra, 1947–1950*, Classics 1173, CD; Big John Greer, *Rockin' with Big John*, Bear Family BCD1554, CD.

COZY COLE (Candy)
February 1949, New York
  "La Danse," Candy 3002, 78 rpm (32b)

BOB MARSHALL/COZY COLE (Decca)
March 2, 1949, New York
  "Milk Cow Blues," Decca 48101, 78 rpm (12b ob behind vocal)
  "The Hucklebuck," Decca 48099, 78 rpm (improv behind vocal, first and last chorus)
  "Red Light," Decca 48099, 78 rpm (ob behind vocal, 8b, 12b, 4b fill at end)

MABEL SCOTT (King)
March 25, 1950, New York
  "Fine, Fine Baby," King 4306, 78 rpm (intro)

Reissue: *Mabel Scott, 1938–1950*, Classics 5068, CD.

WYNONIE HARRIS (King)
May 18, 1950, New York
  No solos

EDDIE "CLEANHEAD" VINSON (King)
May 22, 1950, New York
  "Jump and Grunt," King 4396, 78 rpm (12b)

Reissue: Eddie "Cleanhead" Vinson, *Honk for Texas,* JSP (E) JSP7760, CD.

WYNONIE HARRIS (King)
July 12, 1950, New York
  No solos

MABEL SCOTT (King)
July 15, 1950, New York
  "Willow, Weep for Me," King 4410, 78 rpm (8b)

Reissue: *Mabel Scott, 1938–1950*, Classics 5068, CD.

WYNONIE HARRIS with LUCKY MILLINDER (King)
October 18, 1950, New York
  No solos

WYNONIE HARRIS (King)
October 24, 1950, New York
    No solos

Guys and Dolls: A Decca Original Cast Album
Decca DL 8036, LP
December 3, 1950, New York
    "My Time of Day" (4b muted)

Reissue: Decca Broadway 012-159-112, CD.

COLEMAN HAWKINS (Decca)
February 26, 1952, New York
    No solos

BULL MOOSE JACKSON (King)
April 4, 1952, New York
    No solos

AL HIBBLER
September 30, 1953, New York
    "Anne," Norgran 100, 78 rpm (4b)
    "I'm Getting Sentimental over You," Clef 89095, 78 rpm (intro, ob, ending)

Note: These songs were issued simultaneously on *Favorites*, Norgran MGN4, 10″ LP.

COUNT BASIE
December 12, 1953, New York
    "Softly, with Feeling," Clef 89112, 78 rpm (8b)

Reissue: *The Complete Clef/Verve Count Basie Fifties Studio Recordings*, Mosaic MD8-229, CD; *Ken Burns Jazz: Count Basie*, Verve 314-549-090, CD.

COUNT BASIE
Birdland Era, vol. 1, Duke 1013, LP
January 1, 1954, New York
    No solos

BIG MAYBELLE (SMITH) (Okeh)
January 20, 1954, New York
    No solos

COUNT BASIE
March 15, 1954, live recording, Stockholm Konserthus
    "Blee Blop Blues" (12b 2nd tp solo)
    "Peace Pipe" (12b)

Reissue: "Blee Blop" on Count Basie, *Live in Stockholm*, vol. 1, Tax 3701, CD; "Peace Pipe" on Count Basie, *Live in Stockholm*, vol. 2, Tax 3702, CD.

COUNT BASIE
April 29, 1954, broadcast from Birdland, New York
    "Sixteen Men Swinging" (32b)

"Softly, with Feeling" (8b, 8b)
"Basie Goes Wess" (20b)
"Why Not?" (32b)

Reissue: *Down for the Count*, Jazz Up JU303, CD; *Count Basie All Stars '54*, Moon MCD062, CD.

Note: Joe Wilder was announced during the broadcast as the soloist on "Softly, with Feeling," "Basie Goes Wess," and "Why Not?" Wilder cannot recall why he was the featured trumpet soloist on this occasion; one wonders whether Joe Newman, who normally took the majority of solos, was even present.

THE TRENIERS (Epic; Quincy Jones [arranger])
July 15, 1954, New York
   No solos

FRANK WESS
The Frank Wess Sextet, Commodore FL20032, 10″ LP
August 12, 1954, New York
   "Wess of the Moon" (36b)
   "Wess of the Moon" [alt. take] (24b)
   "Danny's Delight" (32b)
   "Danny's Delight" [alt. take] (32b)
   "Romance" (16b)
   "Frankly the Blues" (12b)
   "Frankly the Blues" [alt. take] (12b)

Reissue: All takes on *Complete Commodore Jazz Recordings*, vol. 3, Mosaic MR20-134, 20-LP set; master takes on Frank Wess, *Wess Point*, Fresh Sound FSRCD469, CD.

RALPH BURNS with LEONARD FEATHER
Winter Sequence: A Seasonal Suite for Rhythmic Reindeer, MGM E270, 10″ LP
September 1954, New York
   "Blitzen" (64b)

Reissue: Ralph Burns, *Free Forms and Winter Sequence*, Fresh Sound FSR2215, CD.

PETE BROWN
Peter the Great, Bethlehem BCP1011, 10″ LP
November 16, 1954, New York
   "The World Is Waiting for the Sunrise" (theme statements)
   "Moonlight in Vermont" (12b, 16b)
   "There Will Never Be Another You" (8b, 8b, 16b)
   "I Can't Believe That You're in Love with Me" (32b)
   "Used Blues" (16b)
   "Tea for Two" (32b)
   "Delta Blues" (intro, 8b, 16b)

OSCAR PETTIFORD
Basically Duke, Bethlehem BCP1019, 10″ LP
December 17, 1954, New York
   "Jack the Bear" (8b 1st tp solo)

"Tamalpais" (8b following tenor solo)

"Swingin' till the Girls Come Home" (3 12b choruses of trades with Clark Terry; Terry leads off)

Reissue: Oscar Pettiford and Tom Talbert, *Bix, Duke, Fats*, Lonehill Jazz 10341, CD.

URBIE GREEN
A Cool Yuletide, "X" LXA-3026, 10″ LP
1954, New York

"Rudolf, the Red-Nosed Reindeer" (4b, 8b, 4b)

"I Saw Mommy Kissing Santa Claus" (16b)

"Santa Claus Is Coming to Town" (intro, 16b)

"Jingle Bells" (16b)

"All I Want for Christmas Is My Two Front Teeth" (16b)

"Winter Wonderland" (16b)

JOHNNY RICHARDS
Annotations of the Muses, Legende 1401, 10″ LP
February 22, 1955, New York

"Part Two" (32b, 4b breaks)

"Part Three" (24b)

Reissue: *Johnny Richards*, Mosaic Select MS-017, CD.

Silk Stockings Original Broadway Cast Recording
RCA LOC1016, LP
March 6, 1955, New York

Wilder plays 1st trumpet throughout.

Reissue: RCA Victor 1102-2-RG, CD.

LUCKY MILLINDER (King)
March 8, 1955, New York

No solos

AL COHN
Jazz Workshop: Four Brass, One Tenor, RCA LPM1161, LP
May 9, 1955, New York

"Every Time" (8b in 1st chorus, 16b in 2nd chorus)

"Rosetta" (16b 2nd tp solo, 4b trades as 2nd of 4 trumpeters)

Reissue: RCA (Spain) 49510, CD; *Al Cohn, Joe Newman, and Freddie Green*, Mosaic Select MS-027, CD.

LENA HORNE with LENNIE HAYTON
It's Love, RCA LPM1148, LP
May–June 1955, New York

"You're the One" (ob)

"Call Me Darling" (ob)

"Love Is the Thing" (intro, ob)

"Then I'll Be Tired of You" (ob)

Reissue: *It's Love/Songs by Burke and Van Heusen*, RCA (UK) 62597, CD.

BENNY PAYNE
Sunny Side Up, **Kapp KL1004, LP**
June 1955, New York
    "Sunny Side Up" (break, 16b)

ERNIE WILKINS
Top Brass, **Savoy MG12044, LP**
November 8, 1955, New York
    "Trick or Treat" (48b following piano solo)
    "58 Market Street" (3rd tp break)
    "Dot's What" (24b 2nd tp solo)
    "Willow Weep for Me" (32b)

Reissue: Savoy 17093, CD.

HANK JONES
November 29, 1955, New York
    "How High the Moon," *The Trio*, Savoy MG12053, LP (32b, 8b)
    "I Think of You with Every Breath I Take," Mort Herbert, *Night People*, Savoy
        MG12073, LP (32b, 8b)

Reissue: "How High the Moon" on Hank Jones, *Bluebird*, Savoy (Japan) 0138, CD; and
Hank Jones, *Bluebird*, Savoy/Atlantic 93009, CD.

Note: Although "I Think of You with Every Breath I Take" was issued on the Mort Herbert
LP, it was recorded during this Hank Jones session.

MARLENE VERPLANCK
With Every Breath I Take, **Savoy MG12058, LP**
November 29, 1955, New York
    "You Leave Me Breathless" (intro, ob)
    "Deep in a Dream" (intro, ob, 16b)
    "We Could Make Such Beautiful Music Together" (ob)
    "I Think of You with Every Breath I Take" (ob)
    "Snuggled on Your Shoulder" (intro, ob, 32b)

Reissue: Savoy 0233, CD; *I Think of You with Every Breath I Take*, Audiophile ACD62, CD.

Note: The Bruyninckx and Lord discographies list Wilder on VerPlanck's December 20,
1955, session as well, but he is not present.

CARMEN McRAE (Jack Pleis)
Torchy, **Decca DL8267, LP**
December 30, 1955, New York
    "Ghost of a Chance" (ob)
    "We'll Be Together Again" (ob)
    "I'm a Dreamer, Aren't We All?" (ob)

Reissue: *Torchy/Blue Moon*, MCA 19392, CD; *The Complete Ralph Burns Sessions Featuring Ben Webster*, Lonehill Jazz 10152, CD.

JOE WILDER
Wilder 'n' Wilder, **Savoy MG12063, LP**
January 19, 1956, New York

Hank Jones (p), Wendell Marshall (b), Kenny Clarke (d)
 "Cherokee" (128b, 64b [4b trades with drummer], 64b)
 "My Heart Stood Still" (64b, 32b, 32b [beginning as 4b trades with piano and drums])
 "My Heart Stood Still" [alt. take] (64b, 32b, 16b)
 "Prelude to a Kiss" (intro, 32b, 16b, coda)
 "Six Bit Blues" (36b, 36b)
 "Mad about the Boy" (32b, 16b)
 "Darn That Dream" (32b, 16b)
 "Darn That Dream" [alt. take] (32b, 16b)

Reissue: All takes on Joe Wilder, *Softly with Feeling*, Savoy ZDS1191, CD; master takes on Savoy SV-0131, CD.

The Most Happy Fella Original Broadway Cast Recording
Columbia 03L-240, LP
May 13, 14, 20, 1956, New York
 Wilder plays lead trumpet throughout. There are no trumpet solos, but he can be heard particularly clearly in Act I, Scene IV (CD 1, tracks 19 and 25) and Act II (CD 2, tracks 6 and 8).

Reissue: *The Most Happy Fella*, Sony Broadway S2K48010, CD.

MORT HERBERT
Night People, **Savoy MG12073, LP**
May 29, 1956, New York
 "Blues for Fred and Faye" (24b, 24b)
 "Mitch's Carol" (48b)

Reissue: Sahib Shihab, *Jazz Sahib: Complete Sextets Sessions 1956–1957*, Fresh Sound 487, CD.

MUNDELL LOWE
New Music of Alec Wilder, **Riverside RLP12-219, LP**
June 12, 19, 1956, New York
 "Tacet for Neurotics" (melody statements)
 "Let's Get Together and Cry" (melody statements)
 "No Plans" (24b melody)

TONY SCOTT
The Touch of Tony Scott, **RCA LPM1353, LP**
July 2, 3, 5, 1956, New York
 No solos

MUNDELL LOWE
New Music of Alec Wilder, **Riverside RLP12-219, LP**
July 19, 1956, New York
 "Suggestion for Bored Dancers" (4b, 2b)
 "Mama Never Dug This Scene" (melody statements)

URBIE GREEN (Johnny Carisi)
All about Urbie Green, **ABC-Paramount 137, LP**

July 31 and August 3, 1956, New York
"Soft Winds" (24b)

Reissue: Fresh Sound 436, CD; *Urbie Green Big Band: Complete 1956–1959 Recordings*, Lone Hill Jazz 10309, CD.

MARY ANN McCALL (Ernie Wilkins)
Easy Living, Regent MG6040, LP
August 14, 16, 23, 1956, New York
"Easy Living" (8b intro melody, ob)
"Mean to Me" (ob)
"In My Solitude" (ob)
"I Thought about You" (8b)
"Deep Purple" (ob, 8b)
"'Deed I Do" (12b)
"It's You or No One" (ob, 16b)
"Something I Dreamed Last Night" (ob)
"It Must Be True" (8b)

Reissue: Savoy 17100, CD; Savoy 93016, CD.

Note: The last two titles were originally issued on *The Girls Sing*, Regent MG6046, LP.

TOM TALBERT
Bix, Duke, Fats, Atlantic 1250, LP
August 24 and September 7, 14, 1956, New York
"Keepin' Out of Mischief Now" (20b)
"Black and Blue" (16b)
"Clothesline Ballet" (32b)
"Bond Street" (16b open tp solo [muted solo is by Nick Travis])
"Candlelights" (32b, 4b)
"In a Mist" (solo passages throughout)
"In the Dark" (solo passages throughout)
"Green Night and Orange Bright" (6b, 32b)
"Do Nothing till You Hear from Me" (8b [trades with alto sax])
"Ko-Ko" (24b, 12b, coda)

Reissue: Modern Concepts 0001, CD; Sea Breeze 3013, CD; Oscar Pettiford and Tom Talbert, *Bix, Duke, Fats*, Lonehill Jazz 10341, CD.

Note: The Bruyninckx discography (copied by Lord) indicates that Wilder does not play on "Do Nothing"; however, he is clearly present.

PATTY McGOVERN (Tom Talbert)
Wednesday's Child, Atlantic 1245, LP
August 1956, New York
"Lonely Town" (24b)
"Winter Song" (intro, ob)
"By Myself" (32b, 8b)
"All in Fun" (ob, 16b)

Reissue: Norma (Japan) NOCD5600, CD.

QUINCY JONES
This Is How I Feel about Jazz, ABC-Paramount 149, LP
September 29, 1956, New York
    No solos

THE BRASS ENSEMBLE OF THE JAZZ AND CLASSICAL MUSIC SOCIETY
John Lewis, composer-arranger; Gunther Schuller, conductor
Music for Brass, Columbia CL941, LP
October 20, 23, 1956, New York
    "Poem for Brass" ("Jazz Suite for Brass") (10b in 2nd movement after Miles Davis
        [flügelhorn] and J. J. Johnson [trombone])

Reissue: Sony (Japan) SRCS5696, CD.

Note: J. J. Johnson was the composer-arranger for "Poem for Brass."

TRIGGER ALPERT
Trigger Happy, Riverside RLP12-225, LP
October 29, 1956, New York
    "Love Me Tomorrow" (16b)
    "Trigger Happy" (32b)

Reissue: *East Coast Sounds: Zoot Sims/Tony Scott/Al Cohn*, OJC 1012, CD.

Note: Also issued as *East Coast Sounds*, Jazzland JLP11, LP.

CHRIS CONNOR (Ralph Sharon)
A Jazz Date with Chris Connor, Atlantic 1286, LP
November 16, 1956, New York
    "It Only Happens When I Dance with You" (8b, 8b)

Reissue: *A Jazz Date with Chris Connor/Chris Craft*, Rhino 71747, CD.

JOHNNY RAY (Ray Ellis)
The Big Beat, Columbia CL961, LP
November 19–20, 1956, New York
    No solos

DINAH WASHINGTON (Quincy Jones)
November 21, 1956, New York
    No solos

TRIGGER ALPERT
Trigger Happy, Riverside RLP12-225, LP
November 23, 30, 1956, New York
    "Looking at You" (16b)
    "I Like the Likes of You" (16b)
    "Trigger Fantasy" (8b, 24b)
    "I Don't Want to Be Alone" (8b melody)

Reissue: *East Coast Sounds: Zoot Sims/Tony Scott/Al Cohn*, OJC 1012, CD.

Note: Also issued as *East Coast Sounds*, Jazzland JLP11, LP.

DINAH WASHINGTON with QUINCY JONES
The Swingin' Miss "D," EmArcy MG36104, LP
December 4, 1956, New York
   No solos

SID BASS
Sound and Fury, Vik LX1084, LP
December 24, 27, 1956; February 18, 1957, New York
   "Sound and Fury" (4b, 4b)
   "Pickin' a Fight" (32b [4b and 2b trades with Charlie Shavers, beginning with Wilder])

Note: Wilder plays in the section on other titles from these sessions.

MUSIC MINUS ONE
Gershwin, Anyone? Music Minus One, vol. 4, MMO1104, LP
1956, New York
   "But Not for Me" [take 3] (24b)
   "But Not for Me" [take 8] (24b)
   "Someone to Watch Over Me" (intro, 48b, ending)
   "'S Wonderful" (intro, 12b, 8b, ending)
   "Fascinating Rhythm" (8b, 8b melody)
   "I've Got a Crush on You" (intro, 16b)
   "Bidin' My Time" (intro, 8b, ending)
   "Somebody Loves Me" (intro, improv passages)

Reissue: Music Minus One J49, LP; Music Minus One J51, LP.

JEAN SHEPHERD (Mitch Leigh/Art Harris)
Into the Unknown with Jazz Music, Abbott 5003, LP
1956, New York
   "Jean Shepherd—Comments" (side 1, track 1) (bugle call on "Call to Post")
   "Socrate's Dream" (16b)
   "Voltaire's Vamp" (16b)
   "Balzac's Bounce" (16b)
   "Jean Shepherd" (side 2, track 9) (bugle call on "Call to Post")

Note: This may be the rarest LP on which Wilder plays; it sold for $1,995 on eBay in June 2003.

HARRY BELAFONTE (Robert De Cormier [a.k.a. Bob Corman])
Island in the Sun, RCA LPM1505, LP
January 26-27, 1957, New York
   "Island in the Sun" [take 2] (fills, ob)
   "Scratch Scratch" (16b, ob)
   "Mama Look at Bubu" [take 2] (intro, 8b, 8b behind flute solo)

Reissue: Bear Family BCD16262, CD (has alternate takes of "Island in the Sun" and "Mama Look at Bubu").

Note: "Mama Look at Bubu" was originally issued on RCA 20-6830, 78 rpm, and RCA 47-6830, 45 rpm.

GEORGE SIRAVO
Old, but New, Vik LX1091, LP
January 31 and February 5, 1957, New York
"Swingin' That Sweet Chariot" (8b, 4b, 8b—all melody statements)

MARILYN MOORE (Don Abney)
Moody Marilyn Moore, Bethlehem BCP73, LP
February and March 1957, New York
"I'm Just a Lucky So and So" (ob)
"Is You Is or Is You Ain't My Baby?" (16b)
"Born to Blow the Blues" (intro, ob)
"Lover Come Back to Me" (16b)
"You're Driving Me Crazy" (16b)
"Trav'lin' All Alone" (ob)
"I Got Rhythm" (16b)

Reissue: Bethlehem (Japan) TOCJ62055, CD; Affinity 763, CD.

A. K. SALIM
Flute Suite, Savoy MG12102, LP
March 21, 1957, New York
"Miltown Blues" (36b)
"Ballin' the Blues" (24b, 4b trades with other horns)
"Pretty Baby" (32b)
"Lopin'" (16b)
"Talk That Talk" (16b)

Reissue: *The Modern Sounds of A. K. Salim: Complete Savoy Recordings, 1957–1958*, Fresh Sound FSRCD474, CD.

BILLY VERPLANCK
Dancing Jazz, Savoy MG12101, LP
March 26, 1957, New York
"Summer Evening" (32b)
"On Top of Old Mountie" (24b)
"I'll Keep Loving You" (16b)
"Day by Day" (16b)
"Oh Gee, Oh Me, Oh My" (16b, 2b break)
"Embraceable You" (ob, 32b)

Reissue: Savoy (Japan) SV0235, CD.

DON REDMAN
Park Avenue Patter, Golden Crest CR3017, LP
April 11, 1957 (and other sessions), New York
"Good Boog Di Goodie" (intro, ob)
"Ballade de Ballet" (6b melody, 8b)
"My Confectionary Baby" (16b)
"My Girl Friday" (ob)
"The Blame's on You" (ob)
"Seedless Grapefruit" (8b)

Reissue: Don Redman, *At the Swing Cats Ball*, Fresh Sound FSRCD393, CD.

HERBIE MANN
Salute to the Flute, Epic LN3395, LP
April 29, 1957, New York
> "When Lights Are Low" (16b 2nd tp solo)
> "Beautiful Love" (32b)
> "Ritual" (16b before Don Stratton 16b solo, 8b before Stratton 8b solo)

Reissue: Herbie Mann, *When Lights Are Low*, Portrait 44095, CD.

MILLARD THOMAS
Harry Belafonte Presents the Millard Thomas Group, RCA LSP1551, LP
May 13–14, 1957, New York
> "Give Me Back Me Shilling" (8b, 24b/16b/16b tp duet with Louis Mucci)
> "'Bye Sweet Dreams" (8b)

A. K. SALIM
Jazz Is Busting Out All Over, Savoy MG12123, LP
July 1, 1957, New York
> "June Is Bustin' Out All Over" (36b)

Reissue: Savoy (Japan) SV0178, CD; *The Modern Sounds of A. K. Salim: Complete Savoy Recordings, 1957–1958*, Fresh Sound FSRCD474, CD.

GEORGE SIRAVO
Swing Hi, Swing Fi, Vik LX1125, LP
July 8 and July 12, 1957, New York
> "Cheerful Little Earful" (8b)
> "Honeysuckle Rose" (intro, 16b)
> "Ida" (8b)

DON REDMAN
Sesac Transcriptions N2101/02/03/04
July 22–26, 1957, New York
> "Ain't Gonna Get Fooled Again" (growl tp passages)
> "Fall Leaves" (16b)
> "Waiting on the Corner" (8b)

Reissue: Don Redman, *At the Swing Cats Ball*, Fresh Sound FSRCD393, CD.

TITO PUENTE
September 12, 1957
> No solos

TONY BENNETT
September 19, 1957, New York
> No solos

BOBBY SHORT
Sing Me a Swing Song, Atlantic 1285, LP
October 18, 1957, New York
> "Ebony Rhapsody" (intro, ob)
> "Wake Up Chillun, Wake Up" (ob)

Reissue: Bobby Short, *Speaking of Love/Sing Me a Swing Song*, Collectables 6843, CD.

BILLY VERPLANCK
Jazz for Playgirls, Savoy MG12121, LP
October 18, 1957, New York
    "Señor Blues" (24b)
    "Miss Spring Blues" (24b)
    "Du-Udah-Udah" (32b)

Reissue: Savoy (Japan) SV0209, CD.

"THE SOUND OF JAZZ" (CBS television series *Seven Lively Arts*)
December 8, 1957, New York
    "Fast and Happy Blues" ("Open All Night") (ensemble)
    "I Left My Baby" (ensemble)
    "Dickie's Dream" (32b 1st tp solo)

Reissue: *The Real Sound of Jazz*, Pumpkin 116, LP; Bandstand 1517, CD; Vintage Jazz Classics 2001, VHS; MVD DJ108, DVD.

Note: Wilder appeared on the show as part of the Count Basie All Stars. He was not present at the December 5, 1957, rehearsal captured on *The Sound of Jazz*, Columbia CL 1098, LP.

DIAHANN CARROLL
Best Beat Forward, Vik LX1131, LP
1957, New York
    "S'posin" (32b)

BOBBY DUKOFF (Charlie Shirley)
Tender Sax, RCA LPM1446, LP
1957, New York
    "Christopher Columbus" (8b)

NEAL HEFTI
Pardon My Doo-Wah, Epic LN3481
1957, New York
    "Coral Reef" (24b with vocal group)

Reissue: *Pardon My Doo-Wah/Hefti Hot 'n Hearty*, Collectables 6876, CD.

DON REDMAN
Dance, Dance, Dance, Urania UJ1211, LP
1957, New York
    "Dum Dum De Dum" (32b)
    "Mad Love Blues" (muted ob)
    "Why Didn't I?" (16b)

Reissue: Don Redman, *Star Dreams*, Drive Archive 41211, CD.

JOE REISMAN
Party Night at Joe's, RCA LPM1476, LP
1957, New York
    "Seven Come Eleven" (16, 8b [trades with Jimmy Maxwell])
    "Bubble Boogie" (12b)

"Light 'n' Polite" (16b [4b trades with Al DeRisi, Bernie Glow, Jimmy Maxwell, with
  Wilder going second])
"Five O'Clock Whistle" (16b)

Reissue: Fresh Sound FSR180, LP.

MICHEL LEGRAND
Legrand in Rio, **Columbia CL1139, LP**
Late 1957 or early 1958, New York
  No solos

Note: Although Wilder (and other leading American jazz artists) are listed as playing on
this album in most discographies, research by Brian Priestly reveals that it was recorded in
Paris with French musicians. See Fernando Ortiz de Urbina, "ND—Michel Legrand:
Legrand in Rio," *Easy Does It* blog, December 16, 2012, available at http://jazzontherecord
.blogspot.com/2012/12/nd-michel-legrand-legrand-in-rio.html.

JIMMY GIUFFRE
The Music Man, **Atlantic 1276, LP**
January 2, 3, 6, 1958, New York
  "The Wells Fargo Wagon" (4b and 2b trades among Phil Sunkel, JW, Nick Travis,
    in this order)

Reissue: *The Jimmy Giuffre 3/The Music Man*, Collectables 6248, CD; *The Complete
Capitol and Atlantic Recordings of Jimmy Giuffre*, Mosaic MD6-176, CD.

Note: The order of the solo trades given here differs from the solo order listed on the
Atlantic LP.

JIMMY MUNDY
On a Mundy Flight, **Epic LN3475, LP**
March 21, 1958, New York
  "Little Girl" (32b)
  "I Found a New Baby" (16b, 8b, 32b)

PEARL BAILEY (Don Redman)
St. Louis Blues, **Roulette R25037, LP**
April 21–22, 1958, New York
  "Way Down South Where the Blues Began" (16b)

MARIAN BRUCE
Halfway to Dawn, **Riverside RLP12-826, LP**
April 1958, New York
  "Lucky to Be Me" (intro, ob)
  "Let Me Love You" (ob)
  "It Never Entered My Mind" (ob)
  "Things Are Looking Up" (ob)
  "Something to Live For" (ob, 12b)
  "Looking for a Boy" (ob)
  "My One and Only" (intro, 16b, ending)
  "A Ship without a Sail" (ob)
  "No One Ever Tells You" (intro, ob, ending)
  "The Gentleman Is a Dope" (intro, ob, ending)

BILLY VERPLANCK
The Soul of Jazz, World Wide MG20002, LP
May 5, 1958, New York
  "Royal Garden Blues" (36b)
  "I Can't Believe It" (32b melody with ensemble, 32b)
  "Where You Gonna Run To?" (48b call and response with ensemble, 32b)
  "Each Side of the River" (48b)
  "You Gotta Be a Good Man" (48b)

LARRY SONN
Jazz Band: Having a Ball! Dot DLP9005, LP
June 24, 1958, New York
  No solos

MICHEL LEGRAND
Legrand Jazz, Columbia CL1250, LP
June 30, 1958, New York
  "Night in Tunisia" (32b 1st tp solo, 4b and 2b trades, beginning with JW)

Reissue: Philips 830-074, CD.

DELLA REESE (Sy Oliver)
The Story of the Blues, Jubilee JLP 1095, LP
July 17, 1958, New York
  No solos

RUTH BROWN
Miss Rhythm, Atlantic 8026, LP
July 30, 1958, New York

Note: Wilder plays only on "Why Me?" The Bruyninckx and Lord discographies list Joe Wilder on another title from this session, "This Little Girl's Gone Rockin'," but no trumpets are audible.

HENRI RENÉ
Compulsion to Swing, RCA LPM1947, LP
August 26, 29, 1958, New York
  No solos

GEORGE SIRAVO
Swingin' Hi-Fi in Studio A, RCA LPM1970, LP; *Swingin' Stereo in Studio A*, RCA
  LSP1970, LP
September 26, 1958, New York
  "Lover" (32b)

Reissue: *Swingin' Stereo in Studio A*, BMG 7432135741, CD.

A. K. SALIM
Blues Suite, Savoy MG 12132, LP
September 26 and October 6, 1958, New York
  No solos

GEORGE RUSSELL
New York, N.Y., Decca DL9216, LP
November 24, 1958, New York
 No solos

STEVE ALLEN
And All That Jazz, Dot DLP3194, LP
November 25–26, 1958, New York
 "Pleadin'" (8b)
 "Walkin' Shoes" (8b)
 "Bluesville" (16b)

Note: Jimmy Nottingham is the trumpet soloist on other tracks. Wilder is unlikely to be present on those titles because there was probably only one trumpeter at each session.

JOE WILDER
The Pretty Sound, Columbia CL1372, LP
December 1, 1958, New York
Urbie Green (trombone), Jerome Richardson (sax, flute), Phil Bodner (sax, English horn, flute, clarinet), Hank Jones (p), Al Casamenti (g), George Duvivier (b), Don Lamond (d), Mike Colicchio (arranger), Teo Macero (arranger)
 "Harbor Lights" (32b, 8b, coda)
 "The Boy Next Door" (intro, 40b, coda)
 "Blue Moon" (16b, 8b, 16b)

Reissue: Joe Wilder, *The Pretty Sound/Jazz from Peter Gunn*, Collectables COL7550, CD.

JOE WILDER
The Pretty Sound, Columbia CL1372, LP
December 3, 1958, New York
Urbie Green (trombone), Jerome Richardson (sax, clarinet), Jerry Sanfino (sax, flute, clarinet), Hank Jones (p), Al Casamenti (g), George Duvivier (b), Osie Johnson (d), Mike Colicchio (arranger), Teo Macero (arranger)
 "Guys and Dolls" (32b, 8b, tag)
 "It's So Peaceful in the Country" (intro, 32b, 8b)
 "Greensleeves" (24b, 32b)
 "Lullaby" (22b, 22b, 8b)

Reissue: Joe Wilder, *The Pretty Sound/Jazz from Peter Gunn*, Collectables COL7550, CD.

CAB CALLOWAY
Hi-De-Ho Man, RCA LPM2021, LP
December 5, 15, 16, 1958, New York
 "Minnie the Moocher" (ob)
 "It Ain't Necessarily So" (ob)
 "St. James Infirmary" (ob)

BOBBY DONALDSON
Dixieland New York, World Wide MG20005, LP
December 15, 1958, New York
 No solos

JIM TIMMENS
Gilbert and Sullivan Revisited, **Warner Bros. 1278, LP**
December 18, 22, 1958, New York
    "Tit-Willow" (32b with ensemble, 32b, 32b with ensemble)
    "We Sail the Ocean Blue" (24b)

Reissue: Hallmark, MP3.

Note: The trumpet soloist on "We Sail the Ocean Blue" is misidentified as Donald Byrd in the liner notes.

REX STEWART and COOTIE WILLIAMS
Porgy and Bess Revisited, **Warner Bros. 1260, LP**
Late 1958, New York
    No solos

PEARL BAILEY
Sings Porgy and Bess and Other Gershwin Melodies, **Roulette R25063, LP**
1958, New York
    No solos

BOBBY BYRNE
The Great Themes of America's Greatest Bands, **Grand Award 225, LP**
1958, New York
    "Take the A Train" (JW recreates Ray Nance's famous solo with Ellington)

ROY HAMILTON (Neal Hefti)
With All My Love, **Epic LN3519, LP**
1958, New York
    "I Miss You So" (intro, ob, ending)
    "Strange" (4b)

Reissue: Collectables 6651, CD.

DONNA HIGHTOWER
Take One, **Capitol T1133, LP**
1958, New York
    "Anytime, Anyday, Anywhere" (ob)
    "I Get a Kick Out of You" (ob)
    "Please Don't Take Your Love Away from Me" (4b intro, ob)
    "Baby, Get Lost" (ob)
    "There, I've Said It Again" (ob)
    "C'est la Vie" (ob)
    "Lover Come Back to Me" (16b intro, ob, ending)
    "Maybe You'll Be There" (ob)
    "Too Young" (8b)
    "Because of You" (8b)
    "Trouble in Mind" (ob)

Reissue: Fresh Sound FSRCD561, CD.

PEARL BAILEY (Don Redman)
More Songs for Adults Only, **Roulette R25101, LP**

1958-1959, New York
No solos

BOBBY SHORT
The Mad Twenties, Atlantic 1302, LP
January 14, 1959, New York
"Heebie Jeebies" (ob)
"I'm Cert'ny Gonna See 'Bout That" (16b with ensemble)
"That's My Weakness Now" (16b, 8b, ob)
"Tiger Rag" (32b)

Reissue: *The Mad Twenties/My Personal Property*, Collectables 6845, CD.

JOE WILDER
Jazz from Peter Gunn, Columbia CL1319, LP
January 18, 1959, New York
Hank Jones (p), Milt Hinton (b), John Cresci Jr. (d)
"Not from Dixie" (32b melody, 32b, 32b, 16b melody)
"A Quiet Gas" (intro, 32b melody, 16b, tag)
"Brief and Breezy" (intro, 32b [trades with piano], 32b, 32b [trades with piano and bass], 16b)
"Joanna" (intro, 16b, 4b)
"The Floater" (32b, 32b, 16b melody, 8b melody)
"A Profound Gas" (intro, 32b melody, 32b, 16b melody)
"Slow and Easy" (12b melody, 24b, 4b melody)
"Brothers Go to Mother's" (32b melody, 32b, 16b melody, tag)
"Fallout" (24b, 60b, fade ending)
"Blues for Mother's" (32b, 32b, 8b, ending)

Reissue: Joe Wilder, *The Pretty Sound/Jazz from Peter Gunn*, Collectables COL7550, CD.

JIM TIMMENS
Hallelujah! Spirituals in Hi-fi Brass, RCA LPM2029, LP
February 10, 19, 1959, New York
"Joshua Fit the Battle of Jericho" (16b)
"The Blind Man" (18b open horn melody with ensemble)
"The Gospel Train" (8b)
"Nobody Knows the Trouble I've Seen" (12b with ensemble)
"It's Me (Standin' in the Need of Prayer)" (2b trades with Doc Severinson, who begins)

Note: The stereo version (RCA LSP2029) is titled *Hallelujah! Spirituals in Stereo Brass*.

VIC SCHOEN with LES BROWN
Impact! Band Meets Band, Kapp KRL4504, LP
February 23-24, 1959, New York
"Oh, Those Martian Blues" (2b trades with Dick Collins, Jimmy Nottingham)

BILLIE HOLIDAY (Ray Ellis)
Billie Holiday, MGM E3764, LP
March 11, 1959, New York
No solos

GEORGE RUSSELL
New York, N.Y., Decca DL9216, LP
March 25, 1959, New York
   No solos

PERRY COMO (Mitchell Ayres)
Como Swings, RCA LSP2343, LP
April 9, 1959, New York
   No solos

Note: Although Wilder is not included in the album credits for this session, he recalls taking part, probably subbing for one of the listed trumpeters: Jimmy Maxwell, Bernie Glow, James Milazzo, or Bernie Privin.

JIM TIMMENS
Showboat Revisited, Warner Bros. W1324, LP
April 24, 1959, New York
   "After the Ball" (16b)

JAYE P. MORGAN (Ray Ellis)
Slow and Easy, MGM E3774, LP
May 18, 1959, New York
   "I Get the Blues When It Rains" (4b intro, ob, ending)
   "I Thought about You" (ob)
   "Just for Two" (ob, 12b, ending)
   "Another Martini, Another Call" (intro, ob)
   "Did I Remember?" (ob)

JOE WILDER
The Pretty Sound, Columbia CL1372, LP
May 22, 1959, New York
Urbie Green (trombone), Herbie Mann (flute), Hank Jones (p), Milt Hinton (b), John Cresci Jr. (d), Mike Colicchio (arranger), Teo Macero (arranger)
   "Caravan" (16b, 64b, 64, fade ending)
   "I Hear Music" (intro, 32b melody with ensemble, 32b, fade ending)
   "Autumn in New York" (32b, 32b, coda)

Reissue: Joe Wilder, *The Pretty Sound/Jazz from Peter Gunn*, Collectables COL7550, CD.

QUINCY JONES
The Birth of a Band, Mercury MG20444, LP
May 26–28 and June 22, 1959, New York
   No solos

WILL BRADLEY and JOHNNY GUARNIERI
Live Echoes of the Best in Big Band Boogie Woogie, RCA LPM2098, LP
June 22 and 28, 1959, New York
   "Beat Me Daddy, Eight to the Bar" (12b)
   "One O'Clock Boogie" (12b)

JOHN LEWIS
Odds against Tomorrow: Original Music from the Motion Picture Soundtrack, United
   Artists UAL4061, LP
July 16, 17, 20, 1959, New York
   "Main Theme: Odds against Tomorrow" (melody statement)

Reissue: MGM 1005697, DVD.

KIRBY STONE FOUR (Jimmy Carroll)
The Kirby Stone Touch, Columbia CL1356, LP
1959, New York
   "Volare" (trades with vocal group throughout)

LITTLE, DANE, AND MASON
Presenting Little, Dane and Mason, Mercury MG20473, LP
1959, New York
   "Fugue for Tinhorns" (intro)
   "Matador" (intro)

MUSIC MINUS ONE
Blues in the Night, Music Minus One MMO1007, LP
1959, New York
   "Birth of the Blues" (16b, coda)
   "Boulevard of Broken Dreams" (32b, 16b)
   "Can't We Be Friends?" (8b, 32b)
   "Sweet Georgia Brown" (32b, 32b [4b trades with rhythm section], 8b)
   "Brother, Can You Spare a Dime?" (4b, 4b, ob)
   "Blues in the Night" (24b, 4b, coda)
   "Louisiana Hayride" (24b, 8b)

DAKOTA STATON (Sid Feller)
Time to Swing, Capitol T1241, LP
1959, New York
   "Baby, Don't You Cry" (intro)
   "Until the Real Thing Comes Along" (ob)
   "If I Should Lose You" (intro, ob, ending)
   "But Not for Me" (8b)

Reissue: DRG 8509, CD.

CREED TAYLOR ORCHESTRA (Kenyon Hopkins)
Ping Pang Pong: The Swinging Ball, ABC-Paramount 325, LP
Early 1960, New York
   "Don't Get around Much Anymore" (4b)
   "Willow, Weep for Me" (4b)
   "Lullaby in Rhythm" (4b)
   "Cheek to Cheek" (8b, 4b)
   "Goodbye" (4b, melody)
   "I've Got My Love to Keep Me Warm" (8b)

JOHN LEWIS
The Golden Striker, Atlantic 1334, LP
February 12, 15, 16, 1960, New York
  "Odds against Tomorrow" (20b opening melody, 14b melody at end)
  "La Cantatrice" (8b melody)

Reissue: *The Golden Striker/Jazz Abstractions*, Collectables 6252, CD.

JACKIE PARIS (Irving Joseph)
Sings the Lyrics of Ira Gershwin, Time 70009, LP
February 23, 1960, New York
  No solos

THE ZENITHS (Richard Wess)
Makin' the Scene, Atlantic 8043, LP
April 13, 1960, New York
  No solos

JANICE MARS (Milton Rosenstock)
Introducing Janice Mars, Baq Room BRR0725-2860, CD
July 25–28, 1960, New York
  "Take Love Easy" (intro, ob)
  "Take It Slow, Joe" (intro, ob)
  "The Inchworm" (ob)
  "Battle Hymn of the Republic" (countermelody throughout)

Note: "Battle Hymn of the Republic" is unlisted on the CD but is track 12.

OSCAR BROWN JR.
Sin and Soul, Columbia CL1577, LP
July, August, October 1960, New York
  "But I Was Cool" (16b)

Reissue: *Sin and Soul . . . and Then Some*, Columbia Legacy CK64994, CD.

HUGO MONTENEGRO
Bongos + Brass, Time S2014, LP
August 9, 18, 22, 1960, New York
  No solos

TITO PUENTE with BUDDY MORROW
Revolving Bandstand, RCA LSP2299, LP
August 29–30, 1960, New York
  No solos

FREDERICK FENNELL
Frederick Fennell Conducts Gershwin, Mercury PPS2006, LP
September 26–27, 1960, New York
  No solos

LAVERN BAKER (Stan Applebaum)
November 14, 1960, New York
  No solos

DIZZY GILLESPIE (Lalo Schifrin)
Gillespiana, Verve 8394, LP
November 14–16, 1960, New York
    No solos

RAY CHARLES (Quincy Jones and Ralph Burns)
Genius + Soul = Jazz, Impulse A2, LP
December 27, 1960, New York
    No solos

BROOK BENTON (Clyde Otis)
Songs I Love to Sing, Mercury MG20602, LP
1960, New York
    "Moonlight in Vermont" (intro, ob)
    "It's Been a Long, Long Time" (intro, ob, ending)
    "Lover Come Back to Me" (intro, ob, ending)
    "Why Try to Change Me?" (intro, ob, ending)
    "September Song" (ob)
    "Oh, What It Seemed to Be" (intro, ob, ending)
    "Baby, Won't You Please Come Home?" (ob, ending)
    "They Can't Take That Away from Me" (intro, ob, 6b, ending)
    "I'll Be Around" (ob, ending)
    "I Don't Know Enough about You" (ob)

Reissue: Verve 000075502, CD.

HENRY JEROME (Dick Jacobs)
Brazen Brass Goes Hollywood, Decca DL74085, LP
1960, New York
    "Theme from *A Summer Place*" (open horn melody)

JOHNNY MATHIS (Glenn Osser)
Johnny's Mood, Columbia CL1526, LP
1960, New York
    "I'm Gonna Laugh You out of My Life" (ending)
    "Stay Warm" (intro, ending)
    "I'm So Lost" (intro)
    "April in Paris" (ob)
    "I'm in the Mood for Love" (ending)

Reissue: *Johnny's Mood/Faithfully*, Sony/Columbia 516020, CD.

The Sand Castle: Music from the Motion Picture
Alec Wilder, composer-orchestrator; Samuel Baron, conductor
Columbia CL1455, LP
1960, New York
    "Swing Music" (8, 4b melody)
    "Ragtime Music" (8b melody)

Since Life Began: Music from the Soundtrack
Alec Wilder, composer-orchestrator; Samuel Baron, conductor

Limited edition LP by *Life* magazine
January 23, 1961, New York

Note: Information about this recording comes from the LP, which lists the credits and recording date. This music was composed for a *Life* film about fashion. Other musicians in the orchestra include Urbie Green, Jimmy Buffington, Bernie Leighton, Milt Hinton, and Sol Gubin. Wilder may be heard playing melody or brief solos in movements 2, 8, 13, and 14.

SAM COOKE (Sammy Lowe)
My Kind of Blues, RCA LPM2392, LP
May 19, 1961, New York
    "Trouble in Mind" (plunger fill)

Reissue: *The Wonderful World of Sam Cooke/My Kind of Blues*, Soul Jam 600814, CD; Sam Cooke, *The Man Who Invented Soul*, RCA 88697921492, CD.

DIZZY GILLESPIE (J. J. Johnson, composer-arranger; Gunther Schuller, conductor)
Perceptions, Verve 8411, LP
May 22, 1961, New York
    No solos

Winston Churchill: The Valiant Years
Richard Rodgers, composer; Robert Emmet Dolan, musical director-conductor
ABC-Paramount 387, LP
June 8–9, 1961, New York

Note: This album includes music composed for the ABC television series of the same name, which aired from 1960 to 1961. Ray Crisara played first and Wilder second trumpet for both the series and the album.

GENE KRUPA (George Williams)
Percussion King, Verve 8414, LP
June 12, 1961, New York
    "Valse Triste" (12b)

Note: Also released as *Classics in Percussion*, Verve 8450, LP.

SAM COOKE (Ralph Burns)
August 9, 1961, New York
    No solos

MARK MURPHY (Ernie Wilkins)
Rah, Riverside RLP9395, LP
September 19, 22, 1961, New York
    No solos

OLIVER NELSON
Afro-American Sketches, Prestige 7225, LP
September 29, 1961, New York
    No solos

GIL EVANS
Into the Hot, Impulse A-9, LP
October 31, 1961, New York
  No solos

FREDERICK FENNELL
Frederick Fennell Conducts Cole Porter, Mercury PPS2024, LP
November 20-21, 1961, New York
  No solos

HARRY BELAFONTE (Jimmie Jones)
The Midnight Special, RCA LPM2449, LP
1961, New York
  "Memphis Tennessee" (ob)
  "Gotta Travel On" (ob throughout)
  "On Top of Old Smokey" (ob)
  "Makes a Long Time Man Feel Bad" (ob)
  "Michael, Row the Boat Ashore" (ob)

Reissue: Harry Belafonte, *3 Originals*, BMG 743217795221, CD.

URBIE GREEN
The Persuasive Trombone of Urbie Green, vol. 2, Command RS33-838, LP
1961, New York
  No solos

The Hustler: Original Soundtrack Recording (Kenyon Hopkins)
Kapp KL1264, LP
1961, New York
  "Bert's Theme" (12b)
  "The Winner" (melody statements)

Reissue: El Records 2932243, CD.

LEONTYNE PRICE (Leonard De Paur)
Swing Low, Sweet Chariot, RCA Red Seal LM2600, LP
1961, New York
  No solos

DELLA REESE (Mercer Ellington)
Special Delivery, RCA LPM2391, LP
1961, New York
  No solos

JOE WILDER
The Sound of the Bugle, Choice MG505, LP
ca. 1961, New York
  "First Call"
  "Reveille"
  "Assemble/Divisions"
  "Mess"

"Stable/Saluting Gun Crews to Quarters"
"Water"
"Guard Mounting"
"Full Dress/General Muster"
"Overcoats"
"Drill"
"Boots and Saddles/Fightquarters"
"Adjutants Call"
"To Arms/Torpedo Defense Quarters"
"Church"
"Recall"
"To the Colors/Morning Colors"
"Mail"
"Boat (Army and Marine)"
"Liberty Call (Marine)"
"General Quarters (Navy)"
"Pay Call"
"Retreat"
"Tattoo"
"Call to Quarters"
"Taps/Evening Colors"

Note: This album, issued by a subsidiary of Savoy Records, consists of Wilder demonstrating bugle calls. Where two titles are indicated with a slash, the first refers to the Army designation and the second to the Navy designation for the call.

GENE KRUPA with BUDDY RICH (George Williams)
Burnin' Beat, Verve 8471, LP
January 18-19, 1962, New York
    "Wham (Rebop, Boom, Bam)" (8b)
    "King Porter Stomp" (24b with ensemble)
    "Night Train" (12b)

Note: "Wham" was recorded at this session but was not issued on the album. All titles, including "Wham" and another originally unissued track, are available on private CD from http://www.jazzlegends.com.

ELLA FITZGERALD (Bill Doggett)
Rhythm Is My Business, Verve 4056, LP
January 30-31, 1962, New York
    "Show Me the Way to Get out of This World" (16b)
    "I'll Always Be in Love with You" (muted fill at end)

Reissue: Verve 559-513, CD.

ETTA JONES (Oliver Nelson)
From the Heart, Prestige 7214, LP
February 9, 1962, New York
    "You Came a Long Way from St. Louis" (16b)

Reissue: OJC 1016, CD.

Note: The OJC CD misidentifies the tracks on which horns and/or strings are present.

TADD DAMERON
The Magic Touch, **Riverside RLP419, LP**
February 27, 1962, New York
　　"Dial 'B' for Beauty" (12b melody with ensemble, 12b, coda)
　　"Bevan's Birthday" (32b, 8b, coda)

Reissue: OJC 143, CD.

JIMMY SMITH (Oliver Nelson)
Bashin': The Unpredictable Jimmy Smith, **Verve 8474, LP**
March 26, 28, 1962, New York
　　No solos

BENNY GOODMAN
Benny Goodman in Moscow, **RCA LOC6008, LP**
July 3–8, 1962, Moscow
　　"Meet the Band" (4b)
　　"I Got It Bad (and That Ain't Good)" (48b, coda)
　　"Swift as the Wind" (16b)
　　"Swift as the Wind" [alt. take] (16b 1st tp solo)

Reissue: All titles except "Swift as the Wind" alternate on Vocalion CDLK 4489, CD; Giants of Jazz 53195, CD. "Swift as the Wind" alternate on *Benny Goodman*, vol. 4: *Big Band Recordings*, MusicMasters CIJ60201 (previously 5017), CD.

Note: "I Got It Bad" is a feature for Wilder with the rhythm section.

PAT THOMAS
Moody's Mood, **MGM E4206, LP**
August 14–17, 1962, New York

Note: The titles on this LP were originally recorded for Verve but were not issued on that label. Although the Bruyninckx and Lord discographies list three trumpets (including Wilder) as present on several titles, none are audible.

THE FOUR AYALONS (Alexander Vlas Datzenko)
Sing Along with Israel, **ATE Records AC633, LP**
1962, New York
　　"Hava Nagila" (solo interlude)
　　"Mul Har Sinai" (8b)

Note: Wilder plays first trumpet on these and all other titles.

MARTY GOLD
24 Pieces of Gold, **RCA VPM6012, LP**
1962, New York
　　"Don't Blame Me" (8b)
　　"You Stepped out of a Dream" (8b)

Sound Tour: France (Kenyon Hopkins)
Verve V6-50000, LP
1962, New York
　　"Train Bleu" (12b, 12b)

"Voyage à Bicyclette" (8b)
"Port de Peche" (8b melody, 8b melody)
"Pays des Bikinis" (4b)
"Scene de Rue" (several short solo passages)
"Theatre (Can Can)" (8b, 2b)
"Place Pigalle" (4b, 12b)
"Café Terrasse" (8b, 8b, 4b)

Note: This is one in a series of four LPs that was produced in collaboration with *Esquire* magazine depicting, according to the album sleeve, "impressions in sound of an American on tour." Wilder, Phil Woods, and Phil Bodner are listed as soloists on this album.

Sound Tour: Spain (Kenyon Hopkins)
Verve V6-50001, LP
1962, New York
"Doves of Majorca (La Paloma)" (4b, 4b)
"Timid Toro" (4b, short melody passages)

Note: This is one in the series of four LPs produced in collaboration with *Esquire* magazine. Wilder, Doc Severinsen, and Hank Jones are listed as soloists on this album. Phil Woods is not listed but can be heard on clarinet and alto sax.

Sound Tour: Italy (Kenyon Hopkins)
Verve V6-50002, LP
1962, New York
"Arrival Milano (Funiculi Funicula)" (4b, 4b)
"Bella Roma (Ciribiribin)" (4b 1st tp solo)
"Sorrento (Torna a Surriento)" (open horn melody statements)
"Seaside (Santa Lucia)" (4b open horn)
"Gondola (Barcarolle)" (16b)
"Roman Nights" (16b, ob)
"Early Morning Song (Mattinata)" (ob)
"All' Albergo" (4b)

Note: This is one in the series of four LPs produced in collaboration with *Esquire* magazine. Wilder, Doc Severinsen, and Phil Woods are listed as soloists on this album.

Sound Tour: Hawaii (Kenyon Hopkins)
Verve V6-50003, LP
1962, New York

Note: This is one in the series of four LPs produced in collaboration with *Esquire* magazine. Although Wilder, Phil Woods, Jerome Richardson, and Phil Bodner are listed as soloists on this album, no trumpet is audible, and it is unlikely that Wilder is present. Wilder's erroneous listing in the credits is probably because of his presence on other albums in the series.

LOUIS BELLSON and GENE KRUPA (Fred Thompson)
The Mighty Two, **Roulette 52098, LP**
ca. April 1963, New York
No solos

AMANDA AMBROSE (Bobby Scott)
The Amazing Amanda Ambrose, RCA LPM2742, LP
August 3, 1963, New York
    "C. C. Rider" (intro, ob, 12b)
    "House of the Rising Sun" (ob)
    "What Are the Parts of a Flower?" (ob)

JOHNNY HODGES (Klaus Ogerman)
Sandy's Gone, Verve 8561, LP
September 5, 1963, New York
    No solos

ETHEL ENNIS (Sid Bass)
Once Again . . . , RCA LPM2862, LP
December 19, 1963, New York
    No solos

MARTY GOLD
Sounds Unlimited, RCA LPM2714, LP
ca. 1963, New York
    "The Donkey Serenade" (4b, 12b)
    "When Your Lover Has Gone" (8b, 8b with ensemble)
    "Canadian Sunset" (8b with ensemble)

Reissue: *Sounds Unlimited/For Sound's Sake*, Vocalion (UK) CDLK4479, CD.

JOE WILDER
Joe Wilder, Trumpet, Golden Crest RE7007, LP
ca. early 1964, New York
    "Sonata for Trumpet and Piano" (Alec Wilder)
    Trumpet Concerto (Haydn)
    "First Concert Piece" (Brandt)
    "The Swan" (Saint-Saëns)
    "Allegro" (Fiocco)
    "A Trumpeter's Lullaby" (Leroy Anderson)

Note: Wilder is featured on all tracks. He was accompanied by pianists Milton Kaye (on "Sonata for Trumpet and Piano") and Harriet Wingreen (on all other pieces).

SHIRLEY SCOTT (Oliver Nelson)
Great Scott! Impulse A67, LP
May 20, 1964, New York
    No solos

JIMMY SMITH (Billy Byers)
Christmas '64, Verve V8604, LP
September 29, 1964, New York
    No solos

BILLY TAYLOR (Oliver Nelson)
Midnight Piano, Capitol T2302, LP

October 13, 1964, New York
No solos

J.J.JOHNSON
The Dynamic Sound of J. J. Johnson, RCA LPM3350, LP
December 9, 1964, New York
No solos

MARTY GOLD
For Sound's Sake, RCA LPM2787, LP
ca. 1964, New York
"Baubles, Bangles, and Beads" (8b)
"Rockin' Chair" (16b, 12b, tag)
"Mood Indigo" (8b with ensemble, 8b, 8b with ensemble, 4b with ensemble, coda)

MARTY GOLD
Suddenly It's Springtime, RCA LPM2882, LP
1964, New York
"Don't Take Your Love from Me" (16b, 16b, tag)
"How Long Has This Been Going On?" (8b)

KENYON HOPKINS
The Reporter: The Original Music from the CBS Television Network Series, Columbia
CL2269, LP
1964, New York
No solos

MORGANA KING (Torrie Zito)
With a Taste of Honey, Mainstream 56015, LP
1964, New York
"Easy to Love" (8b)

Reissue: Mainstream CD0707, CD.

HUGO MONTENEGRO
Montenegro and Mayhem, Time S2176, LP
1964, New York
No solos

Open the Door and See All the People **Film Soundtrack**
Alec Wilder, composer; Samuel Baron, conductor
Fine Recording FR1291, LP (limited edition)
1964, New York
"5/4 Dance" (8b melody)
"Taylor Made Theme" (melody statements)
"Lonely Girl" (14b melody, 2b melody)
"Unbelievable (Version 2)" (14b)
"Dance for B.B." (20b melody)

HAROLD ARLEN (Peter Matz)
Harold Sings Arlen, Columbia OS2920, LP

November 1965, New York
"For Every Man There's a Woman" (ob, ending)

Reissue: Columbia 52722, CD.

STAFF SERGEANT BARRY SADLER (Sid Bass)
Ballads of the Green Berets, RCA LPM3547, LP
December 18, 1965, New York
No solos

RAY MARTIN
Goldfinger and Other Music from James Bond Thrillers, RCA Camden CAL913, LP
1965, New York
"The James Bond Theme" (8b, 12b trades with alto sax)
"Under the Mango Tree" (8b)
"From Russia with Love" (4b, 4b)
"Bond's Lament" (4b, 4b)
"Jamaica Jump Up" (8b)

Note: Although he is known for the style, Wilder has confirmed that the growl trumpet solo on "Goldfinger" is not by him.

SONNY STITT
What's New, Roulette R25343, LP
July 28 or 30, 1966, New York
"I've Got the World on a String" (16b)

LEONARD FEATHER'S ENCYCLOPEDIA OF JAZZ ALL STARS (Oliver Nelson)
Encyclopedia of Jazz, vol. 1: *The Blues*, Verve 8677, LP
November 3, 1966, New York
No solos

LEONARD FEATHER'S ENCYCLOPEDIA OF JAZZ ALL STARS (Oliver Nelson)
The Sound of Feeling and the Sound of Oliver Nelson, Verve 8743, LP
November 4, 1966, New York
No solos

TONY BENNETT (Marion Evans)
Tony Makes It Happen! Columbia CL2653, LP
November 26, 1966; January 12, 18, 27, 1976, New York
"Don't Get Around Much Anymore" (8b)

Reissue: *Tony Bennett Jazz*, Columbia CGK40424, CD.

SCREAMIN' JAY HAWKINS
December 29, 1966, New York
No solos

DICK HYMAN
Brasilian Impressions, Command RS33-911, LP
ca. early 1967, New York
"A Time for Love" (8b)

"Samba de Duas Notas" (8b, 8b)
"Message to Michael" (8b)
"Eleanor Rigby" (10b melody)

PEE WEE RUSSELL (Oliver Nelson)
The Spirit of '67, **Impulse A9147, LP**
February 14, 1967, New York
No solos

LEON BIBB (Artie Butler and Jimmy Wisner)
The Now Composers, **Philips PHM200-249, LP**
July 27, 1967, New York
No solos

LOUIS ARMSTRONG (Tommy Goodman)
What a Wonderful World, **ABC 650, LP**
August 16, 1967, New York
Wilder plays on "The Sunshine of Love" and "What a Wonderful World" but does not
solo.

AL HIRT (Teacho Wiltshire and Paul Griffin)
Soul in the Horn, **RCA LPM3878, LP**
September 16, 1967, New York
No solos

BURT BACHARACH
Reach Out, **A&M SP4131, LP**
1967, New York
"Alfie" (4b intro [JW backed by Thad Jones], melody in first chorus [TJ backed by JW],
ending [JW backed by TJ])
"A House Is Not a Home" (intro, melody)
"Lisa" (ending)

Reissue: A&M 314520297, CD.

EARTHQUAKERS (Issacher Miron)
1967, New York
"Dreaming in the Moonlight," Star 101, 45 rpm (open horn melody statements)

JACKIE GLEASON
Doublin' in Brass, **Capitol SW2880, LP**
1967, New York
"Ti-Pi-Tin" (12b, 12b)
"Cabaret" (12b)

Reissue: *A Taste of Brass for Lovers Only/Doublin' in Brass*, Capitol/EMI 81356, CD.

HENRY JEROME
Henry's Trumpets, **United Artists 3620, LP**
1967, New York
"Alfie" (10b, 6b, 4b, 4b, coda)

KISSIN' COUSINS with LEW DAVIES AND HIS ORCHESTRA (Lew Davies)
Listen to Your Heart, Project 3 PR5008, LP
1967, New York
    "Maybe Today" (ob)
    "Love in Bloom" (8b)

PEARL BAILEY (Louis Bellson)
The Real Pearl, Project 3 PR5022, LP
1968, New York
    "Nobody" (ob)

TONY BENNETT (Torrie Zito)
I've Gotta Be Me, Columbia CS9882, LP
February 25, 1969, New York
    No solos

LES McCANN (William Fischer)
Comment, Atlantic 1547, LP
August 20-21, 1969, New York
    No solos

THE DICK CAVETT SHOW
The Dick Cavett Show: Comic Legends, Shout Factory D4D30164, DVD
September 19, 1969, New York
    Wilder can be seen playing the fanfare of the opening theme as well as on the closing
        theme (disc 1, title 2, chapter 7) on this show, which featured guests Woody Allen
        and Ruth Gordon.

TONY BENNETT (Peter Matz)
Tony Sings the Great Hits of Today, Columbia CS9980, LP
October 7, 1969, New York
    No solos

MOONDOG (LOUIS HARDIN)
Moondog, Columbia MS7335, LP
1969, New York
    No solos

SAVINA
Savina and All That Gentle Jazz, Rave 502, LP
Early 1970s

Reissue: Love 503, CD.

Note: This LP consists of vocals recorded over Music Minus One records from the 1950s.
Although some of the MMO artists are credited (including Wilder, on "Can't We Be
Friends"), there is no mention of the fact that they are not actually accompanying this singer.

TONY BENNETT
Tony Bennett's Something, Columbia C20280, LP
April 2, 1970, New York
    No solos

IRWIN BAZELON
Chamber Concerto No. 2: "Churchill Downs," **CRI SD287, LP**
June 4, 1971, New York
  No solos

CHARLES MINGUS (Sy Johnson)
Let My Children Hear Music, **Columbia KC31039, LP**
September 23 and October 1, 18, 1971, New York
  "Don't Be Afraid, the Clown's Afraid Too" (JW is audible as part of a collective im-
    provisation beginning at approximately 6:10 into the performance and lasting until
    6:45)

Reissue: Columbia CK48910, CD.

GRANT GREEN (Wade Marcus)
Shades of Green, **Blue Note BST84413, LP**
December 16–17, 1971, New York
  No solos

HOUSTON PERSON (Billy VerPlanck)
Broken Windows, Empty Hallways, **Prestige 10044, LP**
March 15, 1972, New York
  "Moan-er-uh-Lisa" (8b)

Reissue: Prestige PRCD24290, CD.

Note: Both the LP and CD misattribute Wilder's solo on "Moan-er-uh-Lisa" to Victor Paz.
This track is retitled "Houston's Blues" on the CD.

DAVID FATHEAD NEWMAN (William Eaton)
The Weapon, **Atlantic 1638, LP**
September 28, 1972, New York
  No solos

DAVID AMRAM
Subway Night, **RCA LSP4820, LP**
ca. 1972, New York
  "Ballad for Red Allen" (intro, solos behind vocal throughout, ending)

JACKIE DeSHANNON
Your Baby Is a Lady, **Atlantic SD7303, LP**
September 20, 25, 1973, New York
  No solos

DICK HYMAN
Ferdinand "Jelly Roll" Morton: Some Rags, Some Stomps and a Little Blues, **Columbia
    MQ32587, LP**
December 3, 1973, New York
  "The Crave" (16b)
  "Black Bottom Stomp" (16b 1st tp solo with ensemble)

Reissue: Dick Hyman, *Jelly and James: The Music of Jelly Roll Morton and James P. Johnson,* Sony Masterworks MDK52552, CD.

The Sting: Original Motion Picture Soundtrack (Marvin Hamlisch)
MCA 390 (later 2040), LP
1973, New York
"Pine Apple Rag" (24b opening melody, 24b closing melody)

Reissue: MCA MCAD31034, CD.

LES McCANN
Another Beginning, Atlantic 1666, LP
ca. May 1974, New York
No solos

YUSEF LATEEF
Ten Years Hence, Atlantic SD2-1001, LP
ca. July 1974, New York
No solos

Note: The original recording was made at Keystone Korner in San Francisco on July 6, 1974; the horn section was added later in New York.

RAY BRYANT
In the Cut, Cadet CA50052, LP
1974, New York
No solos

PETER DEAN (Buddy Weed)
Four or Five Times, Buddah BDS5613, LP
ca. 1974, New York
"Rain" (ob)
"So the Bluebirds and the Blackbirds Got Together" (ob)

Note: Carly Simon is the vocalist on "So the Bluebirds and the Blackbirds Got Together."

DON McLEAN (William Eaton)
Homeless Brother, United Artists 315G, LP
ca. 1974, New York
No solos

MARTIN MULL
Normal, Capricorn CP0126, LP
ca. 1974, New York
"Flexible" (8b)
"You Play Rhythm" (ob)

Reissue: "Flexible" on Martin Mull, *Mulling It Over*, Razor and Tie 82178, CD.

Shenandoah Original Broadway Cast Recording
RCA ARL1-1019, LP
February 2, 1975, New York
Although he did not solo, Wilder played first trumpet for this Broadway show, which ran from January 1975 to August 1977.

Reissue: RCA 3763, CD.

DICK HYMAN
Charleston: The Song That Made the Twenties Roar, Columbia M33076, LP
May 22, 1975, New York
    No solos

LEON REDBONE
On the Track, Warner Bros. BS2888, LP
ca. 1975, New York
    "Desert Blues" (ob)

Reissue: Warner Bros. 2888, CD.

KENNY VANCE
Vance 32, Atlantic SD18135, LP
ca. 1975, New York
    No solos

The Wild Party **Film Soundtrack**
MGM Home Entertainment, DVD
ca. 1975, New York
    Wilder can be heard soloing occasionally on the soundtrack, most notably at 1:05 of
        the DVD.

YUSEF LATEEF
The Doctor Is In . . . and Out, Atlantic 1685, LP
March 1976, New York
    No solos

LEON REDBONE
Double Time, Warner Bros. BS2971, LP
ca. 1977, New York
    "Nobody's Sweetheart" (ob and solo behind vocal)

Reissue: Warner Bros. 2971, CD.

Angel Original Broadway Cast Recording
[No label] GUA001, LP
May 1978, New York
    Wilder played first trumpet in this production, which closed May 13, 1978, after only
        a few performances. Shortly after its closing, the producers made this original cast
        recording, which was issued in a limited private pressing.

NATIONAL JAZZ ENSEMBLE (Chuck Israels, director)
National Jazz Ensemble Series, Big 3 Music 1179, LP
November 19, 1978, SUNY, New Paltz, New York
    "Jitterbug Waltz" (112b)

JIM BARTOW
Ritual Love Songs, Blues Blood 552, LP
ca. 1978, New York
    "Solitude" (intro, ob, 24b)

The Wiz Original Soundtrack
MCA MCSP287, LP
ca. 1978, New York
> Wilder plays in the section on selections on this film soundtrack.

Reissue: MCA MCAD2-11649, CD.

BOBBY HUTCHERSON
Conception: The Gift of Love, Columbia JC35814, LP
ca. March 1979, New York
> No solos

Ballroom Original Cast Recording
Columbia JS35762, LP
1979, New York
> "One by One" (12b)

Reissue: Sony Broadway 35762, CD.

Note: Wilder played first trumpet in the Broadway show, which ran from December 1978 to March 1979.

STANLEY TURRENTINE (Wade Marcus)
Use the Stairs, Fantasy 9605, LP
March–April 1980, New York
> No solos

HELEN HUMES
Helen, Muse MR5233, LP
June 17, 19, 1980, New York
> "There'll Be Some Changes Made" (10b, ob)
> "Easy Living" (ob)
> "You Brought a New Kind of Love to Me" (32b)
> "Evil Gal Blues" (24b)
> "Why Try to Change Me Now?" (ob)
> "Draggin' My Heart Around" (intro, 32b [first 16b with ensemble])

Reissue: Muse (Japan) BRJ4598, CD.

JOHNNY HARTMAN
Once in Every Life, Beehive 7012, LP
August 11, 1980, Franklin Square, New York
> "Easy Living" (32b)
> "By Myself" (48b)
> "For All We Know" (intro, ob, ending)
> "Will You Still Be Mine?" (ob)
> "I Could Write a Book" (ob)
> "I See Your Face before Me" (ob)

Reissue: "Easy Living," "For All We Know," and "I See Your Face before Me" on *The Bridges of Madison County Original Soundtrack*, Malpaso 45949, CD; "By Myself," "Will You Still Be Mine?," "I Could Write a Book," and "I See Your Face before Me" on *Remembering Madison County*, Malpaso 46259, CD.

Note: The film soundtrack versions of "Easy Living," "For All We Know," and "I See Your Face before Me" have been slowed down, so that the pitch is incorrect. Early versions of the Malpaso 45949 CD contain the slower versions; on later versions of the CD, the speed has been corrected. Titles on the Malpaso 46259 CD play at the correct speed on my copy. The altered version of "I See Your Face before Me" was also included on Malpaso PRO-CD-7651, a promotional sampler CD. (See Chapter 10, note 47, for further details.)

42nd Street Original Broadway Cast Recording
RCA CBL3891, LP
November 16, 1980, New York
> Wilder played second trumpet in this production.

Reissue: RCA RCD1-3891, CD.

The Great Space Coaster Original Cast Album
Columbia PC37704, LP
1981, New York
> No solos

DAVID AMRAM
Latin-Jazz Celebration, **Elektra/Musician 60195, LP**
January 1982, New York
> No solos

MICHEL LEGRAND
After the Rain, **Pablo 2312-139, LP**
May 28, 1982, New York
> "After the Rain" (64b, 8b, 8b)
> "Orson's Theme" (40b)
> "Pieces of Dreams" (32b rubato, 68b, 8b, 4b trades)

Reissue (all titles): OJC 803, CD.

Note: Among other errors in their listings for this session, the Bruyninckx and Lord discographies claim that Wilder and Phil Woods do not play on "After the Rain," but they are clearly present.

LARRY ELGART
Hooked on Swing, **RCA AFL1-4343, LP**
1982, New York
> "Bandstand Boogie" (8b trades, 8b duet with unidentified trumpeter)

Reissue: K-Tel 507, CD.

Note: "Bandstand Boogie" is part of the "Hooked on Big Bands" medley.

JOE NEWMAN and JOE WILDER
Hangin' Out, **Concord CJ262, LP**
May 1984, New York
> "The Midgets" (48b 2nd tp solo)
> "Here's That Rainy Day" (32b, 16b)
> "Duet" (2b trades with Newman throughout)
> "Battle Hymn of the Republic" (4b trades, 32b 1st tp solo)

"Secret Love" (32b, 8b melody, 48b 2nd tp solo, 4b trades)
"'Lypso Mania" (32b 2nd tp solo)
"He Was Too Good to Me" (32b melody, 16b melody)

Reissue: Concord CCD4462, CD.

Note: A tape exists of "You Needed Me," an unissued track from this session featuring Wilder with the rhythm section.

TERESA BREWER (Mercer Ellington, conductor; Glenn Osser, arranger)
The Cotton Connection, Doctor Jazz FW40031, LP
January 24, 28, 1985, New York
    "Dinah's in a Jam" (32b)

Reissue: Signature AK40031, CD.

Note: Although the liner notes credit the solo on "Dinah's in a Jam" to Barrie Lee Hall, it is played by Wilder.

The Cosmic Eye Film Soundtrack (Benny Carter)
Journey to Next, Lightyear Entertainment 54168, CD
March 5, 1985, New York
    "Sirius Samba" (16b)

ANITA O'DAY
'S Wonderful, Emily 92685, LP
May 24, 1985, Carnegie Hall, New York
    No solos

BENNY CARTER
A Gentleman and His Music, Concord CJ285, LP; Concord CCD4285, CD
August 3, 1985, San Francisco
    "Sometimes I'm Happy" (32b)
    "A Kiss from You" (16b melody, beginning and end)
    "Blues for George" (24b)
    "Things Ain't What They Used to Be" (36b)
    "Lover Man" (16b, 8b melody, 8b melody)
    "Idaho" (32b melody, 64b, 8b in trades, 16b, 8b melody)

ALLEGEHENY JAZZ CONCERT
Private Treasures from Allegheny Jazz Concerts, 1950s–2000, Jump JCD12-35, CD
August 1985, Conneaut Lake, PA
    "The Man I Love" (64b, 64b [4b trades])

JOHN COLIANNI
John Colianni, Concord CJ309, LP; Concord CCD4309, CD
August 1986, New York
    "Home-Grown" (32b)

DICK HYMAN
The Kingdom of Swing and the Republic of Oop Bop Sh'Bam, MusicMasters
    CIJD60200, CD
July 30, 1987, live recording, 92nd Street Y, New York

"Lester Leaps In" (8b, 64b)
"On Green Dolphin Street" (32b melody with ensemble, 64b)
"When Your Lover Has Gone" (32b melody, 32b, 32b melody)
"Night in Tunisia" (8b, 32b collective improv with other horns, 32b)
"Moten Swing" (32b)

EILEEN FARRELL (Loonis McGlohon)
Eileen Farrell Sings Rodgers and Hart, Reference Recordings RR32, CD
July 12–17, 1988, Charlotte, NC
"I Could Write a Book" (intro, 16b, ob)
"Love Me Tonight" (intro, 32b, ob)
"It Never Entered My Mind" (16b, coda)
"Can't You Do a Friend a Favor?" (8b, ending)

EILEEN FARRELL (Loonis McGlohon)
Eileen Farrell Sings Harold Arlen, Reference Recordings RR30, CD
July 12–18, 1988, Charlotte, NC
"Let's Fall in Love" (intro, 16b, ob)
"Out of This World" (ob)
"Like a Straw in the Wind" (intro, 16b, ob)
"Happiness Is a Thing Called Joe" (36b, ob)
"A Woman's Prerogative" (intro, ob)
"When the Sun Comes Out" (4b, ob, ending)
"My Shining Hour" (24b, ending)

MAURICE (HINES)
I've Never Been in Love Before, Arbors ARCD19240, CD
March 6, 8, 10, 1989, New York
"Sweet Lorraine" (intro, ob, 32b)
"But Beautiful" (16b, ob)

CHARLES MINGUS (Gunther Schuller, conductor)
Epitaph, Columbia C2K45428, CD
June 3, 1989, concert, Alice Tully Hall, Lincoln Center, New York
"Main Score, Part One" (12b plunger solo at 3:45 [11:00 on DVD])

Reissue: Eagle Eye Media EE39171-9, DVD.

EILEEN FARRELL (Loonis McGlohon)
Eileen Farrell Sings Torch Songs, Reference Recordings RR34, CD
July 19–24, 1989, Charlotte, NC
"Stormy Weather" (8b, ob)
"When Your Lover Has Gone" (16b)
"'Round Midnight" (ob, 8b)
"Guess I'll Have to Hang My Tears Out to Dry" (intro, 16b)
"I Get Along without You Very Well" (32b, ending)
"Black Coffee" (ob, 8b, ending)
"Get out of Town" (16b, ending)
"This Time the Dream's on Me" (8b, ob, ending)

EILEEN FARRELL (Loonis McGlohon)
Eileen Farrell Sings Alec Wilder, **Reference Recordings RR36, CD**
July 19–24, 1989, Charlotte, NC
 "It's So Peaceful in the Country" (intro, 16b, ob, coda)
 "Blackberry Winter" (16b)
 "The Worm Has Turned" (8b intro, 8b)
 "'S Gonna Be a Cold, Cold Day" (16b, ob)
 "I'll Be Around" (intro, 16b)

JOE WILDER with MARSHAL ROYAL
Mostly Ellington, **Blue Port NuForce BP-J017, CD**
January 27, 1990, Lyceum Theater, San Diego
Marshal Royal (alto sax), Mike Wofford (p), Bob Magnusson (b), Roy McCurdy (d)
 "It Don't Mean a Thing" (64b)
 "Mood Indigo" (64b)
 "I Got It Bad (and That Ain't Good)" (32b, 16b, coda)
 "Something to Live For" (64b)
 "Perdido" (96b)

Note: The CD includes a companion DVD with the same audio content (no video).

LOUIE BELLSON
A Salute to the Big Band Masters, **MusicMasters 5038, CD**
February 15–16, 1990, New York
 No solos

JOE WILLIAMS
That Holiday Feelin', **Verve 843-956, CD**
June 25, 1990, New York
 "Winter Wonderland" (intro, ob)

JOE WILDER
Alone with Just My Dreams, **Evening Star ES101, CD**
August 6–7, 1991, New York
James Williams (p), Remo Palmier (g), Jay Leonhart (b), Sherman Ferguson (d)
 "But Not for Me" (64b, 32b, tag)
 "Answer Me, My Love" (32b, 16b, 8b coda)
 "Far Away Places" (64b, 64b trades with drums, 16b melody, coda)
 "I Love You" (32b, 32b, fade)
 "Wonderland" (32b melody, 32b, 32b melody, tag)
 "Struttin' with Some Barbecue" (intro, 64b, 32b, tag, ending)
 "It Might as Well Be Spring" (intro, 40b, 16b)
 "What a Wonderful World" (32b, 16b, tag)
 "Alone with Just My Dreams" (32b melody, 16b)
 "I Will Wait for You" (intro, 58b, 58b, tag)
 "Everything Happens to Me" (32b, 16b, coda)
 "Joe's Blues" (12b melody, 24b, 12b melody, tag)

Reissue: Jazz Heritage 513348, CD.

ROB FISHER AND THE COFFEE CLUB ORCHESTRA
Shaking the Blues Away, Angel CDC7-54390, CD
November–December 1991, New York
    "East St. Louis Toodle-oo" (opening and closing plunger solos)

Note: This is the orchestra that was featured on Garrison Keillor's *American Radio Company of the Air* show on American Public Radio. Keillor sings on several tracks.

GARRISON KEILLOR and FREDERICA VON STADE (Philip Brunelle)
Songs of the Cat, HighBridge HBP17399, CD
ca. 1991, New York
    No solos

BRITT WOODMAN, JOE WILDER, and JOHN LaPORTA
Playing for Keeps, GM 3026, CD
January 4, 1992, New York
    "While You Were Out" (20b)
    "Isfahan" (16b)
    "Love for Sale" (64b)
    "Just the Way You Are" (64b, 36b)
    "Chazz" (12b)
    "J.B. Blues" (48b, 6b)

GARRISON KEILLOR
Horrors: A Scary Home Companion, Highbridge 791181, CD
May 23, 1992, Richmond, VA
    Wilder plays in the ensemble on "The Raven."

SMITHSONIAN JAZZ MASTERWORKS ORCHESTRA (David Baker)
Tribute to a Generation: A Salute to the Big Bands of the WWII Era, Smithsonian
    SFWCD40817, CD
July 25–26, 1992, Washington, DC
    Wilder plays in the ensemble on "Song of the Volga Boatmen."

LINCOLN CENTER JAZZ ORCHESTRA (David Berger)
October 10, 1992, Bardavan 1869 Opera House, Poughkeepsie, NY
    Wilder plays in the ensemble on "Take the 'A' Train" (*Jazz at Lincoln Center: They
    Came to Swing*, Columbia CK66379, CD) and "Multi-Colored Blue" (*Jazz at Lincoln Center Presents: The Fire of the Fundamentals*, Columbia CK57592, CD).

Malcolm X: Original Motion Picture Score (Terence Blanchard)
Columbia CK53190, CD
1992, New York
    No solos

SMITHSONIAN JAZZ MASTERWORKS ORCHESTRA (David Baker)
Big Band Treasures Live, Smithsonian RJ0044, CD
May 9, 1993, Washington, DC
    "Raincheck" (8b)

Note: This performance also appears on *Tribute to a Generation: A Salute to the Big Bands of the WWII Era*, Smithsonian SFWCD40817, CD.

MIYUKI KOGA
Dreamin', Concord CCD4588, CD
May 11-12, 1993, New York
  "Do-Do-Do" (ob, 16b)
  "Swing Low, Sweet Chariot" (intro, 32b)
  "When My Sugar Walks down the Street" (intro, 16b)
  "You Made Me Love You" (intro, ob, 16b)
  "I Know That You Know" (16b melody)

KEN PEPLOWSKI
Steppin' with Peps, Concord CCD4569, CD
May 22-23, 1993, New York
  "Lotus Blossom" (16b melody, 16b, 12b melody)
  "Johnny Come Lately" (32b over ensemble, 32b [8b trades with Randy Sandke], 32b
    [4b trades], 16b, 8b over ensemble)
  "Pretend" (8b, 16b, ob)

SMITHSONIAN JAZZ MASTERWORKS ORCHESTRA (David Baker)
Big Band Treasures Live, Smithsonian RJ0044, CD
July 31, 1993, Washington, DC
  "Sepia Panorama" (4b, 4b, 4b)
  "Echoes of Harlem" (JW re-creates Cootie Williams's 1936 solo)

Note: The same performance of "Sepia Panorama" also appears on *Tribute to a Generation*,
Smithsonian SFWCD40817, CD, where the solo is mistakenly credited to Virgil Jones.

JOE WILDER
No Greater Love, Evening Star ES103, CD
August 3, 1993, New York
Seldon Powell (tenor sax, flute), James Chirillo (g), Bobby Tucker (p), Milt Hinton (b),
Sherman Ferguson (d)
  "It's Easy to Remember" (ob, 8b, 32b, 8b, tag)
  "Come On Home" (64b)
  "The Courtship" (16, 8b melody, 36b, 16, 12b melody, tag)
  "Harry Lulu" (32b, 64b [8b trades with drums and tenor])
  "Thinking of Lady" (24b)
  "Samba de Orfeo" (56b melody, 56b, 112b [4b trades with tenor], 32b, 16b melody,
    fade)

JOE WILDER
No Greater Love, Evening Star ES103, CD
August 4, 1993, New York
James Chirillo (g), Bobby Tucker (p)
  "Day Dream" (intro, 32b melody, 16b melody, coda)
  "That's All" (32b, 16b, tag)
  "Dylan" (intro, 24b melody)
  "Love Me Tender" (32b, 24b, tag)
  "God Bless the Child" (38b melody, 18b melody, coda)
  "I've Grown Accustomed to Her Face" (20b, 16b)
  "There Is No Greater Love" (32b, 32b, 32b [4b trades with guitar], 16b, 8b, tag)
  "Prelude to a Kiss" (16b, 8b, coda)

SMITHSONIAN JAZZ MASTERWORKS ORCHESTRA (Gunther Schuller)
Big Band Treasures Live, Smithsonian RJ0044, CD
August 29, 1993, Washington, DC
    Wilder plays in the ensemble on "The Mole."

THE ALL STARS
The All Stars at Bob Haggart's 80th Birthday Party, Arbors ARCD19265, CD
March 11–13, 1994, Arbors March of Jazz party, St. Petersburg Hilton, St. Petersburg, FL
    "Oh, Baby" (32b [8b trades with Yank Lawson], 32b [4b trades with Lawson])
    "Bill Bailey, Won't You Please Come Home?" (32b melody, 64b)

DICK HYMAN
From the Age of Swing, Reference Recordings RR59, CD
May 24–25, 1994, Purchase, NY
    "You're Driving Me Crazy/Moten Swing" (16b)
    "Moonglow" (16b, 16b, 8b, 8b)
    "Dooji Wooji" (12b, 12b with ensemble)
    "'Deed I Do" (24b)
    "I Know What You Do" (16b, 8b)

SMITHSONIAN JAZZ MASTERWORKS ORCHESTRA (David Baker)
Big Band Treasures Live, Smithsonian RJ0044, CD
June 19, 1994, Washington, DC
    Wilder plays in the ensemble on "Hairy Joe Jump" and "Mystic Moan."

SMITHSONIAN JAZZ MASTERWORKS ORCHESTRA (Gunther Schuller)
Big Band Treasures Live, Smithsonian RJ0044, CD
June 24–26, 1994, Washington, DC
    Wilder plays in the ensemble on "Evensong."

SMITHSONIAN JAZZ MASTERWORKS ORCHESTRA (David Baker)
Big Band Treasures Live, Smithsonian RJ0044, CD
July 31, 1994, Washington, DC
    Wilder plays in the ensemble on "Isfahan."

SMITHSONIAN JAZZ MASTERWORKS ORCHESTRA (Gunther Schuller)
Big Band Treasures Live, Smithsonian RJ0044, CD
September 17, 1994, Washington, DC
    Wilder plays in the ensemble on "Evenin'."

STATESMEN OF JAZZ
Statesmen of Jazz, American Federation of Jazz Societies AFJS201, CD
December 20, 1994, New York
    "Open Wider Please" (24b)
    "Just Squeeze Me" (32b duet with Clark Terry)
    "Tangerine" (64b)

SMITHSONIAN JAZZ MASTERWORKS ORCHESTRA (David Baker)
Tribute to a Generation: A Salute to the Big Bands of the WWII Era, Smithsonian
    SFWCD40817, CD

April 29–30, 1995, Washington, DC
   Wilder plays in the ensemble on "Cottontail."

SMITHSONIAN JAZZ MASTERWORKS ORCHESTRA (David Baker)
Tribute to a Generation: A Salute to the Big Bands of the WWII Era, Smithsonian
   SFWCD40817, CD
August 12–13, 1995, Washington, DC
   "Swanee River" (16b)

SMITHSONIAN JAZZ MASTERWORKS ORCHESTRA (David Baker)
Big Band Treasures Live, Smithsonian RJ0044, CD
August 13, 1995, Washington, DC
   Wilder plays in the ensemble on "Blue Blazes."

MARLENE VERPLANCK
A New York Singer, Audiophile ACD160, CD
September 11, 1995, Charlotte, NC
   "That Old Devil Called Love" (intro, ob, 4b)
   "I Looked at You" (intro, ob, 12b [alternating with piano], ending)
   "Good Old Friends" (ob)

DICK HYMAN ORCHESTRA
Mighty Aphrodite: Music from the Motion Picture
Sony Classical SK62253, CD
ca. 1995, New York
   Wilder plays in the ensemble on "When You're Smiling."

RUBY BRAFF
Being with You: Ruby Braff Remembers Louis Armstrong, Arbors ARCD19163, CD
April 15 or 16, 1996, New York
   "Royal Garden Blues" (48b)

SMITHSONIAN JAZZ MASTERWORKS ORCHESTRA (David Baker)
Big Band Treasures Live, Smithsonian RJ0044, CD
July 28, 1996, Washington, DC
   Wilder plays in the ensemble on "Cashmere Cutie."

J. J. JOHNSON
The Brass Orchestra, Verve 314-537-321, CD
September 24–27, 1996, New York
   "Ballad for Joe" (opening melody statement)

Note: In "Ballad for Joe," Wilder reprises the melody he played in Johnson's "Poem for Brass" on the *Music for Brass* LP recorded for Columbia on October 23, 1956.

Everyone Says I Love You Original Soundtrack Recording (Dick Hyman)
RCA 09026-68756, CD
ca. 1996, New York
   "All My Life" (ob)

Note: Wilder plays in the ensemble on other portions of this soundtrack.

TOM TALBERT
This Is Living! **Pipe Dream/Chartmaker PDP14480, CD**
July 1, 7, 8, 1997, New York
 "The Brio Trio" (16b 1st tp solo, 12b plunger solo, 4b plunger solo)
 "Love Is a Pleasure" (16b)
 "A Little Tempo, Please" (32b)
 "Blame It on My Youth" (16b)
 "Echo of Spring" (16b)
 "Our Delight" (32b)
 "This Is All I Ask" (16b)

SMITHSONIAN JAZZ MASTERWORKS ORCHESTRA (David Baker)
Tribute to a Generation: A Salute to the Big Bands of the WWII Era, **Smithsonian**
 SFWCD40817, CD
July 19–20, 1997, Washington, DC
 Wilder plays in the ensemble on "Ill Wind" and "Back Bay Boogie."

THE HEATH BROTHERS
Jazz Family, **Concord CCD4846, CD**
May 29–31, 1998, New York
 "Move to the Groove" (24b)
 "None Shall Wander" (48b)

SMITHSONIAN JAZZ MASTERWORKS ORCHESTRA (David Baker)
Tribute to a Generation: A Salute to the Big Bands of the WWII Era, **Smithsonian**
 SFWCD40817, CD
July 18–19, 1998, Washington, DC
 Wilder plays in the ensemble on "Begin the Beguine," "Mission to Moscow," "Summertime," "Back Bay Shuffle," and "Just a-Settin' and a-Rockin'."

CHARLIE BYRD
For Louis, **Concord CCD4879, CD**
September 10–11, 1999, New York
 "Remembering Louis Armstrong" (20b)
 "A Kiss to Build a Dream On" (16b, 8b melody, 32b, 16b melody)
 "Hello, Dolly" (32b melody, 32b, 32b melody)
 "Tin Roof Blues" (24b melody, 24b, 12b melody)
 "Soft Lights and Sweet Music" (52b)
 "Struttin' with Some Barbecue" (64b, 32b melody)
 "What a Wonderful World" (16b, 16b, 10b)

TOM TALBERT
To a Lady, **Essential Music Group 1000, CD**
December 9, 10, 14, 1999, New York
 "To a Lady Asking Foolish Questions" (16b)
 "'Round Midnight" (16b)
 "Little Girl Blue" (24b, 4b over ensemble)
 "Pavane de la Belle aux Bois Dormant" (4b, 4b)
 "Orange Bright" (32b)

RUBY BRAFF
Variety Is the Spice of Life, Arbors ARCD19194, CD
July 24 or 25, 2000, New York
  "Crazy Rhythm" (16b)
  "Liza" (16b)

MARIAN McPARTLAND with JOE WILDER
Piano Jazz, NPR program
October 18, 2000, New York (originally aired February 13, 2001)
Marian McPartland (p), Rufus Reid (b)
  "It's You or No One"
  "It's Easy to Remember"
  "Samba de Orfeo"
  "How Deep Is the Ocean"
  "Far Away Places"
  "Lady Be Good"

Note: Wilder is featured on all listed tracks. The performance is available at http://www
.npr.org/templates/story/story.php?storyId=91470414.

REBECCA KILGORE with KEITH INGHAM
Rebecca Kilgore with the Keith Ingham Sextet, Jump 12-24, CD
February 26–27, 2002, New York
  "Everything but You" (ob, 8b)
  "Make with the Kisses" (8b, ob)
  "Time on My Hands" (verse, 32b, 16b instrumental feature for JW)
  "He Ain't Got Rhythm" (16b)
  "Trav'lin' All Alone" (ob, 16b, ending)
  "Sing for Your Supper" (12b)
  "There Must Be Something Better than Love" (10b)
  "One, Two, Button Your Shoe" (8b)
  "You're Gonna See a Lot of Me" (16b melody)

JOE WILDER
Among Friends, Evening Star ES106, CD
August 23, 2002, New York
Bill Charlap (p), Chris Neville (p), Russell Malone (g), Bucky Pizzarelli (g)
  "When I Fall in Love" (duet with Charlap) (32b, 8b, 4b)
  "Secret Love" (duet with Charlap) (48b, 48b [8b trades], 32b, 8b, tag)
  "You Are the Sunshine of My Life" (duet with Pizzarelli) (48b, 32b, tag)
  "My Romance" (duet with Malone) (32b, 16b, tag)
  "What Now, My Love?" (duet with Malone) (48b, 40b, 32b, tag)
  "People Time" (duet with Neville) (32b melody [4b trades], 16b melody)

JOE WILDER
Among Friends, Evening Star ES106, CD
August 24, 2002, New York
Warren Vaché (cornet), Frank Wess (tenor sax, flute), Chris Neville (p), Steve LaSpina (b),
Chuck Redd (d)
  "Indiana" (16b melody, 32b, ob, 8b)

"Seventy-Six Trombones" (64b, 16b)
"Only Trust Your Heart" (16, 4b melody, 32b, 8b, tag)
"Centerpiece" (24b 1st tp solo)
"It's You or No One" (64b [8b trades], 32b 1st tp [4b trades with Vaché], 32b improv
   duet with Vaché, 32b, tag with ensemble)

JOE WILDER
Among Friends, **Evening Star ES106, CD**
September 16, 2002, New York
Bucky Pizzarelli (g), Skitch Henderson (p), Jerry Bruno (b), Joe Cocuzzo (d)
   "How Are Things in Glocca Morra?" (duet with Pizzarelli) (intro, 28b, 12b, coda)
   "Lady Be Good" (64b, 32b [4b trades with drums], 16b, 8b, tag)

LIONELLE HAMANAKA
A Jazz Bouquet, **self-produced LH6000, CD**
ca. 2002, New York
   "Some Other Time" (ob)
   "Deep Night" (36b)

STATESMEN OF JAZZ
A Multitude of Stars, **Arbors Statesmen of Jazz SOJCD202, CD**
December 8, 9, or 10, 2003, New York
   "You're Just in Love" (4b trades, 32b)
   "Rockin' Chair" (32b)
   "Just You, Just Me" (32b)
   "Bags' Groove" (24b)
   "Sweet Georgia Brown" (opening and closing melody)

Note: Wilder was the leader on this session, which also featured Warren Vaché (cornet),
George Masso (trombone), Houston Person (tenor sax), Derek Smith (piano), Keter Betts
(bass), and Eddie Locke (drums). "You're Just in Love" is misidentified on the CD as
"I Hear Music."

BOB DOROUGH
Sunday at Iridium, **Arbors ARCD19305, CD**
February 29, 2004, live recording, Iridium Jazz Club, New York
   "Sunday" (ob, 32b, 32b [4b trades with drums], ob)
   "Ain't No Spoofin'" (32b, ending)

GENE LUDWIG with BILL WARFIELD
Duff's Blues, **18th and Vine 18V-1056, CD**
April 10, 2004, live recording, Lehigh University Zoellner Arts Center, Bethlehem, PA
   "Duff's Blues" (24b)
   "Totem Pole" (96b)

TONY BENNETT (Johnny Mandel)
The Art of Romance, **RPM/Columbia CK92820, CD**
2004, Bergen Performing Arts Center, Englewood, NJ
   No solos

ANITA O'DAY
Indestructible! **Kayo 9-10747, CD**
November 3, 2005 (date of JW's overdubs), New York
    "Blue Skies" (8b intro, ob, 32b, ob)
    "This Can't Be Love" (ob, 32b, ending)
    "All of Me" (intro, ob, 32b, ob, ending)
    "Pennies from Heaven" (ob, 16b, ending)
    "Them There Eyes" (intro, ob, 32b duet with tenor sax, ob)
    "My Little Suede Shoes" (64b [8b trades with tenor sax])

BENNY CARTER CENTENNIAL PROJECT (various artists)
The Benny Carter Centennial Project, **Evening Star ES113, CD**
March 13, 2007, New York
JW accompanied by Chris Neville (p), Steve LaSpina (b), Steve Johns (d)
    "The Blessing" (32b, 16b)

Index

Edward Berger is a writer/photographer whose other books include *Benny Carter: A Life in American Music* (with Morroe Berger and James Patrick) and *Bassically Speaking: An Oral History of George Duvivier*. He produced two Grammy-winning albums for jazz great Benny Carter, has been a longtime cohost of *Jazz from the Archives* on WBGO-FM, Newark, and regularly teaches at Jazz at Lincoln Center's Swing University. He retired as Associate Director of the Rutgers Institute of Jazz Studies in 2011, but continues to serve IJS as a consultant.

DISCARD

B WILDER

Berger, Edward.
Softly, with feeling

METRO

R4001232749

METROPOLITAN
Atlanta-Fulton Public Library